The publisher gratefully acknowledges the generous support of the African American Studies Endowment Fund of the University of California Press Foundation, which was established by a major gift from the George Gund Foundation.

Waste of a White Skin

Waste of a White Skin

*The Carnegie Corporation and the Racial
Logic of White Vulnerability*

Tiffany Willoughby-Herard

UNIVERSITY OF CALIFORNIA PRESS

University of California Press, one of the most distinguished university presses in the United States, enriches lives around the world by advancing scholarship in the humanities, social sciences, and natural sciences. Its activities are supported by the UC Press Foundation and by philanthropic contributions from individuals and institutions. For more information, visit www.ucpress.edu.

University of California Press
Oakland, California

An earlier version of chapter 7 was published as "'I'll give you something to cry about': The Intra-Racial Violence of Uplift Feminism in the Carnegie *Poor White Study* Volume, The Mother and Daughter of the Poor Family," *South African Review of Sociology* 41, no. 1 (2010): 78-103.

An earlier version of chapter 3 was published as "South Africa's Poor Whites and Whiteness Studies: Afrikaner Ethnicity, Scientific Racism, and White Misery," *New Political Science: A Journal of Politics and Culture* 29, no. 3 (2007): 479–500.

Library of Congress Cataloging-in-Publication Data

Willoughby-Herard, Tiffany, 1973- author.
    Waste of a white skin : the Carnegie Corporation and the racial logic of white vulnerability / Tiffany Willoughby-Herard.
        pages   cm
    Includes bibliographical references and index.
    ISBN 978-0-520-28086-1 (cloth : alk. paper)—
    ISBN 0-520-28086-5 (cloth : alk. paper)—
    ISBN 978-0-520-28087-8 (pbk. : alk. paper)—
    ISBN 0-520-28087-3 (pbk. : alk. paper)—
    ISBN 978-0-520-95997-2 (ebook)—
    ISBN 0-520-95997-3 (ebook)
    1. Carnegie Corporation of New York—Influence.
    2. Apartheid—South Africa—History—20th century.   3. White nationalism—South Africa—History—20th century.   4. Poverty—Political aspects—South Africa.   5. South Africa—Race relations—History—20th century.   6. United States—Foreign relations—South Africa.   7. South Africa—Foreign relations—United States.   I. Title.
    DT756.W55 2015
    305.809'06809041--dc23   2014017945

Manufactured in the United States of America

24   23   22   21   20   19   18   17   16   15
10   9   8   7   6   5   4   3   2   1

This book is dedicated to Naimah, Yani, Nadirah, Nirandah, Nazarah, Michael, Corey, Damion, Diamond, Dominique, Desiree, Nashon, Diana, Jaylen, Ty-Ree, Brittany, Imani, Sadiya, Thandiwe, Elijah, Mariah, Xavier, Xariya, Kaylei, Megan, Caleb, Crystal, Charles, Shawn Jr., Racine, Tyler, Taylum, Santiago, Sierra, Dakota, Jahmosi, Samyia, Sona, Sweden, Sibulele, Oscar, Tawanda, Amara, Azaan, Salvador, Jacob, Dito, Salim, Solomon, Henry, Sammy, Cyrus, Victor, Ruby Ella, Amara, Tyler, Naveen, Jordan, Marlicia, Jordan H., Hind, Omar, Hady, Atisa, Landon, Riann, Rina, Kirsten, Adalee, Sophia, Arianne, Kavya Anasuya Vihaan, Oscar, Ahvianna, Ariella Zenobia, Bona, Derrick Deon, Dylan, Nevaeh, Darren, Amen, Jihae, Aaron, Anthony, Asa'na Jr., JaKaden, Heriresh, Demi, and Anaya and to the worlds that you will surely create.

All over, we've seen intense oppression. I'm from Detroit, initially, and we've seen a lot of oppression there, historically as well as currently. New York has certainly seen its share. Washington, D.C., has seen its share. So, we don't want to be like people on different plantations arguing about which plantation is worse. What we have to do is to correct the whole problem, and we're about correcting the problem here in Jackson.

—Chokwe Lumumba (1947–2013)

June 6, 2013

A vote for a Democrat is nothing but a vote for a Dixie-crat. . . . Up here in the North you've got the same thing the Democratic party, they don't do it that way, they got a thing that they call gerrymandering. They maneuver you out of power. Even though you can vote, they fix it so you're voting for nobody. They got you going and coming. In the South they're political wolves, in the North they're political foxes. A fox and a wolf are both canine, both belong to the dog family. Now, you take your choice. You gonna choose a Northern dog or a Southern dog. Because either dog you choose, I guarantee you, you'll still be in the dog house. . . . And I hope that when I come back, I'll be able to come back and let you know how our African brothers and sisters feel toward us. And I know before I go there that they love us. We're one; we're the same; the same man who has colonized them all these years, colonized you and me too all these years.

—Malcolm X (1925–1965)

"The Ballot or Bullet," April 12, 1964

King Solomon Baptist Church, Detroit, Michigan

Contents

List of Illustrations

Preface

POSSESSIONS, BELONGING, COMPANIONSHIP, OR DON'T MIND THE GAP

Dean Hutton's image, "The Poverty of Being Unwanted: Danville," draws attention to the political uses of white identity and the possessions and kinds of spaces that typically signal white privilege. Yet the title and the caption refer meaningfully to Mother Teresa and the gap (typically colored white) between privilege and misery.[1] The possessions in question are a tent, a cloth-covered recliner, and a dog. Furnishings, belongings, and kin relations, whether with animate or inanimate things, have a particular resonance with "racial regimes" because of the ways in which they signify ownership, authority, and the realization of self-fashioning.[2] These creature comforts also signify the ability to shelter under the protection of national citizenship through companionship and belonging. The photographic series *"I have fallen": Photographs of South Africa's White Poor* (2013), from which the cover image is taken, highlights individuals, families, and communities, with captions explaining their social activities, names, locations, beliefs, and relationships. Hutton's series documents dimensions of family making, laboring in the informal economy, staking ground, and making a home on the margins, capturing the range of social identities and social locations that impoverished white communities represent. This work provides a powerful frame for this book because of a rare engagement with the genealogy of white feminist antiracism without sentimentality or guilt. Further, Hutton's oeuvre takes combative and radical stances against racial and sexual violence, because of deep familiarity with the process of being marked as a "would-be" white subject. Last, Hutton was politicized into social documentary photography by a group of black people striving to end apartheid without using spectacle to shock, shame, and titillate the white viewing public.[3]

In a different vein, I retrieve the history of white nationalism, segregationist philanthropy, and global racial politics that repeatedly rediscovers the white poor to suture over racial regimes. My work is concerned with the racial logics associated with rediscovering this community to shore up white nationalisms. Where Hutton's goal is to debunk the explicit snarl in the epithet, "waste of a white skin,"[4] my goal is to understand how it functions to prop up antiblack governance and sociality. To do this, I use methods and theories appropriate to race and ethnic politics and political theory, especially critical black political thought, black feminist theories, and black internationalism.

While conducting research in South Africa, archivists queried me, an African American woman, about the origin of my interest in poor whites. They hinted that as an American I would write a book that "othered" South African race relations. Since we had our own experience of segregation, they explained, we should not represent apartheid as exceptional.[5] This reaction was related in part to the history of demonizing and banning African diasporic black activists, Garveyites, missionaries, leftists, and black nationalists and revolutionaries for mobilizing with black revolutionaries in southern Africa and throughout the continent.[6] Black people's history of being movable property can undercut attachments to the possessions, companionship, and belonging entailed in national citizenship.[7] Based on the contingent belonging and kinship that was designed to bring misery under enslavement, this "we" flew apart—especially in the periods of racial state making after apartheid and after enslavement.[8] The archivists who exclaimed at my presence misrecognized me.[9] Further they sought to instruct me on how to use the privilege of being a U.S. passport holder to become an "honorary white."[10]

Should I prove to be a "credit to my race"[11] and carry the tainted legacy of black radicals antagonistic to antiblackness and white nationalism, I could do serious damage to white historical consciousness by studying poor white people. I could write a more humanizing account of impoverished white people that attends to the legacies of racial slavery. But first I had to claim space as a credible witness to racism and white supremacy in the making of white people within white community relations.[12] To write a more humanizing account of impoverished white people, to tend to the legacies of racial slavery, and to claim space as a credible witness, I follow Jacqueline Bobo's concept and methodology of the "black female cultural reader."[13] Although the topic of this book is poor white people in South Africa my main theoretical readings are from the black feminists Saidiyah Hartman, Hortense Spillers, Toni Morrison, Jacqueline Goldsby, Anne DuCille, Joy James, and Ange-Marie Hancock; the black internationalists Cedric Robinson, Pearl Robinson, Cynthia Young, Brenda Gayle Plummer, Gerald Horne, Robin Kelley, Michael West, William Martin, Fanon Che Wilkins, Robert Vinson, Brent Hayes Edwards, and Tiffany Ruby Patterson; and the black feminist internationalists Jacqui Alexander, Dayo Gore, Erik McDuffie, Carol Boyce Davies, and Cheryl Higashida. Why? These scholars have a better understanding of how race and class and gender have been produced transnationally and the violence that has been used to sustain them. They have raised sustained critiques of exceptionalist narratives about white nationalism on the grounds that exceptionalist narratives obscure sexualized racial domination and its role in modernity. Their attention to the complexity of sexualized racial violence (state and interpersonal, embodied and libidinal) more accurately represents a theoretical approach to white poverty. Nikol Alexander-Floyd writes that "illuminating women of color as political subjects and the gender race and sexual politics that impact their lives" is the work of black feminist politics.[14] I extend that work by putting black feminism in conversation with colonial feminism, civilizing missions, and programs of economic development that structure the making of poor whites—and their key role in extending antiblackness. This work contributes to black feminist scholarship by remembering the ways in which black feminism has made the violence and practices of economic injustice central to its concerns. As the experience of black people in struggle is the "basis of consciousness, of knowing, of being[,] . . . [i]t contains philosophy, theories of history, and social prescriptions native to it."[15] I had to bring these theories of struggle against racialized sexual violence to bear to explain the power operations and substitutions at work in the naming of poor white people as a "waste of a white skin." The theories of pathology and collateral damage, ethnic purity and white nationalism, and benign philanthropy that existed contemporaneously to explain poor whites could do nothing against the nightmares that I experienced after reading the five-volume Carnegie Corporation of New York (CCNY) *Poor White Study*, with its horrifying "white" welfare queen rhetoric.[16] As Barbara Christian explains:

> People of color have always theorized. . . . [O]ur theorizing is often in narra-
> tive forms, in the stories we create, in the riddles and proverbs, in the play
> with language, because dynamic rather than fixed ideas seemed more to our
> liking. How else have we managed to survive with such spiritedness the
> assault on our bodies, social institutions, countries, our very humanity? And
> women, at least the women I grew up around continuously speculated about
> the nature of life through pithy language that unmasked the power relations
> of their world[,] . . . though more in the form of the hieroglyph, a written
> figure that is both sensual and abstract.[17]

The caricatures of poor white people and the risks they are alleged to
portend for white supremacy are critical inheritances that enable understanding of what blackness is supposed to be and how and why antiblackness operates as a set of conditions. The language of "waste of a
white skin" captivated me and forced me to ask, What and who were
being wasted? What is the categorical waste that whiteness is being
compared to? What practices of calling history to account could be
brought to bear to tell the story about how poor whites are inextricably
bound with blackness?

When black female scholars conduct international research on white
supremacy their credibility is at stake. The South African archivists
reminded me of this with their questions and their attempts to redirect
me to a more appropriate arena. Perhaps they wanted me to write about
and research black South African women, even though apartheid had
stymied their productivity in the fields of critical theory, political theory,
and political economy. We do not get to claim space in each other's histories simply because we want to or because we have been in political
solidarity. Ethics call for scholars to do otherwise.[18] In the past ten years
black South African women intellectuals (feminist identified and not;
female identified and not) have made decisive and lasting scholarly
interventions in critical theory and history.[19] By their own accounts this
has come at incredible personal cost and enabled them to offer sustained theoretical engagement with the sociological and literary work of
leading lights such as Fatima Meer, Sindiwe Magona, Ellen Khuzwayo,
Lauretta Ncgobo, Dorothy Nyembe, and hundreds of others. Seeing this
situation, I made the ethical choice to not write about and research
black South African women while knowing that as an "American" my
findings would be regarded as more insightful and powerful than those
of women from black South Africa and the diaspora. I am grateful for
that decision. Now, twenty years after apartheid, there have been many
highly theoretical texts produced to reintroduce the political history of

black South African women. I teach them; I cite them; I have felt comfortable conducting original research on black South African women since they have published their work because I have interlocutors from my own generation.

I went to South Africa for the first time in 1999, to write a history of black wildcat miner strikes beginning with Clements Kadalie's 1919 founding of the Industrial and Commercial Union and ending with the 1979 Wiehahn Commission's decriminalization of black union membership using a rapidly changing national archive.[20] In the archives I was literally struck by an organization called the Inspectorate of White Labor, a government agency established to reclassify work categories for "civilized" labor, to make poor whites the mascot for its policies by integrating them into the paid urban workforce, and to demote or fire black people who occupied the jobs. Social histories and political histories of poor whites and the Inspectorate of White Labor often failed to accurately portray the connections to racial segregation.[21] The histories failed to mention that poor whites contributed to the stalling of the black working class. The histories also explicitly blamed black people for white poverty. They got the roots and affect associated with poverty incredibly wrong. Moreover, many of the histories replicated common eugenics and segregationist tropes found in the Carnegie *Poor White Study;* both the published text and the larger research agenda constitute volatile and controversial cultural legacies. These violent narratives of "rehabilitation" and who might benefit from it have been decisively disproven by scholars who have studied gender and race under slavery and the global color line. I was compelled to read this history by people who have had to survive racialized poverty and what Patricia Hill Collins calls its "matrix of domination."[22] Reading the *Poor White Study* gave me actual nightmares for months because of its familiar "welfare queen" rhetoric, extant during the period I began my research. I found myself unconsciously writing "dem po' whites" dozens of times in my dissertation and field notes. Something was happening psychically in my reading as I recognized liberal racism and the rhetoric of civilizing missions. Thomas Noer explains that the nineteenth century closed with the cementing of the philosophy of "Anglo-Saxon solidarity" and a belief in an "Anglo-Saxon world mission," which tried to bring attention to the "characteristics and qualities of Anglo-Saxon nationalities" and the "English speaking race" and thereby normalize the legal practice of white immigration to places where white skin counted for access to legally protected affirmative action for whites.[23] The social histories about poor white people and the visual culture crafted in their defense basically repeated the racist accounts of the Carnegie Corporation.

The archivists could see the impact of my research a mile off. Having been made "an alien in a land called home"[24] and a member of that kin relationship known as the "afterlife of slavery," "born by captives, exiles, and orphans . . . [that] evidenced the wound and the attempt to heal it,"[25] my embodied practice of knowledge production threatened to crack open the mythological history of white settler colonial nationalism.[26] Being an African American woman, in fact, provided key insights. I came to political consciousness through the lessons of exiles who had been tortured into fundamental antagonism with the project of American Empire.[27] I was raised in black Detroit in the 1980s by South African dissident theologians, antiapartheid activists, and civil rights warriors. These people explained what would later become legally defined as "hate crimes" through a lens that linked Soweto to Dearborn. They explicitly hailed the entire population of Detroit as members of the third world radical left. Black internationalist and black feminist ideas offered powerfully different and far more ethical accounts of the materiality and psychic meaning of racialized poverty such that even when implicated in U.S. foreign policy,[28] this national "we" had consistently been concerned with internationalist racial justice, antislavery black consciousness against empire, and black power against white republican nationalism.[29] As a researcher of the intersection of race, philosophy, and international relations, my task was to analyze the process of white racialization, resist seeing South Africa as the super-racist aberrant twin of the United States,[30] and maintain integrity with the project of "look[ing] back" at white people,[31] from the complex positionality grafted onto me through antiblackness. Historically, African Americans have harmed white nationalism by dint of the permanence of a social location of "social death" and an enduring history of carrying forward the "black radical tradition" and pointing out the falsity of "racial regimes." In my own examination of white nationalism I developed new concepts, white misery and global whiteness, to examine the lasting implications of segregationist philanthropy and the attempts to civilize poor white people.

Introduction

Critiques of whiteness studies have warned that attention to white identities displaces examination of the roles that black people have been made to play in the making of the modern world.[1] In the tradition of C. L. R. James's "small whites"[2] and W. E. B. Du Bois's "transubstantiation of the poor white"[3] and foundational to my response to these critiques, I argue that construction of the abject black other and the construction of white poverty are inextricably bound together but not the same. Keeping these critiques in mind, this book is not an ethnography of poor whites. Rather, I focus on the champions of poor whites and the social world they sought to consolidate through domestic and global knowledge projects. In this social world the champions of poor whites marketed the notion of white civilization under periodic threat of white racial degeneration. They also categorically suppressed systematic black vulnerability and gendered black internationalist resistance projects. Such knowledge projects figure "New World black cultures [as] 'counter' to European narratives of history [because] Europe exorcized blackness in order to create its own invented traditions, empires, and fictions of superiority and racial purity."[4] Analyzing these knowledge projects is key to this work.

I argue that this social world predicated on white nationalism, white minority rule, and white republicanism was consistently challenged by black internationalist politics and Third World left politics.[5] Black internationalism and Third World left politics have been concerned with a set of "condition[s] not a place."[6] Black internationalist politics has illuminated the centrality of black people to the making of the modern world through its attention to racial chattel slavery and resistance to it and "the African diaspora as a unit of analysis for the study of world history."[7] This book is informed by black internationalist politics and especially the ways in which this politics understands self-determination, violence, poverty, work, the construction of sexuality and gender, and segregationist philanthropy. Such a critical geography is called for because "forced labor, racial oppression, colonial conditions, and capitalist exploitation were global processes that incorporated black people through empire building."[8] These global processes did not incorporate some uniform "type" of black people; rather "the historical struggle to resist domination" forged black internationalist politics, which "emerged alongside a discourse of difference and discontinuity."[9] Comparative racial politics research has been driven by national-scale comparison, which can serve as the ground for the application of a more theoretical analytic.[10] Reintroducing gendered black internationalism and the Third World left politics that have breathed life into it complicates the rubric of the nation-state and conversations about comparative racial politics that otherwise underanalyze transnational processes.

The figure of the "poor white" and the international campaign to lift members of this group to their "proper" racial-economic standing along the "global color line"[11] provides an enormously useful trope for examining the relationship between race and nation in a new way.[12] This book explores the political origins and the historical impact of the Carnegie Corporation–funded antipoverty research on "poor whites" (1927–32), published as the *Report of the Carnegie Commission of Investigation on the Poor White Question in South Africa* (also referred to as the *Poor White Study*), on the creation of a distinctly racial conception of citizenship, democracy, and work. The *Poor White Study* is a quintessential example of the intersection between segregationist philanthropy and scientific racism. Yet most studies that take up this intersection do not address poor whites as a common currency for U.S. and South African race relations policies.[13] I track the appearance and disappearance of "poor whites" and probe the belief that they are vulnerable to racial degeneration through contact and competition with African people.[14] I find that poor whites have been critical to the consolidation of various forms of white nationalism, Anglo-American solidarity, and white supremacy. Debates about "whiteness in crisis" domestically have obscured geopolitical conditions and played a decisive and enabling role for American Empire and Anglo-Saxon solidarity in the British colonies and dominions[15] via international philanthropy and *race relations technicians*,[16] a mobile community of race relations scholars who endorsed segregation in the United States and South Africa and many other settler colonies in which international philanthropies conducted race relations research. Research funded by the Carnegie Corporation shaped the ideological context and the research agenda that black people could inhabit. This philanthropy trained segregationist race relations experts who gained their expertise about race through personal experience with black scholars, organizations, and higher education institutions. It is little wonder, then, that Pan-Africanists regarding this era understood it as the "transfer overseas of American patterns of social organization . . . [and] extensions of the Corporation's domestic grant-making"—dissemination of widespread Jim Crow and racial colonialism.[17] The philanthropy and its race relations technicians claimed to be experts on black people and race throughout the African Diaspora because of this personal experience. Their "expertise" provided the foundation for academic disciplines and public and foreign policy that created enduring violence and injury for black people.[18]

The outcomes of the *Poor White Study* in apartheid law and the cultural and social organizations that synchronized the local and transnational project of Afrikaner Nationalism compel a reconsideration of the national boundaries of South Africa and the United States—as exceptional "racial regimes."[19] Drawing on archival, historical, institutional, cultural studies, and theoretical registers, I examine the making of national racial histories via global and transnational linkages, practices, philosophies, personnel, and professional associations.[20] I use the term *global whiteness* to denaturalize the existence, spatiality, and temporality of the white settler colonial nation, and to insist, as black radical movements do, that addressing racial politics as if it can be confined to national borders is a point of departure at best.[21] Here I argue that racial politics and its border-crossing features help create and sustain mythic national borders. Thus global whiteness and the mechanisms and processes by which it is sustained and mobilized can be better understood as the geographic contiguity that results from shared and enduring commitments to white nationalism as well as attempts to deny those commitments.[22] Such historical processes are not contained within "national boundaries and the national fictions."[23] Geographic contiguity can be measured through settler colonialism's "origin stories"[24] and white minority rule, the philanthropy dedicated in their names, the racist knowledge production that legitimates their rule, and the myths of black economic premodernity that shore up poor white racial rehabilitation.[25] I aim to deploy Denise Da Silva's analytic of the "arsenal of raciality" that constitutes a global racial order through which modernity emerges.[26] To that end we must understand that the social forces that created the opportunity for this U.S. philanthropy to become an international adviser to local debates about black people's appropriate role, place, and status after the age of empire were constitutive of modernity. Situating the presence of the Carnegie Corporation in Africa extends prior studies of poor whites via key thematics: white nationalism and global whiteness, the discourse of racial degeneration, the nexus between poor whites and increasing anti-black animus, how foundations govern and deploy contexts of racialized violence. Indeed, the supposed national specificity of racial geographies turns out to be in fact porous, permeable, and mutually constitutive of what I call global whiteness. Before we can truly explore the dimensions of global whiteness, let me turn my attention to an important example of white nationalism, Afrikaner Nationalism.

AFRIKANER NATIONALISM AS A VARIANT OF WHITE NATIONALISM: A LEAGUE OF NATIONS FOR RACIAL IMPERIALISM

Though focusing on white nationalism turns attention from the social history and distinctive historical uniqueness of the Afrikaner group, it makes the similarities between the political manufacture of Afrikaner Nationalism and other forms of settler nationalism perceivable. In many ways, the common history of settler colonialism and racial imperialism has been mystified and obscured by attention to white ethnic imagined community. Thus, this redirected focus places Afrikaner Nationalism in the context of a larger trend in settler societies that used white ethnic particularity and myths about autochthony and identity to historicize and naturalize white domination.[27]

In such narratives of white ethnic imagined community we are directed toward national origin stories instead of the ways in which such settler origin stories are historically contingent social formations in modernity. Focusing on white nationalism deliberately turns attention from the exceptionalist race relations history of Afrikanerdom in order to unearth the common history of settler colonialism and racial imperialism championed by white ethnic movements through national origin stories in the United States and South Africa.[28] Crawford and Lipschultz have explained that the manufacture of primordial ethnic identities in the early twentieth century relied on "political entrepreneurs."[29] The patriotic racialism of American president and political historian, Woodrow Wilson, articulated the trajectory of political maturation for these modern white nation-states in a way quite illuminating.[30] Wilson's history of the United States, written during his advocacy of the founding of the League of Nations and his authorization of a generation-long invasion of Haiti, reveled in myths about black inferiority.[31] Not only did Wilson exemplify a kind of national history that relied on an American racial empire, but he articulated a basic sentiment of white nationalism hegemonic among Anglophile historians and political scientists of his day. Ethnic sentiments would give way to national republican ones. Thus when condemning the ethnicity-based electoral organizing of working-class European immigrants, recruited for their ability to reinforce the color line, Wilson wrote, "We have room for but one loyalty and that is a loyalty to the American people. . . . [E]thnic associations [are] subversive."[32] It was precisely this inability to shed the ties of Afrikanerdom that disqualified South Africa from the status of sister republic with the United States that it craved. So, while I am not invested in repeating Wilson's crude ideas about national identity that conflate white nationality with *the* singular political culture of a country—a mythological construction itself—I am concerned with the ways in which attention to Afrikaner identity obscures the production of white nationalism and its attendant commitments to legitimating white authority over black peoples. Viewed as clinging to white ethnicity, Afrikaners were deemed politically immature among other white settler colonies.[33] Wilson argues for one loyalty, nationality, hoping to diminish the significance of ethnic attachments that had the potential to weaken the focus on white authority over black people—a shared interest among white settler colonies.

The national origin stories were mobilized to legitimate white domination and to suggest that white settlers, particularly in southern Africa, were simply one among many ancient "tribes." This idea conveniently erased not only twentieth-century histories of racial state making but also those that preceded them. Earlier histories of racial state making, enlightenment, conquest, militarism, extermination, and Christian cartographies of empire relied on the deployment of settler populations to rationalize the world into a proliferation of modern white nation-states. Thus, considering that the manufacture of white identities coincided with the manufacture of settler colonies as nations, I am more than suspicious of explanations of Afrikaner identity rooted in ethnicity. I propose a radical turn toward considering the shared aspiration to white supremacy that united the sentiments and political ideologies of Afrikaner and British South Africans—to make the African into a Negro.

While the political conflict between the Afrikaners and the British is an important explanatory variable for explaining social and political change in South Africa, since both groups were subject to similar forms of the manufacture of white identities, I propose mapping the term *white* onto both groups to deliberately foreground the emergence of the post–World War II term *ethnicity*.[34]

Clear indications of the manufacture of Afrikaner identity exist in many forms of political advocacy among the Dutch in South Africa. Three arenas provide the best evidence for disrupting fictitious notions about the originality and particularity of Afrikanerdom: Afrikaner spaces, Afrikaner language, and Afrikaner cultural renaissance. Afrikaner nationalism's imitation history of the Afrikaner republics has been disseminated widely. This imitation history excised the numerous Dutch-British marriages and the large numbers of Khoi, Colored, so-called Baster,[35] and African slaves and laborers who traveled with Dutch farmers on the Great Trek (the successive European migrations from the British colonies in southern Africa to the so-called Afrikaner republics, the Orange Free State and the Transvaal, in the 1830s). According to this imitation history the Afrikaner republics were occupied because they were lands without people or time. Such allegedly "Afrikaner spaces" were in fact demographically multilingual, multiracial, and multiethnic while being governed by white minority rule.[36] Moreover, Afrikaner identity was resisted and embraced at key moments in economic and political history—to protect key colonial and postcolonial relations.[37] The Orange Free State and Transvaal were Afrikaner in terms of political and state power but never in terms of the actual constitution of labor, demography, landownership, and social makeup. To perpetuate the idea of these "ethnic spaces" is to repeat a dangerous mythology of racial colonialism and grand apartheid. However, Afrikaner identity was seized upon as a useful political identity to make a claim that a type of racial, cultural, ethnic, or linguistic homogeneity existed among these people when it did not. It is a homogeneity continually breached and restored by the existence of poor whites. Like myths about geographic purity and uniformity, the adoption of spoken Afrikaans as the language of the putative Afrikaner nation illustrates the manufacture of Afrikaner particularity and uniqueness. Afrikaans was the co-opted language of the Khoi people enslaved by the Dutch in

South Africa. The cultural arm of Afrikaner Nationalism published dictionaries and composed national songs and established Afrikaner-medium schools and civic associations. They hosted national festivals, built national monuments, and convened nation-building festivals commemorating the migration from the Cape Colony to the newly founded Dutch Republics. All of these were attempts to establish an Afrikaner literary tradition and a formalized cultural discourse that might legitimate their racial state making.

In an illuminating rendering of this process of white nationalism at work, Cedric Robinson describes the seventeenth- and eighteenth-century flowering and emergence of "the English people," which similarly relied on the creation of standardized English dictionaries, the writing of histories of the English people, writing and dramatization of popular educational "history plays" for the illiterate, translating the Bible into English, and historicizing the world economy from the parochial standpoint offered in the *Wealth of Nations*. The proliferation of these texts and plays and their audiences created spaces for the practice and recognition of this new English national identity, the British Empire project, and the invention of the inferiorized Black—The Negro—to "all step onto the world stage together."[38] "The Negro" they meant to create referred to "Black Africans, the Indians of India, Native Americans, Japanese, and slaves of whatever ancestry."[39] Further these language projects did the work of erasing the history of English people as racial slaves by constantly marshaling the mantra of the British Empire that, as the British military anthem "Rule, Britannia" put it, "Britons never never shall be slaves."[40] Englishness, perhaps the prototypical manufactured white nationalism, was merely a brand for selling white supremacy, power, and capital. In short, Afrikaner ethnicity as a purely manufactured political project helped consolidate and map whiteness onto the Dutch Republics and embraced the "invented Negro" for the rest of southern Africa beyond their borders, suppressing and rewriting the Afrikaners' own history within the global white imaginary. The racial regimes analytic allows us to focus on the politics of the making of Afrikaner Nationalism, while the ethnic paradigm mystifies this process.

WHITE MISERY, WHITE NATIONALISM, AND HISTORICAL CONSCIOUSNESS

White subjectivity invariably includes freedom, selfhood, humanity, desires, forged memory, authority, legitimacy, production, sociality, reproduction, space, and representativeness. As Woods explains, "As a result of slavery, the concept of freedom in the West developed through its negation, unfreedom."[41] "Becoming white" thus requires being rehabilitated for the purposes of becoming the central subject-beneficiary of the modern nation and its "racial contract."[42] Concomitant to this status of being subject-beneficiary, the white supremacist polity and white nationalist ideologies promise white people that they will achieve historical consciousness in exchange for service as the vigilante "paddy-rollers of history"[43] and the "do-gooders" of history.[44] White nationalism protects white subjectivity. White nationalism also provides political and ideological cover for those "impulses to moral action [that have] been slain by fears of racial exile."[45]

Therefore being deemed a "waste of a white skin"[46]—what I am theorizing as white "flesh," or "white primitives," the abject status assigned to poor whites—typically incites a false equivalency that co-opts and displaces contemporary and historical black suffering and black flourishing for the sake of sympathy, albeit with white supremacy.[47] This notion of the white primitive could not elicit such horror, however, without a history of actual white enslavement somewhere in the recesses of psychic memory, albeit a racial history that is transformed into the empowering nostalgia of ethnicity.[48] When white people are publicly reminded of this slave heritage, the reminders are associated with scare tactics about a threatening black presence and the potential for overwhelming black governance and other expressions of "fears" of white racial degeneration.[49]

Such reminders insist on greater white solidarity. As long as white people anywhere can be injured as collateral damage of antiblackness or can be treated like blacks qua slaves white supremacy has limitless possibilities to criminalize, intervene in, and interrupt black racial resistance and to minimize and naturalize black racial suffering. Unsurprisingly, attention to poverty, gender, miscegenation, ethnicity, religion, or bodily difference of whiteness, as occurs in various rediscoveries of whiteness, is often misconstrued as "white disaffiliation from white supremacy" rather than as a recurring "hegemonic configuration of white supremacy."[50] My project examines what I am calling "white misery" as a type of historiographic mischief, the rediscovery of white people as flesh who arrived there through alleged competition with black people reduced to flesh. White misery, thus, allows for a theoretical exploration of the myth that black suffering and black racial resistance are a result of innocent unfortunate circumstances socially constructed without agencies, decision makers, and beneficiaries. White misery also allows for a more careful parsing of the processes of white racialization. I am, therefore, concerned with when and how white misery returns. For whom and how does white vulnerability suggest a relationship of shared status with blackness? In what ways was white vulnerability meant to guarantee black suffering as natural and reasonable while simultaneously rendering black racial resistance as unthinkable? White misery suggests that white vulnerability is another alibi for the "neglect and miscomprehension of the nature and genesis of liberation struggles which already had occurred and surely had yet to occur."[51]

Deeming poor whites a waste of white skin is an authorizing historical gesture undergirded by the accepted belief in the white male republican citizen[52] coemergent with white nationalism as the signature raison d'être of racial chattel slavery.[53] In white nations founded on slavery and founded again through the "progress narratives" granted by emancipation there were also those whites who could not qualify as white. Indeed their existence suggested a temporal and spatial breakdown, and a definitive disjuncture with postemancipation progress narratives. To put it simply, the persistent rediscovery of poor whites undoes the progress narrative. The existence of poor whites made it harder to believe the ideology that a decisive temporal and spatial transition had occurred in national historical consciousness, mode of production, and cultural affect and sensibility. The existence of poor whites made the decisiveness of the shift from colonial and imperial rule to the revolution-minded settler nation far more tenuous. Each of those enterprises was united by an impulse in the tradition of Theodore Roosevelt's "barbaric virtues,"[54] a carefully worded caveat to the notion of the unsullied white republican citizen. Aristotle's defense of the role of the racial slave for the republic provides as good an explication as any for the longevity of poor whites and, more important, for the longevity of the constitutive antagonism between the racial slave and the republic. Slavery was deemed a necessity for economic self-sufficiency for citizen-owners and for the caricatures of humanity deemed "slaves." Enslaved people were rarely expected to achieve the virtuousness of pursuing freedom. Perceived as having "marginal intelligence and development, Aristotle found no compelling reason for inquiry into the ethics, consciousness, or desires of slaves."[55] As a living will-less part of her master's body, the slave could not achieve freedom, pursue it, or birth it, and thus was "disqualified ... from historical and political agency in the modern world."[56] Blackness and antiblackness (construed as the natural status of the slave)[57] have been used repeatedly as "race relations technologies" to inaugurate new historical moments and new national, territorial, and diasporic spaces, along with new peoples to inhabit these moments and spaces.[58] In the modern age republican nation-building projects depended wholly on giving license to white subjects around the world as racist citizens of white minority–rule republics. But such nation-building projects also depended on having the capacity to protect vulnerable white people from slipping into the category of blackness (construed as the natural slave). Such national membership was and is contingent on the ways which the nation is committed to producing blackness and, perhaps more important, on the ways in which antiblackness has produced nations, or in Randolph Churchill's hateful words, "Why do you always worry about our niggers? . . . We don't worry about yours."[59] To deploy a racial politics that takes a particular/given/unique nation and its distraught and needy white bodies at face value, then, misses the mark. Rather, thinking about global whiteness and the ways it has been central to making white minority rule legitimate informs our understandings of black insurgency. When white poverty becomes politically salient it is clear that historical consciousness is at stake.

THE WHITE PRIMITIVE AS A MECHANISM OF GENDERED BLACKNESS

Black people and poor white people are not parallel social locations, even though they are mutually constituted by interested parties and forces claiming to advocate on behalf of white citizens, workers, and women. Indeed tropes about black suffering as comic relief and not as injury fill the gap between white privilege and white misery. The study of the complicated relationship between the racialization of whites and nonwhites, blacks in particular, is stymied by a history of trying to reclaim a sympathetic and humane white position while disavowing the power of antiblack impositions. Moreover, as long as white identity is most often deployed to obscure black suffering, sympathy with whiteness comes again at a cost paid by black people.[60] Zine Magubane rightly admonishes the misstep made by historians who draw a false parallel between poor whites and Africans, making white workers, white women, and the white poor analogous as "savage paupers," "vagrants," and the "heathen at home."[61] This falsification, for instance, allowed British pro-imperialist labor organizers and feminist humanitarians to justify their domestic and international antipoverty campaigns.[62] My work avoids this parallelism by pointing instead to (1) the mechanisms by which white on white racial violence operates; (2) how white on white racial violence uses antiblackness to legitimize the surveillance and isolation of poor whites; and (3) how white on white racial violence creates more intractable forms of antiblack racism. Poor whites are both a social group that is subjected to forms of antiblackness and racialization *and* poor whites are a key to the most pervasive, recurrent, and deeply entrenched practices of antiblackness.

We see the centrality of the cultural work that can be done in ideas about poor white people operating in experimental research on race, poverty, and gender in the United States. In Gilliam's research, interviewees hearing and viewing the same script performed by black and white impoverished women had more extreme antiblack attitudes when they viewed poor white women. Respondents were being cued to comment on their views about the mythological "welfare queen" caricature of antipoverty policy and those deemed the undeserving poor. Each script advocated for long-term and massive state subsidies for the poor. Gilliam explains, "Exposure to the white version of the welfare story also seem[s] to induce whites who describe themselves as having liberal views about gender roles to arrive at extremely harsh views of African-Americans."[63] Depicting a white woman in poverty was a powerful trigger for white respondents, especially white female respondents, in experimental research, because it created cognitive dissonance within several cultural scripts: (1) white women have wealth and are insulated from grinding poverty; (2) black people are inherently poor, as enshrined in public policy; (3) black women and black families are a threat to "normal" and "natural" white family life; and (4) black suffering is unremarkable and black people as subhuman do not experience suffering the same way white people do/would.[64] Poor black women demanding economic justice trigger what Ange-Marie Hancock termed a "politics of disgust," and poor white women demanding economic justice trigger more extreme versions of the same.[65] In the United States in the 1930s, social workers routinely denied impoverished black women public assistance because they believed that black women could always find work as contract laundry workers. This continually repositioned black women as collective laborers for and as the property of white society. Thus the idea of the black welfare queen is an enduring reminder of earlier categories of perpetual wageless black female labor. Julia Jordan-Zachery refers to these "cultural imaginaries" of black women as property as a linchpin for white family life.[66] Viewed as property of the larger society, black women have struggled to access the welfare state provisions designed to guarantee that impoverished white people do not occupy the status of the white primitive. Preventing public consideration of the white poor is a high stakes game, and so they only figure in the public policy agenda when they can function as ciphers for yet another opportunity to trigger and express virulent antiblack sentiment and cover over structural antiblack policies.

Scholars have expended much effort to subject the juridical illegibility of ontological and material black suffering to "re-memory"[67] and "redressing the pained black body."[68] They have written about the challenge to black women's credibility as witnesses and their unique lack of legal standing when championing remedies to sexual violence under enslavement and apartheid, in the workplace, by state officials, and in the prison system.[69] More than tropes or traveling discourses, the suffering of black bodies (libidinal, psychic, material, collective, and physical) continues to mark the nature of the global order and the "terms of order."[70] Importantly, these scholars conclude that black women's status as "unrapeable"—like the status of being always available for household labor—constitutes the arena of white female suffering.[71] Black suffering is made to provide a grammar for empathizing with nonblack suffering. Angela Davis draws attention to this juridical illegibility as it shows up again in the practices of detention and incarceration such as cavity searches, strip searches, and gynecological exams. These practices are necessary for reinforcing the capacity to do violence to black people that shores up their ontological role in the society. Davis concludes that these practices constitute "state sexual assault" and that "prison and police officers are vested with the power and responsibility to do acts which, if done outside of work hours, would be crimes of sexual assault."[72] She elaborates, "If a person does not 'consent' to being stripped naked by these officers, force can lawfully be used to do it."[73] Ayelet Waldman and Robin Levi identified these same practices as part of the continuum of labor and delivery in the narratives of women in the prison system in the United States and revealed the extent to which the prison is a site of gratuitous sexualized state violence.[74] What this teaches us is that one category of bodies can experience injury while another is constructed as not having the capacity for injury.[75] Upon reflection, the parallels that designate all manner of forms of bondage equivalent fly apart when one considers what processes constitute gendered blackness under the modern nation. The relationship between antiblackness and whiteness can thus be understood as that power antagonism which results in white subjectivity doing unlimited systematic cross-generational, structural, material, psychic, social, cultural, and psychological violence to "black bodies reduced to mere flesh," as Spillers would put it. Robinson explains this power antagonism with the phrase "invent the Negro." Through these power operations black people are severed from history, from kinship, and from existence. Such a catechism of horrors comes to mind not simply as a recitation of slights and certainly not to undermine the history of social movements and liberationist visions. Rather it is these things that stand to be remembered when the white primitive no longer engenders feelings of loyalty and defense. Being confronted by the white primitive further legitimates state, vigilante, and interpersonal forms of antiblackness.

INFLUENCE HARVESTING: HOW FOUNDATIONS GOVERN

My work puts the literature on race in philanthropy in conversation with that on race in the social sciences to examine the Carnegie Corporation's influence on the white supremacist polity and public policy making. I use the term *influence harvesting* to draw attention to the practices of "extending the capacity of governance without expanding the national government."[76] By collecting and disseminating abstract national-level data irrelevant to solving neighborhood-scale problems, reform-era philanthropies disincentivized local political mobilization and disciplined elected officials and their constituencies to the need for experts.[77] Influence harvesting includes seeding, founding, funding, and proliferating organizations, institutions, and bureaucratic linkages and associations that actively subvert national and local systems of democratic representation through identifying and containing social forces of resistance to capital and antidemocracy.[78] Foundations produce experts who respond to social problems/crises through the reconsolidation of power via racial regimes. Carnegie-sponsored experts built new public policy organizations that promoted fictional meritocratic antidotes to economic antagonism and structural misery. Foundations produce what the historian Alice O'Connor has called "poverty knowledge."[79] Foundations displace charitable and religious organizations, which more explicitly explain those deemed the undeserving poor as examples of moral failure. Foundations suppress "competing models for social research [especially about poverty] such as female headed holistic localized studies" operating out of community research sites like settlement houses.[80]

The Carnegie Corporation used influence harvesting to "organiz[e] the cultural leadership" of U.S. and South African society and that of other former colonies to promote respectability and deference to the knowledge elite.[81] The Carnegie Foundation's interventions into the domestic policies of former British colonies on the African continent had antecedents in older philanthropic organizations and ideologies about social welfare and poverty common in both the United States and Britain—what I call the "slavery-foundation nexus." Berman writes that "a similar ideology characterized these foundation programs, whether they were undertaken at home early in the century or abroad fifty years later."[82] By "slavery-foundation nexus," I mean the claims made by the older philanthropic organizations to have special purchase on how to promote and organize society by dint of being founded by wealthy people and through their familiarity with the management of slaves in the Americas and in the colonial world. Such cultural leaders dedicated to the uplift of the descendants of slaves were in effect the descendants of the former captains of the industry in slaves. Foundations played a key role in the training of a linked elite that was "efficient, professional, moderate, incremental, and nonthreatening to the class interests of the" super-wealthy and their multiple interlocking projects of elite domination[83] Leonard Harris refers to this would-be elite as the "professionalized status-seekers within academies of culture."[84] The Carnegie Corporation hitched the interests of these new professionals and their organizations to a public function,[85] shaping mass opinion and legitimating capitalism.[86] Such interests were antagonistic to the vindicationist intellectual resistance against the global color line that animated their black contemporaries.

Regarded as the "mid-wife of the Harlem Renaissance," a signature historical epoch in the struggle against the global color line, the philosopher and critical social scientist Alain Locke (1885–1954), a contemporary of Carnegie's early-twentieth-century influence harvesting, briefly served as an evaluator of Carnegie adult education projects in Harlem and Atlanta. Locke had powerful insights into the arbitrariness and ethnocentricism of social scientific empiricism, and the racialism of American pragmatism.[87] Foundation leaders relied on the crudest of racial tropes about societies composed of "the ruled" and "the rulers" that reflected U.S. foreign policy interests that the U.S. military would implement. Locke's flight from the cultural logic of enslavement and racial domination found repeated articulation in the scholarly criticism by black intellectuals of this period whose renaissance approach to knowledge was less calculating and more attuned to opposing racial domination than that scientific interest gauged to retaining racial domination as a foundational means for retaining domestic and international power.

The more consistent nature of foundation-vetted experts was a revolving door through which the "architects of post–World War II foreign policy . . . regularly moved back and forth between corporate headquarters, foundation offices, and state or defense department positions."[88] The Corporation's trustees made grants "which would protect Anglo-Saxon prerogatives, customs, and genes [and] . . . preserve power for people of white, Anglo-Saxon, Protestant lineage."[89] These new forms of knowledge (and the new sciences, departments, and professional associations that they called into existence) masked the oligarchic goals of the foundation sector.[90] These new bases of institutional power in universities and government also drained power, legitimacy, and authority from elected representative government. Consequently at some point governance could not occur without the legitimacy and scientific expertise proffered by foundation experts. Governance of this style in the classical period was known as government by "the best people," or oligarchy. Oligarchy required that property-owning people educated in the narrow interpretations of classical antiquity favored by Andrew Carnegie govern. This particular oligarchy prohibited decision making by immigrants, workers, and, most important, black people. Even when affiliated social scientists (some of whom were trustees and directors of the corporation or other Carnegie agencies) demanded to be allowed the right to decide on their research projects the corporation dictated their topics.

Foundations jumpstart *national industries* and help the idea of the nation cohere. The founding of the National Bureau of Economic Research, for example, provides a profitable illustration of "expertise combined with public education [that] would yield progress and prosperity, but without essential social change."[91] To usher in an era in which everyday people would come to think of their lives in terms of scientific rationality and then would defer to scientists to lead national and foreign policy making required pointing to the "cultural value of science" and the ways that science could be a basis for economic development. Of course this required labeling wealthy individuals' beliefs as scientific innovation in the public service. Since social change from below was the ultimate threat to this oligarchy, influence harvesting as a concept decodes the purported diversity and range of political interests that animated the Carnegie Corporation and those it represented.

THE CARNEGIE CORPORATION IN THE AGE OF LYNCHING

Scholars have described this period as the "Age of Lynching," an era in which major technological shifts in mass transit and communication were enunciated through spectacular acts of antiblack torture and gratuitous violence.[92] Antiblack violence and its commitment to sexualized torture (public and private) formed the routines and everyday practices on which a modern, technologically oriented public sphere could be planted.[93] Black counterpublics responded by mass migration, political mobilization, and the use of print, film, and theater to undercut notions of their subhumanity and advocate for racial equality. Black victims of gratuitous forms of sexualized torture, paradigmatically conceived of as slaves/ex-slaves/freed people, bore the stigma of routinized, often highly technologically rendered violence and lived through the postemancipation global extension and intensification of slavery (albeit through more extensive contract relations).[94] Though such routine violence often could be masked by the aura of scientific progress, economic development, or positivist "knowledge," the racial labor hierarchy rested on the violence itself.[95] Indeed, routine violence bolstered the claim that only certain white men could rebel and only certain rebellions protected liberty.[96] Goldsby writes:

> Violence was part of a cultural milieu that saw westward expansion. . . . [C]ompletion of the transcontinental railroad [would] bring about the Plains Indian Wars of the 1870s and 1880s. Nativist vigilantism against the influx of immigrants from southern and eastern Europe in the Northeast and entry of the Chinese into the West created a lethal synergy with anti-black mob violence. Because labor strikes were often deadly conflicts of interest, workers' battles with corporate bosses were often compared with lynching.[97]

Mass media used flash photography and sound recordings to disseminate images of lynching violence.[98] The federal government, the Bureau of Indian Affairs, and arms manufacturers used the new technology of the machine gun to murder entire peoples and to consolidate American Empire. Guilds, unions, white European minority civic associations, and corporations used early cinema, bare-knuckle boxing, and football to absorb the rage and the wages of the skilled working and clerical classes.[99] Land companies deployed corporate capitalism and railroad construction to facilitate the introduction of black craft workers, entrepreneurs, rural peasants, tenant farmers, domestic workers, and former inmates in the convict lease labor system to solidify a racialized division of labor.[100] The new communication, weapons, leisure, and industrial technologies had audiences and customers only because of the preexisting racial technologies of Negrophobia as basic forms of American entertainment and sociality.[101] These technologies moderated antagonistic social forces and more profoundly entrenched freedmen and freedwomen in the perpetual position of being seen as property of white society: "workers" whose labor was not seen as labor but tribute due to their collective racial superiors. These technologies and the same social forces that popularized them sought to use science, law, economics, and Greek and Roman art and design to obscure, disavow, and continue these forms of violence. These included nullification of the black vote, entrenching and extending slave status after the U.S. Civil War in California, Peru, Brazil, Cuba, New Zealand, Australia, Fiji, and South Africa, and deploying nativist vigilante campaigns enacted by U.S. workers and a U.S. diplomatic plantocracy. This social plan and social design was undergirded by a unifying ideology of liberalism, a white supremacist Anglo-Saxon mandate to govern as white men, an uncanny and disturbing entanglement with presidential administrations, and the continuation of the American Century through ideas about the legitimacy of U.S. coordination and leadership internationally, especially in the former British settler colonies. At the same time visions of Anglo-Saxon liberalism entrenched white supremacy globally in the institutions being organized for global peace.[102] Vindicationists from black internationalist and black nationalist leagues provided an insightful rendering of the antagonism between the darker nations' insistence on racial equality and that of Anglo-Saxon liberalism.[103] By suppressing calls for racial equality, this naive liberalism cloaked a violent context. As the cultural historian Jacqueline Goldsby explains:

> Despite the fact that black people were "lynched" in any number of ways (hanging, shooting, stabbing, burning, dragging, bludgeoning, drowning, and dismembering), similar atrocities that occurred in the course of race riots aren't called "lynching," nor are they factored into established inventories of lynching's death toll. Hundreds of murders and assaults occurred under the regimes of convict lease labor and debt peonage too, the accounts of which often describe what we would consider lynchings. Like the rapes of black women by white men (and Native women by non-Native men), because those atrocities aren't considered part of lynching's history. . . . [There are many] lives lost to us and made invisible by lynching and its cultural logic.[104]

This toxic liberalism suffused everyday practices of leisure, work, and reading the news. As white workers mobilized as political constituencies against robber barons and captains of industry, the national romance with the plantation and slavery was being congealed into notions about how to control and guide oneself, one's household, and the commonwealth. In efforts to recount the many "lives lost to us" in the maelstrom of violence and force that forged this historical moment, the divergent ways in which racialization has operated have been flattened. Returning to the ways in which abject whiteness is inextricably bound to what is the expected and normal position for black people in the social order—wretchedness, suffering, invented Negrohood—relies on honest and careful attention to social death and who is made to occupy it. Further, attention to white on white racial violence provides a more robust account of the ongoing surveillance of poor whites and how this links to more intractable forms of anti-black racism.[105]

CARNEGIE'S FRANCHISE TO GOVERN

Placing the Carnegie Corporation in the context of racial violence both domestic and international ("the Corporations self-imposed mandate to define, develop, and distribute knowledge") and its interest in a "franchise to govern, in important indirect ways" in all of the English-speaking colonies is powerfully informative.[106] While the Carnegie Corporation was designing black education for "underdeveloped peoples" in the United States and in colonized Africa, this franchise to govern reflected the corporation's determination to entrench a global "racial development scheme."[107] At the heart of the ostentatious silences about enduring violence against black people (and all those designated as in close social proximity to black people) in some of the leading work on the Carnegie Corporation is the truth that even a repressive federal government representing the extravagant pathological greed of mining magnates and the descendants of slave owners could not be trusted with the "repression of social forces and social ferment."[108]

For Andrew Carnegie, in the transitional age between British imperialism and American imperialism, progress meant ending the economic caste system among English-speaking persons, though not the racial one. Carnegie used print media coupled with philanthropy as a bully pulpit to provide moral guidance to the poorer classes—throughout the British Empire. In the United States where Carnegie was an employer of tens of thousands people he used print and philanthropy to legitimate racial capitalism. He supported strikebreaking and the economic caste system in the United states but rejected both in Britain. He measured progress by the number of people made into connoisseurs of refined culture and the creation of a commonwealth of public goods that included free libraries, museums, downtown plazas, classical music concerts, and church organs.[109] Thus Carnegie Corporation philanthropy also fostered devotion to an oligarchic class, its culture, social relations, and interests, in a way that claimed no public antagonism with the aspirations of the working classes or those who labored without the status of "worker."

Carnegie's gospel of wealth played well to a certain sector of the Victorian, assimilationist, and racially accomodationist U.S. audience enchanted by the ideology of the Gilded Age, a period of enduring excessive violence. At the same time freedmen and freedwomen, labor leaders, domestic workers, sharecroppers, and migrants to cities in North America, the Pacific, the Caribbean, South America, and Africa championed a different notion of the public and found themselves engulfed by American notions of individualistic freedom and subservient to American corporate interests.[110] Freed people's political interests revolved around addressing the ways in which the new technologies perpetuated bondage.[111] In fact, bondage shaped precisely the ways in which black bodies were incorporated into what Roediger and Esch call the "production of difference." The counterinsurgent political project of the Carnegie philanthropies, birthed in countless moments of militant resistance by workers and freed people, sought to disentangle the idea of white people as workers and the need for associations founded to advance the interests of working people and to redirect white people especially toward white supremacist associational life in order to shore up the racial division of labor and wealth. Indeed, after spectacular wars such as that which occurred at the Carnegie factory in Homestead, Pennsylvania, Carnegie's domestic brand of social education could become far more subtle and yet far more ubiquitous and invasive.

Eugene Debs's 1892 speech, "Crimes of Carnegie: Protest against Condoning Crime in the Name of Philanthropy," details the Homestead Strike of 1892 and Carnegie Steel's attempts to destroy the Amalgamated Association of Iron and Steel Workers.[112] Carnegie Steel was engaged in a project of deskilling their unionized Pennsylvania workers. After a month of striking plant officials called in both Pinkerton Guards and the state militia and installed electrified wire and pipes filled with boiling water that would literally scar and maim striking workers.

Violence and the capacity to do violence constituted the ultimate racial technology. Violence made possible expanding corporate governance while subverting representative government. Having increased production rapidly via new steel plating techniques, the company could wait out the end of the contract and any strike. The Carnegie Corporation used deadly force (private and public) and the Pennsylvania governor's office, which was dependent on Carnegie money, to control workers. The same Carnegie who publicly disavowed the economic caste system and strikebreaking in England resolved the conflict in Pennsylvania by recruiting unskilled black workers to bear the violent brunt of an intraracial battle over who belonged in white supremacy. Thus tens of thousands of skilled white Homestead employees who resided in a planned city that came to be a watchword in late-nineteenth-century corporate capitalism raged against black replacement workers. The tactic of deploying black labor as strikebreakers illustrates the role and positioning of black people vis-á-vis white workers. When plant officials recruited black workers to be the unskilled labor force to complement the new technologies, they signaled their investment in a world in which black bodies were engulfed in economic and industrial modernization. However, these black people were transformed through hypervisibility in a planned white worker colony. Further, these black people were denied access to skill and innovation and the sociopolitical status of worker. This modern industrial transformation was one that black people were deeply familiar with given the nature of slavery in North America. The black people who entered this nexus of industrial civilization were ideologically sutured to the new technological innovations being introduced and the perpetual devaluation of themselves in the workplace and the industrial town as "workers." As strikebreakers—a category of labor that is deemed antagonistic to work, workers, and the ability of "workers" to organize politically and make legitimate political claims—their bodies served as visible reminders of this transformation of workers' status. Plant officials recruited black strikebreakers to frame the conflict with white workers as a conflict about bondage and freedom. Since black bodies always bear the fertile history of wageless, socially dead racial enslavement, white worker political violence could be directed toward them. This response would replay the history of a carceral democracy and demonstrate that white workers' participation in antiblack violence was a major dimension of white workers' freedom.[113] Vigilante violence against black people and blackened racialized groups in many ways constitute the fundamental definition of the political status of the white worker, although not their economic status.[114] The black workers who were recruited in this moment were intended specifically to redirect the political interest of white workers toward gratuitous violence and generalized dishonor of black people. In Homestead, Pennsylvania, and later as a segregationist philanthropy Carnegie officials propagandized that (1) black strikebreakers were the most significant threat to white workers and (2) white workers on strike misunderstood their political status in the racial division of labor. This history illustrates the relationship between a racial division of knowledge and a racial labor hierarchy in which the former provides a comprehensive strategy for influence harvesting and the latter the demolition of the white working class. Each time the white working class failed to link its interests with "white" professional arenas of clerkship for captains of industry, the signature punishment would be the reminder that a white working class would be subject to the risk of the antihuman status that confined black life and death. In this light white people who identified as workers were said to have failed to embrace their sovereignty and rulership or at least their potential for these things. This is not to say that the Amalgamated Association was primed to recruit black people as union members. This is certainly not the case. Ultimately nearly constant monitoring of social relations and manipulation of public opinion through informal political education, whether at the museum, at the public library, or against striking workers, would be necessary to ensure that the white working class came to believe that its signature threat was "cheap" Negro labor. Debs's speech as well as the Strike Committee Declaration warned that the mere memory of something approximating the political interests of a white working class could result in intense white on white violence. Whereas Debs's 1901 speech deemed Carnegie's largesse the "booty of philanthropic piracy," "reckless prodigality," and "alleged philanthropy," Malawian women a generation later, in 1929, were reported to have rejected Carnegie-funded domestic training education that they had been told would be teacher training.[115] These women rejected the supposed largesse of the Carnegie Corporation because of the racialized work and social categories to which they would be confined, thereby synchronizing with other battles by black people against racial accommodationism in social life across the globe. Anticipating sustained battles across the globe against Bantu Education, segregationist philanthropy advocated "education for domination," segregated education, and education which would impose self-negating subjectivities.[116]

At the same time, the United States was engaged in a land grab in the Caribbean, Central America, and the Pacific Islands while also effectively marketing itself as the democratic alternative to British and Spanish imperialism. Carnegie-built institutions made classical culture accessible to the masses without implicating them directly in American imperialism, American nationalism, or the sterilization and genocidal evacuation of populations. Carnegie's appeal to a politics of knowledge that created a new romanticized national identity should be understood as a set of founding noble lies about the legitimacy and permanence of white superiority. Such origin stories shored up racial segregation and justified the brutal practices employed to control labor. As in other racial regimes, American nationalism deployed noble lies about its inherent "sweetness and light"[117] through its ties to the most elitist aspects of Greek experiments with democracy.[118] Such noble lies Robinson explains, prop up racial regimes and "are actually contrivances, designed and delegated by interested cultural and social powers with the wherewithal sufficient to commission their imaginings, manufacture, and maintenance."[119] In the same way that Shakespeare transmitted "classical" culture to give provenance and status to British nationalism, Carnegie's personal writings intended to rewrite the history of the Greeks and Romans in a way that promoted plutocracy. Popular novels that included young strivers, easy prosperity, and land newly "opened" were key to these sanitized histories. Extraordinarily savage acts of state-sanctioned genocide were not included in what was to become the popular history of the new white farming, mining, and drilling class of ragamuffins-become-millionaires.[120] The American Century was launched partly with Carnegie's lofty paeans to progress and uplift for downtrodden whites in the context of massive migrations of recently freed black people to cities, massive migrations from Europe, China, Japan, the Philippines, and the Caribbean, and the shifting racial politics in the Caribbean, Mexico, and Latin America. Carnegie drafted many noble lies about a culture of international harmony to produce a fictional history to expand the influence and power of foundations, their personnel, and their wealthy backers. At the same time American borders and spheres of influence were reshaping and and making national boundaries around the world.

Chapter 1 dispenses with the key frames put forward in the *Poor White Study* in order to situate the failure of domestic policy in South Africa to shore up wages and the quality of life for poor whites. It considers the question, if civic associations and state pressure could not secure the global color line, in what ways might other forces, especially race relations technicians like E. G. Malherbe, catalyze a transformation in the conditions of the South African racial labor hierarchy? Chapter 2 examines the depictions of poor whites to demonstrate how "vulnerable whiteness" and "whiteness in Africa" were deployed in theater, early cinema, political cartoons, and ethnographic photography. Chapter 3 considers whiteness as misery, especially in the thriving legacy of scientific racism.[121] Several questions are at stake: Is white suffering a ruse for displacing black suffering? Does attacking white privilege naturalize the association of blackness with slavery, and to what end?[122] How is antiblackness used to survey and isolate poor whites and create more intractable forms of antiblack racism?[123] When do false parallels between white suffering and blackness emerge and for what set of purposes? Chapter 4 examines the alarming lack of difference between liberal and Marxist historiographies: both misunderstand the relationship between poor whites and black workers through the racialized concepts "job competition" and "cheap labor." Chapter 5 explores how the race for eugenics has been conflated with national scientific achievement in the study of South Africa as a modern *nation*, thereby abetting the manufacture of white citizenship and transforming settlers into *white people*—as a prophylaxis against the travel writer Anthony Trollope's 1877 prediction about South Africa always being a "black man's country." Chapter 6 explains the context that shaped the research agenda for Carnegie philanthropy in Africa. Knowing what research the Carnegie Corporation funded and rejected aids in our understanding of the role of the *Poor White Study* and white poverty as a tool in the global segregationist arsenal. Chapter 7 provides in-depth coverage of one of the research team members, Marie Elizabeth Rothmann (1875–1975). Rothmann's work in the Department of Welfare provides an example of the making of "race relations technicians" and their influence in South African government and internationally. The chapter analyzes why proto–social workers, charity workers, and clergy who proposed the most sympathetic public policy were the faction of Afrikaner Nationalists jettisoned by Carnegie's "scientific" approach to the poor white problem.

CHAPTER 1

Forgeries of History

The Poor White Study

According to the U.S.-trained South African educator Ernest Gideon Malherbe (1895–1982), the *Poor White Study* had its origins in his youthful musings. But, as I investigate here the Carnegie Corporation created Malherbe and the other members of the cadre of "race relations technicians"— a mobile community of race relations scholars who endorsed segregation in the United States and South Africa and many other settler colonies in which international philanthropies conducted race relations research. I consider Malherbe's several attempts to establish himself in the annals of intellectual history. Though his research writings were littered with discussion of his exploits, his career did not begin until he was engaged by the Carnegie Corporation to conduct research.[1] What followed was a lifelong collaboration and the creation of a career in race relations that was largely dependent on his time as a *Poor White Study* researcher. The Carnegie Corporation had an extensive institutional history in South Africa prior to recruiting Malherbe. In addition to the long-standing Dominions and Colonies Fund, the CCNY supported numerous segregationist philanthropic projects.[2] So a study poised to focus on poor white beneficiaries of segregationist philanthropy fit nicely in this research portfolio. The CCNY was interested in propping up Afrikaner Nationalism, which as I am arguing had its most important resonance as a variant of white nationalism.[3]

The CCNY could support Afrikaner Nationalists by extending its long-standing commitments to segregationist philanthropy. Moreover, with its global audiences it could use poor white people as a cover for its segregationist agenda. Poor white people were also of great use as a political football because Afrikaner Nationalism was viewed by the rest of the Anglo-Saxon nation-states as relatively backward and politically immature. At war with itself and quite repulsed by the notion of a "white man's burden," Afrikaner Nationalism could hardly be said to represent a uniform or consistent political ideology or set of policies. Indeed, one goal of the *Poor White Study* was to create a coherent and unified Afrikaner Nationalist elite that could speak with one voice to its global partners. Well-funded race relations technicians, as experts on the social order, were tasked with correcting this nest of problems.

The *Poor White Study* research team gave new life to the uses of the poor white "problem" as a set of political symbols.[4] As framed, this problem had very little to do with effective policy making on wages, employment, housing, or the challenges of urbanization for the poor. Even among the research team definitions of who belonged to the social formation "poor white people" varied a great deal. Consequently in the five-volume *Poor White Study,* researchers numbered the group as being between 58,000 and 300,000 persons. By the 1932 launch of the *Poor White Study* there still remained an astonishing variation in the precise number of persons who made up this population. The study brought together all the prior data gathered about the rural poor white community by government commissions, church antipoverty programs, and local charitable organizations. The 1916 Cradock Congress on poor whites numbered them at 106,518, according to Minister for Agriculture H.C. Van Heerden. In 1923 the number was stated at between 120,000 and 160,000.[5] In 1926 the census recorded the number of unemployed white men who were at least fifteen years old at 58,000.[6] Ultimately, the research team interviewed 49,434 families and administered intelligence tests to 17,000 children, from which they concluded that there were between 220,000 and 300,000 "very poor" white people.

The wide variation in this number is due to several facts that became central definitional concerns throughout the five-volume study. The researchers made a distinction between the deserving and undeserving poor, calling the former the white poor and the latter the poor white. Researchers struggled to categorize the location of families and households as changed employment patterns resulted in profound changes in social relations and family life. Researchers secured a lot of data from charity workers, teachers, doctors, reform school managers, and other members of officialdom. Data that were not gathered from officials and intelligence tests were obtained via invasive interviews in people's homes, where the family's standard of living was scrutinized and a plan was made to offer them appropriate scientifically effective antipoverty aid and work reassignment.[7] Overall the data set and who was identified as numbering among this social group were vastly unreliable.

Some researchers included people from the "Basters" community, one whose political and racial status reflect inconsistencies in the definition of impoverished whites. Some researchers included so-called Colored persons in the data set. Others included, though with much disdain, white women who had married Indian men. Most researchers included people who had Dutch *and* English and non-European people in their family. Held consistent in the enumeration, however, was white people whose lives somehow signaled notions of racial degeneration defined by racial association and social class. In some cases people who were born into poor families were included; in others, only people who had become poor over the course of their own lives were included. Researchers categorized poor white people according to three distinct types: Type A was said to be sinking down into poverty, Type B was said to be intergenerationally poor, and Type C was said to be rising from poverty. Yet since this political constituency was mainly being counted to mobilize and marshal more intense Afrikaner Nationalist public opinion, slipshod counting was useful. The research team's poverty knowledge was created because "the most powerful economic, political, and cultural impulses of [the] social structure impose[d] themselves as codes and desires on the conduct, organization, and imagination of scientists."[8] Parsing out the difference between the material, social, and affective conditions that shaped the experiences of poor white people and the agenda of Afrikaner Nationalist propagandists helps deconstruct how this philanthropic knowledge was produced and how it shaped governance.

Another brand of racial politics played an important role in manufacturing the poor white problem as a crisis. Research team members blamed competition from and dependence on black people for causing white poverty. This blame game covered over the fact that there were hardly any jobs for unskilled white adult male workers. They recommended a decisive end to reliance on hyperexploited black workers whose availability was said to have been a major cause of the continuing problem of white poverty. Feigning concern for black culture and the peasant mode of production, *Poor White Study* researchers claimed that black people's urban industrial employment destroyed African culture. African urban workers had been "detribalized," it was claimed, and suffered "cultural degeneration" in the cities. Education in missionary schools had created "school kaffirs" who posed a threat to African and European society.[9] Such slanderous pseudosympathy was steeped in eugenics and economic parasitism that lacked any concrete commitment to higher wages. Carnegie researchers remained silent about the genuine material threats to African culture: the massive land theft of the 1913 Native Land Act and the colonial laws that criminalized black women's presence in the cities and all black people in the society. Cities and industrialists had decided not to provide enough housing for industrial workers and their families. The jobs and houses that were available existed largely in the informal economy, much of which was criminalized and deemed illicit. Most of the new jobs created in the periodic boom times of South African industrialization were available primarily for single young white women, single young white children, and young black men who were forced to leave their families in the rural areas. Ironically, the main urban housing available to poor white people was carved out of boarding situations with black families establishing rights to the city regardless of discriminatory laws. At issue was the profound dependency of urban poor white migrants on black urbanites. Black urbanites socialized poor white migrants into working-class consciousness.[10] Also at issue was the fact that in the aftermath of the South African War (1899–1902) big capital and landlords had openly agreed to force rural *bywoners* (sharecroppers) into the proletariat. Much of the language about white racial degeneration sought to mystify these forces.

Carnegie researchers concluded that a policy of ejecting black people from the city would preserve unskilled jobs and the scant housing stock for poor white men with families.[11] They further endorsed remanding poor white children to institutional care in trade schools and private domestic work and committing poor white men to labor camps like the Kakamas Labor Colony.[12] Such policy recommendations made it far easier for these researchers to explain white adult male poverty as a function of competition with racial inferiors and fears about white racial degeneration. From corralling people on land settlements to apprenticing/indenturing children, such policy recommendations in effect criminalized poor white people for being poor and made them more available for social control under the guise of rehabilitation via intensive processes of racialization.

PROFESSIONALIZED STATUS SEEKERS AND THE
CULTURE OF LEADERSHIP: ON REINTEGRATING THE
WHITE MENACE

In a June 1921 *Cape Times* article on poor white people, Malherbe explained that his effective lobbying of the Carnegie Corporation and Columbia University administrators had resulted in Carnegie president Frederick Keppel's 1927 tour of South Africa. He neglected to mention that the Corporation's Dominions and Colonies Fund predated his article by nearly a decade. Though Malherbe admitted that the Dutch Reformed Church had also been a prominent advocate for Carnegie intervention into what was deemed an intractable social problem in South African politics, he provided a largely inadequate explanation of why. In a fashion that duplicated the white settler colonial habit of creating a military conflict at treaty borders that required external mettle to "resolve," Malherbe's essay raises many questions. Though founded in a country whose foreign policy claimed to avoid the international entanglements of the imperial age, the Carnegie Corporation had longstanding global interests. Moreover, its international entanglements, both corporate and humanitarian, reflected a powerful tension between U.S. isolationism and expansionism. In these years of transition and decline for the British Empire U.S. economic expansionism financed the political and economic status that enabled national leaders' enthusiasm for isolationism. The CCNY did not expend tens of thousands of pounds and four years of personnel time to study poor whites on the other side of the globe because of the lobbying of a promising young Ph.D.; rather this eminent international philanthropy dedicated its resources to protecting its own interests. Malherbe's skills as an academic and public intellectual were deployed to sanitize Carnegie's franchise to govern after the manner of imperial-age racial politics. While on the one hand Malherbe depicts his relationship with the Carnegie Corporation as emerging casually, at later moments in his oft-written and ever-changing life history, he admitted to his long history of lobbying for intervention by this and presumably other U.S. philanthropic organizations in the domestic politics of South Africa and particularly the thorny social position occupied by poor whites. Malherbe was determined to market his own achievements,[13] the *Poor White Study* was the beginning of his entire career, funded and championed by the Carnegie Corporation, based on segregationist philanthropy.[14] Though Malherbe was a significant functionary linking the CCNY to Afrikaner Nationalism, Frederick

Keppel had already gone to southern Africa to find a means by which U.S. philanthropy might contribute to American expansionism in the British colonies.[15] Researching poor whites provided yet another means by which the organization could explicitly endorse segregationism in the guise of liberal humanitarianism.

By the mid-1920s the CCNY had already supported applied research in the United States and South Africa. Carnegie funded research on large-scale black urbanization, industrialization, and land hunger due to the convict lease system and the Native Land Act. It studied share-cropping and tenant farming, the confinement of the black proletariat to slums, white race riots against blacks, and the suppression of black workers' organizations and black anticolonial movements in the United States and southern Africa.[16] Despite these areas of interest Carnegie research funds were explicitly segregationist and sought to produce leadership among racial accomodationists with male-led white suprem-acy. Unable to fathom the possibility of socially equal black people, the organization used its research to repeat myths about black people's need for white guidance and supervision. In their own bid for paramountcy in Anglophone academia, Carnegie race relations technicians exempli-fied a leadership cohort trained inexplicably by Booker T. Washington but that came to eclipse him as "outstanding authorit[ies] on the prob-lems of education of underdeveloped peoples."[17] Like prominent segre-gationists around the world, CCNY president, Frederick Keppel (1875–1943), was far more compelled to expend substantial financial resources on the *Poor White Study* because of his organization's shared interests with the white nationalist Afrikaner movement. In many ways Keppel's tour brought international prominence to Afrikaner Nationalism and its proponents' intention to lead industry and the state to give poor white people *"eine freie Bahn dem Tüchtigen"* (the unfettered develop-ment of talent).[18] Carnegie officials also were deeply concerned to sys-tematically reintegrate poor whites into the Afrikaner community, because in their current state they were a "menace to the self-preserva-tion and prestige of our white people, living as we do in the midst of a native population which outnumbers us 6 to 1." Malherbe was an expert mouthpiece.[19]

GUARANTEED LABOR/NO GUARANTEES

In 1924 the Pact Government instituted the "civilized labor policy" guaranteeing employment, wages, and hiring preferences for white men qua members of the civilized race. In fact civilized labor was a more complicated policy in practice. It did not mean more high-paying jobs for white men but in fact guaranteed increasing numbers of low-wage jobs for white men and a massive increase in low-wage jobs for white women. This was followed closely by the dramatic increase in informal sector participation by white women. Many low-wage jobs were available for young white women who were also breadwinners for both themselves and their families in the rural areas. Civilized labor also led to the deskilling of white craftsmen as they were more rapidly compelled to join the urban proletariat. There was a high cost of living for small professionals in new cities like Johannesburg and increasing rates of unemployment for older and unskilled white men. The latter could often get jobs on the railways as blacksmiths, carpenters, plumbers, checkers, painters, dumpsmen, watchmen, and other government public relief jobs.

Scholars explain that prostitution, child labor, liquor and diamond dealing, and government concessions wrested from the black informal and formal economy (spirits manufacture, laundry service, and brick manufacture) constituted huge portions of this new white economy.[20] Families depended on the hustling of sex, liquor, and diamonds; young women's factory wages; and rental housing to meet their basic needs. Young urban and rural white women's wages were critical to families' margin of survival.[21] The very dense urban areas lacked basic public amenities like running water and sewage infrastructure. People already living in cramped neighborhoods relied extensively on boarders and renters to make ends meet. Few white male bywoners made it into the mining sector because of their lack of skills. So while white men earned very low wages, black migrant workers earned even less. Black mine workers, though, because of their large numbers, were the main market for white women and black women as independent traders in the informal economy. The very existence of poor whites reflected the unwieldy project of guaranteeing a white men's country.

The Carnegie research team brought together female charity workers, male theologians and female laity, and young social scientists—all committed to proto–social work. However, coming from very different institutions (government, churches, and universities) they were committed to vastly different types of Afrikaner Nationalism. Where in the past, class, profession, and gender mediated the effectiveness of Afrikaner Nationalism to become a potent political force, the Carnegie Commission project flattened debate, mystified varied political interests, and generated a scientific basis for unified political action.[22] In order to cement their "scientific" approach to poverty reduction among whites they agreed that (1) religious missionary work to redirect the moral life of the poor had failed to improve their economic status;[23] (2) "sporadic outbursts of philanthropy"[24] had failed to improve conditions; (3) a wider range of political rhetoric and social welfare treatments would be an improvement; and (4) they would employ a multimethod approach to gathering data that included door-to-door home visits; interviews with school officials, doctors, police, big landowners, and clergy; administering surveys and intelligence tests; and taking ethnographic photos. This comprehensive approach produced a more reliable constituency for Afrikaner Nationalism among the elite and among impoverished white people. And this reliable constituency was critical for smoother international affairs between South Africa and the rest of the world.

Poor whites were often caricatured by the mass media, popular and elite, as anachronistic. The research team trafficked in such caricatures to transform poor white people into white republican citizen workers with family wages. Thus, on the one hand, the published report urged compassion as a more effective means of rehabilitation and insisted that structural economic policies had contributed to the creation of poor whites. On the other hand, the report evinced a promiscuous interest in eugenic explanations for white poverty—especially hereditary degeneration. Researchers judged the character of the poor by whether or not they maintained racially segregated and sexist middle-class standards of living. The same civilizing mission that demonized and later rehabilitated poor whites had to address the fact that poor whites were a despised racial group in South Africa. And yet the antipoverty employment and housing schemes were supposed to transform the deserving impoverished whites into a deserving white middle class and the natural beneficiaries of racial segregation.

The *Poor White Study* pointed to industrialization as a particularly damaging political, economic, and social transition for poor whites—as whites. In response, the joint recommendations of the *Poor White Study* concluded that racially segregated high-quality housing and nonskilled employment in urban areas could alleviate the misery of poor whites. When poor whites—especially unemployed and unemployable males—migrated to the urban areas in search of low-paying "kaffir work" they became the visible face of the social costs of the southern African industrialization and racial labor hierarchy. It was this condition of being reduced to the status that Africans occupied in the racial labor hierarchy that contributed to the *Poor White Study* researchers' scolding of poor whites for being malingerers unwilling to accept manual labor because it was associated with Africans, who often had no choice in whether they were doing the most dangerous and heavy work. While the research team members reproached poor whites for not taking these jobs, they also advocated racial segregation in the workplace so that work crews would be all-white and would receive a "white man's wage" to change the negative stigma attached to working alongside black men in low-paid jobs. As *kaffir* is one of a host of derogatory terms used to describe Africans at the time the study was published, its use helps us understand the rigidity of the "production of difference."[25] Discussion of poor whites obscured discussion of the plight of black workers, who were deemed incapable of becoming modern republican wage earners except under the rhetorics and legal entrapment of Native affairs or immigration restriction. Since blackness was mutually constitutive with being chattel property, even on the African continent, and whiteness with a modernizing standard of living in the modern period, a critique of structural black poverty often did not register outside the black world of scholars.[26]

Race was believed to determine which rights and which quality of life one ought to have. Racial discourse propagandized that all whites should flourish economically. Without meaning to, the *Poor White Study* revealed that the ideology of white supremacy could not guarantee white success.[27] The discourse about inherent white superiority was revealed to be a myth simply by the presence of poor whites and their profound reliance on networks, housing, and economic ties established by African people.

According to white supremacist discourse, poverty among African, Indian, and Colored people was the result of culturally embedded forces and cultural resistance to the modernizing aspects of industrialization. Moreover, ideas about inherent cultural backwardness was alleged to have stymied the ability of black people to profit from industrialization.[28] Ultimately, in these theories, rank in the racial labor hierarchy was directly attributed to proximity to blackness and whiteness. But the available discourse of race, and the ranking of races—often defined in the same way that we use the terms *nations* and *ethnicities*—according to phenotype and "development," caught poor whites in the biologism of scientific racism. Poor whites were also "beaten men from beaten races" in a schema of race that foregrounded the supposed racial differences between Afrikaner and British.[29] Resorting to the eugenic-inspired biological explanations for the existence of poor whites was natural in the context of the proliferating race relations theories about the so-called primitive races, propagated in English-language social anthropology and its mirror social science Afrikaans-language, *volkekunde*.[30]

At issue in the *Poor White Study* was whether poor whites should be considered white and thereby receive all the legal, social, and political benefits of whiteness, considering their otherness and divergence from standards associated with wealthy and middle class whites. The white poor—poor, rural, urban miscegenationists that they were—did not demonstrate the high points of white civilization and so revealed gaps in the narratives upper-class whites told about their own noble origins.

POOR WHITES AND AFRIKANER NATIONALISM

Afrikaner Nationalists often claimed to be the champions of poor whites who were depicted as their pre-modern ancestors. Defending poor whites, then, was used to legitimate and or minimize the anti-human policies orchestrated by the Afrikaner Nationalist movement and its cultural platform. However the relationship between poor whites and Afrikaner Nationalism is far more complicated than this. After the Anglo-Boer War (1899–1902) the English extended credit to wealthy Dutch settlers from the Afrikaner Republics as part of a reparations arrangement that would privilege some Afrikaners while destroying others.[31] Foreign investors and wealthy South African born people of European descent, together, invested in larger industrial scale agricultural holdings owned by fewer families. They transferred concessions (brick-making, transport riding, cab driving, managing sex workers, and illicit diamond dealing) which Kruger had granted to *burghers* (farmers) and bywoners to large conglomerates. Further, they financed substantial land grabs that would find their most aggressive expression in the Native Land Act of 1913. This law (1) forceably removed over 90 percent of the black population and confined them to less than 7 percent of the land; (2) restricted black farming, renting, or purchasing of land to newly mapped and overcrowded "native areas"; (3) outlawed black sharecropping and tenancy in four provinces; (4) compelled black people to give their labor, equipment, and livestock to Boer tenant farmers; and (5) transformed an independent African peasantry into a poor agricultural and urban proletariat.[32] The Native Land Act was a sustained economic and social attack on the African population. But I am drawing attention to how prior to the Native Land Act a series of land grabs had been initiated with the express purpose of making agriculture more capital intensive and making landless white tenants into a wage earning proletariat. These policies hijacked those sectors of the urban informal economy where black people flourished. Though forcing poor white tenant farmers into the proletariat was a communal injury of a different scale and order than the Native Land Act, it is pivotal to understanding the successive waves of communal economic theft from black people, both urban and rural. Both land grabs were deemed harmful but necessary for the racial development of each group: white proletarians poised to become a managerial elite; black proletarians destined to become drawers of wood and hewers of water without the designation of worker. White supremacy needed both processes of proletarianization, and it needed to understand the effect on poor white people and African people in an opposing fashion.[33]

At a historical and conceptual level, South African historiography has foregrounded the struggle between the Afrikaner Republics (figured as economically and culturally vulnerable autochthonous groups) and British imperial (figured as external and capitalist) designs on the continent.[34] This approach obscures similarities between these "competing bourgeoisies"[35] and their shared adherence to white supremacy, separate development, and white paternalism. Both Afrikaner and British political philosophies justified white supremacy through notions about black inferiority, black economic incapacity, and black barbarism, all features of the alleged inherent defectiveness of black self-governance.[36] And both relied on secular and religious justifications for their domination. Indeed myths about the Afrikaner as a white tribe in Africa,[37] rather than an early flank in racial colonial settlement (and theft of established trading networks),[38] have been key to mystifying South African history.

The pedestrian focus on white ethnic imagined community and conflict between the British and the Afrikaners resonates with other accounts of great rivalries between sister republics: North versus South, Boer versus Briton versus Yankee, and even American exceptionalism versus South African exceptionalism provide little insight into the nature of whiteness.[39] Such accounts have obscured the genuine motivating forces for historical change and consciousness in these societies. I argue that historical change and consciousness has in fact been motivated by consolidating racial regimes, naturalizing black suffering, and demonizing militant responses to that imposition.[40] Both liberal paternalists and separate developmentalists were adamantly in favor of political incorporation of black people via robust interlocking forms of permanent exclusion.[41] The actual battle over white supremacy was not occurring between liberal paternalists and separate developmentalists but between white supremacy and black life.[42] Though Cape liberalism, Afrikaner segregationism, and American pseudoanti-imperialism are historiographies in conflict in South Africa, their shared ideological roots undergirded the fashioning of the 1910 Union and the institutionalization of grand apartheid.[43] Called by myriad names across space and time—from the "obnoxious and sinister claims for destiny exhibited by such conceits as German nationalism, British imperialism, [and] the racism of the White Man's burden" to "state racism" to the "Dutch ethical period" to "American benevolent colonialism"—these forms of arranging state power are mutually constituted.[44] Truly, the turn toward writing about black people, black movements, and black collective action as the real South African history by antiapartheid academics since the 1970s has been productive.[45] But even this turn has failed to fundamentally shut down the inadequate historiography that allowed Afrikaner and British conflict to be construed as the genuine motive force of change in that society.[46] Even when the new social histories explicitly motioned toward attending to white raciality and diminishing the claims of white ethnicity, race stood on the same grounds as ethnicity instead of wholly diminishing the specious groundings of white ethnicity.[47] Moreover, when Marxist historicism pushed beyond the white ethnic national imaginary to the category of the white worker, that category colonized all the dimensions of labor, work, consciousness, and maturation of the economic, social, and geographic transformations associated with work. As a concept, "the worker" conveniently excised the majority of sites of work and bodies that labored under its purview.[48] Marxist historicism proffered white worker internationalism as the singularly palatable and representable index of working. All others who did not qualify as workers occupied the status of "flesh."[49] While those designated as flesh could not occupy the precious terrain of being politically conscious workers, the social status of flesh instead makes possible a series of linked conceptions: work to be done; people to be marshaled into doing that work; people becoming conscience of their exploitation; and geographies in which the work of historical consciousness occurs. Beings that have become flesh animate conceptions of the social and thus make possible dubious claims for emancipation of the social position and category of flesh through analogizing white workers and the white poor as being "savage paupers," "vagrants," and "the heathen at home."

By talking about these two social groupings, Afrikaner and British, as white people, we do more than invalidate and flatten the claims to uniqueness and difference that populate their nationalist and imperialist ideologies; we create much needed space to talk about the array of political imaginaries that animated South Africa's black political thought, both domestic and global. Moreover, we shed light on a central animating doctrine that has fed this concern with the growth and maintenance and change over time among white nationalisms—that one white group was effectively reduced to being savage, primitive, and barbarous and needed disciplining, redemption, control, eradication, purification, and renewal by another. Both Afrikaners and British South Africans feared occupying the space of the white primitive.[50] The promise of this work—theorizing South African history in the context of the fear of white racial degeneration—is to dispense with the great white ethnic and national sibling rivalries rhetoric and instead focus on the workings of white on white violence in the service of domination over and suppression of black political imaginaries. Our historiography of race and nation needs to concern itself not with the false consciousness, gyrations, and machinations of these conflicts but with the purpose of their movements.

A study of the competition over which white ethnic imagined community has the political maturation to commandeer national identity misses the point. Each and every one of these distinctive forms of white nationalism needed to manufacture its own poor whites, to decide on a path for their eradication and thus rehabilitation, and to signal that their social and political salience had been managed in order for national republican identity to emerge. White nationalism is an important mechanism for creating cohesion across gender, class, religion, language, national origin, and social status lines among European settler populations. The histories of what each white ethnic imagined nation has claimed as its achievements are more than myths of origin; they are fundamentally unstable and unreliable truth claims or "racial regimes." Racial regimes legitimate proliferation of forms of unfreedom while erasing (and then rediscovering when necessary) Europeans' own histories of being slaves.[51] Such parsimonious, rational, white-aspiring, and male-led national projects were ends in themselves. The focus on Briton and Boer and Yankee positions us to be concerned over which racial regime reflected *greater political maturation,* which racial regime was more *committed to political emancipation,* which racial regime realized a more *humane and beneficient paternalism,* which racial regime more effectively deployed its *civilizational inheritance,* which racial regime had the highest *moral commitment to freedom,* and which racial regime achieved *national manhood citizenship.* These questions distract us from sustained attention to the common and linked histories of settler colonialism and racial imperialism. Such origin stories conceal the ways in which fungible black bodies (as flesh and property) have become the engine for historical consciousness and economic transformation. Paying concerted attention to the white identities, white social locations, and forms of white solidarity reveals how these common racial regimes produced myths about how harnessing black people to the economic and social apparatus of apartheid constituted economic, racial, and cultural advancement. Such white identities, white social locations, and white solidarities in concert with the interests of capital created typologies, both libidinal and material, of racially vulnerable politically immature white voters on the one hand and racially pure politically mature white voters on the other. Given such a context, merely rewriting a history of Afrikaner Nationalism prevents us from considering what such political projects were actually invested in producing: myriad linked, supposedly uniquely founded geographically distinct yet fundamentally continuous white nationalisms. Moreover, territorial boundaries and passports have only very rarely had the capacity to stymy the flow of forms of racial segregation, especially those enacted through empire.

THE RACIAL POLITICS OF MANUFACTURING CIVILIZED LABOR: DISPOSSESSION AND DEPENDENCY

Poor whites were dispossessed of their dependency relations with black people as civilized labor became institutionalized.[52] Through the state-protected whiteness of civilized labor policy they got a new social identity, a new status, and low wages.[53] What might this dispossession have meant for poor white people? Sennett and Cobb explain that white working class and poor people experience upward mobility as a disorienting bundle of affective challenges. Sennett and Cobb's informants reported that being hired as managers and moving to all-white suburbs made them feel greater personal insecurity. They worried about being perceived as not working hard enough. They were "passive in the midst of success because [they] feel illegitimate, [like] pushy intruder[s] . . . to the middle-class world of neat suburban lawns, peaceable families, happy friendships. Despite . . . [having] gained entrée, [they don't] believe [they] deserve to be respected."[54] They internalized blame for feeling ill at ease and unprepared for white middle-class lives. So while their access to coveted and often highly concentrated and scarce economic resources improved, the culture of capitalism and meritocracy affected them very negatively. They believed they had entered a coherent system of opportunities with invisible but high-stakes strings attached. Sennett and Cobb dub this morbid self-doubt "the hidden injuries of class." This morbid self-doubt was propped up by the pursuit of individual achievement, demonstrating that one is different from all the rest, what Sennett and Cobb called "badges of ability." Having become high-potential individuals, informants acknowledged having lost community ties, trusting relationships, and membership in robust communities. Sennett and Cobb's analysis of the psychological costs of upward mobility for white working-class people is illuminating for the study of the "racial nepotism" at work to rehabilitate poor whites in South Africa.[55] Though the civilized labor policy guaranteed new opportunities, it also guaranteed a sense of almost perpetual insecurity.[56] Scholars who have wrestled with the consequences of this insecurity ethically describe it as "the pound of flesh exacted for the right to be excluded from the excluded."[57] Political entrepreneurs fastened onto this economic and racial insecurity to enlist poor whites in a disciplinary rhetoric that made them ardent social patrollers of the whiteness of other poor whites and of all nonwhites.[58] Considering their own impoverished pasts as a mark of shame poor whites became severe racial gatekeepers. Poor white people (supported by massive international attention) viewed black attempts to hold on to meager toeholds in the informal economy as threats to the white standard of living and the project of white racial rehabilitation. In such a context poor whites were depicted as inherently prosperous and black people were depicted as inherently poor and economically backward.

CONCLUSION

Ernest Gideon Malherbe's career as a race relations technician was launched through his association with the *Poor White Study* and with the Carnegie Corporation. His presence and the marketing of his leadership role mystified the basic demographics of the poor white community. His storied association with this research, perhaps, signals how deeply politicized poor white racial politics could become—and its centrality for white nationalism. In a place and time where scarce housing and employment for poor white people in cities would not be provided

Afrikaner Nationalists and professional status-seekers collaborated to conceal the social forces at work. Such race relations technicians with the proper institutional base and funding could suggest that philanthropies were guided more by happenstance and naivete than by hard-nosed corporate calculus. Figures like Malherbe helped distract contemporaries from labor colonies, American expansionism, and economic and social violence against industrializing black people. He could traffic in eugenic explanations about the status of poor white people and sanitize earlier discourses of segregationism through "objective" social science.

Whether the Carnegie Corporation was exporting endorsement of U.S. segregation laws or was tripped up by naive yet damaging humanitarian intentions, the policy recommendations and the long-term obligations, linkages, and associations that emerged from the *Poor White Study* implicated the philanthropy and its donations of financial, educational, technical, and personnel resources in the consolidation of grand apartheid. In addition, the discourse of racial rehabilitation, racial recovery, and racial degeneration that Carnegie researchers engaged to carry out the research agenda of the *Poor White Study* is potent evidence in favor of the interpretation that the Carnegie Corporation was deeply engaged in the politics of Anglo-Saxon solidarity and global white supremacy. Analyzing poor white people and their role in white nationalism is critical to understanding the repetition of the racial wealth divide and the ways in which dispossession of black economies was central to transfers of wealth and status to poor white people. Certainly these social relations forecast the function of nonprofit organizations under contemporary globalization. Philanthropies' continued capacity to constrain transparent, elected public governance is in some ways precisely the meaning of contemporary governance.

The Visual Culture of White Poverty as the History of South Africa and the United States

Repetition, Rediscovery, Playing with Whiteness

When we examine the racial logic of representations of white vulnerability, we find poor whites constructed as a cultural anomaly that is rediscovered and unearthed time and again. I am concerned with how *rediscoveries of white misery* and *playing with whiteness* operated in visual culture as Afrikaner Nationalists of different stripes used such images and symbols to compete for political legitimacy.[1] This visual culture was extended by forces invested in white nationalism far beyond South Africa. The Carnegie *Poor White Study* illustrates how such forces operated through knowledge production, both social scientific and visual cultural. As such, it constructed spaces, social identities, and citizenship in the imaginary of white nationalism. Artists employed a range of genres to comment on the predicament of poor whites. The Carnegie Corporation used these genres to diagnose, sympathize with, and disseminate new knowledge about white poverty. While the *Poor White Study* distracted attention from black resistance to proletarianization and white minority rule, it simultaneously naturalized what Max Weber called the "rational organization of capital and labour." This rational organization of capital and labor is also known as a racial labor hierarchy, where work categories were filled by distinctive racial castes.[2] Impoverished white people were deemed outside of bourgeois ethics, doctrines, and practices of self-management. Their existence interrupted attempts to easily match racial rank to social and work categories. Weber wrote, "To wish to be poor was . . . the same as wishing to be unhealthy. . . . [B]egging, on the part of one able to work, is not only the sin of slothfulness, but a violation of the duty of brotherly love."[3] Such white people in Weber's view symbolized white lack and seemed to mock the idea that improvements in character, vocation, and asceticism would improve production and thereby serve the common good. The very existence of such white people challenged the belief that the racial labor hierarchy was the result of divine order. According to the research team members, also, poor whites lacked ascetic virtue and an appreciation of the white man's burden and thus were incapable of being wealthy, the theological reward for white settlers. Their repudiation of what some argued was their divine historical and national role as white men and women made them both sinful and degenerate in the eyes of social scientists who embraced such moral assessments of the social world.

The *Poor White Study,* then, was able to effect an important kind of historical and representational work by hinging the reformation of poor whites to the project of Afrikaner Nationalism. How could a fit white nation continue to produce generations of white people who failed to identify ideologically with the virtues of vocation and honest work? What accounted for white people who failed to embody and uphold ideologies about bourgeois comportment or the republican working man? White people who lacked a vocation and honest work did not qualify as fit for citizenship domestically and were not legible as republican workingmen in the white global imaginary. The existence of poor whites was a cautionary tale that urged that white nationalism be defended domestically and abroad.

In this chapter I examine E. G. Malherbe's ethnographic photos published as part of the *Poor White Study* (1932), political cartoons by Daniel Cornelis Boonzaier (1920s–1930s),[4] and press coverage of poor whites genre plays and films by a member of the *Poor White Study* research team, dramatist turned propaganda economist Johannes Friedrich Wilhelm Grosskopf (1885–1948). Taken together, these images depict the production of hypervisible, stigmatized, mocked, and sentimentalized poor whites as a social identity and a social problem.[5] Using techniques of visual representation, such as caricature, exaggeration, and humor; framing and captioning; light and shadow; contrast, scale, and texture, these visual representations expose the artifice of the social science practices being used by the Carnegie Commission research team, revealing the limitations of social-scientific objectivity in the context of rampant scientific racism. Moreover, as cultural signifiers these images enable further scrutiny of the historical and material bases of white poverty and the political erasures and consolidations that can be done through it. I end the chapter by turning to another generation of visual framing of poor whites inaugurated by Roger Ballen's acclaimed documentary photographs published in the trilogy *Dorps* (1986), *Platteland* (1994), and *Outland* (2001). Although important aesthetic, technological, and temporal distinctions separate the two periods, poor whites continue to be a compelling subject matter for photographers and filmmakers. Indeed, these latter representations demonstrate the enduring significance of poor white identity to the making of national identity, nationality, and international knowledge production about racialized poverty. In South Africa, advertisements, political cartoons, and ethnographic and documentary photography have all used visual imagery to represent debates over meaning, history, and social relations. Using these sources, I read and examine the practices of the black radical tradition that expose rediscoveries of white misery, playing with whiteness, and the constant need to reconsolidate the unstable racial regime of white nationalism. I offer the language of "global whiteness" to extend the scholarship on racial conceptions of citizenship and democracy and return to the detailed transnational linkages, both institutional and in comparative political thought. The impact and effect of the *Poor White Study* and the philanthropic organization that coordinated it, thus, can best be understood through this framework of global whiteness.

We examine visual culture because, as the cultural studies scholar Raymond Williams explained in a 1978 interview with Edward Said, it is "not a subject separate from history. . . . [It] contribute[s] to the history, and is an active element in the way forces are distributed, the quintessential description of political processes."[6] Visual culture plays an important role in connecting structures of feeling and ideology to the material and social world, for example, by articulating relations to authority, opinion leaders, and social identities.[7] In the context of the *Poor White Study,* the white wealthy did not see the white poor as their racial "kin," their relations, until the Carnegie Corporation demonstrated how the plight of the "deserving" white poor could be used to consolidate white nationalism through visual images. The process by which an external philanthropy could insert itself in ostensibly domestic race relations requires attention to the conditions under which segregationist philanthropy could so readily cross territorial borders. Again, the recurring interest in poor whites raises critical questions about the supposed discontinuity between white settler nations. As this chapter considers visual culture across multiple genres, I begin with a brief turn to how artifice operates in each.

ARTIFICE: POLITICAL CARTOONS, DOCUMENTARY PHOTOGRAPHY, ETHNOGRAPHIC SHOWCASES

"Satirical journalism," as political cartoons are described, uses spoof, satire, and parody to reveal the terms of political debates and the underbelly of public pronouncements.[8] Political cartoons are a type of political discourse that uses visual representations, metaphor, rhetorical devices, catchphrases, and humor to comment on and shape political debate. Andy Mason explains that political cartoons use "over-dramatized postures and expressions[,] . . . vaudevillian characterizations and preposterous settings" in order to criticize policies of the day.[9] Like other genres of visual representation, political cartoons are accused of obscuring the dynamic processes of the past and the present, of causing metaphoric entrapment because they set a rigid frame of associations, and of failing to predict political action because they are focused on tracing ideological flows and shifts.[10] Since so much of political life is guided by the politics of obfuscation while claiming some prophetic capacity to predict or change outcomes, political commentary, including that in political cartoons, proves useful by dispensing with predictions and turning instead to analysis of how things are actually occurring.[11]

In contrast, documentary photography, as Susan Sontag writes, "provides a . . . compact form for memorizing[,] . . . like . . . a proverb."[12] I contend that the greatest contribution of visual representations is their disclosure of the process of artifice that is central to any framing of human events, what Rey Chow calls "writing by overlooking."[13] As Rachel Adams suggests, "the enterprises of exhibiting curiosities and taking portraits are equally invested in the creation of artifice, as they transform the raw material of the visible world into illusions."[14] Visual images projecting otherness and sameness function to "inspire and enhance memory," or criticize the accepted history.[15] The visual is a major site for the battle over history and the invention of social reality particularly with regard to racial blackness. Visual images demonstrate the flexibility of history and its amenability to subterfuge, revision, and marketing.[16] Visual images can also contribute to the politics of restorative justice by repairing people's relationships to their society after uncovering processes of misrepresentation.[17]

Scholars have praised the Carnegie Commission researchers for demonstrating the significant role that social research can play in antipoverty policy making.[18] Even though the Carnegie *Poor White Study* research team members claimed to have the goal of engendering pity

FIGURE 1. "Poor white children served with soup at school. (Northern Transvaal)." From Ernest Malherbe, "Part III: The Educational Report: Education and the Poor White," in *Report of the Carnegie Commission of Investigation on the Poor White Question in South Africa* (Stellenbosch: Pro-Ecclesia-Drukkery, 1932). All rights belong to the Board of Control for Research on the Poor White Question in an agreement with Pro Ecclesia Press or to the estate of the artist.

and thus increasing social equality for poor whites, a racist gaze is evident in their depictions.[19] Sally Gaule describes the "racist gaze" evident in the *Poor White Study* as an inheritance from ethnographic photography's obsession with primitivism and, by extension, its inability to take nonracist pictures even of white people.[20] E. G. Malherbe's photographs included in the *Poor White Study* exist at the intersection of scientific racism and visual theory, encapsulating discourses about civilization, modernization, racial degeneration, and primitivism (figs. 1–6).

Naturalism, realism, and equating people with animals were technical elements that allegedly incorporated the authentic values of poor whites in the backdrop of each photographic scene. The ethnographic descriptions and racism of the *Poor White Study*'s "findings" expose the paternalistic ideas about race and poverty guiding the research team. The meeting between new technology and a continuing humanist obsession with classifying species and documenting order in the natural world birthed documentary photography. Camera technology raises questions about objectivity, point of view, and the false authority of realism. Nineteenth-century scientists attempted to preserve the integrity of the scientific method in their work by exhibiting their ethnographic photos with living sideshows.[21] Trafficking in these modalities

FIGURE 2. "Boy suffering from malaria. His whole diet consists of mealiemeal and coffee—all without sugar or milk." From Ernest Malherbe, "Part III: The Educational Report: Education and the Poor White," in *Report of the Carnegie Commission of Investigation on the Poor White Question in South Africa* (Stellenbosch: Pro Ecclesia-Drukkery, 1932). All rights belong to the Board of Control for Research on the Poor White Question in an agreement with Pro Ecclesia Press or to the estate of the artist.

of entertainment and identifying physiognomic markers of "disease" enabled them to promise cures based on disciplining and civilizing any human types too divergent from uniform national *cum* racial identity. In this way, they saw themselves as safeguarding their own professional expertise and setting it apart from the exhibition of unique cases of racial oddities, gender-bending, and mental and physical abilities for the

FIGURE 3. "Activities of indigent Hostel children in the Kalahari. Preparing for effective rural life. Thrift learnt in a practical way. Display of Savingsbank books." From Ernest Malherbe, "Part III: The Educational Report: Education and the Poor White," in *Report of the Carnegie Commission of Investigation on the Poor White Question in South Africa* (Stellenbosch: Pro Ecclesia-Drukkery, 1932). All rights belong to the Board of Control for Research on the Poor White Question in an agreement with Pro Ecclesia Press or to the estate of the artist.

FIGURE 4. "Activities of indigent Hostel children in the Kalahari. Preparing for effective rural life. Domestic Science: Developing cleanliness and taste in the preparation and serving of the meal and promoting the joy of the household." From Ernest Malherbe, "Part III: The Educational Report: Education and the Poor White," in *Report of the Carnegie Commission of Investigation on the Poor White Question in South Africa* (Stellenbosch: Pro Ecclesia Drukkery, 1932). All rights belong to the Board of Control for Research on the Poor White Question in an agreement with Pro Ecclesia Press or to the estate of the artist.

FIGURE 5. "Canning fruit and vegetables: Laying up stores in times of plenty for harder times to come." From Ernest Malherbe, "Part III: The Educational Report: Education and the Poor White," in *Report of the Carnegie Commission of Investigation on the Poor White Question in South Africa* (Stellenbosch: Pro Ecclesia-Drukkery, 1932). All rights belong to the Board of Control for Research on the Poor White Question in an agreement with Pro Ecclesia Press or to the estate of the artist.

FIGURE 6. "Children on the Diamond Diggings (Lichtenburg). Digger's family. The father had just finished chopping up baby's chair as last bit of firewood." From Ernest Malherbe, "Part III: The Educational Report: Education and the Poor White," in *Report of the Carnegie Commission of Investigation on the Poor White Question in South Africa* (Stellenbosch: Pro Ecclesia-Drukkery, 1932). All rights belong to the Board of Control for Research on the Poor White Question in an agreement with Pro Ecclesia Press or to the estate of the artist.

purpose of leisure. Ethnographic photography was harnessed to many other scientific racist research methods and was a key methodology for eugenic imperialism. As I am arguing, the *Poor White Study* researchers used it to demonize poor whites as racial degenerates, to discipline others who could qualify as "white," and to engender sympathetic sentiments toward poor whites. Representational tactics have been used to intervene in, participate in, and hail audiences for the construction of racism. Scholars have argued that the *Poor White Study* stands out because "white people themselves have rarely been the object of such "anthropological and ethnographic studies of the 'other.'"[22] However, the racist gaze on poor white people operated in a historical context each time they were rediscovered, a context that revealed a crisis in racial power and that animated more vicious forms of antiblack racism while disappearing black people's organized resistance. Thus the Carnegie Commission could cultivate sympathy *and* disdain for poor whites living beneath the "white standard of living" using ethnographic photographs.

While the *Poor White Study* comments minimally on the process of photographing poor whites, the researchers' descriptions and analyses of what needs to be done with and to poor whites confirm their position as racial subordinates. By accusing the poor white interviewees of having psychological problems epitomized by "prejudice" against heavy manual labor jobs, laziness, passivity, and an inflated sense of superiority, the research team introduced subjective characterizations and value judgments. The ethnographic photos provided a permanent visual frame for conflating poor white people with their material conditions.

Texts that purported to explain poverty, like the ethnographic showcases, employed a set of adjectives, definitions, descriptions, and diagnoses that silenced the poor while appearing to closely document and acknowledge them. The poor, like the exhibited Africans, were made present as subject matter but absent as voices. This process was accomplished by the textual means of producing reality effects that employed a ready-made vocabulary of images and metaphors from the empire.[23]

Moreover, these ideologies obscured other interests in expanding U.S. influence in South Africa via Anglo-American solidarity and shoring up white nationalism. With this set of racist ideologies about poverty, it is little wonder that such images mythologized the social and historical forces that created the white poor.

There is a dynamic feedback loop between the way images of poor white people were figured in political cartoons and in the way they were posed "American Gothic" style in the ethnographic photos in the *Poor White Study* and then again in documentary photography and novels. It is best to describe these discursive traces as a relation of persistent and enduring continuity after the manner in which Pumla Gqola renders the distinct yet interlocking historicity of slavery, colonialism, and apartheid. Despite their historical distinctiveness, Gqola explains, slavery, colonialism, and apartheid reflect a continuum of making white nationalisms through antiblackness. Memory and ideology, then, help us see how these spatiotemporal moments are embedded in each other and contiguous, not simply linear. History collects and analyzes consciousness of the past of groups and states, but memory is the broader category that reflects communities' invented selves. This is what Barnor Hesse calls "the ongoing effects and processing of that historical consciousness . . . [and the] political consequences of those social legacies."[24] Thus the question is less one of a tension between the history or memory of poor whites than of "locating and distinguishing between different sources and modes of historical authority."[25] The resonance between these different types of images of poor whites is undeniable: they don't reflect each other but position and pose poor white people in a related fashion. Poor whites are a key ingredient in the making of white nationalism and are reinvoked as necessary to stabilize or destabilize myriad competing social forces. In the postcolonial, postapartheid, and post–civil rights periods the existence of poor whites has been widely used to delegitimate black voting rights, land rights, and legal remedies to correct for white minority rule and all of its effects.[26] But this concern with those who C.L.R. James dubbed "small whites" has a provenance that goes all the way back to postemancipation claims in Haiti, which typically demonize black participation in white minority rule as black domination and insist on nonracial voting rights.[27] It is less important, then, to determine which images came first—even though they are assigned historical dates—and more important to determine how they are communicating and creating an environment for and are key to the deployment of white racialization. White racialization, like other forms of racial domination, is deployed to shore up white supremacy and white nationalism. However, unlike other forms of racial domination, white racialization, as this range of images attests, registers dissatisfaction with the impoverishment of white citizens' obligations to each other and thus naturalizes white kinship and white nationhood as the political extension of white kinship.

This little girl has helped to collect more than £40 at the Alhambra since Monday night for the Mayor's Soup Kitchen Fund.

FIGURE 7. Hungry Girl: The Mayor's Soup Kitchen ad, *Cape Times*, June 26, 1931. Vic Alhadeff, *Newspaper History of South Africa*. Credit: All rights belong to the *Cape Times* newspaper.

HUNGRY GIRL: THE MAYOR'S SOUP KITCHEN AD

A 1931 *Cape Times* advertisement pictured a photograph of a small white girl with piercing eyes and wiry brown hair sitting astride a cooking pot large enough for several children to fit in (fig. 7). The girl is the focal point of the staged image, her skinny legs dangling down the front of the pot, an enormous ladle in her hand. The pot sits on an ornate floor in what appears to be an elaborate Victorian-era building. There are racks of reading material on the left side of the room. Charity workers, both men and women, are posed on the right, standing in a doorway watching the photograph being staged. They are obviously not poor whites themselves but can represent the respectable wall standing between hunger and the vulnerability of a white girl child. The caption reads:

> Fourpence a day will provide stew, bread, eggs, and milk for one person. The helpers in the Mayor's Soup Kitchen will see that only the deserving cases are helped. Can you afford it? Without substantial contributions from the public the Mayor's kitchen must close down.

Though viewers are drawn to the caption soliciting contributions, this image uses race, class, and gender to establish the singular subjectivity of sympathetic white femininity.[28] Tropes about potential "white slaves" undergird fears about the sexual vulnerability of white women in crisis and figure white womanhood and white girls as the quintessential symbol of vulnerable whiteness. These images trigger support for the parental state, vigilante violence, and the extension of coverture-like protections over deserving poor white people.[29] The crisis of urban poverty in the 1930s depicted in this advertisement was made more urgent because a white girl child might possibly slip from the social position of somebody being served food or somebody serving food to others to somebody consumed by hunger. It is not accidental that the face of destitution is female, white, and young. Such images relied on an earlier history of trafficking in images of "vulnerable white women," such as the Afrikaner Nationalist campaigns around the erection of the Boer War Women's Monument (December 13, 1913) and anticipated a later history of the same image deployed in the Empire Exhibition (1936) held in Johannesburg and the countrywide Ox Wagon Trek (1938) celebrations. Each of these national celebrations brings to mind loyalty to a distinctly gendered South African white nationalism. The celebrations reminded white citizens of the twin threats of British imperialism and African military might historicized by annual celebrations of Dingaan's Day and the Battle of Blood River (1838). These public celebrations filled the calendar of white nationalist political theology. In these celebrations, Afrikaners thanked a deity for protection against barbarous black people.[30] In such an environment, the depiction of vulnerable white people, especially vulnerable white women and girls, justified calls to circle the wagons and take care of our own—presumably white republican citizens of the South African nation. Carnegie commissioners trafficked in this freighted context of playing with whiteness by creating such images and gathering empirical evidence that shored up notions of white vulnerability for other purposes.

The "Hungry Girl" advertisement reprises the continued circulation of cannibal images, part of what Robinson and Gqola refer to as the "slavocratic humorous tradition" that transformed the abstract threat of hunger experienced by white settlers into a colonial trope and racial threat about hungry black cannibals.[31] The cannibal image is part of the "visual lexicon not only of South African cartooning but of cartooning in the Western world. . . . The image of a white man sitting in a steaming black pot presided over by a barefooted black chef is one of the standard cartoon images of the twentieth century."[32] By signaling the implied but missing "black primitives," the soup pot featured in this advertisement, big enough to cook a white person, conjures a long legacy of representations of white destitution and black threat, thus obscuring forced labor by black people to feed white hungers, both material and ontological, as Fanon explained when writing that the "settler's city is well-fed."[33] "Invent[ing] the Negro," as Robinson explains, was critical to obscuring white destitution and white intraracial conflict in the metropole when white people were robbed of land and civil status by Enclosure Laws and feudal slavery orchestrated by other white people.[34] What was initially an economic racial threat to white people in the metropole robbed of land by Enclosure Laws and in earlier generations robbed of civil status under British colonialism, feudalism, and slavery becomes an implied racial threat in the colonies and dominions. This frail child is a dictionary of semiotic codes about who is supposed to be poor and why. And white people, particularly white female children, are not supposed to experience this. Thus this frail-looking white female child is deployed pedagogically to reinforce ideologies about irrational black violence and legitimate white self-defense.

Charity workers commenced the Hungry Child Soup Kitchen campaign (1931) the same year that *Poor White Study* researcher and Stellenbosch University professor of economics J. F. W. Grosskopf's film *In die Wagkamer* (In the Waiting Room), one part of a three-act play (*Drie eenbedrywe,* or *Three One-Act Plays*) opened to massive acclaim. *In Die Wagkamer* commented on the social disruption of urbanization for newly urbanized Afrikaners from 1900 to 1925. It depicted a poor white man who found city living far more precarious than being a landless farm worker. The film built on the dramatist's wildly successful play

As die Tuig Skawe (When the Harness Chafes: A Drama in Four Acts), which featured a female protagonist who accepted the chafing harness of marriage.[35] Unlike Grosskopf's 1920 play, *'nEsua: n Bosveld Drama* (Esau: A Drama about the Forest), a story about an "old Transvaal Boer in conflict with the post-Union social order" (which was not received well, according to his biographer), his later works proved that the audience for Afrikaner Nationalist cultural production was expanding, as was that public's stomach for drama about victimized and vulnerable white women. That Grosskopf, one of the signature successes of this theater scene, was the chief economist for the *Poor White Study* offers much for further examination. Grosskopf's claim to fame had been fictionalizing the poor white experience as dramatic fodder. But, like other people recruited as researchers for the *Poor White Study,* his main qualification was his relationship to the major proponents of Afrikaner Nationalism. Grosskopf's ties to Hollywood aesthetics, to be sure, influenced his evaluation of statistical data on the role of poor whites in the South African economy.

When white poverty was addressed in South Africa, it created space for an economic and financial analysis that focused exclusively on the *deserving* white poor by excluding and pathologizing black people as the root of white poverty. Pathologizing black people did nothing to ameliorate poverty for them or for poor whites. The caricatures created in advance of the *Poor White Study* framed the kind of research that could be conducted about this group in the society. Turning to the political cartoons of Daniel Boonzaier, we see meaningful invocations of sympathethic white womanhood as well as characterizations of poor white people as forgotten kin and victims of capital. Ironically, Boonzaier's staunch advocacy of Afrikaner Nationalism allows us to explore the facade of white victimization in more depth than the Hungry Girl Soup Kitchen advertisement and Grosskopf's plays and films.

DANIEL CORNELIS BOONZAIER'S POLITICAL CARTOONS

The South African political cartoonist Daniel Cornelis Boonzaier (1865–1950) was widely featured in both the Afrikaans- and English-language press, despite the fact that he was a strong advocate of cartoonists working in partisan papers.[36] A political proponent of Afrikaner Nationalism, Boonzaier was typically featured in the popularly read Afrikaans-language newspaper, *Die Burger* (The Citizen). And perhaps because he was crafting works of art, he was at greater liberty to admit to fractures within the production of white nationalism. He regularly used the panels of his cartoons to rebut debates in Afrikaner Nationalist circles. His cartoons focused on the mendacity of politicians and intellectuals fighting over poor whites as a potential constituency and the absurdity of the business of influencing others. As H. J. Hofmeyr wrote admiringly in his introduction to Boonzaier's *Rand Faces* (1915), a collection of portraits of elected officials:

> Mr. Boonzaier . . . clothes his subjects with a measure of rotundity, jocundity and profundity which not even in their most grasping moments would they dare to claim. . . . [He] relentlessly drags officials into the limelight of publicity in the following pages[,] . . . mak[ing] the parody an improvement on the original. . . . Many of our politicians completely fill the bill.

Boonzaier's political cartoons captured the everyday consequences of elite policy making, primarily by representing poor whites as speaking back against politicians and their policies. His sympathy for South Africa's poor white communities was evident in these images, but so was his disgust for the politicking around the poor.

One of Boonzaier's favorite subjects was criticism of Jan Christiaan Smuts (1870–1950), an English, university-trained legislator and prime minister who sided both with the British Empire and the Afrikaner republics. Boonzaier used Smuts to explain the ideological battles among various strands of Afrikaner Nationalism, which had much less to do with ethnoreligious conflict and more to do with political entrepreneurs[37] competing to bring the poor white constituency into political alignment. Smuts's vision of South Africa as leader of a great "United States of Africa" required corralling Afrikanerdom into imperial whiteness.[38] A former Jameson Raider, Smuts escaped the taint of having conspired to invade and colonize the independent Afrikaner Republic, the Transvaal, by fashioning himself into an extreme Afrikaner loyalist through a rocky alliance between his former fellow conspirators, the foreign-born whites and "narrow racialists"[39] in the Afrikaner republics, becoming Transvaal's state attorney and later a legislator. While this period of narrow racialism was an important part of Smuts's political posturing and outlook, he ultimately parlayed his role as a loyal son of Afrikaner Nationalism into negotiating the eventual folding of the South African republics into the Union Government. This loyal son of Afrikaner Nationalism went on to "soothe racial feelings in the north" while endorsing and consolidating power for the Union Government, led by its largely foreign-born and pro-imperialist European popula- tion.[40] Smuts's relationship to the Labour Party is best illustrated by his decision to suppress worker strikes with English Dragoon Guards in 1913 on the Rand, with burgher commandoes in 1914, and then again in the spectacular bombings in 1922.[41] Though foreign-born and South Africa–born soldiers repressed striking white workers, the Labour Party allied with the platform of narrow racialism and in 1948 secured a white majority that voted with the Nationalist-Labour alliance. Despite Smuts's role as a global statesman and expansionist diplomat during World War I, South Africa was not regarded as a sister republic to other Anglo-American nations.

CERTAINLY THOSE OF OUR CALLING WILL LET NONE GO DOWN

Published in *Die Burger* on May 12, 1928, *Seker geen vergeefse beroep* (Certainly those of our calling will let none go down (fig. 8) depicted a conversation between Rev. Dr. A.D. Luckhoff, secretary of the Poor Relief Commission of the Dutch Reformed Church and member of the Commission of Investigators for the Carnegie Commission *Poor White Study*, and the once and future prime minister general, Jan Smuts.[42] Fac- ing each other with one man gripping the other's shoulder, they have met to investigate and inspect potential investments, in this case, the poor white family. Using scale and spatial relationships, Boonzaier places the poor family in the background, drawn in streaky lines that make them almost disappear from the cartoon, while using heavy lines to outline Luckhoff and Smuts, who occupy the foreground. Luckhoff and Smuts are larger-than-life figures who literally reach the thatched roof of the house. Bedecked with ties, pipes, canes, and clerical vestments, Luckhoff and Smuts stand in sharp contrast to the crumbling house and the box chair that passes for furniture. Cartoonist Boonzaier captions Luckhoff:

> In the days of the Helpmekaar [Self-Help] Organization one found your fel-
> low Afrikaners so beautifully helping each other to get back on their feet.
> And I'm sure that you won't allow our friend here to go down [go under].[43]

Depicting a decrepit man sitting on a box, clutching a ragged shoeless daughter, beside his blanket-covered haintlike wife, the cartoon repre- sents stock characters in the white community's bleak past, the atavistic face of destitution. In the communal past of white settler history the

FIGURE 8. "Seker geen vergeefse beroep"/"Certainly those of our calling will let none go down." Daniel Cornelis Boonzaier, Cartoon 1928. Black Paint 305 × 249. Signed "Boonzaier." Ashbey's Galleries. Reproduced in *Die Burger*, May 12, 1928. Museum Africa (Johannesburg) File 338.54, Number 72/734. All rights belong to Museum Africa (Johannesburg) or to the estate of the artist.

image of the defeated Noble Boer, "Our Friend," like the aforementioned Hungry Girl trope, established the legacy of the deserving hardworking poor whites, here an image of the pioneering spirit of white nationalist masculinity.[44] The Noble Boer was a stock caricature used by political entrepreneurs to justify the race-making dimensions of colonial policies.[45] This bourgeoisie was interested in protecting the aspirations of white nationalism from the potential racial degeneration, or "going down," that was central to late Victorian racial ideology.[46] A class of aspirant bourgeois proprietors on the make needed the Noble Boer caricature when racial regimes of Afrikaner Nationalism were being constructed. This cartoon in particular demonstrated the synchronicity between clerics and "scientific reformers" protecting the society from their dysgenic offspring. These enduring tropes of white destitution created a bourgeois history of the white settler past that equates poor whites with African people, miserable and tied to the land. And the Noble Boer, with his nobility, served to represent the ultimate fear, the atavism of white civilization, and the blackening of whiteness.[47]

This depiction of physical camaraderie among the elite suggests a feeling of intimate association, a sense of obligation and responsibility for the white poor. Wealthy white South Africans had not been convinced that they had any particular obligation to poor whites. The gentleman commentators look every bit the part of speculators come to investigate and inspect potential investments: a poor white family, specimens that have literally gone down to the lowest rung of human civilization. Though this conversation between men about the masculine virtue of protecting their kin required a minor sermon, the fraternal agreement assures readers that the poor white will be saved.

Luckhoff is a powerful symbol of the campaigns and movements that claim to speak for the poor white, especially before the Carnegie Corporation began its interventions on their behalf. Mediating their reality for the would-be patron, he signifies Helpmekaar as the model solution to the problem. But he represents more than religious devotion to easing their plight; he represents a social group competing for control over the meaning of white poverty and the loyalty of this constituency *cum* congregation.

Boonzaier's cartoon is a sardonic social history of the Dutch Reformed Church lobbying the state to see and reimagine the white poor. Notwithstanding his sympathy for the white poor, Boonzaier is no mere propagandist for Afrikaner Nationalist positions. He intimates that the construction of white identity occurs via conscious, active, strategic partnerships. The spatial relationships in the image—the tired masses below, the cleric above, interceding with secular power—cast Smuts as a potential liberal Afrikaner. This is a strange figuring since Smuts was often accused of being the representative of British Empire, against the making of white republican South African nationhood. In Boonzaier's subtle lines, Smuts is a redeemed sympathetic figure for the Afrikaner reading public of *Die Burger,* one who can hear and respond to poor whites. Thus Luckhoff and his organization negotiate a truce between the poor and the wealthy within not only the Afrikaner *volk* but also the South African white nation because he worked for the Dutch Reformed Church and the Carnegie Commission. Of course, this was still a tenuous relationship in 1928, before the full flowering of the Carnegie Commission's scientism, but in the meantime Boonzaier was sketching and documenting the clergy's attempt to wring some allegiance out of the new academic professional classes.

Conflicts over the definition of Afrikaner Nationalism were waged by national women's voluntary organizations such as Helpmekaar. Other such organizations included the Afrikaner Women's Christian Organization (Afrikaanse Christelike Vrouevereniging, or ACVV), a proto–social work organization through which women asserted a public face for their direct aid to families in need and for their poor white conferences. However, when these self-funded, church-affiliated women's organizations insisted on their autonomy and the right to make decisions, the predominantly male Dutch Reformed Church leaders urged politicians to stymy women's suffrage organizing.[48] Women in the Afrikaner Nationalist movement had to become functionaries for the social regulation of the poor if they hoped to maintain any roles in the public sphere.

Luckhoff's sermon evokes the degeneration of whiteness seen around the world as a consequence of industrialization in the figure of the "savage pauper."[49] Moreover, it captures the paradoxical sentiment of protection for and veneration of the Noble Boer while at the same time perceiving such persons as exemplars of the social problem encapsulated by the notion that they are the "withered branch of a tree," the tree being South African society.[50] Hence the marking of the self-help organization as a preindustrial set of white social relations with a venerable history that ought to be preserved and emulated and, most important, critical to the origin story of Afrikaner Nationalism. I argue that we can trace the process of instructing the white wealthy to see poor whites as racial kin in these images.[51] Rather than concern for the masses of unemployed poor whites, the white business community and municipal officials in general expressed disdain and hostility toward poor whites who were believed to be vagabonding ne'er-do-wells demanding public support for their own individual hangups and failures.[52]

The *Poor White Study* echoed this common trope about poor people, finding that poor whites had wanderlust and adored vagrant life. Vagrancy was seen as a racial marker of inferiority, as traditionalism, and as a refusal of permanent work. Married men who applied for charity faced residency requirements of up to ten years, arrest, eviction from towns and counties, denial of employment and state or charitable housing benefits, and the removal of children from the home. Might we not conclude that such policing *caused* transience? These migrants had existed at the center of the rural agricultural economy in a wide range of migrant labor jobs: tenant farmers, stock herders, sharecroppers, transport riders, and wood and other fuel collectors and dealers. Unwelcomed by the same financial speculators that had pulled them to the cities, poor whites were deemed social parasites at the exact moment when they were capitulating to the urban situation. However, unlike in the theatrical depictions proffered by Grosskopf, Boonzaier's political cartoons do more than propagandize for any particular strain of Afrikaner Nationalism, because they revealed how this form of white nationalism also relied on the eugenic approaches—uplift or social disappearance, whichever came first—embedded in public policy that were essential to legitimizing rights and freedoms through white racial purity. These images, then, made claims about white racial degeneration far more explicitly without masking them behind Afrikaner Nationalism.

THE POOR WHITE IN HIS RIGHT PLACE

Boonzaier's cartoon *Die arme-blanke op sy regte plek* (The Poor White in His Right Place) was published in *Die Burger* in 1923 (fig. 9). Boonzaier indicts General Smuts here for offering land to white speculators that has been taken from poor whites. The commentary is as follows:

> *General Smuts:* Come now, friend, here's a lot of land for you all.
>
> *The 300-Pounders:* But, General, why don't your own people live here?
>
> *General Smuts:* Oh, I sent them/marched them/drove them off to the towns. Aren't the slums the best place for poor whites?

Here Boonzaier is arguing that Smuts alone has caused the removal of poor whites to urban areas, thereby erasing a series of economic decisions made by many other persons. Even when living on the land, most

FIGURE 9. The Poor White in His Right Place/"Die arme-blanke op sy regte plek"/"The Poor White in His Right Place."; Daniel Cornelis Boonzaier, *Die Burger,* June 30, 1923, 8. Museum Africa (Johannesburg), File 338.54, Number 72/3202. All rights belong to Museum Africa (Johannesburg) or to the estate of the artist.

rural whites were poor and did not own the land; those few who did mortgaged it to banks and other creditors after recurring droughts and nonproductive seasons. General Smuts was certainly no friend to the poor, but he was an easy target because he was not a close enough friend of the Afrikaner Nationalists. In this cartoon Smuts is flanked by a baboon representing poor whites. The limit of Boonzaier's sympathy for poor whites, rendered as nonhuman, is revealed.

Boonzaier is sympathetic to the plight of the white poor, but his analysis of the causes of white poverty is so off the mark in this cartoon that he reduces the causes of white poverty to Smuts and foreign capital when other forces closer to home are related to the situation of poor whites. Moreover, Boonzaier depicts the white poor in the same way that social anthropologists in South Africa who study racial and cultural evolution depict the so-called backward races, as being closer to our prehuman ancestors. By 1927, when the Carnegie Commission was gearing up to study the "poor white problem," it began with this same premise: because these people were poor and white, they were both a withered branch of the evolutionary tree and a threat to white civilization. While Boonzaier successfully links land speculation and white

FIGURE 10. "Wat hy in 1907 gese het en wat hy nou doen"/"What you said in 1907, and this is what you are doing now." Daniel Cornelis Boonzaier, *Johannesburg Star*, May 14, 1924. Museum Africa (Johannesburg), Collection No. 731/1297, File 338.54. All rights to image belong to Museum Africa (Johannesburg) and or the estate of the artist.

poverty, he fails to consider the multiple causes of poverty for poor whites alienated from land, or Black people pushed off the land before them. Here, again, Boonzaier draws attention to the plight of poor whites, secures sympathy among wealthy whites for poor whites, inculcates a sense of obligation among the former for the care and uplift of the latter, and lastly, pressures the wealthy elite to demonstrate their commitment to poor whites. But, revealing Smuts to be wooing capitalists carrying suitcases of pounds mystifies how many different nationalities (foreign and domestic) were invested in making money in South Africa.

WHAT YOU SAID IN 1907, AND THIS IS WHAT YOU ARE DOING NOW

Boonzaier's *Wat hy in 1907 gese het en wat hy nou doen* (What You Said in 1907, and This Is What You Are Doing Now) was published in the English-language *Johannesburg Star* in 1924. Boonzaier's caption explains the image with the following:

Transvaal had to be made into a white man's land, but this agenda has not been followed for the last five years. The result is that at one end of the machine millionaires and millions of mine dividends and at the other end poverty and alienation and the streams of the white nation flow out of the land.[53]

Boonzaier accuses General Smuts of not just hypocrisy, but being the force behind the exploitation of the urban white poor. The land is not in the image because by 1924 so many whites had been forced off it that the only appropriate metaphor was a machine that churned out their ground-up bodies in alchemical exchange for a pot of gold (fig. 10).

In this cartoon Boonzaier makes all whites into "poor whites," or *arme blanke*. The 1907 plan he is referring to is one of countless local and national Indigency Commissions conducted by women social workers and the Dutch Reformed Church. Boonzaier conflates the commissions' findings on poverty alleviation with a political agenda of white supremacy because the Transvaal Province and the Orange Free State Province were founded as white homelands. As I have been arguing, such white homelands[54] did not require an end to systematic white on white violence of the class, gender, or racial variety. In fact, the white homelands simply submerged these dynamics. Voting, landownership, and white skin constituted the three qualifications used to guarantee that these places remained domains of white power. Settlers regardless of their European origins could in one generation, or at least this was the promise and expectation, secure the sort of leisured, owning-class lives that they had not been able to achieve elsewhere.

Boonzaier is tracking the transition in Smuts's political pronouncements from those focused exclusively on defense of Afrikaners to those focused on a unified South African nation. This "white man's land" in the Transvaal that Smuts had promised to endorse during his role as a leader in the Transvaal republic was always both white and not white. Its power structure was built to endorse white supremacy despite having bloodlines, family histories, language, culture, and a storied military history that reflected a profoundly amalgamated society—and not simply amalgamated across Dutch-British lines. The so-called Afrikaner Republics were never exclusively Afrikaner. Living in these Afrikaner Republics did not preclude people from marrying people not of Dutch ancestry, and marriage across ethnic lines was very common. European immigrants not only were coming to South Africa in every generation, but they were crucial to keeping South Africa "white." The majority population of these republics was African and Colored—that is, people indigenous to the region—and expanded by those who had migrated as servants, slaves, and reproductive labor during the Great Trek and those who migrated to the mines and farms and marketplaces of the "white" economy. So the reproduction of Afrikaner or British identity in the individual household had far less to do with Afrikaner Nationalist racial purity than with careful choices by adults to represent Afrikaner Nationalism as a pure racial background through the key staging of tea time, the family Bible, family photos, the language spoken in the home, or the coats of arms hanging on the wall. This white man's land was never exclusively Afrikaner, or European for that matter. This paradox is key to examining this political cartoon. Ostensibly, the political cartoon is about the destructive role of the British Empire and financial capital in South African society. While the British Empire and foreign capital played an undeniably important role in South Africa, what we have here is little more than a popularly repeated and carefully staged externalization of internal racial conflicts.

Prior to 1913 most European-descended South Africans spoke, wrote, and read either Dutch or English. Well into the 1940s, linguistic evidence demonstrates that national Afrikaans-language preservation cultural organizations still struggled to capture the imagination of the Dutch constituency. Afrikaans was a *konbit*—a kitchen language spoken by the African and Colored coreligionists, traders, tenant farmers, domestic servants, slaves, and farm workers brought by Dutch migrants to the Transvaal.[55] Afrikaans creolized Dutch- and African-language grammars, as well as Arabic, and German, and so on, which is of importance as we consider the pledge to build a white men's land that General Smuts was supposed to be in need of reminding about. The first book in Afrikaans was a translation of the Qur'an by a Muslim prisoner of war on Robben Island. And according to Solomon Plaatje's evidence about his role as a translator in Parliament, black people played an important role in the official translation of all the languages spoken in South Africa.[56] One could even infer from Plaatje's testimony that without black speech and translation as an intermediary, European languages would not have been able to imagine the white men's lands that they hungered to develop. So much for a white men's land and a white mens' language. Though Afrikaans did indeed become the adopted language of the oppressive system of grand apartheid, its multiracial origins were hidden from the people who spoke from the position of command. This stolen language helped secure a racial regime that would guarantee their role in a system of domination. Any such white men's land with a borrowed language that relies on politician's pledges to secure reflects not only its manufacture but also its tenuous grip on social relations.

Between 1913 and 1918 many Afrikaner Nationalist cultural organizations and events were established, including language festivals like the one hosted by the Reverend Johannes Rudolph Albertyn (1878–1967), prominent member of the *Poor White Study* research team, in 1916 and the launching of the first Afrikaans-medium high school at Willowmore. The effort to standardize the language was for the purpose of representing Afrikaner identity as an ancestral and authentically ancient one. However, even at the infancy of the Afrikaans language movement many people refused to speak it because they had been raised speaking Dutch or English. Parents rejected single-language Afrikaans education because they wanted their children to be bilingual in Dutch and English. Afrikaans was rejected as a European language. In fact, until the 1930s people were still campaigning to get Parliament to hire Afrikaans-speaking translators and stenographers because it was not deemed a complex enough language for use in parliamentary discussion and record keeping. This white men's land relied on the language of African traders and that of its slaves, farm worker,s and domestic servants, and whites had to be repeatedly convinced to speak their "own" language. There was still a great deal of debate over who actually counted as an Afrikaner; political leaders like Smuts continued to insist that all whites were Afrikaners, while Hertzogite leaders in Transvaal and the Orange Free State insisted that foreign-born whites and British-descended white South Africans did not fit into this category. Not until the mid-1930s did J.B.M. Hertzog announce categorically that Afrikaans speakers who were not white would be excluded from being considered Afrikaners. It is ironic that the people referred to as "Colored" in South Africa had their language demeaned, then taken out of their mouths, and then were denied whatever claims that they might make as the original speakers of the language.[57] The struggle over Afrikaans as the ancient language of this supposed white men's land demonstrates the persistent racialization and manufacture of this language. The pursuit of white men's lands rested on harnessing a set of myths about white racial purity to specious land claims. So while a cartoon such as this ostensibly condemns the cannibalism of capitalist relations, British imperialism, and a multiplicity of industrial and economic conflicts, the condemnation relies on a fallacy of a promised white men's land in Africa. Smuts supposed betrayal of a divine covenant to protect white men's land relied on an ongoing practice and promise of genocide and racial subordination. The proper context of these particular capitalist relations, then, is white on white violence, in the attempt to secure white supremacy over all black people.

There are some other things to consider in this cartoon besides the failure of the political class to manifest a white men's land. For example, the cartoon conflates the white poor with all whites. In 1922 the Smuts government dropped bombs on striking mine workers who waved banners and chanted for "white men's wages." This infamous moment in South African history is known as the Rand Revolt. The mythic white men's land that was being planned and championed in Canada, New Zealand, Australia, the United States, Central and South America, Tangyanika, Southern and Northern Rhodesia, and South Africa comprised a roving, predominantly male workforce of miners born in Scotland, Wales, other parts of Europe and positioned as settler-residents of the colonial predicament.[58] The Scottish and Welsh miners in particular brought with them to South Africa the tradition of resisting British capital. As recurring economic slumps in the price of South African gold and droughts in 1915, 1917, and 1918 continued to ravage the global economy, these miners used their claims for white men's wages, white republican citizenship, segregation, and immigration restriction (which was really whites-only immigration) to organize against British capital and the British Empire that had created the conditions for their mobility. By "imperialists," Boonzaier is signaling foreign mining capitalists like Cecil Rhodes and Alfred Beit who both conspired to overthrow the independent Afrikaner Republics but also funded their financial development for generations. Boonzaier is indicting the political machine that encouraged European and European-descent white workers to come to South Africa without whom the political vision of keeping South Africa white would have been impossible. Such charges against British imperialism fall apart when held up against the fact that such white workers were themselves deeply implicated in the politics of empire. Even among the "native-born whites," a strange ahistorical social identity that emerged in every settler society, the realities of exploitation were far more common and local than international. Thus the charges against the British Empire often functioned as a shibboleth to obscure intractable local forms of white on white conflict that was racial (focused on power) and not ethnic (focused on identity) at all.

PRIME MINISTER'S CHOICE

Boonzaier's cartoon *Ons Eerste Minister se Keuse* (Prime Minister's Choice) was published in *Die Burger* in 1923 (fig. 11). Boonzaier puts the following words in Smuts' mouth:

FIGURE 11. "Ons Eerste Minister se Keuse"/"Prime Minister's Choice." Daniel Cornelis
Boonzaier, *Die Burger*, July 7, 1923, Museum Africa (Johannesburg), File 338.54,
Number 72/3202. All rights belong to Museum Africa (Johannesburg) or to the estate of
the artist.

> How can the wretch now expect me to bestow my time on him when I am
> mingling in such high society.

Smuts, the betrayer of white Afrikanerdom, was an easy target, having
snubbed the white urban poor and their supposed representatives in the
Labour and Nationalist Parties. Henry Ford's presence in South Africa
is signaled by the presence of his automobiles parked along a tree-lined
pathway.[59] The difference in status between the wealthy white and the
white poor is aptly illustrated via opulent dress and smug disdain for
the poor white beggar in patched pants. The wealthy woman is draped
in feathers, cape, gown, gloves, and umbrella. Smuts is similarly dressed
for high society, sporting a top hat, tails, and cane. However, this critique of fancy clothing and cars stands in for a systematic analysis of the
outcomes of the economic conference and other meetings that did not
have white poverty on the agenda. The successes and failures of that
conference are utterly mystified in what becomes a rhetorical site
intended to capture a power relation. The woman wears the banner of
the economic conference, confusing what we know about the role of

women in antipoverty advocacy in this period. The beggar's unwelcome proximity to the wealthy couple provides the emotional tension. But his very existence is as disturbing as his proximity. With their eyes at the same level, the beggar returning the gaze of the wealthy couple and their bodies at the same height, the poor man presents a stoic antithesis to the elite. I argue that white racialization is occurring in this picture because the supposed unity between whites is being broken down. Viewers are led to be shocked by the lack of a fraternal connection. So while Boonzaier uses the return of the gaze to reveal that the supposed cross-class unity between whites does not exist, he reasserts their unity in a politicized whiteness brokered by Afrikaner Nationalism.

FROM BERKELEY TO WHITE AFRICA: THE AESTHETICS OF POVERTY

To turn to the present enables us to consider the longevity of images of the white poor and the ways in which the Carnegie Commission shaped debate about them. Half a century after the *Poor White Study* was published, the documentary photographer Roger Ballen drew on it. Though Ballen's photographs of rural and poor white people have been compared to those of the American antipoverty photographers Walker Evans and Dorothea Lange, they depart both from this genealogy and the more immediate one in which it was located, the 1950s through 1970s antiapartheid documentary photography produced by Peter Magubane, Ernest Cole, Finbarr O'Reilly, David Goldblatt, Alf Khumalo, and Omar Badsha, all of whom centered their work on the carnage of apartheid and militant, humanistic, resilient resistance to it.[60] Ballen's subject matter and his formalist and hyperaesthetic approaches reflect the distance and the proximity between pictures taken of black people by whites and black photographers in South Africa.[61] Magubane, for example, squarely represents the contest over history and the vitality of the black radical tradition in South African aesthetics and visual culture, while Ballen absents his work from this political context.[62] Where Magubane's pictures reflect resilience, revolt, and rural poverty as a consequence of apartheid, Ballen's concern for poor whites was profoundly transformed by the legacies of photographic technology and the relationships that it stages between audience and photograph and photographer and object. These characteristics show up repeatedly in the context and the images in Ballen's work. Ballen, as he himself indicated in a 2002 interview, had drawn on the knowledge base of the

Carnegie Commission: "The Carnegie thing is very rich. . . . [T]here are stories about the diamond diggers in the Platteland in that introduction. The stories . . . capture the richness of that community that fundamentally captured my interest. In a way, it was like a disappearing tribe I was trying to capture."[63] Ballen, like many South African commentators concerned with social relations, identity, and poverty, insisted that the *Poor White Study* had produced a sympathetic rendering of poor whites. He does not comment on the uses of racial demonization and dehumanization via intelligence testing, for example, to secure that sympathetic rendering.[64]

> They're almost like the primitive Africans, in their own way, a lot of similarities in their culture. I mean they eat mealie meal for their food. They have a lot of kids and the big families. . . . [T]hose people spent most of their time in the countryside and then they moved to the cities in the 20s and 30s and they couldn't get work in the countryside and their lands were split up and a lot of the farms were divided among the families so they didn't become very economic. . . . [A] lot of these communities are really the only true mixed white/black communities in the country.[65]

Ballen's comments about an exotic, isolated, and colonial white South Africa in the 1970s pivoted on his own location among white American vagabonders on the African continent.

> South Africa's changed a lot in the last thirty years in all sorts of way. When I first came here in the early 70s I crossed Africa, and [South Africa] was very colonial in its own way[,] . . . also a very isolated country . . . [with] very few highways. . . . It had a unique visual landscape.[66]

As a recent University of California, Berkeley graduate in geological sciences, Ballen's African exploration, though it occurred at the height of the period that the historian Cynthia Young describes as the confluence of the "U.S. third world left" couldn't have been more different. While the international black consciousness movement rocked places like Oakland, California—the root of the Free Speech Movement—Ballen's relocation to South Africa isolated him from the most critical period of recent twentieth-century U.S. history, one characterized by vibrant black and Third World left internationalism.[67] Many black people in this period were fleeing from South Africa, from the bantustans, and arraying themselves on the battlefront that became the frontline states. Ballen's work secured a high-profile position for him as a cultural arbiter beyond these many battlefronts for racial justice while inadvertently and uncritically recirculating one of the central logics of antiblackness: the racial vulnerability of white people. Ballen's inspiration, the *Poor White Study*, recapitulated the missionary solidarity of global whiteness and fantasies of colonialism—how settlers write themselves into and upon the history of the places they come to occupy. As Ahluwalia explains, settlers become natives through the "indigenization" of white conquerors.[68] Thus Ballen's positionality in this long history of photography of poor whites also reiterated settler colonial processes of settlers making themselves indigenous.

In the corpus of photography that documents rural poverty, Ballen is distinguished by a devotion to aesthetic formalism: the complexity and range of visual ideas conveyed in each photograph is far more significant than the social or political ideas and relationships that might make a photograph compelling. Though he conceded that the introduction to *Platteland* verged on a political commentary on the failure of apartheid—as demonstrated by the physical degradation of the subjects of his photographs—he insisted that the entire corpus, from *Dorps* to *Platteland* to *Outland*, reflects the development of his aesthetic sense and his capacity to bring together complex visual themes. Ballen explains:

> I don't discuss the meaning of the photograph, the meaning is visual. Does the meaning have anything to do with anything political? What is this picture about [points to one picture in *Outland*]? What is this picture about? Is it about the lines on the tent is it about the fins of the fish is it about the fishes dying. Is it about this man's dying? Is it about the tire on his chest? What is it about? . . . If you go back to this, this is about maybe a poor white's cabin. This documents an aspect in the early 80s. I didn't move anything or change anything. This is the way this place looked. In this picture did this boy put this wire around his neck or did I put it on his neck? There's a tension there. Fifteen years ago I wouldn't have put a wire or it wouldn't have made any sense to have a wire around a neck; that was going too far.[69]

The methodology of aesthetic formalism requires us to consider the series, then, as various forays into comprehending what it means to envision this hyper-visible and hyper-remembered community as *forgotten*. In *Dorps* (1986) envisioning was reflected in choices to consider features of the rural household and its shape, composition, contrast, repetition, movement in space. Thus the heightened attention in *Dorps* to the formal elements of architectural entryways (doorways, gates) was pealed back a layer when in *Platteland* (1996) Ballen entered one-bedroom cabins to reveal rough-hewn faces hinged to depleted bodies loafing, exploding, contorting, and exposing themselves but never masking anything. This formalism persisted in the composition of *Outland*

(2001), where images of grimacing men hanging themselves with copper wire augurs how many people in that collection would be dead by the time it came to publication. Ballen mentioned most sympathetically that two fellows he had photographed for that collection had died. These haunting geometries and fictions of light stops and shutter speed are supposed to be excised from the forces that made their faces not windows to tortured and beleaguered souls but vast expanses of soullessness.

Documentary photography most fulfills the goals of aestheticism when the novelty of viewing something taboo shifts attention from the circumstances being viewed. The enduring philosophical debate between realism and aestheticism remains unresolved because individual photographers decide whether or not to disclose the way that the camera alters and transforms. The quest for objectivity explains why photographers and audiences most value images that capture the elusive essence of a social problem, through individual nameless but authentically suffering people, ironically thereby removing the emotional connection that humans would otherwise have when they inhabit or witness each other's pain. Nakedness, hunger, desperation, hollowness haunt the world of documentary photography.[70] Other scholars discount this largely libidinal explanation of attraction to shocking visual images representing the universal horror within, opting instead for a material explanation that asks: Why do some bodies get designated as objects of visual curiosity?[71] What structural relations of power are captured when some bodies can only fit into the racial and sexual economy in this way? Nevertheless, there are a wide range of goals among documentary photographers and a wide range of impacts of their work for the state, particularly in attempts to document racialized poverty and mobilize more equitable distribution of the national wealth.[72]

My main concern with Ballen's formalism is the lack of distinction between the human form and the physical form because I would contend that this body of work hauntingly depicts people in a way that has the effect of negating their humanity. They are photographed in intimate moments of hosting an important guest and display glee, trust, hope, and very little else. There is no masking at all for these people, just the most intimate invasions of the shape and form of their private desires, except there is no desire in them and they have been figured as incapable of injury.[73] Part of the quintessential project of "white writing," such images are disturbing because of their echoes in the colonial-racial-slavocratic obsession with humans without divine agency, the soulless.[74]

For Ballen, discomfort with these images, even the one that is the most well known globally, an image of two men dressed as members of the constabulary, one drooling, comes from repressed psychosexual urges that exist in the subconscious. As a psychoanalyst of the colonial predicament Frantz Fanon distanced his anticolonial method of analysis from psychoanalysis and the explanation of all conflict as repression of sexual desires because he recognized how much of racial colonial violence was constituted by expressed and acted upon sexual violence, with hardly anything done by those in power that exists mainly or only in the psychic territory of repression and the unsaid. Rather than a thinly veiled schema of *unconscious* hatred and violence, the colonial world was marked by explicit acts and rigid spatial demarcations of systematic sexual degradation, humiliation, natal alienation, and gratuitous violence.[75] Such spectacular violence against black bodies, of course, not only had the capacity to spread beyond the actual terrain of those figured as inhabiting antihuman bodies—black people—but of course could only function if it surged beyond these boundaries and executed the cannibalistic impulse upon its authors. Not only is resistance largely absent from Ballen's human subjects. The contention that people disturbed by these invasive representations are merely repressed doesn't sit well. The images—of exaggerated physical features all out of proportion; pictures of boy children with guns and girl children with tattered dolls; drooling adults; adults infantilized, pictured with their dolls; and imagery that revolved around the dirt poor, the freakish, and the silly— are potent reiterations of the notions in the *Poor White Study* about racially degraded white people who deserve their lot. That they are white does not make the pictures less or more problematic. Instead, they signal a racial and sexual economy that always makes this set of images antiblack, and in this instance white.[76]

Ballen dubs concerns with what these image do as cultural texts a "projection" and "merely sociological." He insists that those who cannot look at his pictures or those who see exploitation where others see empathy are people afraid of their own id. My project has been animated by my familiarity with such photographs of black people around the world that inspire photographers to flatten experiences of horror and turn them into experiences of human innocence qua primitivism. I am sympathetic with Ballen's subjects because there are distinctive historical reasons—which unfortunately endure and are redeployed at critical moments in the life of racial regimes—for their poverty that have everything to do with their systematic dehumanization and experiences of torture and oppression. Their "willingness" to sit for photographs cannot take away the fact that the only pictures they are invited to sit for are images of squalor and degradation.

The second aspect that marks Ballen's work is the unmistakable exoticization of poverty and the practice of decontextualizing racialization beyond recognition. In this aspect, the more appropriate way to understand his photographs is through the context of worlds' fairs, nineteenth-century circus exhibitions, freak shows, and other cultures of spectacle and menagerie that were designed to cultivate a sense of national identity by providing representations of species. The bearded lady, for example, is not just an individual with different hormone levels; she is more a representative for a tribe, a people primitivized by their performance and by the discourse of perversity that drew their audiences. Ballen says:

> [I]n South Africa they were shocked at *Platteland* and *Platteland* was a very very controversial book here. I got everything from death threats to tv talk shows and everything else. It really shook the white population here. . . . The white situation they had never encountered it and they had done what they could to uplift a lot of the whites. But the situation in 1985 was a lot different than in 1955 or in 1935 because the government had proactively tried to alleviate white poverty to a large degree. . . . But the poorer part of the population tends to maintain the cultural heritage more definitively than modern middle class individuals. So what interested me in this group of people was that they actually had; there was something very rich in their heritage in terms of the white man's relationship to Africa. And the white man's . . . relationship with the land, with their mythology, with their community, I think like you might find in Appalachia. I think that's an interesting something that's really unique about this group of people culturally. And maybe I wouldn't necessarily say visually because you can find these things anywhere in most countries.[77]

Ballen acknowledges in this comment that it is something about the people themselves that makes them artistically significant. The formal aligning of characters and objects in a setting is meaningful aesthetically because of what white barbarism means. Ballen's publications played a historical role in South Africa and the global art market; marketing whiteness in Africa. The artist explains after the fashion that the *Poor White Study* did: he links upper- and middle-class white South Africans to a racialized kinship with white poverty, again making the photographs a proxy for a political analysis that is hard to disavow.

A third aspect to be considered is the idea that poor whites reflected the original and authentic culture of white South Africans because South

Africanness as a settler colonial national fantasy was manufactured for the consumption of middle-class white people. National ceremonies and rituals to rededicate themselves to pioneering ancestors reflected the formation of the South African white middle class as citizens in the period of the consolidation of white nationalism under study here. This logic of authenticity is the same racial logic that Bantu Affairs used to justify separate development since black people who participated in urban commodity culture were said to be in danger of losing their culture. The poor whites were not primitive. They were not remnants of a prior historical time. And probably long before Ballen came to photograph them, they knew that other white people had the consumer attributes of white status and a white standard of living—suburban homes, garbage disposals, self-defrosting refrigerators, self-cleaning ovens, Afrikaaner Taal Festivals (language celebrations), and Great Trek celebrations—even when they themselves did not have access to them. It is naive to conclude that since middle-class people have such commodities and consumer practices they are more modern. After all, most often the commodities that signified middle-class status, such as the time-saving appliances in middle-class homes, were operated, maintained, and used by black women and men who worked as domestics. So they were time savers and status securers only inasmuch as the invisible black people signaled in Ballen's photos operated them; but such possessions and possessing them did not make one modern. Ballen's preoccupation with poor whites as Noble Boers did not grant them any more moral authority or political space. This is simply a mystification that enables us to exploit them with misplaced sympathy. The sympathy ought not to be for their culture, which is rarely critically engaged, but for the hardships that they face as a direct result of being exploited by wealthier whites in their society and in societies beyond their own. This story is absent. In many ways, because the context of exploitation has been erased, these photographs participate in the same process that the Carnegie Commission on White Poverty engaged in, that is, depicting poor whites as an eternal, unchanging cultural group that deserves sympathy but for the reason that they are ugly and deformed rather than for the reason that they reflect racialized and gendered exploitation and ill-gotten gains by upper-class white South Africans. Ballen's work, then, revels in ugly bodies via pornographic projections. Audre Lorde theorized the pornographic as "emphasiz[ing] sensation without feeling" and as "defin[ing] human need to the exclusion of the psychic and emotional components of that need, suggesting that formalism on its own faces profound limits.[78] The people as pictured appear devastated, lost, happy, and moronic because Ballen's formalism has erased their humanity and their natural desire to be clothed in something akin to dignity and self-recognition. Their main, or only, emotion is tragicomic dysfunction. Except it is not funny to watch a grown man drool, or an old woman so wasted away in her bed that viewers can only expect to witness the transformation from dust to dust. And perhaps a moral conversation has to be had with these photographs and their makers—over many many decades—to deconstruct the mythology of aesthetic beauty that mystifies them.

The exhibition of the so-called tribe of poor whites in South Africa tells a particularly ill-fated story about Europeans in Africa. The first snatch of the story makes them unfortunates and dependents on others for their survival. The second snatch of the story makes them victims of the undeniable atavism that results from Africa itself. That place of prehistoric origins always wins, and poor white skin cannot bear the burden of civilizing.[79] Ballen's uncanny reproduction of the race-making categories of the *Poor White Study* so many years later reveals a precarious balance between aesthetic composition and objective realism typical of the genre. Moreover, the ease of reproduction suggests that the *Poor White Study* researchers tapped into a volatile and persistent ideological canon, not an objective reality. Depictions of the racialized white poor that draw on clichés of scientific racism launched Ballen's work in the international art market. What stories must be told to make the people photographed appear so vacant and so available for the viewer's consumption? What must be done to people to make them so disinterested and to make them appear as if they want nothing at all? Is it, as suggested, that they are part of an old culture, a tribe that has been found? Or is it that viewers are witnessing a replication of a familiar rhetoric of primitivism.

THE LONG HISTORY OF POSTRACIAL DISCOURSE

The larger project of the Carnegie Corporation of New York in South Africa in the 1920s and 1930s, and its enforcement of racial accommodationism, suppression of black radical thought, and idealizing racial liberalism, was an anticipation of and participation in early-twentieth-century discourses of postracialism and color-blindness. As a political project, the Carnegie Corporation participated in a kind of mischievous conflation of liberal racism and the black radical tradition. Black radical discourses on race, even those profoundly compromised by their allegiance to a structural and cultural embeddedness in Victorian ideologies about the human and civilization, at root have been concerned with expanding the social space for liberation. Coming out of material conditions of institutionalized gratuitous antiblack violence, black radical discourses constitute a break with white supremacy. On the other hand, the false history provided about poor whites by the Carnegie Corporation served explicitly to conceal the role of white on white racial domination, the violence of domestic (South African–born) white capital, and to obscure the racial relations of power by producing a racial subject vulnerable and sympathetic primarily because of its lost white entitlement. No black racial subject could compete with this—because despite whatever depredations black people were compelled to absorb and suffer, their blackness could be and was used to explain why black people were alienated from sovereignty, humanity, subjectivity, citizenship, freedom, housing, mobility and permanency, personal security and safety, control over the social reproduction of kin and family relations, social and financial supports, land, education, food, wages and benefits, and electrical, water, and sewage infrastructure. Thus at the very moment in which new photographic technology was being used explicitly to create ethnographic images to map the spatial dimensions of the racial labor hierarchy, to entrench the international campaign for eugenic imperialism, to paper over the cruelty of racial capitalism, and to insist that Britons would never be slaves under the regime of Anglo-American solidarity, the Carnegie Corporation of New York used visual culture to produce and rediscover white misery, vulnerable whiteness, and whiteness in Africa/African whiteness. This chapter has reconsidered the way that the figure of the poor white has been deployed by two antagonistic worldviews—one energized by the "forged memory" created by the Carnegie Corporation and one intent on dismantling the ways in which white poverty was used to legitimate antiblackness.

CONCLUSION: PLAYING WITH WHITENESS

The Carnegie Corporation of New York furthered the ideology of white racial kin via scientific racism using a volatile visual regime with a complex representational and cultural politics. Where clerics and playwrights and women reformers had failed, the approval of Americans creating a sense of racial kinship among white people across the geographic lines of would-be sister republics succeeded. Thus the Carnegie

Commission resolved earlier debates about white identity and the paradoxical presence of poor whites. I have pointed to the ethnographic photographs, plays, films, and documentary photographs made available by the *Poor White Study* in order to point to the groundwork of the uses of the figure of the poor white as a tool in the politics of Afrikaner Nationalism across later genres. I have discussed the way that sympathy for poor whites was deployed to unite Afrikaner Nationalist elites and working-class people. By examining representations across genre, we become more familiar with the process by which whites were taught to see white identity as a vulnerable and victimized identity. While Carnegie commissioners construed poor whites as a social problem to be rehabilitated, Daniel Boonzaier's 1920s and 1930s political cartoons disavow apartheid's cultural nationalism and rejected the call to rehabilitate white people as a crass politicization of white poverty. Unlike these South Africans concerned with showing how structures of power were organized to give certain white people unearned privilege, American immigrant to South Africa, Roger Ballen used documentary photography to experiment with and traffic in some of the most provocative racializing images of whites as poor people in the English-speaking world. In comparing these different types of representations of the debate over "poor whites," I undercut the ready explanation of white urban poverty as a plight caused by either British imperial and capitalist policy or competition with the black majority and reveal how apartheid failed as a system for guaranteeing economic and political uplift for the poor while galvanizing white supremacy. Where apartheid did not fail was in structuring a racial regime that could rely on complex visual triggers. Boonzaier's political cartoons render poor whites as a politicized community in the 1920s and 1930s, racially vulnerable to competition by black workers, "foreign" capitalists, and British imperialists. While Boonzaier focuses on elite decision makers and their failure to address the problems of the white poor and to prohibit white urban migration, the economist and dramatist Johannes Friedrich Wilhelm Grosskopf produced numerous plays that were released theatrically and one groundbreaking film about the plight of South Africa's poor whites. I have analyzed these dramatic works as well and the significance of an economic historian's role in scripting the history of the racial economy as a story about white loss and white deprivation. Plays and films about the plight of poor whites in South Africa contributed significantly to the consolidation of views about poor whites and the idea of the need for a muscular, masculinist, and violent type of racialized South African citizenship. The documentary photographer Roger Ballen offers another wedge into the conversation about visual materials tracing the history of photographic depictions of poor whites in the antiapartheid era of the1970s and 1990s and the first postapartheid generation. His photographs reveal the staying power of stereotypical tropes about white poverty as an ethnic and/or cultural/tribal formation and the social and cultural work that aestheticization of racialized poverty via documentary photography does to suppress other struggle-oriented uses of the technologies of documentary photography.

Though the racist gaze is evident in the depictions of poor whites in South Africa—most of which are characterized by the deployment of scientific racism to engender pity for the white poor—there are also critiques of Afrikaner Nationalism and the discourse with which it frames poor whites. The Carnegie Commission could cultivate sympathy and disdain for poor whites living beneath white standards; the latter made them that much more sympathetic. In contradistinction to the analyses of white poverty in the Carnegie Commission—which attempts at times to refute the racist logic of social science in the 1920s—the visual representations of white poverty reveal the consequences of the politicization of white poverty. By concluding that poor whites were victims of misguided clerical philanthropy and mismanaged state public welfare schemes instead of hereditary failures, Carnegie researchers made elaborate claims for scientific management of the poor while simultaneously noting that poor whites were genetic embarrassments. While the Carnegie commissioners construed poor whites as a social problem to be rehabilitated and a genetic racial problem to be eliminated, Boonzaier's political cartoons rejected a strictly apartheid historiography of white poverty by revealing its manufacture in visual culture. Moreover, these examples demonstrate that references to ethnicity, minority rights, and the volk are inadequate explanations for white identity in South Africa. Instead, a more comprehensive theoretical framework is necessary to understand images of poor whites.

Boonzaier's political cartoons and Ballen's documentary photography are compelling examples of the disavowal of white privilege and the redeployment of whiteness as inaccessible to poor whites through the creation of a popular discourse about the meaning of white identity. Whiteness materializes as a new social identity through the dissemination of the Carnegie Commission "findings," academic and elite depictions of whiteness, and the placement of Carnegie Commission researchers in key policy-making positions in the Afrikaner Nationalist government. But popular visual representations of whiteness also pro-mulgate a new type of whiteness: one that speaks back to the gaze of the entire professional class of scientific experts, charity workers, and theologians that made up the champions of the poor. Elites did not simply generate propaganda for distribution to the masses. Rather, new knowledge about the shared ideology of white poverty was created by elites and by the popular classes.

At the root of these various representations, policy driven and academic on the one hand and artistic and popular on the other, is the irony that in South Africa, where white supremacy has dominated as an ideological and structural frame since the colonial era, whiteness has been available for manipulation. Nevertheless, the crises posed by the massive amounts of wealth to be had on world markets in the 1920s as they intersected with national interest in transforming white supremacy into grand apartheid collided in the public debates surrounding "white poverty." Concealed in this debate over white poverty and its discourse of racial purity, miscegenation, and slum clearings was an overriding anxiety that white South Africans would organize and collaborate with Africans and Indians and Coloreds who had been mobilized by urban activists in the black radical tradition in South Africa for at least two generations by the 1920s.

The White Primitive

Whiteness Studies, Embodiment,
Invisibility, Property

In 1960 the Carnegie Corporation continued its investments in scientific racist research in South Africa with the Mobile Testing Laboratory for Research on Mentality. The mobile testing unit was equipped with several long trucks with brightly lit laboratories and staffed by research scientists.[1] The April 1960 correspondence between Johannesburg's National Institute for Personnel Research and Carnegie staffer S.H. Stackpole featured black-and-white photographs and slides of the mobile labs traveling South African roads and two photographs of scientists. In one image a male scientist displays his instruments on a desk; in the other a female scientist administers a test to a white man using a rock as a desk. The latter photograph could easily be in a museum installation called "the meeting of civilization with tradition"; the scientist, clad in lab coat, and the test taker, clad in burgher clothing and a wide-brimmed hat, epitomize the type of work being conducted and with whom. The mobile testing unit is both an obvious throwback to the era of mental hygiene and evidence of its longevity. Such research on white people provides a window into the racial logic of white vulnerability and its relationship to the project of whiteness studies.

The contributions of whiteness studies[2] and the critique of scientific racism[3] have provided new registers[4] for examining the political and theoretical significance of the Carnegie Corporation's *Poor White Study* of 1927–32, during a period of white minority rule in southern Africa and at the height of the American eugenics movement.[5] In this chapter I use whiteness studies and the critique of scientific racism to demonstrate how the *Poor White Study* was a significant precondition to the geopolitical consolidation of Afrikaner Nationalism.[6] Moreover, the international eugenics movement profoundly influenced national political cultures, associational life, racial politics, and antipoverty policy in each of its member states.

Taken together whiteness studies and the critique of scientific racism expand our understanding of the political, cultural, and social projects that were animated by and attached to this social group, poor whites, which was the subject of the *Poor White Study*. For the most part, whiteness studies has historicized the manufacture of white identities, documented the intersection of ideologies of race, class, gender, and nation, and analyzed whiteness as unearned privilege, stolen property, and a particularly ostentatious form of provincialism.[7] Further, whiteness studies bear witness to suppressed histories of racial violence that have shaped the world and "invented the Negro" as an alibi for such a world.[8] Key metaphors that pervade whiteness studies view whiteness as investment and property, as invisible privilege, and as a juridical and social construction *distinct from* the racial, genetic, heritable body that was the central figure in eugenics. Alternately, we can also understand the nature and function of whiteness as a risk-laden, hypervisible, and biologically sanctioned political and philosophical set of meanings. Poor whites, as it turns out, are a racialized group that white supremacy used to transform itself into a vulnerable, protected, and almost sacred political category. These alternative ways of thinking highlight the nuanced relationship between the actual social formation of impoverished white people and the privilege assigned to white nationalists allegedly working in their defense. It is precisely this nuanced relationship that requires us to take up both whiteness studies and the critique of scientific racism. Whiteness studies scholars, with their attention on white privilege and white supremacy, have infrequently drawn from the critique of scientific racism. I argue that the pseudoscientific language about biology and physiognomy deployed in the international eugenics movement that is usually linked to scientific racism must be brought into conversation with the literary, historical, legal, and cultural analysis of whiteness studies to be a more effective scholarly rejoinder to white supremacy. In addition, whiteness has played an important role in the constitution of the social sciences,[9] so if we are concerned with decolonizing knowledge production practices and decolonizing knowledge itself, having a proper account of whiteness is imperative.

Thinking about whiteness as risk-laden, hypervisible, and embodied is not to exclude the ways that whiteness functions as privilege and supremacy but to offer an account of the status of contingent whiteness or semiwhiteness and its uses. Taking up the problematic of embodied, hypervisible, risk-laden white racialization enables us to turn to considerations of the cultural work done by poor whiteness, or the racial logic of white vulnerability.[10] Whiteness as privilege and supremacy is the root of antiblackness.[11] At the same time, poor whiteness can be a genuine target of antiblackness, and white supremacy cannot be fully understood without attention to the monitoring and regulation of the poor white body. White misery was harnessed to white nationalism and rediscovered at moments of crisis, such as during the height of scientific racism in South Africa, in order to legitimate antiblackness. The mechanisms and processes that shift the meanings attached to vulnerable whiteness and the uses of its rediscovery concern me here.

Far from the postracial histories circulating the globe,[12] I am asking that we look again at the white poor as a category subject to intermittent antiblackness and its disciplines and discourses. While poor whites have been designated as the beneficiaries of apartheid and as the social and political justification for the legitimacy of apartheid, ideologies about their potential for racial degeneration have been underexamined. Thus I argue that one important mechanism in the creation of apartheid, in addition to the displacement, murder, and dehumanization of African, Colored, and Asian peoples, was the establishment of systematic procedures for the regulation, constraint, and racial marking of poor whites as irretrievable and degenerate, as "like the blacks." I foreground the racial policing of white identity, rhetoric about white racial degeneration, and the enduring strands in the political origin story of white nationalism animated by the "white primitive" and the "white poor."

I do not focus on poor whites to displace the harms to black people or to minimize those ongoing, extraordinary, quotidian intergenerational practices that structure black bodies as antagonistic to the human ontologically. Rather, I wish to examine how white selfhood faces its own internalized racism, slave past, and self-hatred. Put simply, where whiteness scholars have been mostly concerned with whiteness as privilege and unearned rights, I am concerned with whiteness as misery.[13]

If white selfhood was premised on misbegotten claims to having the only access to humanness and power, then that constitutes a perverse and ultimately flimsy premise for rationality, achievement, virtue, capacity, social advancement, and historical change. This is what I refer to as diminished and diminishing white selfhood. Scholars who have commented on the making of racial blackness and the notion of the human have used concepts such as "fundamental antagonism," "inventing the Negro," and "the dead do fly planes" to explore the idea that white selfhood occupies the only location of rationality, achievement, and capacity worthy of defense and the designation "human."[14] However, I mean to trouble this notion by delinking the terms *white* and *selfhood*. Selfhood is not exclusive to white people, and not all white people have access to selfhood.

EUGENIC IMPERIALISM

Eugenics was an international campaign resulting from a highly self-conscious and mobile white settler community invested in propping up and underwriting rickety white minority-rule polities and the cultural platform that obscured the workings of power in them. Edwin Black's use of the term *eugenic imperialism* in his magisterial study *War against the Weak* (2012 [2003]) conveys the international nature of the eugenics campaign from 1907 through the late 1930s. Our temporal distance from the formal eugenics movement and its organizations, principles, and partisans has made it much easier to view it as pseudoscience, as have the many scholarly debates that have sought to delegitimize it. However, its lasting global legacy and its imprint on various institutions of and ideas about social welfare, commonwealth, and the public good are ignored to our own peril. Indeed, impulses toward a eugenically defined empire have been some of the most enduring epistemological claims taken up in order to hijack the human aspirations and potential of the poor. The proliferation of eugenics organizations, government administrations, and immigration restriction laws in Germany, Norway, Sweden, Britain, France, Italy, the United States, and New Zealand during this period hinged on three critical political goals: extending American influence, supplanting charitable and government aid for the poor with sterilization and other restrictions on individual bodies, and reinforcing the idea of pure citizenries by disappearing huge segments of the population through confinement and incarceration, sterilization and child theft, and racial reclassification.[15] By offering direct financial support to individual scientists, groups of scientists, and governments, the Eugenics Records Office, the International Federation of Eugenics

Organizations (IFEO), and the Carnegie Foundation were able to capitalize on the racial self-consciousness of whites in countries where political power was lodged exclusively in the hands of whitened settler-citizens. National eugenics committees wanting to join the international organizations spearheaded by American eugenicists had to agree to introduce policies similar to those passed in the U.S. Congress and in numerous U.S. state governments. Coming from every continent, national leaders who facilitated the introduction of formal institutional relationships between researchers and policy makers in their countries and American government agencies, foundations, and organizations needed to echo the mantra of the head of the American Museum of Natural History, Henry Osborn, namely, that "the true spirit of American democracy that all men are born with equal rights and duties has been confused with the political sophistry that all men are born with equal character and ability to govern themselves."[16] Each new organization also had to agree to lobby against providing all manner of social supports for the poor because such social supports only delayed the hoped-for eventual genetic disappearance of such people. Finally, each new organization had to contribute a statement about white supremacy and the protection and vulnerability of white civilization to internal racial degeneration.

Eugenics continued undeterred into World War I, viewed as significant both for achieving international recognition in science and for meeting international good governance standards. In the waning years of the British Empire, the logic of empire became an emboldened strain in the democratic politics of a world of theoretically sovereign white minority-rule states. This showed up as the erosion of self-determination, political participation, and basic self-rule in matters of reproduction. Workers seeking social welfare and the right to organize clashed with an elite that believed most workers could not govern themselves and were not likely to survive the transition to industrial civilization. With its goals of protecting white civilization, eugenics campaigns used a host of terrible treatments (genetic monitoring, sterilization, child abduction, mental testing, forced removals, and detention) in poor white communities to civilize poor whites—quite often through disappearance.[17] These treatments were regimes of misery, punishment, torture, public humiliation, and racial demonization. They were publicly condoned measures of disciplining and punishing; the important distinction between the political regimes of disciplining and punishing centering on whether bodies are viewed as mere flesh.[18] Those deemed as mere flesh occupy an ontological status of social death constituted by the inability to end naturalized and ubiquitous suffering upon which life, citizenship, belonging, membership, character, achievement, morality, aesthetics, innocence, mobility, and family ties are predicated for those not deemed mere flesh. But even in this context of social death and the inability to end naturalized and ubiquitous suffering, at least two forms of response to structural violence obtain—one organized by those deemed mere flesh and another by those deemed alive. The former is typically organized around the sign of "uplift"; the latter, around the sign of "rehabilitation." It is a mistake to conclude that the eugenics movement was not deeply involved in monitoring both responses. Eugenicists were concerned that energies devoted to uplift would be wasted on people deemed to be mere flesh. They also countered that energies devoted to rehabilitation would be better spent on forcibly limiting biological and social reproduction of such people so that it would be less costly to administer coercive forms of exclusion. They insisted that environmental and social contexts like poverty and homelessness could account to some extent for the misery they identified. But, ultimately, their interests revolved most around protecting property, advantage, and power among those deemed legitimately and meritoriously socially alive. Under the global racial contract, blackness is subject to generalized dishonor, confinement, natal alienation, criminalization, gratuitous violence, and decayed constricted spaces. It is often convenient to distinguish between those disciplined (rehabilitated/alive) and punished (uplifted/confined to the status of ontological mere flesh) as white and black. This convenience, however, does not account for the related reproductive directives associated with disciplining and punishing because those disciplined are encouraged to reproduce and those punished are discouraged from reproducing. The disciplined are said to disappear and become rehabilitated when they no longer exist, while the punished are said to be unable to disappear—for should they disappear, then the rest of the world would disappear with them as their suffering is the ground on which one imagines redemption for those to be disciplined.

These regimes functioned in tandem with the ideological, institutional, and material mechanisms to transform African lifeworlds into entries on account ledgers and to literally destroy Africans in southern Africa.[19] This does not mean that African people lacked a work ethic, workers' consciousness, or elaborate systems for making their labor and products alternately available and scarce.[20] Instead what I am analyzing is the ways in which scientific racism as a racial regime promoted the devaluation of the work, labor, and products of its racial targets—as well as the makers of that work, labor, and production.[21]

Poor whites have been conceptualized by scholars as the remnants of a flourishing white civilization, as evidence that white civilization is vulnerable to internal disintegration and degeneration,[22] and at the same time as a group that can be rehabilitated—exploited but not subject to gratuitous violence, natal alienation, generalized dishonor, and myths about seduction into state sexual violence.[23] Thus the complex array of approaches to solving the social problem that their very existence represents tends to focus on rehabilitation and their potential upward mobility to the neglect of theorizing about or even acknowledging the ways that racialization first and foremost is about inculcating shame and guilt in the white mind through practices of highly scripted body modification and surveillance of the body,[24] as well as suppressing guilt about complicity with an antihuman social order.[25]

Racism, in its first and last instance, I argue, is about controlling white people: reinforcing an amoral self-abnegation and attenuating moral accountability in order to exact compliance with the administrative, ideological, and material annihilation of black and non-black people.[26] The policing of the borders of whiteness among whites, a "consensual hallucination . . . located in real space,"[27] was a critical terrain on which to map South Africa's racial hierarchy and to demonstrate the Carnegie Corporation's race relations technical expertise. White selfhood organized through these social forces is a diminished one and reveals a profound misunderstanding of the nature of human life. Despite premature death and systematic intergenerational suffering, blackness reflects a better understanding of what it means to live. The difference between these two worldviews cannot be accounted for without accounting for the white self-annihilation that is embedded in white privilege. Moreover, the annihilation and premature death of black peoples is resisted and survived through multiple forms of radical resistance, recognition of fundamental antagonism, identification with the dead, mimicry, signifying, prophecy, obeah, rebellion, and imaginative assertion of the praxis of the "decolonial imaginary,"[28] "race traitorship"[29] and "abolitionism."[30] By "race traitorship," I am referring to the process by which white people abandon the dictates of white privilege by militantly sabotaging all dimensions of whatever might constitute legitimations of innocence or veracity or fellow feeling or logic or charity imbricated with whiteness; it is the only contingent way out of reproducing white supremacy. Following M. Jacqui Alexander, I am pointing toward a selfhood that does far more than turn its back on axes of advantage and call out antiblackness. Alexander proposes that selfhood be understood as becoming "oneself in the process of becoming one with the Sacred"and through "mutual embodiment," defined as "Divine desire work[ing] to prod the self into believing that it does not exist of its own accord, free will notwithstanding."[31] These concepts about cosmology are not meant to avoid the practical sites of power that social forces operate through but to reveal some of what has been traded in for the mess of pottage that constitutes white nationalism and to explain again how many fields black revolutionary protocols operate through.

THE EMBODIMENT PROBLEM: ENVIRONMENT, HEREDITY, AND UPLIFT

In 1931 R.W. Wilcocks, a South African psychologist and author of volume 2 of the *Poor White Study*, provided an example of the enduring ambivalence about poor whites' status being better explained by hereditary degeneration or environment. In his presidential address to the South African Association for the Advancement of Science, "Intelligence, Environment, and Heredity," Wilcocks claimed that "on the whole, then, it may safely be said that . . . heredity is an important factor in determining the level of intellectual efficiency."[32] Here Wilcocks echoed other hereditarian thinkers of the contraception movement who argued that poor whites were not "victims of circumstance . . . but [were] inherently degenerate, a threat to the very survival of white supremacy, and beyond rehabilitation by environmental amelioration."[33] Wilcocks's presidential address began with a nod toward the relationship between genes and crime illustrated by the notorious upstate New York Jukes Family Study, an entire family of hundreds who had all been remanded to reform schools and jails due to their "criminal disposition."[34] Wilcocks commented on research by mental hygiene experts and argued that people with low IQs[35] should be directed to vocational schools and denied high school–level education. This precise set of measures would be used a generation later for the supposed benefit of Africans by the highest-ranking educational official in South Africa, E.G. Malherbe, a former *Poor White Study* researcher.[36] After reviewing dozens of studies in the United States and South Africa on the IQ of twins, siblings, and parents and children, Wilcocks concluded that environmental modification made very little impact on the intelligence of children (1931). Six decades later, wrestling with the inconsistent and ambivalent embrace of eugenics by South African academics, historians of eugenics[37] suggested that "Wilcocks ascribed this decline [poor white children's IQ fell in tests from age 10 to 13] to the unfavorable environmental conditions under which poor white children lived" and stated that "intelligence test scores could not truly represent their inherent potentialities."[38] However, despite public denunciation of eugenics by some South Africa–based social scientists, many of them went on to become apartheid technocrats who were profoundly influenced by genetic pathologies as reasons to further restrict black social status. Most liberal "Friends of the Negro," such as Malherbe, John David Rheinallt-Jones (1884–1953), Thomas Jesse Jones (1873–1950), and Charles Templeman Loram (1879–1940), lent critical support to Jim Crow and the most accommodationist pro-colonial tendencies in the writings of Booker T. Washington (1856–1915) and James Emmanuel Kwegyir Aggrey (1875–1927). But for many the introduction to eugenics and separate development came through their research on poor whites.[39] Though the *Poor White Study* resulted in improved social status and provision of social welfare and minimal (though highly publicized) government-funded employment for this social group, the intense scrutiny of poor whites was part of a civilizing mission to eliminate them as a distinctive community of whites who were also members of racially integrated urban areas, families, and households.[40] In exchange for complying with the prescriptions and requirements of whiteness Afrikaner Nationalism hoped to erase contingent semiwhite people and communities.

Though Wilcocks ends his volume of the *Poor White Study* (1932) with recognition of the importance of environment on intelligence, he insisted throughout it and the 1931 presidential address that "the intelligence of an individual was preponderantly determined by inherited factors." Wilcocks's deep ambivalence about environmental and hereditary explanations for white poverty—and the difficulty that even historians of racial segregation have accounting for this ambivalence—is precisely why a theory of the racialization of poor whites is necessary. Despite their allegiance to environmental and structural causes for explaining white poverty, the Carnegie Commission not only "enter[ed] directly into a serious dialogue"[41] with the methods and principles of eugenicist theories, but their speeches, writings, political organizing, and public pronouncements explicitly endorsed the conventional definitions of eugenic imperialism. By using conceptual frameworks such as hereditary failure, organic shiftlessness, and a native "tramping" way of life, the Carnegie Commission caricatured poor whites as biological inferiors.[42]

With their obsession for measuring the intelligence of poor whites in every part of the country, taking pictures of them, and documenting their everyday habits, the *Poor White Study* researchers erected a significant section of the long campaign against European and non-European racialized subjects. The five-volume *Poor White Study* included ethnographic photographs and appendixes on the physiological basis of poor white identity that sought to illustrate what racial degeneration looked like and the way that being a poor white scarred the white body. By suggesting that mental testing, the search for the missing link, removal of children, work retraining programs, forced removal of whites from integrated residential districts, and sterilization of whites were all linked to the set of administrative practices and procedures that reinforced the ideology of black inferiority, I am arguing that whites also were racialized in an embodied fashion. Mental testing in particular, though now disregarded by many as a flawed attempt to measure intellectual capacity, functioned by attacking the body. Sterilization campaigns functioned by attacking the body and made powerful distinctions between the genes of wealthy and poor whites. Even Race Welfare Society opponents of contraception who argued that contraception promoted race suicide among wealthy white people argued that poor white people as members of the "lower orders were . . . reckless, self-indulgent and destined by their nature to breed uncontrollably."[43] Eugenicists argued that key aspects of the human character could be measured by physical attributes such as bone or face structure but also by psychological tests of IQ and political opinion tests of commitments to nationalist pro-natalism. Such tests reinforced white as well as nonwhite bodies being made into subjects of a racial hierarchy. Laws, policies, and scientific knowledge all get enacted on specific bodies, both white and nonwhite. These practices of embodiment go a long way toward explaining the nuanced way in which whiteness operates.

In each interview that was conducted, *Poor White Study* research team members gave poor whites access to a very sophisticated scientific racist conversation by subjecting them as both "model subjects" and "errant subjects" to scientific racist testing. Therefore to call the hierarchy of races among whites predominantly a popular culture, narrative, and representational event[44] minimizes the effects of this study on the interviewees, who understood it as a threat, a type of upper-class elite harassment, and an imposition on their bodies. This was not merely a cultural or class imposition, but a racial imposition. When some interviewees made clear their absolute resistance to the process of being scrutinized as poor people and as "white" people by not answering questions, by turning the questions back on the interviewers, and by challenging the imposition of being scrutinized in their homes, they were indicating a resistance to being understood as white in the ways that the research team members conceived of them.

Whiteness can paradoxically and simultaneously constitute unmarked privilege and marked/commented-upon discrimination. Whiteness always carries with it colonial imaginaries and tropes obsessed with static suffering bodies like the "detribalized African" and the "white primitive" that need missionary rescue and sympathy for their very existence while enthusiastically suppressing political identities.[45] Meanwhile these colonial archaeologies rarely imagine white bodies suffering under the regime of white supremacy, because membership alone in white group identity is supposed to guarantee unfettered expression of subjectivity and the ability to observe, name, and theorize about the other. There is a way of describing white racialization that is not parallel to the forces racializing black people. And that way of describing white racialization requires pointing to the ways in which white racialization functioned to produce more antiblackness. And yet passing for white among whites comes with its own set of disasters.

THE INVISIBILITY PROBLEM

The workings of white privilege and white supremacy have been theorized as being invisible and unmarked features of an extant visual and aesthetic regime of power. Part of this supposed invisibility has been enshrined in social prohibitions and actual laws against black people publicly commenting on the structural and interpersonal workings of white privilege and white supremacy.[46] For example, for much of its history the South African Native Affairs Department enshrined a policy that prohibited black people from taking photographs of white people, using the logic that the "act of looking and photographing people was the preserve of the white person[,] . . . keeping Africans, or those others[,] in the position of object of scrutiny."[47] Similarly, American literary critics have argued that black novelists who wrote about white characters have faced penalties and ostracism in the literary establishment for not remaining within the appropriate domain of writing about blacks.[48] While black people have been largely restricted from commenting in the world of arts and letters on the practices of white supremacy, the treatment of black bodies is a hypervisible index of technological breakthrough, territorial and military expansionism, and sanction-free leisure and entertainment meant to transmit coherent meanings about these shifts.[49] Though tortured black bodies have been available for visual consumption, the white body has been typically protected from such surveillance and scrutiny.[50] Folks who deny the existence of an antiblack social order also deny the existence of these forms of scrutiny, admitting to racist animus only in individual acts against individual black and other nonwhite people. Such denials turn the racialization of space and transfers of wealth from black people to nonblack into incidental material harms. Investments in liberal individualism and meritocracy prop up processes like land theft, criminalization of black landownership, deindustrialization, downward mobility, theft of the tax base, and tax laws that make black savings a financial reserve for white investors. What follows from arguments in defense of the invisibility of white supremacy and white privilege is that revealing white complicity with white supremacy and black disadvantage is tantamount to a major and fundamental shift in power. But black people both observe and comment on the existence of white supremacy and suffer the imposition of being cast as "the invented Negro." For whom is a call for making white power visible most productive? Indeed "black people watch white people with a critical 'ethnographic' gaze . . . [and] think critically about whiteness."[51] The most important feature of white privilege and white supremacy, then, may be its regularly criticized hypervisibility. Scrutinized by nonwhites, contested by "lesser whites," and constitutive of the major mediating frames for discourse about all manner of social crises, whiteness propels sensible people to consider who it is that can't perceive white privilege.[52] And how does the script on invisible white supremacy function? How does a notion of invisible whiteness invoke some aspects of structural antagonism and mask others? When theorists argue that whiteness is invisible they inadvertently sideline the generations of scholars who have scrutinized white raciality, where white identities come from and how and when white identities are produced.[53]

The types of prohibitions against looking at white people are not characteristic of the *Poor White Study,* which, in fact, looked at, documented, and theorized about whites. Even more, the *Poor White Study* points to an international social science project of looking at poor whites in order to contain excessive or degenerative whiteness, to comment on and regulate this racial social location, and to use its deficits to shore up white nationalism.

There are other political stakes in claiming that white supremacy is invisible besides marginalizing the research of black people who have indeed considered this question. If white supremacy is invisible, it means that white people cannot or have not generated a tradition of white race traitorship, that is, taking the blows of antiblackness meant for black people. By suppressing traditions and genealogies of white race traitors we miss the possibility that "anti-black racism . . . is a tool to legitimate decisive transformations in power relations, not a universally inherent code of belief."[54] Such genealogies and traditions force us to hone in on the makings of black resistance in each historical moment of Negrophobic impulses,[55] blackness being the signature of philosophies and practices that destroy antiblack conceits. For nonblack race traitors white supremacy is hypervisible, and naming its operations is an antiseptic preparation for examining the roots of its power. They also avoid the mistake of false parallels between white poverty and black suffering.

One particular branch of nonblack race traitors emerges from among militant antiracist feminist traditions.[56] From Klan Watch activists to neo-abolitionists to historians of black women's militant resistance, antiracist feminist social criticism and activism examines the ways in which forms of white violence and pleasure-seeking participate in black suffering masquerading as gender justice.[57] These nonblack feminist race traitors illustrate how poverty, class status, colonial consciousness, domesticity, motherhood and families, and sexuality constitute the violent power relations of gendered whiteness. They illustrate how masculinity, colonial femininity, *baaskap* (governance by white minority rule), and fatherhood are linked in a toxic fashion to colonization of the domestic and the national.[58] These thinkers foreground the loss of human dignity associated with benefiting from white supremacy. Exemplars point to the ubiquitous complicity of white womanhood with white supremacy especially through white female colonial practices imagining non-European women as sexual territories for female-led progress.[59] Avoiding the much-criticized tropes of white female helplessness, vulnerability, sympathy, sentiment, and innocence, the most effective of these race traitors explain that to be white and poor is a misery because one is a racial other not because it is paradoxical for whites to be poor.

If white supremacy and white privilege are actually hypervisible, drawn upon to authorize and extend faltering white nationalisms, and have been rejected by militant black and nonblack people, then the international project that prioritized the crisis of poor whites in South Africa was implicated in sanitizing, naturalizing, and lionizing Afrikaner Nationalism.

THE PROPERTY PROBLEM

Cheryl I. Harris's pathbreaking essay "Whiteness as Property" (1995) argued that whiteness has become an inalienable property that has been accruing wealth since the explicit racialization of slavery. Courts in North America accepted the notion that white status was something of value, though they were often conflicted about how exactly to value the property in white skin and what other criteria had to be met to value the property in white skin as asset. Because legal recognition of a person as white carried material benefits, "false or inadequately supported claims were denied like any other unsubstantiated claim to a property interest."[60] Taken together, scholars in the whiteness-as-property school reflect on whiteness concealed in legal discourses in order to track the way that whiteness is property, about the wealth associated with citizenship, via slavery, antimiscegenation, and immigration/citizenship jurisprudence. In those instances when the history of scientific racism is accounted for in critical whiteness studies, such as the legal analysis of Ian Haney-Lopez, the whiteness-as-property trope has been qualified by the suppleness of legal doctrine in settler colonies/racist democracies in order to explain the resulting white exclusivity of eligibility for citizenship. Courts have drawn on contradictory logics of "common knowledge" and "science" to prohibit non-Europeans from accessing citizenship benefits.[61] Haney-Lopez describes non-Europeans trying to access citizenship by showing proof that they are indeed white according to the biological standards of the day. Thus the whiteness-as-property scholars have focused on nonwhites passing for/as white and also nonwhites suing to be relieved of the burden of laws written specifically to constrain the activities and life chances of non-Europeans.

The major limitation of the idea of whiteness as property comes through the inherent risks associated with the practices of passing and the conceptions about passing as a set of practices of limited expression of agency and trickery. Instead, access to the temporary mobility that passing offers is a poor consolation and a survival strategy of last resort when faced with the self-degradation that constitutes whiteness.[62] Harris illustrates her theory of whiteness as property through a family story about her grandmother, a sharecropper who passed for white in order to secure employment as a clerk at a department store. This poignant tale spends a great deal of time talking about her "grandmother's choice" and the economic coercion and race subordination that constitutes it. These latter two social forces compel us to think hard about the risks associated with passing. If passing is not a choice and is not an expression of liberty, then shouldn't we also begin to consider the contingency of what one is passing in to?

> The attempts to lay claim to whiteness through "passing" painfully illustrate the effects of the law's recognition of whiteness. The embrace of a lie, undertaken by my grandmother and the thousands like her, could occur only when oppression makes self-denial and the obliteration of national identity rational, and in significant measure, beneficial. The economic coercion of white supremacy on self-definition nullifies any suggestion that passing is a logical exercise of liberty or self-identity. The decision to pass as white was not a choice, if by that word one means voluntariness or lack of compulsion. The fact of race subordination was coercive, and it circumscribed the liberty to define oneself.[63]

Once one is presumed white, access to employment is no longer precluded by blackness.[64] Whiteness relieves people of scrutiny and is a shield reinforced by juridical and social power, and yet the phenomenon of passing, which is based on the coercion and seduction of being safe as white, highlights the paradoxical lack of safety to be found in white skin. But how can such circumscribed, one may even say nonexistent, liberty for self-definition be anything but the riskiest sort of property or investment? Such a shifting commodity requires coercion and damaged selfhood. This movement in Harris's work illustrates and foregrounds the violence that Jill Nelson called "volunteer slavery" done to people to make passing in white professional cultures an "option."[65] Nelson refers to passing as a "volunteer slavery" because it has substantive advantages over regular slavery: presumably, choice, opportunity, mobility, the absence of sexualized torture, and wages and benefits extracted for work exchanged.[66] Harris agrees that the economic coercion and racial subordination faced by her grandmother reveals passing to be the opposite of choice, therefore the requirement that one exchange employment and being able to feed oneself and one's relations with the damage that constitutes passing reveals how dangerous trafficking in whiteness and white security actually is. Certainly, Harris's grandmother experienced passing as a traumatic survival strategy that carried forward at least two generations. Whiteness attained is no secure ground.

Some might say that as investments go, whiteness, like real estate, is a certain and stable one because it creates access to the acquisition of property, the basic building block of capitalism. And as we know, property has a color. But whiteness is also a risky investment because for all of its returns it so thoroughly dehumanizes those who aspire to achieve it. The pursuit of whiteness leaves people less human, less capable of accountability for their own debasement, and yet thoroughly meritorious in their own view because by standard markers of socioeconomic status they are successful. Whiteness is the ultimate Midas touch, a wealth that enraptures, encases, and ultimately entombs. In George Lipsitz's words, "While one can possess one's investments, one can also be possessed by them. . . . [T]he artificial construction of whiteness almost always come to possess white people themselves unless they develop antiracist identities."[67] Lipsitz fastened on one of the more sinister impacts of whiteness, that it binds and cages whites. Their moral sense so confined, they continually lay up treasures on earth that will rot their souls. Lipsitz defines the possessive investment in whiteness as "a poisonous system of privilege that pits people against each other and prevents the creation of common ground."[68] Calling whiteness a poison is a way to reveal its soul-killing character. Whiteness causes profound losses in human development, especially the loss that can be measured in racial violence and hatred.[69] These losses can be quantified in socioeconomic status, underdevelopment, and maldistribution of resources and wealth. But for Lipsitz, the most losses are losses in the human ability to be responsible and accountable and to exist in the social world with wisdom. These are the associated risks of whiteness.

The risk of investing in whiteness is aptly described by James Weldon Johnson in *The Autobiography of an Ex-Colored Man.*[70] Johnson's protagonist realizes simultaneously that his motivation to become a race man—an exceptional example of black success and status mobility that is an exception to the race—might make him little more than someone who exploited black poverty for his own sense of self *and* that to live the life of an unremarkable and invisible white man would make him a pitiable human being because of a lack of any noble aspiration. Nevertheless, he chooses the latter because it enables him to become invisible, to meld into European high society. For the protagonist such invisibility is a coveted treasure, and yet it yields an intense sense of mediocrity and self-erasure. These incredibly high costs of whiteness are valued highly because of the kind of life that his children will be able to inherit; rather than being property, they will become inheritors. At the same time, the protagonist's children are disinherited by being kept ignorant of their father's and mother's defiance of segregation and antimiscegenation laws. Johnson's protest novel is on one hand an attempt to glorify the "folk" often degraded by black Victorians in their various uplift projects. But just as importantly, it characterizes whiteness far more accurately by focusing on it as a comforting vacuum and an absence.

CONCLUSION

Unlike other antiracist thinkers who seek to challenge whiteness, I am not convinced that talking about whiteness as benefit or accomplishment is the only operative strategy. Instead, I suggest that we begin to talk about whiteness as pathology, whiteness as diminished selfhood, whiteness as soul injury, and whiteness as death. When black people see whiteness they see empty unearned privilege and therefore a worthless existence crying for the opportunity to live actual life. It is the pursuit of white supremacy, the racial contract, and life motivated by preservation of Herrenvolk democracy that has caused the devastation and suffering of human existence. We cannot undo the attractiveness of the pursuit of white supremacy by talking about how it always wins and how it always satisfies human greed. Instead, we must begin to talk about white supremacy as being antihuman in the sense that it creates premature death for those designated as black and in close proximity to blackness and requires "miserabilism" and "dehumanization" for those designated after long processes as white.[71]

Work such as I am doing, bringing together critical whiteness studies and scientific racism studies, hopes to tie together the nodes of an international social science of race bent on creating a racialized poor white in South Africa and in many other settler societies.[72] Simply saying that whiteness is unmarked or invisible continues the pathologization of blacks for existing, for not being white, and for being the mythical "black problem." This construction normalizes the hypervisibility of blackness and obscures how much of racism functions to constrain white behavior and diminish white capacity and accountability. Saying that whiteness is invisible erases the many ways in which whites create impossible self-negating requirements that other whites must meet to qualify for even limited membership in white privilege. Ultimately, saying that whiteness is invisible also erases the process by which poor whites become another racial target. By calling attention to poor whites, I have stepped into a crack in the literature on critical whiteness studies, a crack that is productive and meaningful and helps us articulate the relationships between scientific racism and whiteness studies. First, I am laying out the project of a critical whiteness studies that needs a better genealogy that explicitly links the past and contemporary biologism of scientific racism. Second, to be a more effective refutation of white supremacy, such a critical whiteness studies must track the institutional and professional investments in the creation of white supremacy and white nationalism through various colonial relations across geographic and territorial space. Racist biology has been made complicit in making white bodies perfect, beautiful, and adored bodies and nonwhite bodies degraded and subhuman bodies. The reduction of the black body to "flesh" can occur only if there is a similar misapprehension of the white body, a sculpting, categorizing, cataloging, and dissection that objectifies and exoticizes white people's bodies. White people did not become white solely through popular interpretations of segregation laws; white people became white through monitoring and manipulation of their bodies. In settler societies, practices such as unsanctioned murder, torture, rape, beating couple with residential redlining, electoral gerrymandering, antimiscegenation laws, anti-immigration and white-only immigration campaigns, racial profiling, English-only policies, and name changing that have all contributed to a massive rescripting of white identity and white language and new understandings of the white body in space. Such practices serve to contain the white body through protectionist policies. But all of these policies have biological corollaries and depend to a great extent on social scientific and biological discourses about cleanliness, superiority, and capacity. Policies such as redlining and gerrymandering have biological origins in theories about cleanliness and genetically or group-linked diseases. Similarly, English has been promoted throughout the colonial era as not simply a lingua franca, but as a superior tongue that can carry modern concepts and modern ideologies better than other languages. The deliberate scientization of the experience of poor whites in the transition to urban industrial life in the *Poor White Study* illustrates that the existence of a contest among whites over position in the racial hierarchy has been repeatedly resolved by biology-based categorization and classification of race. Though whiteness has often been defined as that which normalizes and predicts white privilege, and white capacity to possess, study, and make a spectacle of the Other, the *Poor White Study* functioned by demonizing poor whites, making a certain type of whiteness hypervisible and subject to increased scrutiny.

CHAPTER 4

The Roots of White Poverty

Cheap, Lazy, Inefficient . . . Black

In 1931 Carnegie Corporation Overseas Visitor Grant recipient, C.S. Richards of the University of Witwatersrand, reported that South African productivity could be transformed if its entrepreneurial culture changed from one based on charisma to one based on U.S. models of scientific management. He added that such scientific management would free South Africa from the "soft cushion of African labour."[1] Richards suggested that African labor was inefficient and African laborers themselves were incapable of industrial work, but white labor and machines could develop South Africa along more internationally recognizable lines. Richards's reasoning sought to guarantee the job security of a white standard of living, variously articulated as "a white wage" and "civilized labor," based on white "efficiency" and black "inefficiency."[2] However, black labor was essential to South African economic development and not merely as "cheap" or "inefficient" workforces.[3] Like those of Richards, the *Poor White Study*'s policy recommendations called African workers an unfair economic threat rather than the backbone of the South African economy. Competition with blacks was said to drive down white wages by "encroaching" on "white jobs." Such arguments staged African women and men as having a purely ornamental function in the history of South African industrialization, as being a volatile threat to "civilized laborers" and a threat to whiteness. Though Afrikaner Nationalism claimed to reject "the soft cushion of African labor" publicly, it could never have taken advantage of industrialization in

South Africa via such an eviction of African workers from labor and wage markets. The scientific management of labor, in practice in both the United States and South Africa, often relied on the "soft cushion of inefficient native labor."[4] Richards's comparative study concluded that U.S. business practices were reliable and should be emulated while simultaneously erecting a deafening silence about the U.S. addiction to the same so-called soft cushion of African labor.

Bolstered by an international debate about building white men's lands, white male entitlement to waged work became the political status quo. As Annabel Cooper writes of New Zealand, no longer did British immigrants expect simply to be "male providers" if they were skilled, but "proletarian providers." The social world around them came to expect that this new norm, while it was really the global historical exception. Unions and courts agreed that the white male working class had a right to a living wage "whether married or single."[5] The living wage sought was the "family wage," which would enable these men to support themselves and large families. South African miners drew on their identity as settlers and members of workers' organizations in Canada, the United States, Australia, and Britain to develop South Africa's white male working class even while subordinating South Africa's white female working class. Their adherence to this wage and the set of policies and court decisions that redistributed wealth and opportunities to them to guarantee this wage made them *expensive* labor.

In addition, they believed that their hard work and thrift should be rewarded by state-guaranteed access to democratic political participation. Marilyn Lake and Henry Reynolds write, "In the New World encounters of diverse peoples, the masculine democracies of North America and Australia defined their identity and rights in racial terms: the right of Anglo-Saxons to self-government and the commitment of white workers to high wages and conditions, against those they saw as undermining their new-found status, whether they be aristocrats or 'coolies.'"[6] From bans on Chinese, Indian, and African people owning mining rights to endorsement of job protection and reserve labor systems, the laws were organized to privilege the white male republican worker.

Notions about black productivity and inability to develop economically were crucial rhetorics through which poor whites' proximity to blackness was debated—especially since poor whites had been observed living "at a standard almost as low as that of the Negroes in their community."[7] Poor whites were viewed as especially vulnerable to "parasitic" blacks.[8] And black workers were viewed as lacking worker consciousness and therefore not as "true workers."[9] Afrikaner Nationalism and mining capital deployed a set of racial ideologies about vulnerable white workers that made black work, black wealth, and black resistance to mere proletarianization invisible, and when visible, pathological. By the 1920s, as colonial power had failed to "detach [African] labor power from its social roots," mine capital and white nationalists of every ideological stripe reintroduced the language of tribal atavism, economic stagnation, and black incapacity to make socially meaningful economic decisions.[10] Thus when black people were placed in an economic relationship to poor whites that was said to undercut poor whites' entitlement, the very notion of black people as workers was obscured by the myth of the "soft cushion of African labor."[11] This set of relationships explains why the Carnegie *Poor White Study* took up a range of extant tropes that suggested that white poverty was caused by unfair job competition with black people. This chapter examines the meanings attached to labor, work, productivity, and products when done by black bodies and how ideas about poor whites were mobilized to negate the role of black people in the political economy of South Africa.

The *Poor White Study* played a decisive role in shifting the frame of the international conversation about South African development while at the same time maintaining the old explanation for South Africa's weak productivity: the African presence. Africans were reputed to be inefficient workers because they regularly articulated individual and collective rejection of the terms and conditions under which "industrial civilization" was pursued and their circumscribed role in it. Still having access to land, Africans were deemed savage and semiproletarianized.[12] Thus a research agenda focused on producing a stable white workforce and consolidating white nationalism did not need to pay attention to African people as workers. The notion of the "African worker" in some quarters remained something of an oxymoron. Moreover, a research agenda focused only on moderate improvements[13] to the quality of life of white workers actually needed to render black people as incompetent, inefficient racially, incapable of doing "white jobs," permanent migrants, natural servants, ugly female beasts of burden, dandies, lazy, criminals, vagabonds, American slaves, strikebreakers—anything and everything, except workers.[14]

The notion of parasitic, freeloading, and idle black pseudo- or nonworkers creating and being an economic problem for threatened, vulnerable, and pathos-evoking white workers—already always under-stood as upwardly mobile and economically productive—occupies a venerated and iconic ontological location across political ideologies: liberal, Marxist, imperial, and so on. Ideas about poor unskilled whites under economic threat from blacks come not only from Afrikaner Nationalists and liberal imperialists but also from historical materialist analyses. The accounts are reproduced in toto with very little change. From the former slaveholders turned abolitionist humanitarians[15] who made up the bulk of philanthropic segregationists in the Jim Crow United States and colonized Africa[16] to the rotating throng of white male charity scholars *cum* "experts on the Negro," including Thomas Jesse Jones (1873–1950), Charles Templeman Loram (1879–1940), Ernest Gideon Malherbe (1895–1982), and John David Rheinallt-Jones(1884–1953), accounts about black economic threat were shaped by a cast of vipers. Such liberal missionary educators and their pro-nouncements entrenched racial capitalism in slave and colonial societ-ies.[17] Their absurd accounts of the origin of white poverty provided an endlessly flexible justification for white nationalism. Union members, white workers, politicians, charity workers, and social researchers used the concept of unfair black job competition to explain white poverty.

Ideas about unfair black job competition were popular across the political spectrum, showing up in the writings and political rhetoric of Afrikaner Nationalists, imperialists, and liberal philanthropists, as well as historical materialist analyses of the origins of white poverty. Among labor historians this notion of unfair black job competition is consis-tent. Lis Lange writes, "The unskilled labour market was dominated by not yet fully proletarianized, cheap African laborers against which most white laborers could not compete";[18] and again, "The reports of the Inspector of White Labour again pointed to an old problem in the Rand's labour market: unskilled White men were facing serious compe-tition from black workers on the mines";[19] and finally, "Unemployment intensified the competition between white and black labor for unskilled jobs."[20] These racist and gendered narratives about work, poverty, and the sympathetic and unsympathetic poor have shaped economic politi-cal thought in South Africa.[21]

In the words of the summary report of the 1932 Carnegie research team:

> Unrestricted competition on the labour market between the unskilled non-European and the poor white, and the low wages the European then receives, create conditions of poverty which have a demoralizing effect on the latter.

Measures for restricting such competition should aim at countering this demoralization.[22]

This mythology buried black work and black labor consciousness in a mystified and permanent era of premodernity that could be corrected only by preventing African "detribalization." Black labor, black work ethics, black agricultural markets, and the black body have been used as potent symbols for mobilizing empathy for white workers.

According to Robert H. Davies, "Throughout the first four decades of the twentieth century, ['poor white' unemployment] was one of the provincial issues discussed and debated within the various forums of the bourgeois state."[23] These included the Transvaal Commission of 1906–8, the Select Commission of Parliament of 1913, the Transvaal Provincial Commission of 1916, the Select Committee of 1916, the Dutch Reformed Church Conference of 1916, and the Unemployment Commission's three reports in 1921 and 1922. The "poor white problem" was also a major feature of numerous departmental reports, internal committee reports, parliamentary debates, debates at annual and regional Dutch Reformed Church conferences and the 1914 Economic Commission. In each of these historical moments poor whiteism was rediscovered and deployed by complicated social and political forces but with a repetitive set of explanations for the origins of white poverty that were intimately tied to larger discourses and investments in global whiteness.[24]

RACIALIZED STANDARDS OF LIVING: "LONG SERVICE AFRICANS" AND "BOSS BOYS"

The unfair black job competition myth rested on a racialized standard of living in which wage, political, and social rights were valuable to white men to the extent that they were restricted from all others. As African miners acquired skills beyond their job classification and racial caste status their position in a racialized labor hierarchy was caricatured as a black economic threat causing white vulnerability. Their intermediary contract status and opportunities for upward mobility as "long service Africans" and "boss boys" made them workplace intermediaries likely to earn wages much closer to those earned by white miners than those earned by the majority of African miners and structurally positioned them to benefit from skilled white miners' consistently weak negotiating position.

First class African laborers or highly skilled African workers were to consist of the remaining twenty percent and were to be remunerated at the *discretion* of each company. The latter class of African labor presented mine managers with endless problems because it constantly *threatened* skilled white miners, engine drivers and all the other remaining skilled white workers (emphasis mine). . . . On many mines some Africans had acquired special skills despite their positions as helpers and not apprentices and managers generally found it desirable and economical to encourage and make special provisions for such cases. Some mine managers went so far as arguing that all Africans who had worked a few months and had become "fair to good drillmen" should be considered skilled but paid less than white men doing or supervising the same job.[25]

Migrant workers, mining engineers, missionaries, liberals, and historians have been key in the circulation of ideas about a racial labor hierarchy that rendered industrial civilization and development as the gift of the European world to the non-European world.[26] Europeans were to be the beneficiaries of the living standard and stewards of the wealth that was generated. Myths about black laziness, black docility, and black culture that needed protection from the taint of economic development accompanied these ideas of subordination. While Africans were burdened by industrialization Europeans were supposed to have the mental capacity to endure the loss of culture, group identities, and ties to community that came with the individualism and independence of the modern industrialized economic system.[27] No matter how many positions were granted to so-called long service Africans and boss boys,[28] their level of indebtedness both social and financial meant that they would always be viewed as usurpers undeserving of either employment or wealth equality. And there was no guarantee that their wage would be paid at a certain rate or on a consistent basis. Wages were set by their white managers. Semiskilled blacks were said to threaten skilled whites. Comparisons of black income, as opposed to comparisons of white wealth, are notoriously useless. Therefore, the class orientations, aspirations, economic social forces, and agency that motivated black workers to migrate to new work locations and to organize as workers were deemphasized.[29] The debate about what black workers could expect as a result of their wages and what black workers could expect as a result of their employment in the migrant contract system was silenced. There was little discussion of what black workers were entitled to. Other historiographical lapses were aided and abetted by the migrant labor system, the necessity of walking away from harsh employers and bad conditions, and the volatility caused by the firings of black men.

Though historical materialists and social historians provided much-needed correctives to arguments like that made by Katz by writing African workers back into South African economic and industrial history, they sometimes argued that black culture was the primary and singular terrain for resisting their position in racial capitalism.[30] Sometimes these social historians simultaneously documented African worker protests and erased their existence as a "true working class."[31] Having provided ample evidence that African workers in Durban, for example, faced a number of structural disincentives[32] to their recognition as workers,[33] scholars who characterized black struggle in terms of class tied their explanations to highly racialized notions about African culture.[34] Noting that the origins of labor migrancy and the backbone of South African industrialization were to be found in African economic goals that successfully provided economic constraints on mining capital, they further insisted that "Africans were involved in both commodity production and migrant wage labor" before the diamond boom at Kimberley, suggesting that Africans had not been simply waiting for Europeans to bring industrialization to them.[35] Despite these correctives, by designating complicated commodity exchanges—both products and labor—as "pre-industrial, cultural/social" in the case of Africans and "industrial, economic, structural" in the case of whites, even these antiapartheid scholars echoed powerfully enduring racist ideas.[36] By asking "how in this hostile environment Africans survived as autonomous human beings with a culture[37] of their own within the white master's world . . . [and how] these processes entailed the making of an African working class," they conflated the African working class with African culture, which was generally miscast as stagnant and static, and simultaneously conflated the European white working class with industrialization—the embodiment of progress, innovation, and vision. Frederick Cooper has argued that class struggle was about "avoiding becoming generic sellers of labor power [and] retaining a bounded, culturally rooted sense of difference and particularity"—a way of life.[38] The impulse to interrogate African culture came to stand in for looking at African economic organization.[39] Further, the impulse to look at African culture would have been better paralleled by a view into European culture, which was obscured.[40] A question like, What were the expressions of African agency that contributed to the making of an industrialized South Africa?, may have challenged the false dichotomy between industrialization and culture.

I now turn to the question of value as another trope to produce the myth of unfair black job competition. The social value of a laborer is critical. Part of becoming generic sellers of labor power was an assessment of the social costs or "value" of a laborer, which pegged social status and social location to fairly rigid and permanent wage hierarchies and salaries. As Robert H. Davies put it, "Under capitalist relations of production the income of the direct producer (the wage) is not directly determined by the value which the worker creates in the process of production, but rather by the value of his or her labour power—the socially determined costs of reproducing the worker in his or her normal state."[41] Wages were determined by a racialized labor hierarchy.[42]

The Carnegie Corporation's summary report had a similar criticism:

> Under European rule the native population has greatly increased in numbers. In many cases the areas inhabited by them have become too small to support them all; and they have, in addition acquired civilized needs to an ever-greater extent. Hence natives seek wage-earning employment in increasing numbers within the economic system of the Europeans. But a considerable number of them do not need to support their families from such wages alone. For this reason, and on account of their low standard of living, they have established a low scale of wages for certain forms of unskilled work. This naturally depresses the scale of wages of the unskilled European.[43]

But the belief of the white male republican was that black people, as undeveloped peoples and descendants of slaves, were collaborators with capital, unfit for self-governance politically and dangerous in the market for wages. Black people were trapped in the trope of laziness for resisting proletarianization, and when they were proletarianized, black people were trapped in the trope of being willing or happy slaves or conspicuous consumers but never a true working class or artisanal class with an "African work ethic."[44]

COMPETITION AND RACIALIZED PATHS TO PROLETARIATIANIZATION

Scholars have argued that there was a key difference in the process of proletarianization of African workers and unskilled white workers.[45] For example, Davies writes that the proletarianization of "the unskilled whites ... had not directly been sought by capital at all ... but had come about largely as an indirect consequence of the spread of capitalist relations in the white rural areas."[46] Such scholars would have us believe that poor whites did not face significant coercive or repressive apparatuses and so therefore had nothing compelling them to become a proletariat.[47] These "indirect consequences" are described by Davies as private appropriation and capitalization of land and capitalist agriculture sold to the mines. These indirect consequences resulted in "exclusion of certain whites from economic ownership" and inoculated poor whites from racial capitalism.[48] The premise of this erroneous claim is that racialization of poor white people is not a potent social force. Furthermore, because poverty has been assigned to blackness and wealth to whiteness, poor whites' transformation into an urban proletariat was benign and should be considered an actual public good. In fact, the coercive and repressive apparatuses deployed against poor whites included deliberate financialization of land; calling in heavily mortgaged subsistence-level land; diminished access to credit for stock, seeds, tools, and grazing contracts; laws that medicalized pastoralism; fencing; railways; taking advantage of ecological crises in ways that disadvantaged poor whites; interrupting and then killing the transport riding trade; and keeping the cost of South African–made goods high in order to exploit the domestic market. The consequences of not accepting the proletarianization were being committed to labor colonies that were essentially reeducation camps and being deemed criminally neglectful or criminally burdensome. Significantly, the seemingly invisible hands behind the forces that made poor whites into a proletariat are deemed as having been driven by no particular sector's interests.

In this way of crafting the history, Africans were subjected to numerous deliberate practices, policies, and laws to drive them into proletarianization, while unskilled whites became proletarians as a result of forces but not through compulsion or systematic violence.[49] This misrecognition provides the roots for the belief that unfair black job competition—which implied the potential to acquire wealth that could eliminate poverty and give one access to the status of self-governing, self-representing, possessive individualism—explains white poverty. Africans were proletarianized through the following discriminatory laws designed expressly to prevent them from being self-sufficient: (1) taxation in rural areas; (2) pass and vagrancy laws in the towns and urban areas, which forced them to sell their labor power at very meager rates to pay mounting legal fines for violating these laws to be employed; (3) criminal and penal codes, which turned black resistance in towns into insubordination and desertion; (4) the migrant labor system; (5) living in hostels where heterosexual family life was mostly prohibited; (6) meager amounts of food, heat, and furnishings; and (7) suppression of even the most minimal educational or artisanal aspirations.[50] According to Davies, poor whites, in contrast, were proletarianized by mistake. As the redeemable sympathetic poor, poor whites were not supposed to be poor, and if they were, certainly no one made them that way deliberately. Coercive and repressive apparatuses that rendered the white proletariat were viewed as beneficial public goods, while the coercive and repressive apparatuses used to constrain black people were seen as limited instruments for improvement of blackness, which was believed to be an impossible, unforgivable condition. As Vic Alhadeff writes:

> Jobs were created. There were sewerage pipes to be relaid, dams to be built, properties to be guarded. The South African Railways absorbed thousands of the unemployed: in 1924 the S.A.R. employed 4,760 white labourers; by 1929 this figure had soared to 16, 248. Under the Work Colonies Act anyone found guilty of begging or forcing his family to beg was committed to the colony for at least a year.[51]

Unskilled whites were viewed as a ready market for political representation, professional advice, technical expertise, social guidance and uplift feminism, and social welfare. If none of these processes was deliberate, then poor whites could be a natural proletariat whose social value had not been driven down. By claiming that poor whites were not "subject to any particular exploitable institutions associated with the migrant labour system, and that they had no base in any 'reserve' economy," scholars miss a whole range of expressions of biopower sites of violence.[52] "The net effect, therefore," according to Davies, "was that the unskilled white proletarians confronted capital not as potential migrant workers but as an urbanized proletariat totally separated from any means of subsistence, whose reproduction costs would thus in the long term (if not in the short term) necessarily have to be related to the subsistence requirements of an entire family unit."[53] But isn't it true that poor whites failed to urbanize in significant numbers until well into the twentieth century? So to what extent were the advance guard of young white South African women sent by their rural families to enter domestic service, the textile factories, and other forms of secondary industries counted as a migrant labor force?[54] Scholars acknowledge that poor white families drew on the income of young women, children, and wives as landladies and laundresses and produce dealers, selling alcohol, diamonds, food, and sex—and yet this process is described in ambivalent and confusing fashion. Davies argues that black people's wages were low because capital had calculated what they actually needed to live on as migrants. Meanwhile white wages were higher because capitalists had calculated what poor whites actually needed to live in heteronormative, patriarchal, aspiring middle-class white households.[55] While the fact that white men could have wives, consorts, and families made their situation vastly different from that of black migrant men, whose wives and kin were criminalized, few poor white men could get jobs in the mines well into the World War I period.[56] A combination of subpar wages and irregular informal economy participation did not a middle-class home life make. Thus, this white male wage did not function in the way that Davies describes.

In the period leading up to 1910 we see the state institutionalizing the political project of transforming poor white people into viable white workers. From 1906 to 1909 the Department of Mines hired the Inspectorate of White Labor to (a) survey employees and unions who would not include poor whites and (b) set up agricultural schools and mine training schools to replace recent European immigrant workers.[57] In addition to the idea that poor whites were proletarianized by mistake, the mining capital sector actively campaigned against the idea of hiring poor whites. In 1913 a Chamber of Mines report claimed that hiring poor whites at the wage of 7 shillings 6 d per shift would result in the closing of sixteen mines; at the wage of 10 shillings per shift, twenty-six mines; at the wage of 12 shillings 6 d per shift, thirty-five mines; and at the wage of 15 shillings per shift, forty-one mines. The mining sector also argued that low-paid white workers would eventually unionize and demand higher wages of the sort that would close mines. It was these tendencies toward demanding fair wages and the fact that white men were said to be harder to supervise because they were naturally "hostile," "slovenly," and "uncivil" when forced to work for others that would make them difficult workers. This assessment of unskilled white workers implied by extension that African workers were docile, malleable, and lazy and therefore preferred.[58] These character assessments again constructed poor whites as vulnerable to Africans but only because Africans were said to be servile and willing to be exploited and thus unmanly. This was a gendered and raced caricature of workers' identities embedded in existing power relations.

Davies identifies phases of pressure and response to the colonial demand to hire poor whites in mining. From 1899 to 1903 the British said that hiring poor whites would create more political stability and make South Africa like the rest of the empire, all the while importing Chinese workers from 1901–3. By the 1903–7 period the Het Volk political bloc had defeated the mining capital bloc in elections and demanded responsible government and higher wages for unskilled whites that they argued would be justified by increased efficiency in mining production. From 1907 to 1908 government organized experiments similar to previous ones to see if natural white "efficiency" justified a white labor policy.[59] F.H.P. Cresswell, manager of the Village Main Reef mine, later a leader of the Labour Party and a cabinet member in the Pact Government (1924–33), argued that mechanization at particular stages in production could make whites more productive. As a result gangs of twenty to thirty African hand drillers were reduced to smaller numbers of groups of machine drillers. The machine drill process that previously had five to six Africans with two drills and one white supervisor was transformed so that one skilled machine man supervised one or two white helpers. Cresswell confidentially noted that white helpers would be made to work if the white foreman and supervisors struck. But Cresswell's experiments revealed that even the Gordon drill, known as the "white man's chance," could not make white workers more efficient than Chinese or African workers.[60] "Various other proposals for employing unskilled whites in more mechanized labour processes likewise proved, by and large, to be less profitable than the continual use of Africans."[61] In 1907 the Department of Labor and the Inspectorate of White Labor were founded. By 1908, 108 unemployed white skilled miners and nearly 2,500 unemployed white unskilled general laborers had registered with them.

In all these phases of pressure to hire white workers and to build a "White Rand" the notion of "job competition with African workers" mystifies the reality of "securing and controlling native labor."[62] I am making a very subtle but important point here about job competition, namely, that unskilled whites imagined that their real competition was with African workers and not with owners was a myth because African workers were only employed at wages that were certain to ensure that they remained destitute and without political rights, wages that would destabilize their access to wealth building for generations. In other words, white workers had a misunderstanding of their role as white men but also in terms of a racial wealth divide that consistently prohibited black workingmen from acquiring wealth. But more than false ideology, the notion that there was a cohesive and united white labor force in South Africa was a sinister way to hitch unskilled whites into defense of state, philanthropic, and party forces that would have them endorse the belief that they had the capacity through their income to become viable competitors against people whose concern was accumulation of big capital and that they were in competition with people who like them had no access to wealth at all.[63]

From 1903 to 1904 the lowest-paid white mine workers earned 13s 9d per shift and the highest paid earned 29s per shift. These included many artisanal recruits from Europe who came with their own unions. Mining capital did not want to remove these whites from production because their artisanal skills made them valuable and because they served as enforcers of white supremacy in being "indispensable in the exercise of control over black workers." Yet the same mine owners wanted to minimize white work in the mines.[64] In an Aristotelian hierarchy of types, white workers were meant to be the brains of all operations, to conceive and coordinate, while black workers were meant to do the "merely muscular work" that was "given to races willing to be considered inferior."[65] The irony is that this hierarchy of status could very easily work in favor of the employers where "merely" workers and "merely" supervisors could easily be replaced. Thus the struggle was not to eliminate white workers but to keep them in "petty bourgeois mental and supervisory places" while blacks were inserted in the "productive manual labour."[66]

This productive manual labor included the *finding*—as in the discovery—that rock drilling could be done by Chinese and African people as early as the 1904–7 period, with whites functioning to fix broken drills and deciding where to place the holes. Davies notes that by 1914 Africans were *found* to be capable of coordination by people whose economic historiography was still quite wedded to ideas about African economic incapacity. In 1922–26 it was *found* that white rock breakers could supervise three different skill areas. Even in areas that required more "competence" and more mechanical skill, such as machine managers, drivers, and operators of engines, hoisting equipment, bowlers, and so on, after the 1913 strike it did not have to be men with long histories of mining. Before the strike and after, white men were increasingly replaced in these fields while rhetorics about "competence" still circulated and reinforced white supremacist ideology. By not problematizing these racial rhetorics, our economic history is handing us a far less usable past than we might have thought.

CONCLUSION

Explaining the complexities of the relationship between black and white economic opportunity via the social costs or value of reproducing that labor doesn't get us very far, primarily because poor white men were never paid enough to reproduce themselves. Now I am not suggesting that the set of coercive and repressive apparatuses that shaped black people's existence was the same as that shaping poor whites' existence. But I am suggesting that the targets of antiblack racism were also poor whites and that the spread of capitalist relations in the rural and urban areas deeply influenced black existence. In other words, the way most labor historians have explained white poverty overestimates white authority over blacks and underestimates black negotiation with capital.[67] I am suggesting, in short, that job competition tells us very little about the significance of race in the making of class. Moreover, job competition fails to reveal the ways that class struggle, to paraphrase Adam Przeworksi, has much less to do with struggle between classes and much more to do with struggle about the meanings of class.[68] Put another way:

> What, one wonders, is the best way to define "class" in South Africa given that our society is complex, diverse and interdependent? . . . We also need to enquire about the nature of the class structure of South Africa and whether all class structures can be investigated in the same way? . . . And finally, it is important to examine whether ascriptive or achievement related markers of class and stratification are more acceptable?[69]

Pointing out that respectability and status—or ascriptive achievement-related markers—are class concepts and that if you want to talk about the poor and the way that middle-class people attempt to hail them and legitimize social welfare violence against them is important: "Respectability is a class concept, one which builds on behavioral difference between top and bottom while asserting the possibility of movement in between."[70] The state and capital had to come up with ways to incorporate these people who were resisting and failing at becoming white wage laborers. The state was very concerned about the supposed racial degeneration of whites both in the sense of the "barbarizing effects of power unrestrained"[71] and in terms of an "index of culture."[72] From labor bureaus to industrial schools to "apprenticeships" as domestics to the Kakamas Labour Colony, the state, clergy, social workers, and proto-feminists lobbied for the empowerment of poor whites. Opportunity was supposed to transform poor whites into respectable people—concerned about the approval of their betters. It was supposed to shame them into new aspirations and new demonstrations of self-discipline, self-control, and moderation. In short, opportunity was supposed to make them white: white in terms of class status, appropriate gender relations, race, associations, consumption patterns, standard of living, political loyalty, and their role in economic history.

But in each of these sites of opportunity the state relied on extant debates about white industrial civilization, racial hierarchy, criminalization, and the racialization of poverty to enforce a strict discipline of agricultural training, bans on dancing, swearing, filthy language, immorality, laziness, and untidiness. By claiming their indigeneity and their status as "of Africa," Johan Geerstema argues, Afrikaners had a historical problem to resolve, that of demonstrating that they possessed the essential cultural attributes that would enable them to shift their awe of nature and the cosmos to the modes and practices of rationality, observation, data gathering, and the reification of culture and civilization. From John Philip to C.D. De Kiewiet, the critique of Afrikaners supposedly failing to submit to reason and failing to orchestrate the submission of "nature" to culture, civilization, and rationality has shown up time and again. According to Enlightenment precepts, the white man's burden was dominion over lands and peoples to promote commodification and wealth and harmonious social order. So Afrikaners had a particularly thorny problem in terms of their role in South Africa. This is because to be "of Africa" meant to be in need of civilizing, development, capacity building, and guidance. So what was to be done with white people who were in need of such racialized help? As a problem of the ontology of whiteness and a problem of power, fine distinctions about the whiteness of poor whites and their vulnerability to a *swaart gevaar* (black horde) has had to be reiterated and has become a kind of default explanation of their "failure." Though competition is a key process through which capital transformed people into "cheap" and "expensive" laborers and set them in opposition to each other, it is an inadequate framework for explaining white poverty. Competition as a concept implies agency, not entrapment; it encourages us to analyze income, not wealth; and it delinks proletarianization from other processes of categorizing people that shape their role in the economy.[73] As a paradigm, competition fails to explain economic structures that of necessity produce long-term racialized prosperity and long-term racialized poverty. The idea that white poverty, in particular, was caused by blacks flattens categories of whiteness and blackness in order to generate naturalizing notions about entitlement to and coherence with racial capitalism for would-be whites and incapacity for and distance from capital for those deemed black. Since the proponents of unfair black job completion traffic in notions that are neither natural nor historical, I have considered how racism has shaped the way we understand the making of "natural" and "unnatural" sectors of the proletariat.

Countless South African scholars have taken up the question of the supposed paradox of poor whites, all sharing the same assumption that whiteness coheres with productivity and profit and that blackness coheres with poverty, laziness, and docility. This seeming paradox gives rise to the racial demonization inherent in phrases like "white trash" and "waste of a white skin." But what most concerns me is how those moments when white poverty is linked to black people and false notions about black agency, black opportunity, and black competition for jobs with white people operate to entrench antiblackness.

The myth of job competition and the understandings about white people made vulnerable by antagonistic black people mystify the larger structure of wage determinations, monopolies, Industrial Conciliation Boards, government ministries, and chambers of Commerce and their shared investment in appearing to be benefactors, not architects, of repressive apparatuses that racialize poverty using antiblack laws, policies, and sedimented institutions.[74] As we consider the process through which white people became expensive labor and black people became cheap labor we do ourselves a serious disservice by not examining how wages were meant to be a momentary pathway to civilization for white workers and merely a supplementary income for black workers, who were understood to be inherently confined to their natural mode of production as agricultural workers on white-owned land. Therefore, wages were not simply a currency exchanged for selling one's labor but also represented the social meanings that were attached to the identities of each type of wage earner. Higher wages, in this case, signaled that white workers were being recompensed for existing—as white people—farther up the group developmental scale and the corresponding lower wages signaled that black workers were being recompensed for existing—as black people—lower down on the developmental scale. Though employers hoped to benefit from a reserve workforce that no longer had an independent means of production, they also insisted that black people were permanently agricultural. Black people were seen as existing atavistically in an earlier stage of economic unfolding. Employing black workers was seen as a necessary evil to promote capital and profitability. But to the extent that paying black workers' wages could theoretically, though not actually, destabilize white upward mobility and white standards of living, black workers' wages could be eliminated or slashed. In other words, that the social value understood as necessary to reproduce black and white life itself was coded so differently is as important to the economic historiography as our understanding of the constitution of classes and class formation.

Though black wages were paradigmatically lower than white wages and could be construed as competing with white workers, black workers were not in fact or in practice a competing force against white workers. Competition implies a type of agency and benefit to black workers that was constrained in nearly every aspect of social relations. The *Poor White Study* was a critical data set for policies of racial segregation that had not yet found their fullest elaboration. Black workers were mischaracterized as the cause for white poverty, and whites were seen as vulnerable to black participation in the modern economy. So if black people participated in the economy in any fashion except as slaves, white people would not be able to earn enough or accumulate enough to live. The main flaw in the job competition myth is that it presumes that equally positioned workers come to the employer with various valuable attributes through which they compete for the opportunity to be hired. This logic is then extended to racial groups that are said to have more or less comparative advantage in the job market. However, how workers are viewed in the job market has much more to do with which groups of workers are seen as truly belonging to the society and which workers are seen as *permanent foreigners, human property, or slaves whose unremunerated labor is meant to benefit the entire society—albeit of white citizens.* I say this because white capital used this idea that black workers were the cause of white poverty to avoid being accountable for underpaying black workers and white workers. Moreover, the claim that black workers were the cause of white poverty talks about the payment of salaries to black workers as if blacks were culturally backward and did not have a right to be earning any kind of salary anyway; in this configuration only whites had a right or an entitlement to salaries. Black salaries were so low compared to white salaries that they could not be the cause of white poverty. But because whites were said to be deserving of economic opportunity—and their very low paying jobs did not guarantee upward mobility—and blacks were supposed to be the tools, instruments, and raw material of white economic opportunity, any form of remuneration in cash given to blacks for their labor was seen as a social and economic problem. White people, both poor and rich, could not imagine that black people could or should have access to capital, land, themselves, or other forms of wealth. Blacks with wealth that could be transformed into land or capital were the problem.[75] This idea of black labor competition causing white poverty concealed the absolute contempt that whites have when blacks have anything. This is why black ownership or successful possession of wages is so utterly reviled and why black participation in consumption is represented as pathological, deviant, and self-destructive. Blacks and other racialized subjects with consumer goods are constantly being told how best to use their money and scrutinized and surveilled by whites who are simply upset that blacks own the clothes on their backs—let alone own their own skins. Whites invested in this racially exclusive mode of economic development because they stood to gain significantly from the creation of a white-only democracy that would eliminate most black sovereignty and create super-white supremacy. The myth of black competition became the arbiter of social, political, and economic relations in which black people's actual position of vulnerability was mystified, erased, and denied. As black people in South Africa were more likely to be stripped of the most basic rights necessary for taking home a reasonable portion of their wages and earnings, the notion of white vulnerability caused by black competition turns accumulated advantages that whites benefited from into accumulated disadvantages.

In order to make people into generic sellers of labor two processes occurred. Those blacks who refused to submit to "free labor" were called a threat to the economic system and were racially depicted as backward tribes. Those whites who refused to submit to "free labor" were surveilled, regulated, and controlled through the mechanisms of social work, the juvenile detention facility, the jail, the mental institution, the poor house and work colony, and the criminalization of survival strategies in the informal economy. By ignoring the attack on poor whites, we miss the processes by which freedom comes to mean subordination, order, and submission.

By examining the racialized mechanisms that constitute proletarianization and charitable/philanthropic uplift as related instruments used by big capital at different stages of corporate development we have come to understand that those who own the semi-independent base of "the wage" have profound limits on upward mobility via mastery of skills or inclusion in the wage labor market. Scholars who examine the wage and the racial wealth divide explain that wages mean very little in terms of shifting social status; wages are not enough. Achola Pala writes:

> First, in considering the issue of the impact on women of colonial and/or neocolonial socioeconomic processes, it is well to bear in mind that, although such processes have enslaved women in the reserves and exploited their labor while withdrawing men to work in wage-earning jobs, in reality wages alone cannot constitute an argument that men have benefited from those systems of oppression.[76]

In this sense, then, the wage has never been considered the substantive force for changing the status of individuals and communities in economic development. Because proletarianization and charitable/philanthropic uplift share a group of meanings and roots in capital, these two mechanisms in concert with other social formations and transformations produce at least two outcomes for a person's and a community's life chances: either to be seen as redeemable, having dignity, self-respect, and the capacity to legitimately pursue a higher social status or to be seen as irredeemable, poor, resistant to work, lazy, and in need of guidance about how to achieve dignity and self-respect. But the racial lines that demarcate these two positions bleed into each other in substantial ways. At the very least we are left with the irretrievable fact that those deemed irredeemably poor, resistant to work, lazy, and fundamentally incapable of achieving dignity and self-respect are not in competition with those legible as respectable—even those legible as contingent and semiwhite in their respectability.

CHAPTER 5

Origin Stories about Segregationist Philanthropy

Scholars have debated[1] whether Carnegie Corporation philanthropy in South Africa is an example of imported American Jim Crow social science[2] or whether it was an example of an exceptional South African form of segregationism.[3] Such "origin stories" have been critical for many white nationalisms and their ability to repair fragile "racial regimes."[4] This pivot around the question of the origins of segregationism prompts us to ask the wrong question. The Carnegie Corporation intervened in South African intellectual life and parliamentary politics in order to suppress black radical viewpoints and legitimate white nationalism.[5] Trying to locate the origins of segregationism and the scientific racism that animated it in either British-American liberalism or Dutch-Afrikaner racialism undertheorizes the impact of the *Poor White Study*. Thus the notion that South African scientific racism was a local discourse is less illuminating than the geopolitical conditions that require that we consider (1) whether segregationist philanthropy and liberal paternalism promoted underdevelopment (economic, social, and political) for black people; (2) whether and how scientific racism was used to regulate black and white people; and (3) whether white misery[6] is as important to white supremacy as white privilege. This chapter takes up the limits of the various exceptionalist origin stories of segregationism. I aim to redirect our attention to the ways in which the Carnegie Corporation navigated the global racial order in order to correct the contradictions produced by white on white violence. Across the colonial world "cross-cutting cleavages" proliferated in order to temper such contradictions and protect the global color line.[7] These organizations ranged from those that deployed the political salience of class and gender to those that propped up white kinship through religion and trade. In order to protect the geographic mobility of "white" settlers and a legal and juridical system that guaranteed them citizenship and property rights throughout the British Empire, such organizations sought to repair breaches created by white nationalisms at war with each other. Drawing on their shared identities as settlers, soldiers, and union members in Australia, Canada, the United States, and New Zealand, migrants relied on the "global sexual racial contract" to develop the white working class and republican citizenship.[8] They further flourished through concrete policies that guaranteed immigration restriction and segregation.

THE AMERICAN INHERITANCE

The development scholar C. J. Groenewald argued that the *Poor White Study* initiated all South African social science and that its methods constituted the earliest and most substantial antipoverty research,[9] essential to industrial productivity, liberal governance, and stabilizing social antagonisms.[10] By implication, Carnegie's overall social research, in this view, was not racist, and if it had racist outcomes they were imported from the land of Jim Crow.[11] Moreover, Groenewald calculates that since the bulk of Carnegie's expenditures were for the benefit of black people and not for poor whites the charges of racism fail.[12] However, white scholars and colonial administrators in segregationist societies deployed such funds[13] to detain and pacify black people and black reproduction.[14] Ultimately, the data gathered, the advocacy campaigned for, and the laws changed were all in the context of racial accommodation by black people under racial colonialism.[15] In this framework, antipoverty social research promotes uplift and is innocent of colonial, racist, and imperialist modes of consolidating power.[16] And black failure to benefit from liberalism reflects the "indebtedness of blackness" as well as the "wages of whiteness" conceived by Du Bois.

REHAB FOR FALLEN WHITES: BLACKS AS THE REAL TARGET OF SCIENTIFIC RACISM

While Groenewald asserted that the *Poor White Study* along with other Carnegie social research derived from American and British social science, for Saul Dubow segregationist thought in South Africa was a distinctive and national formation[17] that emerged from the "selective absorption" of scientific racism from the international intellectual movement known as "eugenic imperialism."[18] The "selective absorption" of British- and U.S.-generated segregationist ideology and practice, in this line of reasoning, created space to articulate South African exceptionalism. By tracing the data gathering, publishing, authorizing, institutionalization, and professionalization of South African eugenic thought and practice, Dubow emphasizes South Africa's unique national racial history and "provincializes" British/American projects of racial segregation.[19]

Concerned with promoting autonomy from both British and American academia, South African social scientists, including E. G. Malherbe, touted "South Africa as an experimental laboratory in racial and cultural relations."[20] To that end, while the Carnegie Corporation marketed its technical expertise in the scientific management of racially segregated labor forces and its proficiency in coordinating white minority rule, South African eugenicists focused on building white national consciousness in Africa and capitalizing on Africa's singular role in the international debate on human origins, primitivism, and the "missing link."[21] These eugenicists and liberal segregationists hoped to capitalize on the view that southern Africa was perceived as an important site for potential exploitation and extraction. Moreover, attention to poor whites as cultural defects in white civilization provided the context for sanitizing the inherent violence of white settler expansionism in Africa. According to popular Eurocentric notions of the day, African peoples were living examples of prehuman existence. Allegedly embodiments of prehistory and primitivism, African people constituted the basis on which Eurocentric notions of human being were built.[22] While such Eurocentric notions of human being were contested sharply from the Enlightenment to the interwar years during which the *Poor White Study* was conducted, philosophers, clergy, artists, and politicians from camps liberal, Marxist, imperialist, isolationist, and psychoanalytic consistently wrote histories of human being in which Africa and African people served as the "missing link" and thus prompted the political and social imaginary of white peoples.[23] Dubow analyzed the *Poor White Study* but concluded after a few lines that it was not really "that racist"[24] and resulted in decades of financial benefits and improved social status for poor whites. He writes, "Suggestions that the poverty of whites was natural and ineradicable were entertained, but ultimately rejected."[25] Since scientific racism is so inconsistently understood as a tool for racializing whiteness, we can understand Dubow's replication of this theoretical gap. Unlike black people, white people were to be socially rehabilitated and politically empowered through the application of scientific racist doctrines and policies. According to Dubow, scientific racism only targeted blacks, so poor whites caught up in its dragnet were an anomaly.[26] However, as we have learned, even policies that result in substantive political gain for the racially stigmatized poor are not divorced from enduring forms of racial subordination.[27] Regardless of attempts to distinguish a South African national science, the racial colonial legacy could not be erased. Ironically, "South Africanization of science" would have been "African science."[28] But whites in South Africa did not conceive of themselves as Africans. The geography of white South African experiences, the particularity of their identity in diasporas, and their mobility should have made them Africans, not "Afrikaners."[29] But the lack of distinction in their own pedigrees was submerged in order to make them white: citizens of the republic and members of the settler colonial world.[30] Thus Dubow's "South Africanization of science" might best be understood as a prophylaxis against Trollope's 1877 prediction that South Africa would always be a "black man's country," revealing the contingent nature of inadequate whiteness.[31] South Africanization of science as the attempt to identify a "national" science actually makes a whole cohort of African scholars *white*—based precisely on their ability to articulate the differences between themselves and so-called primitives both black and white. The Carnegie-funded research on poor whites helped European settlers in Africa fix the problems that such "problem people" revealed.

Indeed, the pursuit of an autonomous South African national identity through a science of the management of the purportedly "uncivilized world" relies precisely on South African *nationality* being produced by the existence of a global racial contract through which the social is constituted. Since the international standard of science was primed to study "subject races" and ultimately study the discreteness of blackness and whiteness the national project fails to capture the dynamics of the global racial project. Thus South Africa's intellectual autonomy was achieved through participation in a long-standing attempt to justify white supremacy and black subordination, not through "new science." When South African social scientists demonstrated that despite (or because of) their intermingling and cohabitation with Africans as a settler community, they, too, could reproduce a colonial science, they were accredited and approved as producing new knowledge for a new white nation. South African intellectuals were complicit in eugenics—in ways continuous with and more similar to that which intellectuals developed in and across other settler societies.[32] Demonstrating a South African national identity by debating the weakness or strength of the South African style of eugenics is a dead end that prohibits analysis of the complexity and dynamics of racial segregation and the uses of white raciality globally. The Carnegie Corporation could traffic in white misery on another continent because white misery fit well into the logic of the global racial contract through which nation-states are made.

POOR WHITE CHARITY BEFORE THE CARNEGIE CORPORATION: WORK, HOUSING, AND HEALTH

Primed by the existence of prior campaigns in defense of poor whites, the South African voting populace already knew that poor whites were vulnerable, in need of charity, and potent symbols of their own mythic Afrikaner Nationalist prehistory. Whenever poor whites were memorialized and championed they represented a complex nexus of aspirations for recognition as a legitimate sister republic to the United States and a potential "wedge against British control."[33] Thus if and when poor whites were *kept around* as a potent representation of the frailty of Afrikaner Nationalism, they served as "living fossils."[34] As living fossils and proof of bias against the trodden upon Afrikaner nation, poor whites were carriers of a venerated past and a new national social scientific language. Turning them into a cause célèbre and a social problem that needed well-funded science and experts meant shifting the conversation toward the financial impact of relying on so-called primitive, nonproductive[35] African workers and the deleterious social effect "detribalized" and "diseased" African city dwellers were supposedly having on poor whites.[36] Building on a powerful ideological substrate that had failed to guarantee that white supremacy would result in categorical white wealth, the Carnegie Corporation conjured a lasting win in the war on white poverty.[37]

Overall, prior campaigns to uplift poor whites materially had been spotty at best and totally ineffective at worst.[38] In job creation, party politics, public health, and housing, the social forces that hoped to enhance the lot of poor whites faced long-standing resistance by both British and Afrikaner voters, elected officials, and businesses.[39] Though government officials expressed fear that poor whites would be ready recruits for class revolt, their ultimate state policy belied their public statements of concern. Invoked numerous times between 1907 and 1934, the Afrikaner Nationalist movement failed in their campaigns to use poor white identity to increase social supports or to effectively mobilize poor whites into a reliable political constituency.[40] Despite their exhortations and lobbying, the Dutch Reformed Church and the Catholic Women's League, the Transvaal Indigency Commission, the National Union of Railway and Harbor Servants (NURAHS), the Pact Government, the Labour Party, and the White Labour Department failed to secure reparations guaranteed by the Treaty of Vereeneging for whites who were imprisoned during the South African War (1899–1902).[41]

The White Labour Department faced considerable resistance to their lobbying for the hiring of poor whites as replacement workers on the railways.[42] In response to the White Labour Inspector's demands, railway executives argued that poor whites were unskilled and were unlikely to stay on the job for long. They reasoned that poor whites wanted excessively high wages for the social *penalty* of working alongside blacks. Commenting on the multilingualism of their African and Indian laborers, railway management hesitated to train (white) men whom they believed were dishonest and idle to replace their loyal, honest, respectable, skilled, multilingual, acculturated to industrial practices and modes of living and surviving, and, of course, lower-paid non-European employees. While railway management agreed to retrench Africans and Indians in exchange for whites, they compromised by paying whites only slightly higher wages. Instead, they reclassified their jobs making them accessible to whites only. The railways had a revolving door policy of firing black employees, reclassifying job categories, and hiring poor whites in those jobs, then firing poor whites and replacing them with the rehiring of longtime black employees. In exchange for the job security of "white by custom" work, white workers had to accept wages far below government subsistence levels. The South African Railway promoted over three thousand poor whites by 1916 and could then hire more whites to work in manual labor jobs. Though the railway complied with government demands by establishing "white by custom" work categories, by 1924 there were still only three thousand white railway employees. This was exactly the same number of white employees working for the railways in 1909. The rewards of white nepotism for poor whites were largely affective and symbolic.

White workers could not afford to rent in the private housing market but instead depended on the rail companies to build barracks-style hostels (or they rented from others, predominantly black people) and were not compensated for moving their work camps. White railway workers continued to rent their tools, tents, and water and were regularly defrauded by managers who sometimes stole the whole gang's wages. Last, white workers had to pay for their own return tickets if the work on a site took less than three months. Such company policies were set with the black worker in mind, a person whose status as worker could be shifted to that of illegal nonresident vagrant when employers wanted to discharge them quickly. The minimal increases in actual white wages for the railways did not include benefits or subsidies that would substantively distinguish white from black economically. Thus the railway set clear boundaries on how far it would be obligated to poor whites. This echoed sentiments in South African society, which generally rejected Afrikaner Nationalist claims that poor whites were part of the white national family.

There was just as much white resistance to housing poor whites as there had been to hiring them in jobs previously held by black people. From 1919 to 1934 urbanization was taking a severe toll on Johannesburg residents. Substandard housing and limited to no access to clean sewage or water were some of the more dramatic consequences of this rapid urbanization in a city that had no intention of providing public services to the working poor, particularly since the greatest majority of working people in Johannesburg was black. Johannesburg city health officers, Dr. Porter and his successor, Dr. A. Milne, called the idea of a poor white housing shortage fallacious. City health officials objected to the need for subsidized poor white housing; instead they favored decent housing for Africans outside city limits, in the so-called native villages or locations—a policy that obtained in a more formal fashion as the model for the post-1948 apartheid city. "Race mixing" and the presence of black people in the industrial city was a far more sinister public crisis according to Johannesburg officials in the Labour Party.[43] Failing to secure newly available federal money for housing subsidies, the Johannesburg Town Council, while being very sympathetic to the plight of the urban poor, framed the issue of housing as an enforcement of the 1923 Natives (Urban Areas) Act that forced Africans living in the city to move. They found that this framing of the problem of poor white housing loosened purses and provoked local political will considerably. In the 1930s Native Affairs Department officials forcibly removed thirty thousand African workers from Johannesburg and relocated them to three thousand substandard municipal homes, constituting the largest pre-1948 housing boom. Scholars reflecting on municipal housing for African people have argued that it was wholly unsatisfactory—referring to municipal housing as "barn-like shelters."[44] This particularly aggravated the living conditions for African women, who never qualified for municipal housing in the African locations or in the city proper. These evicted African tenants found themselves in the unenviable position of having to move back to the city multiple times, facing repeated evictions and fines. In the meantime, twenty-five thousand more whites moved into Johannesburg, mostly male and single, at the behest of the mining and railway companies and the Pact Government's "civilized labour policy"—despite that same government's refusal to provide housing for this workforce.[45]

By reframing the debate on housing in terms of the alleged threat that black people posed to public health, health officials deployed the proposals from reports about the slums in Jeppestown, Fordsburg, Doornfontein, Newlands, and other places where white workers were said to have no shelter at all or to live in dire conditions of overcrowding, subletting rooms and half rooms from relatives, strangers, and Africans. By reframing demands for subsidized poor white housing in this way, city health officials and national policy makers could continue to pursue evictions of black Johannesburg residents rather than build adequate housing. If a housing shortage existed, that problem, they agreed, would be corrected by exacting the toll from Africans and the public policy apparatus responsible for their management, the Native Affairs Department. The campaign to house poor whites thus provided an ever-expanding role for the Native Affairs Department in local and national policy making and governance. City and national health officials were simply endorsing the long-standing policies toward social problems facing whites. They reasoned that once blacks were removed from Johannesburg proper, the poverty and lack of drinking water and sewage and other facilities that had created the conditions for the 1904 plague outbreak and the 1918 influenza epidemic would remedy themselves. Here, the relationship between white poverty as a phenomenon that exacerbates antiblackness is on full view. Health officials were more concerned with proving the "scientific linkage" between blacks and disease than with making the city habitable for residents. Consequently, they demonstrated the lack of interest in poverty reduction schemes that benefited poor whites specifically. Since black people were the reputed disease carriers, according to these racist public health and city planning sciences, the priority was to cordon off a contagion that was coded as racially black. Public health and city planning fulfilled state mandates for specific groups of white citizens, and Native Affairs policies that understood African people as antagonistic to public health fulfilled state mandates for producing and protecting white life.[46] The government was very concerned to ensure that any resources for the poor went to Africans in order to reinforce the idea that *blackness was the living standard of poverty* in South Africa. Regardless of the social problems, public policy reverted to the default mechanism, social and political control of the African population, a "racial contract." White people became citizens and members in the nation through systematic dehumanization of African people as individuals and as group members. Consequently, the same hyper-empowered white people had to be figured as the ones really most vulnerable to racial attack by the "swaart gevaar," or black threat.

While it took an entire generation to proliferate the vocabulary that captured these dynamics, their roots are to be found in the interwar years, the international eugenics movement, and the expediency of the U.S. manifestation of Anglo-Saxon solidarity and expansionism. In short, this disruptive and disastrous set of policies failed to produce enough shelter to house the poor in Johannesburg, and it had the tragic effect of displacing African Johannesburg residents while drawing many more whites and "Colored" South Africans into the desperately underserved urban center. *Poor White Study* researchers commented negatively on ineffectual slum clearance policies by pointing to the miscegenation rife in urban areas because of the lack of proper housing and improper social education. They reasoned that the Native Affairs Department was the appropriate bureaucracy for improving the working and living conditions of Africans and hoped that the White Labour Department would have as much authority over the lives of poor whites as the former had over the lives of African people. Carnegie researchers hoped to convince upper-class South Africans that poor white workers were in danger of becoming even worse off than Africans. The Carnegie Commission learned from and hoped to reinforce the notion that insisted that all social problems were associated with being African.

If the resistance to hiring and housing poor whites created political dilemmas for Afrikaner Nationalism, collaboration with the Labour Party in Johannesburg—elected on a platform of housing reform—proved to be an ineffectual means for transmitting the Afrikaner Nationalist message.[47] While the national Pact Government launched a new agency, the Central Housing Board created by the Housing Act of 1920, by 1934 the Labour Party proved better at recruiting poor whites to cities than at housing them. The Johannesburg Town Council failed to utilize national funding allocated for housing development in the urban areas.[48] Securing no more than 346 homes in over a decade, the Labour Party revealed how difficult it was to make appeals for social supports unless they were making claims for whites *as whites*. The Labour Party, like other housing advocates, found that until it championed the expulsion and eviction of African city dwellers, they had no access to public health officials' recognition and no access to national funding for building low-income housing.[49] The CCNY took advantage of the Labour Party's initial reticence to deploy racism to spotlight the failure to get more housing for whites.

The push to find work in the cash economy and the pull of jobs on the Rand consigned city dwellers of all races to urban wretchedness. Notwithstanding, the varied attempts to invoke poor white identity centered on the degradation of the so-called white race and the *unnatural* situation of living near and in the same households as black people. If social and political campaigns prior to Carnegie philanthropy for poor whites all desired to name whites as the rightful beneficiaries and inheritors of the incredible wealth being produced on the Rand they were stymied by the fact that voters, electoral officials, and business owners did not feel any particular solidarity with poor whites. Lofty expectations aside, the currency of shared whiteness guaranteed very little except more hardship for black people. While arguments about being the dispossessed kin of their wealthy white employers failed, arguments that castigated black and Indian employees as those taking the wealth out of white hands were more likely to make their mark. Whiteness, then, was not a familial tie of status and privilege but more akin to a shared ideology of antiblack and anti-Indian bias. That white people were poor denied them full access to white identity. Poverty and whiteness were contradictory identities, regardless of their reality in people's everyday experiences. However, those white people who claimed allegiance to distorted views of Africans and Indians found succor and all manner of public and private assistance. The big difference between the CCNY study and prior campaigns to uplift poor whites was the former's success at moving toward pseudoscientific and technical legitimations for antiblack reforms more quickly (even exclusively) than the prior campaigns. In the *Poor White Study,* the CCNY found in South Africa a ready market for its technical expertise on poverty management and regulation, not to mention a ready market for race relations management. Through complex manipulation of the "facts" of poor white identity, Afrikaner Nationalists could argue that Africa and proximity to Africans were destroying white civilization—the evidence lying in the existence of poor whites, an existence that had to be repetitively reenacted.

The conflicts among Afrikaner Nationalist theologians, charity workers, and academics prohibited Afrikaner Nationalism from maintaining a solid unified power bloc that could balance British power in the region. One major way that all Afrikaner Nationalists made their arguments about the poor white was attention to their supposed biological inferiority and genetic failure. Considered a menace of Western civilization and the "withered branch" of the European evolutionary tree, poor whites became the focus of Afrikaner Nationalists, seeking to secure their allegiance and extracting proof of their political devotion. The reality was that this first generation of poor whites in urban South Africa relied extensively on the social, housing, employment, and health care networks established by African, Indian, and Colored workers. Afrikaner Nationalists fastened on this material dependency and geographic integration and raised the specter that poor whites would become eventual political allies of their neighbors, who they had begun to marry and rent rooms from. The prominent educator and *Poor White Study* researcher Ernest G. Malherbe wrote, "We saw the poor white was often a *victim* of his environment. But just as often he was the cause of his deteriorating environment."[50] Malherbe's conclusion directly challenged the ecological and structural explanations of poverty, reducing poverty (and white poverty especially) to a moral, psychological, or biological concern and a disease of proximity to blackness.

One of the major impacts of the *Poor White Study,* then, was to shift the terms of debate among Afrikaner Nationalists and introduce psychological and economic theories to deal with a common concern. It is not surprising then that Afrikaner Nationalism began to undergo a shift toward more articulate ideological divisions and, ultimately, a cohesive philosophy after the *Poor White Study.*

Nevertheless, taken together, these earlier campaigns had three crucial results. The first was building the ideological infrastructure that the Carnegie Commission could then use to initiate a more sanitized, academically approved discourse for racial colonialism and racial domination. The second was getting an ineffectual but popularly supported Labour Party elected to the Johannesburg Town Council. And following from that, the third was the decisive turn away from class-based organizing to race-based organizing through which the Labour Party piloted the course toward a superbly overblown white identity constantly in need of bolstering. The consequence of this use of poor white identity was the suppression of calls by both black and multiracial campaigns for economic justice.

CONCLUSION: THE SLAVERY-FOUNDATION NEXUS

The Carnegie Corporation's liberal antipoverty schemes were less examples of projects of black economic improvement (as Groenewald has claimed) and more examples of what the American sociologist John Stanfield calls "philanthropy and Jim Crow." Detailed analysis of where Carnegie funds were used suggests that the money set aside to benefit blacks was actually used to train a cadre of white nationalists, English and Afrikaans speaking, who coupled their academic training and prestige to conduct eugenic research on tens of thousands of white and non-white South Africans. Their formal training and association to segregationist philanthropy gave the social scientific seal of approval to grand apartheid. Scholars have demonstrated that the relationship between philanthropic organizations and the racial segregationism that characterizes racial colonialism and chattel slavery troubles the possibility of the philanthropic sector being considered as purely benign factors in the economic development of postemancipation societies, which typically remain grounded in systematic and institutionalized racial subordination.[51]

By the end of apartheid, historians of social anthropology and its Afrikaner variant, *volkekunde,* came to raise instructive questions about the poorly analyzed celebration of Jim Crow social science, the philanthropies that paid for it, and the claims to having benefited blacks through its research and advocacy.[52] The chief architect of volkekunde, the study of the "forms of social life of the primitive races," Alfred Reginald Radcliffe-Brown, began to teach social anthropology at University of Cape Town in 1921, just three years before Raymond Dart's 1924 finding of Taung Man put South Africa on the map as an "experimental laboratory" and an international exemplar in the social anthropology field. The consequences of this competition to prove that South Africa could also reproduce an original academic social science paradigm rested on proving the primitiveness of African people. It also rested on demonstrating the primitiveness of poor white people. Native Affairs administrators and White Labour Department officials used a process of "selective absorption," of social Darwinism and eugenicism, to resolve the Poor White Problem and the Native Problem and establish an empirically measurable justification for apartheid as a model of political and economic development.

Ironically, the ability to talk about scientific racism as a national phenomenon or a project of the devoted parental state exclusively and not an imperial phenomenon of global proportion is part of what creates the space for the cadre of new social scientists and bureaucracy builders in racial democracies to claim that the register on which they are establishing the terms of order is somehow decidedly divorced from colonial administration and the practices of the Home Office. However, attention to the international context of racial capitalism suggests that supporting institutional linkages for U.S. empire in South Africa would prove to be pragmatic and stable pillars for entrenching racial advantage and disadvantage.[53]

An entire generation of South African scholars had their scholarly training disciplined by a context in which they were to be the agents and personnel driving and protecting the fantasies of unchallenged white supremacy in South Africa and the United States. Thus we are left with a historiography of one of Carnegie's major interventions, the *Poor White Study*, that largely pivots around the wrong question. Asking whether the institutionalization of racial segregation in South Africa in urban welfare policy and the social sciences comes from within or from without fails to register the complex global racial contract and generations of suppressing the black radical tradition, often by identifying and creating eminently deployable classes of white people—both among the aspiring academic elite and the desperately unpedigreed poor.

As human being and the realization of human rationality in the aspiration toward and the achievement of the nation and the bureaucracy that organizes it is imagined, the racial politics that rely on black people as the fundamental antagonists of human being and the nation must continually erect new racial regimes and forgeries of memory to paper over this relation. The study of poor whites, white poverty, and the idea that poor whites were an intractable social problem was one such racial regime. That the racialization of poor whites could occur both as privilege and misery is fundamental to the workings of this relation. In this chapter, I have examined and theorized the relationship between white misery and the kinds of cultural service it is enabled to do to secure white men's countries and more important the white global imaginary.

My analysis of Carnegie's *Poor White Study* concurs with other findings about the failure of liberalism to articulate a political agenda for black liberation.[54] Paul Rich argues that instead of providing political leadership the anthropological research on African culture and the so-called problems of culture contact and ethnic conflict actually attached prominent liberals to the segregationist political project of Afrikaner Nationalism.[55] Despite a proliferation of civic organizations and the training of multiple cadres of scientifically trained race relations experts, the white liberals who rejected apartheid nevertheless failed to articulate a value system in opposition to apartheid that had room for a black radical tradition. Indeed, their decades-long interest in suppressing the widest possible range of African public opinion, radical African-led political and civic organizations, and an African public sphere made them enervated intermediaries for and handmaidens of Afrikaner Nationalism.

CHAPTER 6

Carnegie in Africa and the Knowledge Politics of Apartheid

Research Agendas not Taken

In 1947[1] Carnegie Corporation of New York president Devereux Josephs invited Cornelis De Kiewiet (1902–86) to investigate "how Carnegie might profitably renew its support of undertakings in South Africa."[2] De Kiewiet returned with a research proposal on the impact of proletarianization on black people in the year immediately preceding the Afrikaner Nationalist takeover of government.[3] Noting that there were mounting social and racial problems there,[4] he argued that the CCNY could be as helpful as they had been in the 1930s. CCNY staffer Whitney Shepardson shelved De Kiewiet's proposal allegedly because the philanthropy sought to avoid involvement in South African domestic affairs.[5] Of course, the Carnegie Corporation had been deeply involved in South Africa through dozens of segregationist antipoverty projects,[6] the *Poor White Study* perhaps having the most decisive impact on domestic affairs and providing lasting precedent for lobbying within party politics and academic circles.[7] Arguably, a study on black people and racial capitalism would have intervened in the 1948 election of the Afrikaner Nationalists to parliamentary power in South Africa—which ushered in grand apartheid. Wedded to antiblack foreign policy and U.S. expansionism, the philanthropy's leaders had not anticipated undertakings that might give voice to black militants.[8] For segregationist philanthropy white nationalism at war with itself had required international intervention, but black subordination, viewed as a domestic concern, required no comment.

In the earlier period Carnegie intervention in South Africa was seen as critical for creating a tractable black elite and suppressing organized black revolt.[9] The interwar years proved to be a period of "hitchhiking imperialism" in the British dominions and colonies.[10] The *Poor White Study* played a decisive and enabling role for U.S. commercial interests, which could more effectively supersede Britain in South African governance and bureaucracy, and raise the profile of America in the global imaginary by waiting in the wings while British "practical subjugation" and Christian zealotry operated on the African continent.

This chapter explains the context that shaped the research agenda for Carnegie philanthropy in Africa.[11] The questions I want to address are as follows: Why was the CCNY interested in South Africa? Why was the Carnegie Corporation persuaded that the "poor white problem" was a priority? Which South African social groups most stood to benefit from this research agenda and how? How did Carnegie Corporation president Frederick Keppel (1875–1943) and the CCNY come to be allied with the chief intellectual architects of Afrikaner Nationalism, both English and Afrikaner? The Carnegie Corporation intervention represented a stage in the development of South Africa's legalized "separate development," or grand apartheid. I demonstrate that a shared commitment to global whiteness was central to shared conceptions of democracy in the region and in the world system.[12]

The introduction to the *Poor White Study* is noticeably silent on these questions,[13] using happenstance and coincidence to obscure Carnegie Corporation decision making. It is written as if the Carnegie Corporation researchers ended up on the wrong side—read: the white supremacist anti–Union Government side—of the conflict *by mistake.*[14] Evidence to the contrary is to be found in the correspondence between research team members and Keppel,[15] where we find that Carnegie personnel used their influence to press the Union Government to do more on behalf of poor whites. The Union Government had tried to balance support for the white poor without fueling the Afrikaner Nationalist political platform and so offered in-kind gifts but did not commit cash financial resources for the *Poor White Study.*[16] Though R.W. Wilcocks, secretary of the research team,[17] assured Keppel that the Union Government would pay the L1,000 to print the document in English and Afrikaans, later memos indicated the Carnegie Corporation paid for that as well. Through the *Poor White Study,* segregationist American foreign policy revealed its alignment with the Dutch Reformed Church and the development of Afrikaner Nationalism.

By funding certain kinds of projects and scholars, especially those indebted to the Carnegie Corporation's largesse, this philanthropy linked the shared projects of capitalist industrialization to the parental state. Capitalist industrialization, on the one hand, was committed to scientific management of labor based on a rigid racial and gender hierarchy, which meant fitting each racial group and its gendered components to their appropriately complex or appropriately mundane task in mechanized society.[18] Zine Magubane explains this labor hierarchy by critiquing the "social body" concept: "Viewing society as functioning in ways analogous to the human body was useful in that it provided a way of thinking about how one portion of an organism could be dependent upon another, yet still superior."[19] The parental state, on the other hand, was committed to a system of education that would produce malleable subjects for industry (workers) and for society and governance (citizens). Industries in the United States and South Africa were deeply invested in producing such subjects and staged elaborate Americanization ceremonies for their American and South African workforces to literally bake in a social identity.[20]

When the CCNY allied itself with the economic development of poor whites, a group that came to be known as the "withered branch of the tree" in the evolution of the white race,[21] it agreed that the most pressing problem in South Africa was white people living beneath their true standing in the racial hierarchy. The *Poor White Study* was part of a larger political and cultural project to promote and institutionalize Anglo-Saxon solidarity and the myth of the "pound per day" white wage earner. Carnegie's segregationist philanthropy promoted racial accommodation by black people to white political guidance and co-optation of the "black radical intelligentsia" whether in the U.S. rural South or the entire continent of Africa.[22] Since "few white South Africans were willing to consider the African a political or social equal . . . [and since African people were] assumed to be incapable of self-government, the black African was entitled to the paternalistic guidance of the white race."[23] From the African Methodist Episcopal Church championing South Africa as a "black man's land" (1903–5) to the black revolts in 1906, white commentators regarded such articulations of a black political agenda against accommodationism as the seeds of a race war.[24] Prompted by the founding of the National Association for the Advancement of Colored People (NAACP) in 1909 and the African National Congress (ANC) in 1912 and given a complicated intellectual dependence on a "Washingtonian philosophy" that converged all too neatly with a racial labor hierarchy, Carnegie Corporation philanthropic efforts in 1911 were scrambling to respond to black political militants.[25]

Corporations and foreign policy officials in the United States relied heavily on the soft power and influence of American and South African race relations scholars, whose interest in white poverty simultaneously endorsed white liberalism as a force for public good and a means to distract from the organizational energies of black radicals who had inherited a "theory of black radicalism . . . through their work and study in the mass movements of Black people."[26]

Urged by Keppel himself, the CCNY paid for and printed the five-volume *Poor White Study,* receiving only in-kind support from a reluctant South African government.[27] The CCNY's support for poor whites presents a fascinating puzzle about the intersections of the politics of knowledge, international relations, and race since poor whites and the framing of them as a social problem was a cause célèbre for the segregationist Afrikaner Nationalist political and social campaign. Poor whites, though unfortunate, were not unlike the urban poor in other industrializing nations and fared categorically better than the black urban and rural poor in South Africa during this period. Support for poor whites enabled the segregationist Carnegie Corporation to intervene in South Africa and legitimize the interests of racial capital in both countries under the guise of humanitarian assistance in Africa.[28] While the first generation of Carnegie-funded researchers were credentialed by ties forged during slavery, abolition, and the bureaucracies established to contain emancipation, the second generation cut their teeth on eugenic imperialism by gathering data about the social lives and communities of the racialized poor. Carnegie's study of poor whites in South Africa trained a second generation of highly mobile race relations technicians.

THE SLAVERY-FOUNDATION NEXUS AGAIN

Many scholars have identified the role that white supremacy plays in philanthropy and social science and in promoting an accommodationist political culture.[29] The Carnegie Foundation's interventions into the domestic policies of former British colonies on the African continent had antecedents in older philanthropic organizations and ideologies about social welfare and poverty common both in the United States and in Britain.[30] The irony of former captains of the industry in slaves wedded to the uplift of their descendants should give us more than pause.[31]

One such philanthropy, the Phelps-Stokes Fund had a history of connection to the black Victorian branch of the racial uplift movement in the United States and also in the missions set up by the American Colonization Society.[32] Carnegie Corporation–sponsored agencies in South Africa that co-opted black radical leadership relied on those black Victorians who endorsed white political rule for Africans.[33] Indeed, black American interest in Africa, even among Garveyites, revolved to some extent around redemption and regeneration of African people via white political control at the same time that scandalous reports about abuses of black farmworkers by white settlers in South Africa proliferated.[34] Embodied by the training of uplift-oriented black missionaries, segregationist philanthropy was driven by accomodationism, racial conciliation, patriotism, asceticism, bourgeois individualism, patriarchal domesticity, withdrawal from the public sphere and political life, and the tacit support of the pursuit of American empire that could result from a pacified black populace sometimes confused with self-help and in-group cooperation.[35] Seeking to repatriate black people who had themselves been slaves and or were actively engaged in antislavery campaigns would provide conduits to increase U.S. influence. If Africans from the diaspora could be enjoined to lead "their own people" much of the burden of dealing with the multiple crises caused by the enslavement of generations of Africans could be exported out of the Americas.[36]

In the 1830s, the Phelps-Stokes family began to fund missionary and educational projects through the New York State Colonization Society to export Africans in the United States to Africa. Anson Greene Phelps funded this campaign despite the vocal and militant political campaigning by free and enslaved Africans in the Americas against racial chattel slavery. As Cedric Robinson notes, the U.S. government designated $100,000 to fund colonization of free people of color, but the political project of ejecting them undermined their usefulness. The existence of free people of color could also be explained as proof of the benefit of slavery as a civilizing instrument for so-called African savages living in the Americas.[37] Indeed, the money they earned and their political advocacy could easily be and often had been turned toward further entrenching enslavement because of family ties between free and unfree. For much of the first half of the nineteenth century free Africans rejected colonization because "they were poised to make claims on their rights as American citizens," but by the 1850s and the enforcement of the Fugitive Slave Act they too faced the unhappy reality of having to concede that emigration might be the best hope.[38] The existence of free

African abolitionists created big problems for white supremacy, and yet their existence was important for maintaining slavocracy in the United States and expanding its tentacles along with the aspirations for American empire; thus the long-term financial and social interest in and commitment to removing this social problem. The Phelps-Stokes family, then, were exemplars of the "cruelty and paternalism [that] could be expressions of the same class position."[39] The Carnegie Corporation extended the planter philanthropy legacy of the Phelps-Stokes family. In many ways the Carnegie Corporation was simply extending the linkages formed in this earlier period of white rule, or as Edward H. Berman puts it, the origins of the Carnegie Corporation in Africa was the legacy of the Phelps-Stokes family in slavery. Such a long history provides a more adequate context to the insight that

> the conceptualization of these foundation educational ventures coincided with the demise of the colonial empires of Britain, France, and the Netherlands after 1945. The resultant educational and cultural programs were a reflection of the belief that America's post–World War II interests could be served by aligning the evolving third world nations to the United States through the provision of social services (particularly education), which had been limited by the former colonial powers, thereby fulfilling an articulated local need and at the same time prodding these nations from flirtation with socialist [and anticolonial] doctrine. The extension of a sophisticated form of cultural imperialism also had the advantage of obfuscating the continuance of discredited and crude forms of economic and military imperialism.[40]

While liberal scholars like Cornelis De Kiewiet[41] and Carnegie director Newtown Baker acceded to the institutionalization of apartheid by saying that no other settler society had to deal with the economic burden of a majority population that was still "backward" and "primitive," most white liberal scholars also failed to simultaneously analyze the demographic reality that every settler society relied on indigenous labor, political institutions, technology, commercial relationships, and land—while still ultimately experiencing greater productivity than South Africa.[42] Thus we find the international concern that something was wrong with South Africa, and, of course, quite possibly it was South Africa's European-descent settlers themselves who caused the stalled economic productivity.

Though many argued that U.S. interwar support for colonization in Africa was motivated by "a more supportive American commercial policy," not support for colonization alone, "it is impossible to separate America's sense of mission from its belief in economic expansion . . .

[and] the civilizing impact of commerce."[43] Consequently, the United States found itself caught off guard when no South African consumer market emerged and the British colonial administration exacerbated racial segregation.[44]

With their commitments to expansionism and the uplift of a reputedly savage race, the United States and Great Britain also found compatibility in their shared commitments to white supremacy and imperialism as key features of the diplomatic and economic strategies for securing white nationalism.[45] Businesspeople, missionaries of all races, and African Americans all labored to get the African continent on the U.S. foreign policy agenda, claiming that their entrepreneurial, Christian, and diasporic beliefs and resources had led them to a particular charge on behalf of the continent and its people.[46] All pressed the State Department to consider the economic possibilities of the African continent, to support the conversion of the "unsaved" masses, and, in the case of African Americans, to recognize the transnational racial linkage shaped by a shared history of enslavement and subsequent segregationist noncitizenship.[47] Du Bois "argued [that] South Africa was the inevitable result of white colonialism. White rule, whether in America or Africa, meant racial exploitation."[48] Nation building for these "white men's countries" rested on a fundamental antagonism to black lives and a retrograde mythology (i.e., uplift) about protecting and caring for black people.[49] In South Africa this racial antagonism took the form of laws that created intergenerational wealth for the majority of white people and intergenerational poverty for the majority of black people through a continuous transfer of wealth from black people to white people. The Native Labor Act of 1911 criminalized leaving a job for black workers only. The Mines and Works Act of 1911 confined black workers to unskilled labor categories that criminalized and made invisible the black artisanal classes. The Native Land Act of 1913 confined black landownership to 13 percent of the land in the country. The Pass Laws, both local and national, enshrined residential segregation and discrimination in mobility, transportation, and the provision of all public services.[50] The Natives Urban Area Act (1923) forced black people living in cities, the industrial centers that their labor had built, to move outside of them. The Color Bar Act of 1926 excluded black people from the skilled trades, again. Such laws obviously could not contribute to economic or social uplift but were claimed to do precisely that.[51]

There was also tension between black Victorians and black radicals. The former had endorsed accommodation to white political rule via individualism, masculinist conformity, uplift, and loyalty to empire only to find that once Britain had complete control it did not grant more rights to African people. Between 1911 and 1914 black Victorians had to acknowledge that "assumptions that British control would lead to 'uplift' and 'civilizing' of the black African were . . . erroneous. . . . Britain had proved as willing to sacrifice the rights of blacks for unity between Englishman and Afrikaner as the United States had been to tolerate segregation to help heal tensions between North and South."[52] On the other hand, black radicals had always argued that the white man's burden was about how to secure black adoration for white people and white rule and how to ensure that white people were regarded as morally pure while insisting on white rule and black death. In their criticisms of accommodationism to white leadership, they raised the question of black people's fundamental rights and the history of organizations that championed black people representing their own interests, black people having fundamental rights, Ethiopianism, black nationalism, and black militancy.[53]

RESEARCH AGENDAS NOT TAKEN

Near the end of his life, Andrew Carnegie insisted that some portion of the funds set aside for grants for public education, universities, libraries, and the establishment of other mass cultural educational centers be donated to the British Empire's possessions, echoing his own support for "the Anglo-Saxon world mission," which tried to bring attention to the "characteristics and qualities of Anglo-Saxon nationalities" and the "English speaking race."[54] This portion of the money, called the Dominions and Colonies Fund, found its way into the hands of European settler populations, who found yet another international patron for their massively subsidized projects of white nationalism in Africa.[55] The fund set aside $10 million as an endowment exclusively for work in the British Empire's possessions, Canada, and the United Kingdom[56] and started a new agency based in Washington, DC, on July 10, 1917, to make international donations.[57] Budgets in the period 1911–41 indicate that the Carnegie agencies spent massive sums in segregationist settler colonies (see Appendix A) where African people, Indian people, and so-called Colored people were legally prohibited from using any of the facilities the CCNY built.

The Overseas Visitor Program, a signature project of this fund, paid for exchanges for white scholars from the colonies and dominions to study in Europe and the United States: "These overseas university programs . . . were designed to train a coterie of *indigenous* experts who internalized western norms" (emphasis mine) and interests and who, once certified by external supposedly objective gatekeepers of progress and civilization, [would] become leaders in their societies and guarantee that "local currency is pegged to one of the world currencies and secure favored-nation trading status for western states."[58]

As a consequence, the research reports produced under the auspices of the Overseas Visitors Program often sung the praises of U.S. higher education and its progress-oriented social mission while shedding little light on education and its role in the making of political identities and histories. The Carnegie Overseas Visitors Grants, according to Edward Berman, yielded a crop of inexpensive lobbyists and advocates for seg-regationist U.S. higher education as a model of social harmony for the colonies and dominions.[59] When confronted with examples of racial violence that countered the progress-oriented narrative about the U.S. higher education system, Visitors Grant researchers like W.M. Robb either remained silent or insisted that racial prejudice was an aberrant, foreign, and temporary issue.[60] By recruiting, training, facilitating, funding, and publishing such scholars, the CCNY endorsed and proliferated segregationist higher education that mirrored Anglo-Saxon colonial education.[61]

For example, Professor C.S. Richards's trip to France to study the graduate programs of management and business administration was scheduled during the academic recess.[62] To compensate for the lack of actual educational data, Richards remarked that materials were sent to him. Despite such lopsided research conditions, Richards and fellow Overseas Visitor Grant researcher H.M. Robinson both concluded that South Africa and Australia, respectively, should adopt the practices that they saw in the United States. In a report following up on fifteen years of CCNY philanthropy for building libraries, librarian Robinson reported that the CCNY had offered a revolutionary approach to librar-ies whereby they could help in the national project of rationalizing European identities into white identities.[63] As in the United States, new programs of public or informal education often deployed through libraries and museums were central to creating coherent national identi-ties, evidence of the inherent opportunities available to the self-made individual in such white men's countries. Public educational institutions participated by providing adult education programs of all sorts in the classic Carnegie style: contributing to the "making of America" through "giving civic training."[64] CCNY-founded libraries in South Africa sponsored new programs such as Children's Book Week and informal educational programs on art and travel. Library staff attended rural and community events and developed study courses and winter schools for workers, revamped mobile libraries and library depots at schools, and participated in Afrikaner cultural festivals. Robinson noted that the South African white community had eventually "rallied behind libraries and supported them with their provincial town budgets, built new libraries, complied with compulsory contributions by local governments for their own libraries, created free accommodation for the library, and affiliated local libraries with the provincial library service."[65] He admitted that despite the many successes of new programs and the communities that now supported local libraries without provincial or federal aid, libraries were difficult to maintain because of the prejudice among librarians against the white Transvaal residents. Members of his own staff were of the opinion that libraries that were "designed for the *platteland* [countryside] where high cultural standards do not and never will prevail would fail."[66]

Overseas Visitor grantee Austin Roberts lobbied for CCNY funding for South Africa's museums by complaining about a lack of scientific training and pointing out that studying animals was key to white civilization, agriculture, and animal husbandry.[67] Roberts's convoluted logic linked the absence of advanced vertebrate zoology to the poverty of the white population, which he claimed was "fifty percent poor people" unable to support such educational institutions. The various forms of South African backwardness and exoticness were to be continually rediscovered and marketed to access international philanthropy.[68]

Reflecting on the anticommunist purges nearly a generation later, De Kiewiet stated that Carnegie philanthropy and most other area studies educational research was an instrument of U.S. foreign policy in Africa.[69] From CIA interventions in decolonizing Africa in 1951 to explicit requests to provide cover for U.S. intelligence agencies to trustees of the American University and the American Council of Learned Societies who were CIA agents, De Kiewiet revealed, the Carnegie Corporation had a long history of intervention in Africa.[70] The pattern established before World War II of defending white supremacy included funding scholars like Robb, Richards, Robinson, and Roberts.

Examining a small sample of the research conducted through the Overseas Visitors Program by Robb, Richards, Robinson, and Roberts has been a means to assess the motivating factors guiding the Carnegie

Corporation's interest in South African social relations and the principles that guided it. Though Keppel would have been familiar with outstanding research by scholars in the black radical tradition, he allied Carnegie philanthropy with the chief intellectual architects of Afrikaner Nationalism, continuing a long tradition of Anglo-Saxon solidarity.

Research projects that brought more nuanced approaches to the study of black people as members of black freedom movements, migrants, workers, and gendered subjects like De Kiewiet's, which was shelved, reveals much about "racially mediated hierarchies affect[ing] access to data and determined success" in international studies.[71] These racially mediated hierarchies were the organizing principles that led to a shared *politics of knowledge about black people.* Research institutions, whether public or private, were populated by highly influential scholars who constituted an academic intelligentsia. These people and the organizations that supported them claimed to be the ultimate arbiters of scientific and objective knowledge about black people and Africa. Acting as gatekeepers, research project agenda advisers and evaluators, the various tiers of competing scholarship, were in position to build and to tear down whole departments and research groups and the scholars associated with them. Members of these racially mediated hierarchies were familiar with each other and debated each other and were part of the same epistemic community.[72] And yet the gentlemanly conduct of academic professions assiduously excluded discussion of the material conditions under which black academics conducted their research.[73] These material conditions included the fundamental power differential and resource gap across the racialized tiers of academic scholarship.

Coupled with the expansionist vision of race and empire that animated even the most isolationist members of this elite, such racially mediated hierarchies were particularly devastating to black academics and black institutions of higher education enmeshed in the slavery-foundation nexus type of relations of liberal paternalism. Keeping in mind that the development of scholarship about Africa in the English-speaking world was influenced by the subordinated status of black people globally, we can begin to more robustly consider why African Studies that concerned itself with black liberation remained a very low priority.[74] Liberal champions retained the African diaspora concept and kept its peoples in their place in the global racial hierarchy. Liberal consciousness almost universally defined race relations as racial accommodation and conciliation by black people to criminalization, dangerous working conditions, crowded and nonexistent housing, inferior schools and hospitals, and white-only representation in the halls of legislature and the judiciary. Ultimately, such racial conciliation and the influential interracial friendships that were its premise relied on antiblack Victorianism. Liberal friends of the Negro and friends of the Native did not endorse the many moments of armed resistance to economic depression and state bombardments by striking black workers and students in the U.S. and South Africa in the wake of race riots.[75] Armed resistance by black people revealed widespread social instability, potential economic disaster for American expansionists, and strong support for bypassing the devoted attentions of mostly impotent white spokesmen. Social scientific theories based on "race contact," "social distance," "defense of the disappearing black 'folk,'" and "customary law," coupled with Carnegie resources, actually prohibited scholarship that might have done real and permanent good.[76]

Scholarly work undertaken by Solomon Plaatje, Alain Locke, Samuel Molema, W.E.B. Du Bois, Horace Cayton, St. Clair Drake, Ralph Bunche, and Jack and Ray Simons provide reliable exemplars of the principles and analytic frames of the black radical tradition, scholarship that was attuned to the pursuit of the most radical imaginings for human freedom by fighting all ideas and practices that legitimated human chattelization. Identified as the black radical tradition, these principles and analytic frames were just one feature of the dynamic forms of resistance against a wide range of systemically brutal white nationalisms. Moreover, the black radical tradition in this instance of the production of social science research on the dynamics of power, white nationalism, and empire that are enmeshed in and created by the global racial contract is evidence of antagonist world visions. One vision of the world was of white over black and a personnel that could effectively link the administration of multiple white nations. Such partisan policies of national and wealthy class interests sought to explicitly demobilize and impede the decision making, problem solving, and organized resistance of the disadvantaged black people that they claimed to aid. Another vision of the world was one in which black emancipation was fought for. Such white nationalisms were particularly adept at playing the white vulnerability card and thereby deploying the racial logic of white vulnerability against those who were repeatedly cast as marauding black antagonists of human civilization. When non–South Africans supported the Afrikaners as segregationists and the British South

Africans as liberal race relations advocates they provided an international and scientific stamp of approval for white supremacist forms of governance and social organization; they helped resolve a set of intraracial conflicts, long mischaracterized as based on ethnicity, within these white men's countries. Disavowals of these motivating factors, principles, and values have led to undertheorizing the relationship between the rediscoveries of white misery and antiblackness.

CHAPTER 7

"I'll Give You Something to Cry About"

The Intraracial Violence of Uplift Feminism
in the Carnegie *Poor White Study* Volume,
*The Mother and Daughter of the Poor
Family*

A new knowledge politics about poor whites has emerged from feminist criticism of women's roles as agents of apartheid. The postapartheid concern among South African feminist literary critics about the politics of guilt, innocence, and culpability among white women, in particular, can be viewed as a new iteration of this examination of poor whites, albeit with a decided investment in the postcolonial feminist political project. This new way of thinking about the meanings of whiteness has important implications for the examination of the racial group poor whites and the making of gendered power relations. A central figure in the debates on White women's role (guilt) in apartheid is Afrikaner Nationalist propagandist and Carnegie Poor White Study researcher, M. E. Rothmann.

Here I am concerned both with this feminist literary criticism about white women and the feminist historical scholarship on poor whites and gender relations.[1] Both literary critics and the historians take up the question of how white women in South Africa have been represented historically, and have insights into how to understand the Carnegie Corporation's *Poor White Study* (1927–32), the international research project on poor Whites. Both literatures are also engaged in a political project of remembering the history of gender relations and feminist politicization in ways that reckon with the durability of white supremacy and with failed attempts to unmask white privilege. I proceed in the following with a reading of Marlene van Niekerk's *Triomf* ([1994]

1999) and M.E. Rothmann's *The Mother and Daughter of the Poor Family* (1932), with the express intention of complicating the grounds on which this attention to white women in the history of apartheid is being understood. By guilt/innocence/culpability, I do not mean good deeds and bad deeds but instead a cultural logic that normalizes: (1) white-on-white violence, (2) poor whites articulating themselves as white subjects apart from black people, and (3) middle-class female uplift ideologists. This cultural logic abets white supremacy and the proliferation of antiblackness.

The practices of subordination and the racialization and feminization of poverty that haunt South Africa and constitute premature death still require much more than the anachronistic and often useless handwringing of white guilt. Calls to remedy legal injuries in the postapartheid era have their origins in the very nature of the racial colonial order. Challenges to old and new forms of racial colonial order continue to face postracial disavowals by the globalized right wing.[2] While the study of white culpability for racial domination has a history, I am concerned with the ways in which white-on-white violence is consistently overlooked in the pursuit of guilty parties, in terms of individuals, groups, and state-sanctioned violence. Concern for black suffering is disingenuous in a world that relies on its extension and claims to be innocent of black suffering all at the same time. Feminist literary critics, writing about guilt/innocence/culpability, are seriously engaged in the work of demythologizing the grounds on which claims for white innocence can be made. And yet the grounds for demythologizing white innocence do not rest solely in violence toward black people; they also rest in claims made, but yet to be legible, about those whom we might call "would-be" white people. Nevertheless, like the material stuff that the racial contract consists of, tears shed over black suffering by non-black people transform little about power or social relations.

Feminist scholars coming out of the 1970s and 1980s participated in the historiographic shift toward "history from below" in South Africa, finding that African women were the most significant contingent of women to actively make a claim to participation in nationalism, to confront the state on the basis of membership in nationalist political movements. In this historiography, black women's political agency and organizational acumen stood out as especially distinctive—and especially representing the social location of white supremacy's imagination of "below"—by opposing it to a set of tropes and myths about demure, passive, Afrikaner Nationalist women. At the same time, many of these feminist scholars were trying to confront the historical writings in which Afrikaner women were depicted as tools of masculinist Afrikaner Nationalism, who deferred to male decision making and a male architecture of Afrikaner Nationalism. Afrikaner women had been characterized as having accepted the role of assistant, caretaker, and nurturer in the domestic arena, only to perform as directed toward Afrikaner Nationalist goals. Signature departures, such as historical research by Marijke Du Toit, demonstrated that Afrikaner women were actually actively engaged in political organizations that drove the direction of Afrikaner Nationalism. But despite this corrective, a more complex gender analysis of leadership by Afrikaner Nationalist women must include an examination of the race, class, and gender dimensions of the Afrikaner Nationalist women's agenda. Upper-class women were driven by uplift feminism, which guaranteed them public political identities and the role of policing the bodies of the poor. By "uplift feminism," I mean practices of identifying poor whites as a social problem that required explaining and translation, social training and rehabilitation, and vigilant articulation of the markers of appropriate forms of whiteness and white subject formation. The goal of uplift feminism was to transform this group of social anomalies or to diminish their impact enough to further reinforce the normalization of the segregated society necessary for Afrikaner Nationalism.

In addition, these feminist scholars began to articulate a consistent challenge to the discourse of responsibility for civilizing poor whites that emerged from colonial feminism.[3] Under the regime of colonial feminism and uplift feminism, poor women were driven to prove that they wanted to be rehabilitated, both in the household and in female-dominated workplaces. The amounts of charitable aid available to them were minuscule yet critical components of their household budgets, when combined with prostitution, low-wage and dangerous factory jobs, child labor, and liquor and diamond dealing. These were the combined resources available to address the vulnerability their families faced because of poverty.[4] And yet in interviews, parliamentary reports, and news coverage, the voices of poor women were most often distorted by the compulsion to vocalize their assent to Afrikaner Nationalism through adherence to uplift feminism's antiblack race rhetoric. Caricatured as people who readily accepted their genuine economic crisis and were comforted by the adherence to masculinist Afrikaner Nationalism, the class and race dimensions of whiteness provide important opportunities for historical reconceptualization. Scholars have also commented that depictions of poor whites in the *Poor White Study* differed substantially from the "respectability," "historical authenticity," "manliness," and wholesome rootedness in the land (a quixotic holdover from Calvinist explanations for settler indigeneity) produced prior to this study and contemporaneous with it.[5] While histories written by aid societies, clergy members and poverty bureaucrats flourished, critiques of the social science of racialized poverty would be minimized and marginalized and largely suppressed. Much of this critique has focused on community life and fuller elaborations of women's survival strategies in industrial South Africa. They were published first and emerged in fully elaborated form in 1970s and 1980s feminist social histories and feminist labor histories.

The first plank in the comprehensive challenge by feminist and gender scholars has been to assiduously reject the stereotype of the "man-made" Afrikaner. According to this stereotype, Afrikaner Nationalist women played a supplementary role in the orchestration and ideological architecture of apartheid. Thus Afrikaner women's lives needed no serious interrogation, and they could not be held accountable—or even capable of having political agency and will for that matter—for the legal injuries of racial segregation. But because both literatures, the account focusing on "man-made Afrikaner women" and the account attempting to correct that, avoid theorizing how the maternalist philanthropic work of Afrikaner Nationalist women was a type of intraracial violence as well as an expression of suppressing class conflict, they do not fully analyze the masculinist domination waged by upper-class white women. By "intraracial violence," I mean the practices of domination and subordination that are intimately connected to and part of the dynamic constitution of interracial violence, the racialization and feminization of poverty, and the social science of poverty but that operate within a racial group. In the rush, then, to demonstrate that Afrikaner Nationalist leaders were self-made women there seems to be too much valorization of a few women in history for having made it into the historical record and not enough critique of the masculinist practices that accompanied their acquisition of political leverage in the public sphere.

"Man-made" Afrikaner Nationalist women did exist, but they were poor white women made by Afrikaner Nationalist female leaders, who created public political identities for themselves through their toxic caretaking of their poor female charges and through their suppression of working-class Afrikaner women's political organizing around wages, employment, and housing.[6] While "made" by Afrikaner Nationalist female leaders, it would be incorrect and oversimplistic to call this power dynamic only "maternalism" because masculinity and male domination is never only merely enforced and embodied by males. More robust examination and theorization of the meanings of whiteness and white femaleness across class is absolutely integral to this debate. I argue that one of the more productive data sets available for theorizing ideas about white female political identity, culpability, innocence, and guilt is available in the vignettes, oral histories, and life histories collected for inclusion in the *Poor White Study*. In many ways, the *Poor White Study* stands as a very powerful site of the elaboration of the history of intraracial politics, because of its role in knowledge production, policy formation, and the constitution of the social science of poverty. While feminist literary critics in the postapartheid era are examining white female political identity and the idea that one has to be a perpetrator to enter history, too much of the political project is contained within frameworks where white women's political action always pivots around myths about black peoples' dependencies, needs, and vulnerabilities. This must be coupled with attention to the ways that whiteness has been constituted through white-on-white violence. When stern parents threaten weeping children with even worse punishments by saying, "I'll give you something to cry about," the desired effect is to silence the vocal expressions of sadness about having been punished and the indignity of having another's will proscribe one's actions. The power of the threat is that some other worse punishment could quite easily be devised and administered, and in an ageist modern world children usually comply, power relations being what they are in the domestic sphere and in all the spheres in which the social reproduction of communities occur. Such white-on-white violence, also, relies on having the socially legitimated use of force over one's charges. Unlike the arena of guilt, the affective position through which postapartheid scholars are criticizing the "man-made Afrikaner woman" concept, the threat of giving someone something to cry about is more direct. Guilt, so say these postapartheid critics, is evidence of a politics of white women's resistance to being figured as the caretakers and social guardians of black people. My hope is to redirect this concern with guilt toward intraracial violence and my capacity to give elite wealthy women something to cry about. I do not minimize black suffering at the hands of white domesticity but encourage postapartheid critics to do more decolonizing work so that the tears that are being spent will not be spent on hand-wringing and apologies about cannibalizing black people's lives in order to extend white domesticity. Instead, I have more faith in the capacity of postapartheid critics to address the intraracial politics of violence spurred by attempts to reproduce white domesticity. In the case of white guilt, disingenuous tears are often spilled to avoid rectifying and correcting legal and material injuries against black people. Paradoxically, expressions of white guilt are best understood as a rhetoric of empathy, with an implicit call for black people to take care of, witness, validate, and forgive innocent and vulnerable white people—crying. Thus the effects of antiblack violence are blindsided by the implicit call to recognize white guilt. The true victims in such cross-racial exchanges are then positioned as white people, and white women in particular.[7] Sometimes even quite astute politicized people engage in what Audre Lorde critiqued as "Oppression Olympics," what Andrea Smith has quite usefully recast as the "three pillars of white supremacy." and what Zenzele Isoke has called "structural intersectionality." Rather than deploy what Ange-Marie Hancock has called "intersectional solidarity" in order to highlight the quite complex and different ways that logics of white supremacy affect differently located and differently constituted racial subjects, people demand that their weeping be acknowledged and witnessed by black people.[8] There is certainly weeping to be done over the continued legacies and reproduction of forms and dynamics of apartheid, but some of those forms are misrecognized because of false ideas about who is supposedly immune to the vagaries of white supremacy and antiblackness. Poor white people are not immune to antiblackness. If antiblackness is indeed a world-making concept, then it constitutes, shapes, and affects many different locations and racial subjects.

Discussing the race, class, and gender dynamics of the racialization of poverty among poor whites requires delinking naturalized racial formations/social identities and political categories that constitute whiteness. Poor whites were an essential racial ingredient in the manufacture of Afrikaner Nationalism as a gendered national project. A critical reading of Marie Elizabeth Rothmann's *The Mother and the Daughter of the Poor Family* tells us both about the politicization of poor white identities and the great women philanthropists who articulated a maternalist and paternalist Afrikaner Nationalism—but instead of valorizing them, such a critical reading enables us to *de-stool* (remove and impeach) them and redirect the practices of feminist historiography. Rothmann's report for the *Poor White Study* provides a cartography of how the history of philanthropy and welfarism bound poor white women and upper-class white women together in a dynamic of intraracial violence that profoundly extends the theorization of white female guilt and culpability. I find that the feminist literary critical interest in culpability and questions of white female guilt has a profound resonance with the valorizing of Afrikaner Nationalist feminist historical figures like Rothmann among feminist historical scholars. Thus, to reiterate, I seek to make visible white privilege and white female culpability that enables us to analyze white women as perpetrators of racial, class, and gender violence, with the target being poor white victims. In this way I distinguish how poor white Afrikaner women were made into tools of Afrikaner Nationalism by other women: more privileged, higher-status Afrikaner Nationalist women like M.E. Rothmann. Poor white women were the "man-made" women[9] that South African feminists have labored so long to challenge in nationalist historiography about men. Some feminists have valorized the life and work of Rothmann, and the cohort of women she mobilized is a critical location for this analysis. Close examination of the role played by Afrikaner Nationalist feminist historical figures suggests that they functioned not only as promoters of what I designate as uplift feminism but also as key theorists of Afrikaner Nationalism and, paradoxically, as suppressers of poor Afrikaner Nationalist women's political organizing.

For example, feminist literary critics have rejected the sentimentality that created a guileless, innocent white femininity, especially in post-apartheid analyses of fiction about the apartheid era.[10] Georgina Horrell has noted:

> The elaborate masquerade of the feminine is a means of deflection, the means of covering up a crime, theft: illicit acquisition of power. . . . Masquerade, the necessary performance of guiltless, innocent, self-effacing, and self-sacrificing white femininity is . . . an 'obsession' or 'narcissistic insurance' which remains implicit in the writing of white women.[11]

Similarly, in Irma Du Plessis's estimation, in order to become a subject of history there must be the possibility of being represented as a perpetrator, not simply as a tool of another's political imaginary or an innocent victim. At the same time that much attention is being paid to guilt, these scholars have begun the process of identifying Afrikaner feminist rejection of racialized colonialism. Thus in Marlene van Niekerk's literary criticism and novels there is an antiracist, antisexist history worthy of recuperation that has been suppressed by masculinist Afrikaner Nationalism. Each of these major scholars on the race, class, and gender dynamics of whiteness and Afrikaner Nationalist whiteness takes up white women's agency and role in white supremacy in ways that require serious attention to the manner in which white women have in the past (and in the present) entered history. These feminist literary critics theorize the race, class, and gender dynamics of white women in the historiography of Afrikaner Nationalism.

Horrell and Du Plessis argue that white female culpability is essential to theorizing the investments in white supremacist political organizing by white women. While Horrell is concerned mostly with the representations of whiteness produced during the era of the Truth and Reconciliation Commission and with the writings of white female antiapartheid activists, Du Plessis is concerned with the domestic world as a site of colonial encounter. Furthermore, Du Plessis makes visible the ways in which white female charity—especially as directed toward nonwhite children—produces female dilemmas enshrouded in the language of philanthropy and welfarism. White female charity invokes familial interdependence in ways that obscure feminist political organization and antagonistic interests. In the scripts available for white women, their role is to be the ever-faithful helpmeets of Afrikaner Nationalism, whose ethics emerge only when confronted with the chance to treat nonwhite children as indulged pets[12] or as inevitable "baby maids."[13] Du Plessis urges more examination of the sites and practices where white female authority and power are expressed. Furthermore, she points to the ways that notions of sisterhood and familial language mystify white female authority and power. Such notions mask power inequalities, cultivate false dependencies, and prohibit mutuality, solidarity, and interdependence.

Like Du Plessis, I follow Marlene van Niekerk's fiction for the actualization of this theoretical search for white female culpability and guilt. By foregrounding the dynamic relationships between white Afrikaner women across race and class divides, van Niekerk's fiction functions as a critical theoretical text on white women's role in the history of apartheid.[14] In the case of *Triomf* (1994), as in the case of *Agaat* (2006), which Du Plessis examines, one important site of white female culpability is in the politics of dependence and care in the household. In *Triomf*, however, the targets of similarly damning representations are the social workers who monitor the one female member of an impoverished white family, Molly. The experience of being made into white people through the forces of masculinist nationalism offers numerous trajectories for politicization, most requiring taking on sensibilities of whiteness such as deservingness and bourgeois morality and decoupling from complicating interdependencies with black people and blackness. But, as a "black female cultural reader,"[15] I am again assiduously concerned about those whites for whom relations to and with blackness most profoundly reveal the white supremacist project.

I depart from Du Plessis by reading *Triomf* rather than *Agaat*. In *Triomf*, we are not presented with a heroic white woman on a mission to save everybody, as in *Agaat*. Nor are we offered seductive moralistic identifications with victims of antiblack racism, also as in *Agaat*. Nor are we given a protagonist who consolidates her class status as a white woman of advantage through her identifications with black people, as in *Agaat*. Instead, in *Triomf* we are confronted with petty, annoying, silly, even foppish attempts at uplift feminism, coupled with the failures of poor whites to represent supremacy and power. Thus van Niekerk compels the reader to consider white female guilt and culpability in two new ways: the guilt and shame of racialized poverty and the guilt of social workers and proselytizers with churches, charity organizations, and the Nationalist Party. This is an example of the interconnected guilt caused by revealing white poverty and white privilege and intraracial brutality and white on white subordination.

In van Niekerk's *Triomf* poor white women—like the protagonist Molly—are represented as taking responsibility by bearing the guilt of their circumstances openly. Her family is guilty simply by virtue of being *poor and white*. Their abject condition then creates the space for upper-class white women's claims to racialized and gendered innocence. As a member of the racialized and hated white poor, this protagonist's white femininity is the equivalent of debt—a debt she cannot ever be innocent of. She embodies shame and remorse and silences. As a poor person, she lacks the power and privilege of self-protection. Molly experiences social silencing in the household, yet as the narrator of this novel she is represented through a constant inner life of long talks with her dog. Ultimately, this constant mumbling banter does not compensate for her silencing. Marlene van Niekerk does not allow Molly innocence.

Molly and her family are othered by the white people in their community, such that there is no possibility for them to claim any ground in innocence. Being poor does not make them innocent of complicity with antiblackness. Instead, being poor whites—the kind of people who are not supposed to exist—highlights the ways in which intraracial violence among white people is so critical to maintaining white supremacy. Innocence belongs to people who have class standing, legitimacy, status, and reputations to protect. The poignancy of the configuration of this family and this imprisoned female character is created precisely through their inability to be the "deserving poor." All the members of the Benades family are pariahs in their community. Pariahs cannot use the ground of innocence to make their resistance. Figuring poor whites' pariah status in the forefront of the novel reminds us that there are no clear breaks with the past. Postapartheid reconciliation happens through remembering, albeit differently understanding but still remembering the past, particularly the era that led up to grand apartheid, which offers much to consider about the circulation of the scientific justifications that granted people like the Benades the chance to become "good white victims." Once innocence and good white victims are done away with, there might be a chance for a white writing in South Africa that can complicate the study of whiteness by paying attention to the ways in which white poverty constituted a dangerous visibility to philanthropists and social workers as agents of social control.

If white female relationships with black men and black women always turn white women into long-suffering victims who are unaware of their exercise of privilege and abuse, how can we fully theorize guilt and culpability? What if we were to consider other locations or sites, such as social work discourse, and practices where white women exercised authority and power over white people? And what if we were to consider locations or sites where the exercise of authority and power is almost always misread as beneficial, uncontroversial, and noble, a site of culture and state functioning that has been decolonized only by its nonwhite racialized victims and not by its primarily white female agents and functionaries? Those concerned women who were in a position to ameliorate or surveil and regulate the situation of poor whites came from political parties, journalism, theater and the fine arts, higher education, the clergy, banking and credit institutions, and social work.[16] In addition, they tapped into an international philanthropic investment by the Carnegie Corporation in segregationist economic development among racialized groups.[17] Despite such vastly different material and social interests, these social forces converged with an American philanthropic organization to draw the global color line.

Social work discourses, practices, and personnel have played a decisive role in demonizing the poor and racializing poverty, so that nonwhite poverty comes to be seen as normal and culturally appropriate while white poverty comes to be seen as a paradox or a civilization-threatening social crisis. Racialization of poor whites, I argue, entails the demonization of this group through the code words and empirical data-gathering techniques of scientific racism, in order to identify and assess them and demonize them and thereby claim them as an important social problem in need of assistance and rehabilitation. Further, racialization of poor whites involves "decontamination" of poor white subjects from their complex dependencies on nonwhite subjects. Ultimately, the racialization of poor whites characterizes their disappearance as a benign or beneficent act.

The racialization of poverty is constructed by a nexus of meanings, whereby being poor means lacking the capacity for self-governance, both in a democratic and in an individual sense, and, thereby, being a target/beneficiary for nonstate and state actors' surveillance relentlessly described as charity.[18] Elite Afrikaner Nationalist women had power; they even fought to have power. They were not silent but left records in scores of conference records, case histories, and vignettes about families and children that constituted a record of state surveillance. Indeed, Afrikaner Nationalist women provided what they considered a public good but what most feminists would consider toxic caretaking. Their vignettes and case studies stood in as the signature legitimation of state intervention in the lives of poor whites. A scholar who has considered this public record explains:

> Vignettes, like many discursive constructions, produce and are produced by the practices and populations they supposedly describe. . . . The magazines produced by the child rescue movement were intended to inform, with the aim of eliciting donations from the reader, but they can also be understood as propaganda, reconstituting the everyday phenomenon of the street child as an object of pity and a victim of vice and neglect, and a threat to and the embodiment of the future of nation, race, and Empire. In addition, they modeled the behavior of the reader, encouraging benevolence in the rich, and establishing norms of child care amongst the poor.[19]

Benevolence and care of the poor through social work were cornerstones of an ideology that granted authority to upper-class women in their role as champions of the colonial racial order. They relied on the propaganda about poverty to signal familiar frameworks and concepts that demonized the poor, ostensibly to rehabilitate them. In other words, in order to deconstruct what has become a major myth about how race, class, and gender have functioned in Afrikaner women's political organizing—that Afrikaner women were simply unthinking tools of Afrikaner nationalist men—we have to examine white female culpability and guilt in the colonial past, not only in the 1950s through 1990s era. White female culpability and guilt thus have to be understood not only as the postapartheid masquerade of vulnerable femininity but also in the context of coloniality, where white women's political identity rested on ideas about illicit theft of power and propaganda about the proper way to behave. Those practices and ideas that enabled some Afrikaner Nationalist women to create public sphere political identities for themselves also constituted abuse of other, poor Afrikaner women.

In addition to the structural and everyday atrocities borne by black men and women in the households of white people, there is a set of everyday atrocities borne by poor white people. A host of supposedly life-sustaining public welfare institutions and their private iterations in actuality created more harm than good for the racialized poor. These include the reserve, the compound, the labor colony, the industrial labor school, the welfare agency, the hospital, the jail, and the sanatorium, as well as the kitchen/parlor/cement-floor backhouse. Critics agree (now that we have agreed that apartheid was wrong) that the reserve, the compound, and the kitchen/parlor/cement-floor backhouse were institutions designed for premature death. There is a lack of consensus, however, on the racial logic of institutions such as the labor colony, the industrial labor school, the welfare agency, the hospital, the jail, and the sanatorium, in part because these are recuperated as modern, sanitary expressions of biopower. If we take seriously the race, class, and gender dimensions of these latter institutions, we find that, like the first category, they are profoundly racialized and profoundly death driven.

When we begin to think about whiteness as loss and misery rather than privilege alone, we can more carefully analyze systems, patterns, and practices of intrawhite violence that are as much at the root of white supremacist power as antiblack violence.[20] In other words, to not consider what white people are willing to do and have done to each other in the pursuit of constructing fully coherent whiteness is to continue to miss the complicated ways in which most "would-be" white people are drawn into white supremacy. Even though the historical record on working-class and unskilled putative white people indicates that as a group produced through racial subordination the greatest majority of white people are hailed by white supremacy, I am arguing that we are misrecognizing the actual ways in which white supremacy draws in and utilizes many different kinds of would-be white people.

MOTHERING POOR WHITES: THE POLITICAL TRAJECTORY OF MARIE ELIZABETH ROTHMANN

Both the biography of Marie Elizabeth Rothmann—valorized extraordi-

nary woman—and the ethnographic vignettes that she recorded constitute a data set about the politics of personal responsibility, which I now
explore. I focus on her biography and the ethnographic vignettes that she
related in her volume of the *Poor White Study, The Mother and Daughter
of the Poor Family,* to demonstrate how and why attempts to examine
white female culpability/innocence/guilt can be enhanced through attention to earlier historical intraracial practices of inequality. As more historical work has been done on Rothmann, even her name has changed.
For example, by 1932 convention she was known publicly in print by her
initials to diminish the significance of her gender for readers, but historians no longer do this, partly as a result of the labor of feminist historians.
Class was expressed in Afrikaner Nationalism in three ways: blaming the
racialized poor, moral panic, and the politics of disgust. So while male
Afrikaner Nationalists claimed to be advocates for vulnerable poor whites
and hoped to garner support via pity and sympathy, their female counter-
parts trafficked in the disciplinary regime of shame. Rothmann's life no
doubt signals the extraordinary achievements of a female social scientist
and political leader in a time when women were actively prevented from
rising to their full potential. However, what I would call the achievement
feminism model did not really enable poor women's voices or critiques of
economic systems or economic decisions to be foregrounded. Moreover,
Rothmann's leadership did not promote destabilization of the gendered
class politics of Afrikaner Nationalism, which were organized around the
white standard of living, domesticity, and upper-class aspirations.

Rothmann was a founding theorist of Afrikaner Nationalism and a
key figure in the consolidation of a mass movement to secure political,
cultural, and social power and status for Afrikaner Nationalists. She
published a number of books about the life of the traditional *trekboer*
(pastoralist tenant farmer) communities and as a journalist and architect of key aspects of Afrikaner Nationalism—especially with regard to
the role of women in the domestic sphere and all arenas of feminized
labor. She identified many ways in which the domestic sphere and feminized workplaces could be sites for the Afrikaner Nationalist political
project. An analysis of her advocacy for poor white women to adopt the
white standard of living provides an insight into the politics of uplift
feminism. It also reveals a depoliticizing of poor white women, and perhaps surprisingly a practice of reinforcing white poverty. Though upper-
class Afrikaner Nationalist women may not have been "man-made
women," they secured their privileged access to leadership and public
identities by making an entire class of man-made women among poor

white women.

In addition to her journalism, political fiction, and use of elementary education as a principle venue for the transmission, mobilization, and theorization of Afrikaner Nationalism, Rothmann was organizing secretary of the Afrikaanse Christelike Vrouevereniging (ACVV), an Afrikaner Nationalist women's charity and mutual assistance organization. At this time her interest in the home life of the Afrikaner family reached it highest point. Rothmann's ACVV work consisted of organizing nursing, maternity homes, libraries, rural schools, and training for social workers in rural areas. Each of these are key nation-building sites, albeit not sites for promoting democracy. Rothmann's experiences and history of leadership of female and male social workers and educators made her the most appropriate woman to be appointed to the Carnegie Commission's *Poor White Study,* which provided an international audience that was deeply committed to white supremacy and segregated racial regimes as a solution to both the "Negro Problem" and the "Poor White Problem," as they were understood globally.

In 1933 Rothmann's devotion to the National Party won her election to the vice presidency of the main committee of the party in the Cape. She contributed greatly to the dissemination of the findings of the *Poor White Study* as a member of the continuation committee of the 1934 Volkskongres, which established the paradigm for the national Department of Welfare.[21] She wrote up the history of the ACVV in 1954 in the books *Ons Saamreis* (Our Journey Together) and *Ons Voortgang* (Our Moving Forward). In 1966 she was the recipient of a Carnegie Corporation Overseas Visitors Grant, which she used to conduct research comparing white poverty and interactions between black and white people plein the rural woodcutting areas of Kentucky in the United States and Knysna in South Africa.[22] Carnegie commissioners, like their British philanthropy forebears, understood the world and historical change to be directed by white people.[23] I have argued that Carnegie commissioners contributed to the articulation of scientific justifications for a global color line, in which race relations consisted of white people with "barbarian virtues" using force and necessary violence to civilize the world of nonwhite people. This is precisely why poor whites in the United States and South Africa would have seemed to have some traits and experiences worth comparing.[24]

Rothmann's activity and leadership were essential in so many Afrikaner Nationalist cultural, media, and women's and political organizations that I would argue it is quite appropriate to consider her the

mother/female originator of post–Anglo-Boer War Afrikaner Nationalism. She said of herself that her "long history of sympathy" with poor
whites enabled her to discern and offer terms and frameworks for categorizing them, a categorization in which she differentiated between
those whose economic failure was the result of individual problems and
those whose economic failure was the result of cultural location and
geographic isolation. She noted that clergy and doctors quite often took
her to visit families who posed the greatest problems for them. Rothmann's role was understood by these clergy and doctors as amplifying
sympathy for poor whites and propagating a cultural shift wherein poverty was seen as a condition to be ashamed of.[25] In fact, Rothmann
clocked more hours, covered more territory, and visited more families
and communities than any of the men on the *Poor White Study* research
team. She did, as it turns out, spend more time in the field, but this did
not necessarily give her more discernment.

Rothmann visited 462 homes as part of the Carnegie *Poor White
Study,* 322 in the Cape and 140 in Transvaal. Of these she estimated
that 126 (27 percent) were poor because of "personal defect." Although
she contradictorily noted that to classify 30 percent of Afrikaners as
poor because of personal defect would be an overstatement, her data
confirmed this generalization.[26] This approximately one-third of the
population that was undevelopable and incapable of rehabilitation
through economic opportuny, social guidance, or moral training
required some other means of treatment. Something else would be
required for dealing with them. Rothmann's was a classic racialized culture of poverty explanation. Her hundreds of interviews caricature poor
whites. Like other members of the *Poor White Study* research team,
Rothmann failed to examine how the stringent and punitive policies
attached to charity and aid articulated with the structural explanations
for poverty in order to focus on reproducing middle-class white domesticity.

Rothmann described the problems associated with those whites who
failed to become upwardly mobile as (1) laziness, (2) immorality in the
household (especially signaled by syphilis rates among mothers), (3) isolation from cultural and uplifting pursuits, (4) wanderlust and an inability to stay in one place, (5) expectations of living too well, and (6) men
who deserted their families. She failed to address some of the reasons
families were on the move: families feared their children would be taken
away and institutionalized; men moved from place to place in pursuit of
jobs in order to provide for their wives and children; and charity orga-

nizations had residency and character reference requirements and also required proof that a person was not trying to "get over" on the system.[27]

Like most other commentators, Rothmann missed that her charges-*cum*-informants were long-term outsiders to the system. It was obviously quite hard not to be seen as taking advantage and refusing to participate in the sacrificial, self-respecting success that Afrikaner Nationalism required of its members. Each place they started out seemed reasonable and open because, of course, with black people confined to reserves the land seemed empty." But starting out in each new place was difficult, as securing credit for seed, or having the money to purchase tools for irrigation, often was not forthcoming. Indeed, many towns were quite happy to evict any poor white families who arrived, and referrals to Rothmann's agencies could also mean being sentenced to any number of labor colonies.[28] Rothmann condemned the roving life of new town dwellers who seemed to lack work. Yet as a charity and welfare organizer, she knew intimately the rules for applying for state and church aid, and most likely had written many of them.

Rothmann's descriptions in *The Mother and Daughter of the Poor Family* follow the genealogy of particular families to point to the degree of degradation and the moment when the families' prospects for self-sufficiency collapsed. Organizing her case studies around loss, she focused on how most of the families that she interviewed had been financially independent owners of the means of production only one generation before. Rothmann's attention to genealogy emerged from an understanding about family wealth that assumes first that people have it and second that it will remain within a family from one generation to another. None of this genealogical research commented on recurring economic and environmental collapse endemic to capitalism or structural economic decisions such as fencing, the elimination of trusts, the expansion of the railroads and the consequent elimination of the transport riding industry, or the negative economic impact of removing young women and men from family economies via apprenticeships and factory work. These endemic events and structural economic decisions had many soothsayers among the very same proponents of Afrikaner Nationalism. The fact that families did not have wealth or previously had wealth in land and livestock and other real property and had lost that wealth coincides far too neatly with Afrikaner Nationalist historical myths about the prosperity and wealth that was supposed to be the natural station of Afrikaners. While this set of notions powerfully reinforced a political theology (of divine inheritance), it was relayed by Rothmann outside of economic history in a way that made Afrikaners the natural inheritors of wealth, regardless of global, regional, or local economic conditions or shifting laws, conditions, or capital ventures. This rendering of Afrikaner economic history reproduced mythologies that harmed poor whites.

When Rothmann commented on immorality in the home, she described women's immorality or the wife having syphilis, but there was no mention of the husband also having syphilis. In some sense her understandings of such health crises were confined to the belief that the mother and wife was the "angel in the house," the arbiter of morality and sexual habits of all members of the household. If the mother and wife was not in that position, she was failing her husband and children. Indeed, if she had married a man with a disease as socially stigmatized as syphilis, again, she was to blame for choosing a future of degeneration. This gendering of the household subordinated women.

Among the observations Rothmann made was the high number of children who had been institutionalized in each home, taken away to be taught to work, but she never asked critical questions about how the parents she interviewed felt about the removal of their children. Rothmann strongly endorsed the breakup of families, because, she argued, being apprenticed offered a better chance for the children. Rothmann's analyses unfortunately pitted child welfare against family welfare and delinked children from families and communities in order to redirect their affiliations and loyalties to the Afrikaner nation. Perhaps she was not disturbed about the institutionalization of her interviewees' children because she was more concerned with decorum, proper homes, efficient work patterns, and the white standard of living. Nor did she inquire about the availability of public education for the parents or what means they used in the informal economy to secure food and shelter. In many ways the questions Rothmann asked, and the questions she did not ask, set the stage for a very long valorization of Afrikaner Nationalist women in leadership and a prolonged and profound disciplining, silence, and subordination of poor white charity recipients.

In the description of the X family, Rothmann registers again and again her shock at the unkempt, dirty house where they lived and their visibly unkempt, dirty bodies and clothes. She was repulsed by a story told to her by one woman during an interview about her husband running away to live in a "kaffir" village, to get the "dirty kaffir women's" diseases. Rothmann asked her interviewee the following questions: Why had the woman married such a man? Why had her mother permitted her to be involved with such a man? Why had an unmarried sister lived in the same one-room house with her and her husband?[29] Rothmann's series of questions strike me as biased and intentionally avoiding the precarious economic circumstances of her informants. Through her questions she is redirecting the cause of poverty to a moral culpability. Her life commitment to Afrikaner Nationalism, clearly demonstrated by her biography and political trajectory, biased her research.

Meanwhile, the woman Rothmann interviewed compared herself to black people, expressing gratitude that she, at least, was not as wretched as black people. Rothmann took this antiblack declaration as a sign that the woman had a measure of self-respect and some moral, racial, gender, and class aspirations. Expressing such antiblack sentiments was key to being taken as the sympathetic and striving poor. The interviewee's expressions of racist attitudes and a belief in white supremacy proved, for her interlocutor, her adherence to whiteness.[30] However, as Du Toit has argued, many of the interviewees and other poor white women who sought to supplement their food, clothing, and shelter budgets with tiny amounts of aid from charity organizations deployed antiblack Afrikaner Nationalist rhetoric and loyalty in exchange for that aid. In essence, I am arguing, and Du Toit's findings concur, that many of Rothmann's interviewees deployed antiblack rhetoric as the currency of exchange for receiving the aid and advocacy of upper-class social workers. This aid and charitable support functioned as a small part of a complicated income stream for household and family budgets.

In addition, antiblack sentiment and rhetoric were seen as key to their rehabilitation and reform—from the social failure of white poverty. Furthermore, antiblack sentiment was the one thing that poor white women could deploy to demonstrate their commonality with Rothmann and other middle-class social workers materially, culturally, or socially.

One clue that the members of the X family were not actually that concerned with measuring up to the standards of whiteness that the *Poor White Study* was teaching was the provocative disclosure about a family member who had been convicted for stealing from an African employer. So while Rothmann's interviewees were mouthing complaints about certain kinds of work being beneath a white man's dignity, Rothmann's assurance that such work was perfect for them—as poor whites—was missing the joke that the interviewees were playing on her.[31] They expressed antiblack views and at the same time pointed to their traffic with, interactions with, and dependency on black people for wages and income. While one could argue that such interview disclosures should be read as poor whites lamenting never being able to be proper white people and being degraded by being surrounded by and dependent on black people, it is also true that these dependencies and interrelationships with black people, while not properly called solidarities, were certainly as essential to income, food provision, housing, employment, and household income as the highly scripted and regulated attempts to gain support from middle-class whites.[32]

But there is another noteworthy dimension of this antiblack rhetoric. By responding to the cue that they knew social workers wanted to hear, these interviewees were deploying an age-old strategy of dissemblance and "signifying" among the racialized poor who are dependent on state income supports. It is not unusual to be suspicious of these claims of superiority to Africans, especially since the claims contain the rhetorical slippage of being jealous of and also being employed by these same black people.

PROVING LOYALTY TO THE GOVERNMENT AND THE AFRIKANER NATIONALIST MOVEMENT

Part of the rhetoric of poor white women was a written or verbal exchange of performed deference and loyalty to the government and the Afrikaner Nationalist movement and to whatever political parties claimed to be providing the needed food, land grant, stock loan, housing, clothes. There was a "commonly expressed declaration of political loyalty."[33] It was important to demonstrate that one intended to do as told and to follow the signals that would make one deserving and respectable as a recipient of such aid. What we do not have in Rothmann's study is a record of poor women's protests against the expectations of deference and loyalty.[34] Why did poor white women have to say they were loyal to a national or provincial government or church authorities that clearly failed to provide for them? Given the race, class, and gender dynamics of the stringent welfare controls, one should expect to find poverty rights and welfare rights campaigns flourishing around the world. Poor white women "paid" the national, provincial, municipal, and church authorities with their deference, loyalty, and gratitude. Their deference was recorded and required by upper-class white handlers whose philanthropic identity depended on the degradation of their poor white charges. Poor white women walked a very narrow discursive tightrope, because they had to demonstrate their loyalty and work ethic while listening to female social workers transmit the message that as white women they were entitled to be in relationship with other white people and with other people who lived at a certain class level. But poor white women must have known and had the experience that state and church aid could just as easily be taken as it was given and that they would have to supplement the state aid to be able to live. Moreover, they could also see that receiving church and state aid put them in a separate social category from other whites and did not guarantee that they would be accepted as whites or that they would emerge decisively from poverty into whiteness with property rights, privileges, and status.

In the material sense, to be able to guarantee that they would qualify for food and monetary aid poor white women had to have the capacity to speak out of both sides of their mouths. They had to satisfy the currency of antiblack rhetoric that was important for Afrikaner Nationalist social workers, and they had to report that they were in close enough contact with black people to be in danger of becoming the kind of social problem that the same social workers would consider a major social crisis. The *Poor White Study* interviews indicate that these were mischievous interactions that document much more about the creation of a racial other than about the stated aim of the research project—discovering the origins of white poverty. As historical documents, these interviews should be understood as representations that signify on a symbolic economy that determined whether one was institutionalized (in the labor colony, the industrial school, or somebody's kitchen) or allowed the misery and volatility of employment as free labor (in factories, kitchens, or the informal sector).

Rothmann's descriptions become mere caricature of two categories: the good poor and the bad poor. These naturalized categories are premised on the belief that charity and assistance are beneficial and a heavily mortgaged public good for which the poor should have been grateful. The requirement that people demonstrate self-respect in a highly scripted fashion that really only had one feature that could very easily link poor whites to upper- and middle-class whites—vocal expression of antiblack opinion—seems a strange means by which to measure their economic status. However, the requirement that interviewees denounce black people was clearly a very essential monitor of their need-worthiness and character.

In addition, the focus on genealogies of wealth accumulation allowed Rothmann to reinforce ideas about the angel in the house or that mother whose task under nationalism is to maintain and reproduce the highest moral standards in the domestic sphere and thereby produce new citizens. Blaming women for marrying bad men, encouraging young women to work as domestics so that they would have training in proper middle-class standards of living before marrying, prevented Rothmann from recognizing that her would-be charges were actually being victimized by the requirement that they comply with a whole battery of social welfare expectations. Moreover, this set of ideologies prevented her from realizing when her interviewees were speaking back to her role as an agent of the state. And yet it was these poor white women who were precisely the sort that Rothmann and the ACVV were determined to transform, not just in their rhetoric, but also in their expectations. Rothmann's pitch, because these home visits and interviews were also about the goal of teaching poor whites how to behave by asking them intimate questions about their standard of living, was to get them to articulate that they would become good stewards of white privilege and white power. Thus, by securing verbal assent, Rothmann and her fellows could avoid issues like land tenancy and equal wages for women.

Rothmann details how successful uplift can be by talking about a poor white woman she had heard of who had been tested as subnormal, yet become an orderly and neat housewife who was able to save to buy good furniture. These criteria—neatness, domestic bliss, and good-quality furniture—do not reflect very much objectively. But the meanings attached to these things were the intangible features of whiteness that Afrikaner Nationalism was trying to cultivate in poor whites in order to whiten them. What sort of relationship or fate would Rothmann have expected for the same woman had she not been able to achieve these things? Perhaps evidence of her sympathy even when tinged with raw repulsion was Rothmann's statement that many poor whites were "shrewd, not mental[ly] subnormal."[35] Here she signaled that poor whites sometimes were motivated by a criminal-like conniving instinct rather than by genetic degeneration. Certainly one person's conniving is another's thoughtful way to guarantee their income stream.[36]

CONCLUSION

Studying Rothmann's engagement with interviewees during the Carnegie Commission is very instructive as to her viewpoints on their material conditions and status. Rothmann-like parliamentary debates and most popular and academic renderings of poor whiteism posed the same distinction between the poor white and the white poor. The "poor white" and "white poor" language used by the Carnegie *Poor White Study* was indicative of this powerful class and race divide, as one indicated the sympathetic poor and the other indicated the unsympathetic poor. In the 1914 publication, *White and Black: An Inquiry into Africa's Greatest Problem*, E.J.C. Stevens anticipated the typology of poor whites that was used later in the Carnegie *Poor White Study*.

> There are three types of poor whites. The first [being] the deserving poor without skills that are trapped in manual labor. These people are willing to work but need education and skills. The second are those who have lost self-respect and the ambition to lift themselves and their families. The third are born into poor whiteism with an atmosphere that corrupts their morals. These are likely to become criminals but could become useful members of society if they are rehabilitated.[37]

In these ways, this engagement with poor and working-class women constituted a "poverty knowledge" that was was highly racialized through the logics of scientific racism. Like uplift feminism throughout the British Empire, the colonial dimensions of racial hierarchy shaped the imaginary of feminist political action and the political agenda of feminists. By making careful, almost typological distinctions between themselves and the type of whiteness that they inhabited and cultivated and that which was available to their wards, Afrikaner Nationalist feminists participated actively in the racialization of poverty. For Rothmann, as for the other Carnegie *Poor White Study* researchers, to be the deserving poor was to be those who had been put on a downward spiral of poverty through no fault of their own. To be the undeserving poor was to be among those whose deliberate and willful acts of self-destruction should be condemned. Rothmann did not hedge on her conclusions about this. She argued that those who did not have the will to change their situation—to become white consumers, to become white mothers—had to be targeted the most aggressively for rehabilitation/disappearance. She hesitated to suggest direct control over their reproduction but was quite frank about her belief that every effort had to be made to prevent poor white young women from marrying just to get out of the house. Instead, Rothmann argued that domestic work, especially for women, could be a sort of saving grace that would give them higher expectations—through their contact with the objects, furnishings, manners, and social expectations of those who could afford domestic workers—about how their lives ought to be.

Families depended on the hustling of sex, liquor, diamonds, young women's factory wages, and renting housing to meet their basic needs.[38] Many poor white families supplemented their low wages through charity organizations, disability pensions, and dependency relationships with black people.[39] Thus, as Du Toit has indicated, poor white women had to claim Afrikaner identity to access Afrikaner Nationalist charity organizations as sources of jobs, food, and clothing. Poor whites came from rural areas where work habits and practices were shaped by dependency relations with black sharecroppers, tenant farmers, midwives, other domestic servants, and woodcutters who had been forcibly removed and cheated out of their land. Cross-class ties among whites had to deny and suppress the significance of these relations of dependency between black and white rural people. This means we should all be quite skeptical about the role played by Afrikaner Nationalist uplift feminists who certainly did not see poor whites as their social or racial equals.[40]

While much important social history on the work, community, and family life of poor white women in Johannesburg and Cape Town is available in the research that has been conducted, too much of that data is overshadowed by an unwillingness to deal with poor whites as a racial and gender grouping. When poor whites have been taken up as a complicated community, they have been analogized to blacks or uncritically folded into the politics of Afrikaner Nationalism.[41] What I have done here is to begin from theories of representations about white people and histories of toxic care and supposed benevolence, which reflect intraracial harm. Moreover, I have examined the race, class, and gender dimensions of the making of poor whites as a racial group by taking seriously the uplift and achievement feminism of upper-class Afrikaner Nationalist women. I have characterized the interests of poor white women hailed by Afrikaner Nationalism as shaped by dependencies on precarious income streams, rhetorical affiliation with Afrikaner Nationalism, and antiblack sentiments. I have taken into account the lack of sustained attention to social welfare, bullying, and domestic ideology within the study of Afrikaner Nationalism and poor-whiteness. And I have turned away from the overdetermined view that poor white Afrikaner women entered history vis-à-vis authority and privilege over black women. I have instead turned my attention to their subordination by Afrikaner Nationalist women. Attention to this subordination enables a more thorough examination of white female culpability, guilt and innocence, and its legacies in the postapartheid era. I have presented a model for how and why to use the *Poor White Study* data about poor white women to think through the role of intraracial violence and adherence to white supremacy.

The implications of considering the *Poor White Study* in the examination of guilt/innocence/culpability are that we begin to more soberly assess the ways in which white-on-white violence constitutes the grounds for cross-racial violence, in particular antiblackness and the fear of contamination by the differential proximities to blackness. Indeed, the project of white supremacy profoundly relies on poor whites articulating themselves as white subjects independent and innocent of meaningful social and economic and cultural linkages to black people and the persistent presence of upwardly mobile female strivers enthusiastically deploying masculinist social regulation. To have to whiten white people suggests that intraracial violence is a kind of durable interracial violence.

Conclusion

Race Makes Nation

A racial attack on black people sits at the heart of global affairs and the emergence of social science; this attack has used analytics that disavow racial suffering and allegedly provide analytics for understanding its costs. While radical black activists sought to produce a world in which black peoples' lives could be made livable in the face of wholesale genocide, lynch law, incarceration and forced labor, the horrors of enduring forms of enslavement, dispossession of land and forced migration, and transformation of whole communities into citizenship-less plantations for humans made chattel, this U.S. foundation found a home in social research in South Africa that was at its root about blackness and whiteness and yet consistently disavowed its investments in white supremacy. Being involved in South African domestic and southern African regional policies on racial segregation enabled philanthropies in the United States to have a purchase on the continent and thus to expand and legitimize the role of an outward-looking and expansionist United States. The various agencies and organizations sponsored by the Carnegie Corporation in South Africa and on the continent had the twin goals of silencing black radical opposition and training an international elite enthusiastic about membership in the U.S. sphere of influence. As champions and funders of educational programs for patient accomodationism with white supremacy, interracial cooperation, and vocational education in the United States the Carnegie Corporation supported decades of research that applied separate developmentalist policy measures to black people throughout the world. Not only did the Carnegie Corporation philanthropies provide the intellectual discourse (the racial regime of language and tropes) for the industrializing United States, but they provided the most expensively trained and erudite expressions of white supremacy on the African continent.

I raise questions about how international debates on race and race relations effect domestic racial citizenship. Or to use Edward Berman's words, "No serious student of politics, of whatever ideological persuasion, would attempt to disassociate foreign policy formulation from domestic considerations."[1] Yet in the case of race, the racial in the domestic scene has so powerfully been positioned over the racial in the global scene that it has resulted in an often stilted research agenda that amasses and identifies cases of racial domination without a fully elaborated reason or purpose. Rather than compare racial democracies and their engagement with scientific racism it is appropriate to describe U.S. strategic interests in South Africa as a "civilizing mission," because Anglo-American collusion and collaboration resulted in the crafting by both states of a mostly continuous and orderly noncontentious race relations social order that simultaneously propped up white supremacy and claimed to be concerned about racial equality. "The Carnegie Corporation ... ," Plummer writes, "informed W. E. B. Du Bois that it adhered to a policy of deferring to racist and imperialist opinion—euphemistically termed 'Dominion advice'—on matters pertaining to South Africa."[2] As editor of *The Crisis,* Du Bois argued that there was "an obvious parallel between white rule in South Africa and the American south. The South ... served as an example to South Africa of the necessity of terror and violence to preserve white supremacy. In both ... the white man's commitment to justice was only rhetoric."[3] Thus in dozens of cases African Americans were prohibited from shaping U.S. foreign policy even though they commented on it and had their public opinion shaped by it fully. Consequently, African Americans were contained and detained within U.S. national identity, while their existence and advocacy manifestly undermined the legitimacy and political authority of this variant of white nationalism.[4] Lest we mistakenly imagine that this was a situation confined to North America:

> For years British authorities had limited Afro-American travel to and residence in British Africa with the sympathetic cooperation of U.S. officials. . . . The Colonial Office sought to disrupt a long history of communication between African nationalists and Afro-Americans. After the death of Booker T. Washington and the demise of militant Garveyism, British colonial author-

ities sometimes permitted African students to train as teachers and low-level functionaries at black American colleges. . . . Lincoln University alumni, for example, included future leaders Kwame Nkrumah and Ako Adjei of Ghana, and Nnamdi Azikiwe of Nigeria.[5]

While deeply grounded in the particularities of South African historical experiences, the *Poor White Study* suggests that racial formations like "the poor white" are profoundly shaped by complex and contested international agendas such as prohibitions on travel among advocates of principles such as "rights for national minorities," "racial equality," "self-determination," and "equality of nations."[6] The black people who advocated such things were met with a towering wall of Anglo-American repression that prioritized domestic sovereignty and the protection of the nation-state against any and all other interests that shaped the international scene. In addition, they had to confront doctrines about the nature of what constitutes the international sphere. In Abebe Zegeye and Maurice Vambe's observation, the transnational race relations analytic routinely avoids narrow-minded "bantustanised" political theoretic analysis that figures "ruled and rulers . . . as possessing uniform or similar subjectivities at all times . . . [which results in] gross misprepresentation[s] of the geopolitics of the African diasporas."[7] Thus I argue that comparative approaches to racial politics that foreground states miss the significant impact of international politics, mistakenly buy into white nationalisms, and avoid critique of the exceptionalist and imperialist imaginary of white nations as they shape domestic racial politics and scripts of national identity. Indeed "civilizing missions" enacted by foundations and philanthropic organizations, for example, function both within nations and across national borders. Ann Stoler suggests that we contend with the issue of why we study the colonial state. Is the colonial state simply an extension of the national political culture of different European countries? Is the goal of comparative colonial studies simply recataloging European nationalities? Using Foucault can get us to think about which categories seem to be commensurable and which comparisons seem appropriate to make, so that finally we can "trace circuits of knowledge production which cut through and across imperial axes and which may refigure nation-bound histories and conventional units of analysis."[8] Some of the many categories that get ignored are how race is constructed, how mixed-race is constructed, and how and where colony and metropole are located. Since colonies are places erroneously construed as causing "death by culture" via wholly unique forms of racial and sexual domination and metropoles are construed as offering the conditions for emancipation, disrupting that particular binary is central to refiguring the boundaries of the nation.[9] Some of the most productive turns in scholarship of this kind are marked by the following names: African Diaspora Studies, comparative racial politics, racial politics, comparative political thought, non-Western political thought, and studies of race and nation. All seek to correct the marginalization of sustained black political imaginaries and campaigns opposed to racism and white supremacy in international affairs. Caught within national identities more often characterized by second-class citizenship and a lack of substantive racial equality, African Americans, in particular—but certainly not only—have a long history of participation in an ethical international foreign affairs.[10] Reading African Diaspora Studies through the lens of political diaspora, by which I mean identifying mutually reinforcing global racial conditions of anti-blackness and the organizing of black consciousness solidarity campaigns throughout the world, is a central protocol for this long history and differs in decisive ways from culturalist diaspora. To draw on Frederick Cooper's insights on this: "Anti-colonial and anti-apartheid movements were truly border crossing," drawing on the "multidimensional involvement of different African American organizations [and] . . . movements within Africa itself."[11] Such movements were critical to articulating the moral imperative that "colonialism and apartheid were wrong." Such organizing has often been a proactive and consistent response to national identities that guarantee bureaucratic and legal exclusion and forms of legalized confinement and detention. Rather than accept such national identities as reasonable African Americans in the hemisphere have an enviable documented history of international and transnational solidarity with important theoretical implications that was heavily regulated and rejected by colonial states.

Subnational groups have prioritized international action to hinge their criticism of domestic segregation to racial colonialism and to register their discontent and moral condemnation of state-sponsored colonial and neocolonial violence domestically, abroad, and in international relations. As Charles P. Henry attests:

> Many of these key events demonstrate that racism at worst and ethnocentrism at best have been at the center of U.S. foreign policy. . . . [T]he spread of democracy in the nineteenth century was integrally linked to a rise in racism. Moreover, this racism grew with the development of science, not in spite of it. Thus, such concepts as manifest destiny, the White man's burden, eugenics, and racial hierarchy are central to the development of the "national interest" of the elites that controlled U.S. foreign policy.[12]

The comparative political thought and comparative racial politics that emerge from African Americans' engagement with diaspora—despite those culturalist, linguistic, sociospatial, and region-bound assumptions that do not translate—provide a more sound road map for understanding the details of how racial groups have come to know themselves and how their existence has been used to shore up racial regimes. Reconsidering key themes in European political thought such as rights, democracy, sovereignty, interest, justice, and nation through their ties to slavery, genocide, social death, and premature death, U.S. philosophers such as Charles Mills have called for a political thought far more engaged with world and international history than that previously offered.

In the United States European immigrants and settlers had to become white in order to enjoy the fruits of the state, including legible state-recognized citizenship and personhood. However, the process of whitening of individuals and groups and the juridical definitions of citizenship and democracy can be better understood through an analysis that captures transnational linkages, global racial hierarchies, and philanthropic institutions. By this, I am arguing that domestic race relations "problems" are only inadequately and partially analyzed within national borders. Furthermore, the research agenda of the Carnegie Corporation in this area offers comparativists a rich bounty of underanalyzed archival materials on racial politics. Finally, the nature of the influence of the *Poor White Study* suggests greater attention to the processes through which racial politics became a commodity and language and policy framework for internationally prominent social scientists.

Acknowledgments

Support for this research was provided by the University of California President's Postdoctoral Fellowship; the University of California, Santa Barbara (UCSB) Interdisciplinary Humanities Center; the UCSB Graduate Division; the Democracy and Governance Group of the Human Sciences Research Council (South Africa); the Mellon Foundation Future of Minority Studies Project; the Department of Ethnic Studies at UC Riverside; the Department of Anthropology at UC Berkeley; the Academic Senate Council on Research, Computing and Libraries Special Research Grant at UC Irvine; UC Humanities Research Institute Grant; Working at Living Working Group; the UC Irvine ADVANCE Program, and Dean Vicki Ruiz. Vital research assistance was provided by Rosie Bermudez, Tiffany Andrews, Ryan Davis, Ashley Hughes, Erika Chan, and Andrea Slater, La Shonda Carter, Eddie Rodas, and Armand Demirchand. Laura Holliday and Diane Belle provided excellent editorial assistance. I owe a huge debt to the editors at the University of California Press, Neils Hooper, Kim Hogeland, Francisco Reinking, and Sheila Berg for their time, wise counsel, and serious engagement.

The many librarians and archivists at the Kimberly Africana Library, the William Cullen Historical Papers Library, the National Cultural History/African Window Museum, the Africana and Government Publications Libraries at the University of Cape Town, UNISA Archives, the Human Sciences Research Council, the NG Kerk Archives at Pretoria, the South African National Archives Pretoria and Cape Town Depots, the Killie Campbell Library at the University of Kwa-Zulu Natal, and the University of California, Santa Barbara, have shaped this work profoundly. I want to especially thank Michelle Pickover, Hloni Dlamini, Nellie Sommers, Diana Wall, Kathy Brookes, Jonathan Frost, Elda Grobler, Carin Pesler, Kienkie Froneman, Vida Allen, Herma Niekerk, Elize Sutherland, Karen Sefenhuysen, Buks Gronewald, Sylvia Curtis, Alice Harris, Gary Colmenar, Maria Coetzee, Wei Ling Dai, Sherri Barnes, Rebecca Imamoto, Christina Woo, Pauline Manaka, and Lucia Snowhill.

Over the years many colleagues have spoken with me about my research, read chapters in draft, and asked me detailed and important questions that have contributed to this work. I have been a member of a number of important intellectual formations in the process of completing this research. All have been spaces where I could experiment with talking about the genesis and history of this project and my understandings about it to different audiences: scholars concerned with feminist philosophy, race, indigeneity, settler colonialism, empire, queer transnationalism, women of color feminisms, identity politics, critical ethnic studies, comparative political thought, black politics, and feminist politics. Some have provided funding, but most have not. Most have used incredibly low-tech modalities to claim space to build and protect autonomous geographies to speak across disciplinary formations, methodological divides, and histories. Most have borne the weight of my hesitant participation *and* overenthusiasm with great kindness. All have shared insights about the quotidian impact of economic violence and the ways that it provides an index for the making of racial and social and gender and spatial analytics. In each of these spaces I showed up time and again because documenting the complexity of a world that pretends to know itself and its others has been my preoccupation since I was taught to read. In this book, and in the many varied intellectual, artistic, and activist formations where I have held a seat and done my work, I know I carried forward some of the best practices that we have inherited as survivors of the many middle passages of the past, present, and future. Each individual and institution in the "roll call of names" and the vast archives of liberation mentioned here represent modes of inquiry and languages worthy of study and reflection. May the bearers of these names always know how deeply their wisdom has touched me.

For sound advice and good questions, I thank Cedric Robinson, Elizabeth Robinson, Avery Gordon, Abebe Zegeye, Oyèrónké Oyěwùmí,

Denise Da Silva, Vicki Ruiz, Nancy Scheper-Hughes, Eileen Boris, David Roediger, Jeffrey Stewart, Ed Keller, the National Conference of Black Political Scientists, the Association for Black Women in Politics, and the Race and Ethnic Politics Section of APSA, the LOUD Collective, Maylei Blackwell, Erica Edwards, Aisha Finch, Mishuana Goeman, Grace Hong, Arlene Keizer, Jodi Kim, Deb Vargas, Mignon Moore, Sara Clarke Kaplan, Sarah Haley, Dayo Gore, Sarita See, Andreana Clay, Dana Wright, Nancy Aldritt Julietta Hua, Asta Svensdottir, Kasturi Ray, Hermon and Sylvia Lee, and Deborah Terry.

For struggling by my side, I thank Jon Hyslop, Mary Simons, Marijke Du Toit, David Goldblatt, Omar Badsha, Dean Hutton, Judith Tayler, Greg Cuthbertson, Louwrens Pretorious, Roger Ballen, Robert Krieger, Rehana Ebr.-Vally, Emmanuelle Gille, Chris McAuley, Jane Duran, Kum-Kum Bhavnani, Stephan Miescher, Christopher Newfield, Aaron Belkin, Laurie Freeman, Kathleen Bruhn, Linda James, Frederick Backman, Anita David, H.L.T. Quan, Marisela Marquez, Tu Huynh, Kris Peterson, Francoise Cromer, Crystal Griffith, Ilya Ahmadizedeh, Najda Robinson, Gerard Pigeon, Sharon Hoshida, Joanne and Otis Robinson, Earl Stewart, Irene Nexica, Alison Kafer, Chris Bickel, Gail Bluitt, and Jill Meredith.

For reminding me to ask the ancestors first, I thank Lisette Arnette, Jennifer Hughes, Santos Roman, Phindiswa Flepu, Janine DeBruyn, Riann van der Berg, Berma Choonoo, Elaine Jacobs, Stanley Bapela, Mary Hames, Catherine Cole, Catherine Burns, Kwame Braun, Thea Dixon, Ilsa Koning, Dawn Citto, and Ermias Guta.

For opening every meeting with a clear understanding of the stakes of our survival, I thank Jan Furman, Amita Shastri, Robert Smith, Ricky Green, Michael Mitchell, David Covin, James Martel, Joel Kassiola, Tanji Willoughby, Robert Williams, Greg Simmons, Dominick Varsalone, Pam Narcisse, Wendy Henderson, Nancy Lawler, Mike Hughes, Asa'na and Evelyn Akoh, Rachel O'Toole, Ann Kakaliouras, Tamara and Janice Austin, George Scheper, Diane Ganz-Scheper, Bob Moeller, Doug Haynes, Linda Vo, Catherine Liu, Cecilia Lynch, Louis De Sipio, Jim Lee, Julie Cho, Ayumi Chandler, Claire Jean Kim, Raul Fernandez, Bill Maurer, Tom Boellstorff, Valerie Jenness, Setsu Shigematsu, Sora Han, Katherine Tate, Thomas Parham, R. Radhakrishnan, Sohail Daulatzai, Lilith Mahmud, Laura Kang, Jenny Terry, Tesha Sengupta-Irving, Darryl Taylor, Bridget Cooks, Sheron Wray, Jessica Millward, Jared Sexton, Nahum Chandler, Frank Wilderson, Ulysses Jenkins, Linda Martín Alcoff, Satya Mohanty, Joseph Jordan, Kia Lilly-Caldwell,

Tracy Fisher, Michelle Tellez, Tamiko Nimura, Michael Hames-Garcia, Ernesto Martinez, Brian Thomas, Gaile Polhaus, Zenzele Isoke, Darryl Thomas, James Jennings, Tony Affigne, Diane Pinderhughes, Cathy Cohen, Leonard McNeil, Curtis Stokes, James Lance Taylor, Wendy Smooth, Niambi Carter, Nadia Brown, Melina Abdullah, Julia Jordan-Zachery, Duchess Harris, Nikol Alexander-Floyd, Greg Thomas, Mark Schuller, Elizabeth Currans, Molly Talcott, Dana Collins, Karl Bryant, Emily Davis, Alex McKee, Madelyn Detloff, Huda Jadallah, Deanna Kara'a, Gail Bluitt, Jill Meredith, Iyatunde Folayan, LaPia Willoughby, Tanya Willoughby, Francois Herard, Corey Willoughby, Dr. Charles G. Adams, Rev. Mangedwa Nyathi, Sibongile Nyathi, and the communities of Hartford Memorial Baptist Church of Detroit, Michigan, Christ Our Redeemer A.M.E. of Irvine, California, and Second Baptist Church of Santa Barbara, California.

For breathing for me when I could not breathe on my own and for decades of militant self-sacrifice, I thank Barbara Herard. For always asking the hardest questions and for her exacting standards and fearlessness, I thank Jeanne Scheper. As for the mistakes and missteps, the rough ground and the bitter pills, these have also been very important teachers, for which I am thankful.

Appendixes

TABLE I

	Year(s)	Amount	Investment
McGill	1941–43	$7,200	Neurological Institute
Montreal	1940	$8,000	Library of Botanical Institute
University of Cape Town Scientific Research	1937	$45,000	
Montreal University (Canada)	1940	$8,000	Library of Botanical Institute
University of Puerto Rico	1939	$13,500	School of Tropical Medicine Library
University of Puerto Rico	1941	$4,500	Bacteriological equipment
Queens University (Canada)	1934	$3,000	Biochemistry
Queens University (Canada)	1939	$9,000	Physics and biology
Saskatchewan University (Canada)	1935	$4,500	Professorship in physics
Saskatchewan University (Canada)	1937	$2,500	Biological research
University of Sydney (Australia)	1936	$4,500	Chemistry
University of Sydney (Australia)	1937	$25,000	Allocation
University of Toronto (Canada)	1921–26	$24,500	Helium and low temperature research
	1922–26	$29,000	Insulin
		$4,800	Professorship in physics
Western Australia University	1937	$4,800	Paleontology

TABLE 1 *(continued)*

	Year(s)	Amount	Investment
University of the Witwatersrand	1936	$54,750	Geophysics
Australian National Research Council	1927	$25,000	Endowment
Australian and New Zealand Association for the Advancement of Science	1936–38	$4,750	
East African Research Institute (Amani)	1930	$10,000	Science library
		$50,000	Endowment
Research Grant Board of Union of South Africa	1928	$50,000	Support
	1933	$30,000	Research
Royal Society of Canada	1927	$25,000	
	1932–41	$124,335	Scholarships

SOURCE: Robert M. Lester, *The Corporation and the Promotion of Science: 1911–1943* (January 15, 1944), CCNY Printed Material, Box 3, File 3.9.

APPENDIX B: COMMONWEALTH FUNDING HISTORY

TABLE 2

	Year	Amount
ETS psychometric fellowships	1953–60	$11,050
Africa to U.S. Institutions	1928–60	$852,451
South Africa	1928–60	$1,329,160
Nigeria	1932–61	$701,761
Kenya	1925–55	$163,653
Rhodesia and Nyasaland	1928–61	$298,353
Sierra Leone	1940–54	$10,735
Sudan	1937	$1,325
Tanganyika	1930–34	$60,000
Uganda	1928–60	$236,380
Zanzibar	1936	$5,000
Asia		
Ceylon	1934–37	$10,300
Hong Kong	1953–57	$55,165
Malaya	1934–57	$93,113
Australia	1927–60	$1,528,118

SOURCE: Stephen H. Stackpole, *Commonwealth Program 1911–1961* (New York: CCNY, 1963), 23–60, CCNY Printed Material, Box 3, File 3.13.

APPENDIX C: COMMON TERMS

Rev. Johannes Rudolph Albertyn (1878–1967)—Staunch supporter of Afrikaner Nationalism, probably along with Grosskopf the most extreme nationalist in terms of his sense that Africa was really for the Afrikaners, organized and founded several Afrikaans Taal or language festivals, organized and founded Afrikaans-only high schools.

CCNY—Carnegie Corporation of New York.

Dominion and Colonies Fund—Carnegie Corporation of New York fund designated for the British Empire. The majority of the awards went to settler colonies.

Dutch Reformed Church—Has been argued to be the most stalwart pro-apartheid religious group because of its Calvinist philosophies of predestination and racial separation.

Johannes Friedrich Wilhelm Grosskopf (1885–1948)—Economist and playwright, taught at University of Stellenbosch, wrote the *Poor White Study* volume on land and economic deprivation.

Thomas Jesse Jones (1873–1950)—Official with the CCNY-coordinated funding for the Phelps-Stokes Fund, which along with the Institute of Race Relations represents one tendency of the work done in the liberal English-speaking community.

Frederick Keppel (1875–1943)—President of the Carnegie Corporation of New York.

Charles Templeman Loram (1879–1940)—Columbia University graduate, member of the *Poor White Study* Board of Control, director of Malawi Jeannes Schools, Natal director of education, and member of the Native Affairs Commission.

Ernest Gideon (E.G.) Malherbe (1895–1982)—Columbia University Teachers College liberal Afrikaner intellectual, founder of the National Bureau for Educational Research (later named the Human Sciences Research Council), and author of the *Poor White Study* volume on education. He was the most prolific member of the research team in terms of his writings and self-conscious historicization of the *Poor White Study* and was strongly in favor of bilingual education, though his family participated in many Afrikaner Nationalist cultural festivals.

Poor White Study—Conducted from 1927 to 1932 to establish the systematic response to white industrialization and urban poverty and to eradicate poverty among whites in South Africa. The only national commission on race, culture, and development established that was funded exclusively by the Carnegie Corporation of New York. Despite requests over a period of two years, the South African government refused to contribute moneys. All other similar endeavors were funded by a combination of international organizations and the South African government or solely by the South African government. This study is a classic case of how race, culture, and development research was conducted in South Africa in the two decades prior to 1948 grand apartheid.

Name, Dates, Memberships	Emphasis	Age in 1927	Years in Bloemfontein	Years at Univ. of Victoria (later known as Univ. of Stellenbosch)	Father DRC Clergy	Training/International Experience in Europe/United States
R.W. Wilcocks (1892–1967) *Woordeboek* Project	Psychology	35		1909–12 1918–54	Yes	1912–17 Ph.D. Univ. of Berlin
J.R. Albertyn (1878–1967) f. 1916 Afrikaans Taal Fest., 1934 Volkskongres, f. Hoerskool Diamantveld, Federal Council Poor Relief	Theology	49	1906–26 Willowmore 1926 Kimberley	1903 Seminary	Pastor himself	1904 B.Div. Princeton
J.F.W. Grosskopf (1885–1948) Published largely in *Ons Vaderland* and *Het Volksblad*	Agricultural economics	42		1904–6 M.A. 1920–48 Econ. professor	Yes, German missionary, paternal/ maternal	1908 Ph.D. Univ. Leiden Law
M.E. Rothmann (1875–1975) Active member of ACVV, FAK, Voortrekker, OssewaBrandwag, published largely in *Huisegenoot, Boerevrou*	Women, Charity	52		Univ. Cape Good Hope	Unknown	1966 Carnegie Overseas Visitor Kentucky

E. G. Malherbe (1895–1982)	Education	32	b. Orange Free State	1913–19	Yes	1924 Ph.D. Columbia
New Education Fellowship, 1929–30; Dir. Natl Bureau Educational Research (Human Science Research Council), 1939–45; Dir. SA Census, 1945; Military service—research on soldiers, 1945; Dir. Military Intelligence, investigated Ossewa Brandwag and Broederbond as Nazi orgs.; 1945–65 principal Univ. of Natal; 1951 SAAAS; 1966–67 pres. South African Institute of Race Relations						
W.E. Murray	Medicine	NA	NA	NA	NA	NA

ACVV—Afrikaanse Christelike Vrouevereniging (Afrikaner Women's Charity Organization), publisher of *Huisegenoot* (Homemaking) serial

Boervrou—*Boer Woman*, serial

FAK—Federasie van Afrikaanse Kulturrverenigings (Federation for Afrikaner Culture)

Het Volksblad—*People's Paper*, serial

Hoerskool Diamantveld—Diamond Fields High School, an Afrikaans-only school

Ons Vaderland—*Our Fatherland*, serial

Ossewa Brandwag—Oxwagon Trek, an annual nationwide festival to commemorate the Great Trek

SAAAS—South African Association for the Advancement of Science

SAIRR—South African Institute of Race Relations

Volkskongres—People's Congress

Woordeboek—Afrikaans Dictionary

Notes

NOTES TO PREFACE

1. Mother Teresa wrote, "We think sometimes that poverty is only being hungry, naked and homeless. The poverty of being unwanted, unloved, and uncared for is the greatest poverty." Mother Teresa, "At His Disposal," in *Mother Teresa: Come Be My Light: The Private Writings of the Saint of Calcutta,* ed. Brian Kolodiejchuk (Rochester, NY: Image Press, 2009), 259.

2. Cedric J. Robinson, *Forgeries of Memory and Meaning: Blacks and the Regimes of Race in American Theater and Film before World War II* (Chapel Hill: University of North Carolina Press, 2007), xiii; Gargi Bhattacharyya, *Tales of Dark Skinned Women: Race, Gender, and Global Culture.* (New York: Routledge, 1998), 119, 128; Hortense Spillers, "Mama's Baby, Papa's Maybe," *Diacritics* 17, no. 2 (1987): 64–81; Cedric Robinson, *Terms of Order: Political Science and the Myth of Leadership* (Albany: State University of New York Press, 1980).

3. Tiffany Willoughby-Herard, "'Revolt at the Source': The Black Radical Tradition in the Social Documentary Photography of Omar Badsha and Nadine Hutton," *African Identities* 11, no. 2 (2012): 201.

4. Marlene Van Niekerk, *Triomf,* trans. Leon de Kock (Johannesburg: Jonathon Ball Publishers, [1994] 1999); Carnegie Corporation, "Joint Recommendations and Findings," in *Report of the Carnegie Commission of Investigation on the Poor White Question in South Africa* (Stellenbosch: Pro-Ecclesia-Drukkery, 1932), 2, 3, 16. *The New York Times* commented on South African writer—the most famous of her day—Sarah Gertrude Millin's statement that the Europeans in South Africa "were destined to capture the sympathetic imagination of a world that had just finished tolerantly laughing at them." Afrikaners appealed to the United States as a "sister republic" but were regarded as white outsiders in the Anglophone global imaginary made up by the civilized nations.

John W. Crawford, "South Africa Is a Confused and Very Confusing Place: Sarah Gertrude Millin Writes an Illuminating Study of Its People and Their Problems," *New York Times,* April 3, 1927, BR3.

5. Through this seemingly innocent question, archivists hoped to restrict and redirect my access to the South African archival materials. However, they inadvertently reminded me of black scholars' sustained century-long intellectual project to challenge black people's detained condition within white nation-states; black scholars' investments in Pan-Africanism and in diasporic, anticolonial, international, and transnational modes of analysis. According to a member of the Council on Foreign Relations and former president of the African Studies Association, Pearl Robinson, though submerged and largely unacknowledged by white academia, black scholars have resisted being locked out of academic research and have produced an entire world of black diaspora vindicationist scholars. See Pearl Robinson, "Area Studies in Search of Africa," in *The Politics of Knowledge: Area Studies and the Disciplines,* ed. David Szanton (Berkeley: University of California Press in collaboration with e-scholarship, 2004), 1–41. This diasporic understanding insisted that South Africa was best explained as a consequence of a global racial order. Many organizations were founded in the Black Power era to challenge knowledge production about racial discrimination as being a national phenomenon rather than a global one. In North America these include the African Heritage Studies Association, the National Conference of Black Political Scientists, and dozens of others. The archivists' question was not innocent. It was a direct result of historical practices of excluding black scholars from scholarly resources and materials and silencing and marginalizing the finalized research of black scholars. White radical roots in the struggle against racial domination in academia is a critical part of the history especially since so often white scholars contributed to silencing black scholarship. Neil Roos, *Ordinary Springboks: White Servicemen and Social Justice in South Africa, 1939–1961* (Aldershot: Ashgate, 2005); Joshua Lazerson, *Against the Tide: Whites against Apartheid* (Bellville: Mayibuye Books, 1994); Pierre Hugo, "The Silence of the American Academic in the Segregationist South," *South African Historical Journal* 38 (1998):183–99; Pierre Hugo, "The Politics of Untruth," *Politikon* 25, no. 1 (1988): 31–55; Thomas J. Noer, *Briton, Boer, and Yankee: The United States and South Africa, 1879–1914* (Kent, OH: Kent State University Press, 1978), 133.

6. Robert Vinson, *The Americans Are Coming! Dreams of African American Liberation in Segregationist South Africa* (Athens: Ohio University Press, 2012); Zine Magubane, *Bringing the Empire Home: Race, Class, and Gender in Britain and Colonial South Africa* (Chicago: University of Chicago Press, 2003); Brenda Gayle Plummer, *Rising Wind: Black Americans and U.S. Foreign Affairs, 1935–1960* (Chapel Hill: University of North Carolina Press, 1996).

7. Thus scholars have argued that black peoples' being literal property and debt has created strong resistance to ever being made into movable property again—sometimes through the insulation of a desire to appear wealthy. This embodiment of the trappings of wealth is always then underscored not as a phenomenological site of knowledge production and dealing with the contradiction of being the debt at the center of a world based on racialized property but as mere folly and foolishness.

8. Frank Wilderson, *Red, White, and Black: Cinema and the Structure of U.S. Antagonism* (Durham, NC: Duke University Press, 2010); Pumla Gqola, *What Is Slavery to Me? Postcolonial/Slave Memory in Post-Apartheid South Africa* (Johannesburg: Wits University Press, 2010); Gerald Horne, *The White Pacific: U.S. Imperialism and Black Slavery in the South Seas after the Civil War* (Honolulu: University of Hawai'i Press, 2007); Gerald Horne, *The Deepest South: The United States, Brazil, and the African Slave Trade* (New York: New York University Press, 2007); Katherine McKittrick, *Demonic Ground: Black Women and the Cartographies of Struggle* (Minneapolis: University of Minnesota Press, 2006); Jennifer Morgan, *Laboring Women: Reproduction and Gender in New World Slavery* (Philadelphia: University of Pennsylvania Press, 2004); Julian Kunnie, *Is Apartheid Really Dead? Pan-Africanist Working-Class Cultural Critical Perspectives* (Boulder, CO: Westview Press, 2000); Saidiya Hartman, *Scenes of Subjection: Terror, Slavery, and Self-Making in Nineteenth-Century America* (New York: Oxford University Press, 1997).

9. France Winddance Twine and Jonathan W. Warren, *Racing Research, Researching Race: Methodological Dilemmas in Critical Race Studies* (New York: New York University Press, 2000); Ralph Bunche, *An African American in South Africa: The Travel Notes of Ralph J. Bunch, 28 September 1937–January 1938,* with contribution by Robert J. Edgar (Athens: Ohio University Press, [1992] 2001).

10. Robert Vinson, "Citizenship over Race? African Americans in American–South African Diplomacy, 1890–1925," *World History Connected* 2, no. 1 (2004): 37, http://worldhistoryconnected.press.illinois.edu/2.1/vinson.html. Accessed October 14, 2013.

11. Comedy about black people as property is ubiquitous. The illogic of phrases such as "You are a credit to your race" is always an expression of microaggression. Derald Wing Sue et al., "Racial Microaggressions in Everyday Life: Implications for Clinical Practice," *American Psychologist* (May–June 2007): 271–86, www.consumerstar.org/pdf/RacialMicroaggressions.pdf. Accessed June 20, 2014. It may have been one of the many talented comedians on *Def Comedy Jam* (HBO series produced by the media mogul Russell Simmons from 1992 to 1996) or someone long before this era who first told the joke with the punch line, "You can't buy a couch with a 'credit to your race,'" to mock the uselessness of white attempts to congratulate black people in economic language for countering some of the intrinsic debt that makes up our lives in racist societies.

12. David Roediger, *Black on White: Black Writers on What It Means to Be White* (New York: Random House, 1998); Robert Fikes, "Escaping the Literary Ghetto: African American Authors of White Life Novels, 1946–1994," *Western Journal of Black Studies* 19, no. 2 (1995): 105–12; Toni Morrison, *Playing in the Dark: Whiteness and the Literary Imagination* (Cambridge, MA: Harvard University Press, 1992).

13. Jacqueline Bobo, *Black Women as Cultural Readers* (New York: Columbia University Press, 1995), 42. See also Manthia Diawara, "Black Spectatorship: Problems of Identification and Resistance," in *Black American Cinema,* ed. Manthia Diawara (New York: Routledge, 1993), 211–20.

14. Nikol Alexander-Floyd, "Disappearing Acts: Reclaiming Intersectionality in the Social Sciences in a Post-Black Feminist Era," *Feminist Formations* 24, no. 1 (2012): 19.

15. Cedric Robinson, *Black Marxism: The Making of the Black Radical Tradition,* 2nd ed., with a foreword by Robin Kelley (Chapel Hill: University of North Carolina Press, 2007), xxxv.

16. Greg Cuthbertson, Interviews by author, June 7 and May 31, 2002, UNISA.

17. Barbara Christian, "Race for Theory," *Cultural Critique* 6 (1987): 68.

18. And despite the burden of carrying the story of humanizing impoverished white people into spaces in which black people's suffering required a kind of painful suspicion of belief and action, I was obedient to my guides and to the work put in my hands at that time. As the only black girl in an elementary school of all-white Catholic eastern and southern European second-generation immigrant children, an identity I still carry with me, I could claim knowingness and a particular intimacy with what it meant to be made into a "waste of white skin" by my classmates and teachers. I was made to know and sympathize with their making in deindustrializing Detroit by seeing what their new and wholly unfamiliar experience of blackening was said to mean. Supposedly when all the white men lost their jobs in that community my classmates would become as wretched as "me." But we weren't wretched. My mother was a teacher descended from a long line of civil rights activists in the U.S. internal colony and my father a Haitian immigrant professor at a historically black college founded by fellow graduates from the Sorbonne who were also graduates from torture and exile in the Third World writ large and in neat particularities. The costs to black people of the deindustrialization of Detroit has been told by many. I have yet to tell and remember the costs to black people, that group of radicals/escapees/multilinguals/warriors/survivors, and what they bore in their houses and on their bodies and in their children's eyes when working-class white people were made into waste in Detroit and its little all-white suburbs.

19. In addition to paradigm-shifting single-author texts, several authors have published exquisitely researched and carefully selected essays, poems, and reflections for anthologies and special issues of journals on black women in South Africa. I would be remiss if I did not mention Yvette Abrahams, whose work with Zola Maseko on Sara Baartman has literally rerooted black women's thought by enrobing bodies and stories, as well as Shelley Barry, Philippa Yaa de Villiers, Lucille Greef, Myesha Jenkins, Aryan Kaganoff, Percy Mabandu, Maserame June Madingwane, Makgano Mamabola, Makomele Manaka, Napo Masheane, Lebogang Mashile, Sabata Mpho Mokae, Natalia Molebatsi, Makia Lueen Ndlovu, Khethiwe Ntshangase, Otumile Shupinyaneng, Simphiwe Dana, Pumla Gqola, Zethu Matabeni, Caroline Wanjiku Kihato, Nomboniso Gasa, and Nthabiseng Motsemme. I also want to recognize the communities that raised and sustained them whose names and numbers can never be fully counted. See Caroline Wanjiku Kihato, *Migrant Women of Johannesburg: Everyday Life in an In-Between City* (New York: Palgrave Macmillan, 2013); Zethu Matebeni, *Black Lesbian Sexualities and Identity in South Africa: An Ethnography of Black Lesbian Urban Life* (Saarbrücken, Germany: Lambert Academic

Publishing, 2012); Natalia Molebatsi, *We Are: . . . a Poetry Anthology* (Johannesburg: Penguin), 2011; Gqola, *What Is Slavery to Me?;* Rebekah Lee, *African Women and Apartheid: Migration and Settlement in Urban South Africa* (London: I.B. Tauris, 2009); Sandra Jackson, Fassil Demissie, and Michele Goodwin, eds., *Imagining, Writing, Re(Reading) the Black Body* (Pretoria: UNISA Press, 2009); Devaraskshanam Govinden, *"Sister Outsiders": The Representation of Identity and Difference in Selected Writings by South African Indian Women* (Pretoria and Leiden: UNISA Press and Koninklijke Brill NV, 2008); Nomboniso Gasa, ed., *Basus'iimbokodo, bawel'imilambo/They remove boulders and cross rivers: Women in South African History* (Pretoria: Human Sciences Research Council Press, 2007); Pamela Brooks, *Boycotts, Buses, and Passes: Black Women's Resistance in the U.S. South and South Africa* (Amherst: University of Massachusetts Press, 2008); Reitumetse Obakeng Mabokela and Zine Magubane, eds., *Hear Our Voices: Race, Gender and the Status of Black South African Women in the Academy* (Pretoria: University of South Africa Press, 2004); Wendy Woodward, Patricia Hayes, and Gary Minkley, eds., *Deep Histories: Gender and Colonialism in Southern Africa* (Amsterdam: Rodopi, [1994] 2002); Zmitri Erasmus, *Coloured by History, Shaped by Place: New Perspectives on Coloured Identities in Cape Town* (Cape Town: Kwela, 2001); Rehana Ebr.-Vally, *Kala Pani: Caste and Colour in South Africa* (Cape Town and Maroelana: Kwela Books and South African History Online, 2001).

20. Unsurprisingly, one of the negative impacts of the legacy of apartheid was the isolation of South African social historians and labor historians, which led to the lack of communication with a rapidly expanding scholarship on black consciousness, African Diaspora studies, and black feminisms, all of which were explicitly shaped by political resistance (civil disobedience and direct action) to apartheid. Another dimension of this isolation could be seen in publishing. For the most part, scholarly publication lagged, and most research presented at seminars and conferences was not published until long after and could be accessed only in South African research libraries and archives.

21. Elaine Katz, "Revisiting the Origins of the Industrial Colour Bar in the Witwatersrand Gold Mining Industry, 1891–1899," *Journal of Southern African Studies* 25, no. 1 (1999): 79; Deborah Posel, "Whiteness and Power in the South African Civil Service: Paradoxes of the Apartheid State," *Journal of Southern African Studies* 25, no. 1 (1999): 99–119; Robert Morrell, ed., *White but Poor: Essays on the History of Poor Whites in Southern Africa, 1880–1940* (Pretoria: UNISA, 1992); David Harrison, *The White Tribe of Africa: South Africa in Perspective* (Berkeley: University of California Press, 1983); Martin Legassick, "The Mining Economy and the White Working Class," paper presented at the Conference on Southern African Labor History, African Studies Institute, April 8–10, 1976; Elaine Katz, "White Workers' Grievances and the Industrial Colour Bar, 1902–1913," paper presented at the African Studies Institute Seminar, University of the Witwatersrand, Johannesburg, 1973; Union of South Africa National Archives, Pretoria Depot, Poor White Collection, Inspectorate of White Labor Files (1915), Reports from the Inspectorate of White Labor, CCNY, Box 3, File 3.5.

22. Patricia Hill Collins, "Black Feminist Thought in the Matrix of Domination," in *Black Feminist Thought: Knowledge, Consciousness, and the Politics of*

Empowerment (Boston: Unwin Hyman, 1990), 221–38, www.hartford-hwp .com/archives/45a/252.html. Accessed June 20, 2014.

23. Noer, *Briton, Boer, and Yankee,* 13, 38. Promotion of white immigration and restrictions against black and Chinese immigration were central to the making of white nationalism and the very notion of the modern republic. At the national level this has been described as affirmative action for white people; and at the global level, the global color line. Ira Katznelson, *When Affirmative Action Was White: An Untold History of Racial Inequality in Twentieth-Century America* (rep. New York: Norton, 2006); Marilyn Lake and Henry Reynolds, *Drawing the Global Colour Line: White Men's Countries and the International Challenge of Racial Equality* (Cambridge: Cambridge University Press, 2008).

24. Derrick Bell, *Gospel Choirs: Psalms of Survival in an Alien Land Called Home* (New York: Basic Books, 1997).

25. Saidiya Hartman, *Lose Your Mother: A Journey along the Atlantic Slave Route* (New York: Farrar, Straus and Giroux, 2008), 6.

26. Ibid., 64–69. With regard to the trade in people, Hartman describes in horrific detail both how enslaved black people's bodies were measured in transferable alienable units for sale—the Portuguese *braços* (unit or arm) the Spanish *pieza de India* (a mercantile unit of human flesh that often comprised more than one person) and the Dutch *leverbaar* (a healthy deliverable male or female slave). She also describes the acts of torture and dissection that were part of "St. George's world" that reduce living people to those with "annulled lives, transformed . . . into dead matter, and then resuscitated for servitude." Here the question of the aspiration to be an owner, a successful member of the bourgeoisie through accumulation of wealth, cannot be separated from the fact that the wealth is the black body, the black body kept alive only for the purpose of creating wealth—what Jennifer Morgan *(Laboring Women)* calls the "prospect" of the black woman's womb that guided speculation and financialization of human chattel and their progeny. It is cannibalism to the highest degree. So it enables us to ask the important question, What acts of violence make it even conceivable that the children of the slave owners and the children of slaves see the world in/on/after/over the same terms?

27. Cheryl Higashida, *Black Internationalist Feminism: Women Writers of the Black Left, 1945–1995* (Champaign: University of Illinois Press, 2013); Dayo Gore, *Radicalism at the Crossroads: African American Women Activists in the Cold War* (New York: New York University Press, 2012); Erik McDuffie, *Sojourning for Freedom: Black Women, American Communism, and the Making of Black Left Feminism* (Durham, NC: Duke University Press, 2011); Maylei Blackwell, *!Chicana Power!: Contested Histories of Feminism in the Chicano Movement* (Austin: University of Texas Press, 2011); Michael West, William Martin, and Fanon Che Wilkins, eds., *From Toussaint to Tupac: The Black International since the Age of Revolution,* (Chapel Hill: University of North Carolina Press, 2009); Dayo Gore, Jeanne Theoharis, and Komozi Woodard, eds., *Want to Start a Revolution? Radical Women in the Black Freedom Struggle* (New York: New York University Press, 2009); Pamela Brooks, *Boycotts, Buses, and Passes: Black Women's Resistance in the U.S. South and South Africa*

(Amherst: University of Massachusetts, 2008); Carole Boyce Davies, *Left of Karl Marx: The Political Life of Black Communist Claudia Jones* (Durham, NC: Duke University Press, 2008); Vijay Prashad, *Darker Nations: A People's History of the Third World* (New York: New Press, 2008); Cynthia Young, *Soul Power: Culture, Radicalism, and the Making of a U.S. Third World Left* (Durham, NC: Duke University Press, 2006); Penny Von Eschen, *Satchmo Blows Up the World: Jazz Ambassadors Play the Cold War* (Cambridge, MA: Harvard University Press, 2006); Nikhil P. Singh, *Black Is a Country: Race and the Unfinished Struggle for Democracy* (Cambridge, MA: Harvard University Press, 2004); Robinson, "Area Studies in Search of Africa,"), 1–41; Charles P. Henry, ed., *Foreign Policy and the Black (Inter) National Interest* (Albany: State University of New York Press, 2000); Penny Von Eschen, *Race against Empire: Black Americans and Anticolonialism, 1937–1957* (Ithaca, NY: Cornell University Press, 1997); Brenda Gayle Plummer, *Rising Wind: Black Americans and U.S. Foreign Affairs, 1935–1960* (Chapel Hill: University of North Carolina Press, 1996); John Henrik Clarke, ed., *Dimensions of the Struggle against Apartheid: A Tribute to Paul Robeson. Proceedings of the Special Meeting of the Special Committee against Apartheid on the 80th anniversary of the Birth of Paul Robeson, 10 April 1978* (New York and Washington DC: African Heritage Studies Association in cooperation with the United Nations Centre against Apartheid, 1979).

28. Stephanie Batiste, *Darkening Mirrors: Imperial Representation in Depression-Era African American Performance* (Durham, NC: Duke University Press, 2012); Yogita Goyal, *Romance, Diaspora, and Black Atlantic Literature* (New York: Cambridge University Press, 2010). These scholars offer examinations of pro-imperialist African diasporic formations.

29. West et al., *From Toussaint to Tupac;* Prashad, *Darker Nations;* Von Eschen, *Satchmo Blows Up the World;* Singh, *Black Is a Country;* Robinson, "Area Studies in Search of Africa"; Henry, *Foreign Policy and the Black (Inter) National Interest;* Plummer, *Rising Wind.*

30. Gaye Seidman, "Is South Africa Different? Sociological Comparisons and Theoretical Contributions from the Land of Apartheid," *Annual Review of Sociology* 25 (1999): 419–40; Seymour Lipset, *American Exceptionalism: A Double-Edged Sword* (New York: Norton, 1997); Donald Culverson, "Rumors of Apartheid: Myth and Stereotype in U.S. Foreign Policy toward South Africa," in *Tales of the State: Narrative in Contemporary U.S. Politics and Public Policy,* ed. Sanford F. Schram and Phillip T. Neisser (Lanham, MD: Rowman and Littlefield, 1997), 199–211. Politicians and scholars have trafficked in exceptionalist narratives and claimed South African and American exceptionalism as key variables to explain the distinctive racial system in each place both to advance and to undercut apartheid and Jim Crow. As both viewpoints pivot around the question of the geographic origins of this segregationism, a more fine grained account is required.

31. bell hooks writes, "White students respond with disbelief, shock, and rage[,] . . . with naive amazement that black people critically assess white people[,] . . . that black people watch white people with a critical 'ethnographic' gaze . . . that subvert[s] the liberal conviction that . . . [embracing the belief that]

we are all just people . . . will make racism disappear. They have a deep emotional investment in the myth of 'sameness' even as their actions reflect the primacy of whiteness as a sign of informing who they are and how they think." bell hooks, "Representing Whiteness in the Black Imagination," in *Black on White: Black Writers on What It Means to Be White,* ed. David Roediger (New York: Schocken Books, 1998), 41. Similarly, Steve Biko noted that "white people should become attuned to heed what black people had to say in order to defeat the main problems whites struggled with: their presumed superiority." Biko, cited in Abebe Zegeye, *Youth and Societal Change in South Africa* (Pretoria: UNISA Press, n.d.), 20. Houston Baker's "Completely Well" documents a similar experience. After reading everything in the "colored" library he enters the newly desegregated white library and infuriates the librarian, who "turned redder and redder" on realizing that young Baker had read all the books she offered him and committed them to memory. Baker goes on to note that the bias toward "classics" that existed in his black undergraduate and white graduate training reflected little more than "superstition," "tastes and inclinations," and a "minute fraction of the best the world has to offer." Houston Baker, "Completely Well: One View of Black American Culture," in *Long Black Song: Essays in Black American Literature and Culture* (Charlottesville: University of Virginia Press, 1990), 8, 9, 10.

INTRODUCTION

1. Robyn Wiegman, *Object Lessons* (Durham, NC: Duke University Press, 2012); Pumla Gqola, *What Is Slavery to Me? Postcolonial/Slave Memory in Post-Apartheid South Africa* (Johannesburg: Wits University Press, 2010); Zine Magubane, *Bringing the Empire Home: Race, Class, and Gender in Britain and Colonial South Africa* (Chicago: University of Chicago Press, 2003); Georgina Horrell, "A Whiter Shade of Pale: White Femininity as Guilty Masquerade in 'New' (White) South African Women's Writing," *Journal of Southern African Studies* 30, no. 4 (2004): 765–76; Vincent Crapanzano, *Waiting: The Whites of South Africa* (New York: Random House, 1985).

2. C.L.R. James, *Black Jacobins: Toussaint L'Ouverture and the San Domingo Revolution* (repr. New York: Vintage, [1938] 1989), 33–34.

3. W.E.B. Du Bois, "Transubstantion of a Poor White," in *Black Reconstruction in America: 1860–1880,* introd. David Levering-Lewis (New York: Simon and Schuster, [1935] 1992), 237–324.

4. Tiffany Ruby Patterson and Robin Kelley, "Unfinished Migrations: Reflections on the African Diaspora and the Making of the Modern World," *African Studies Review* 43, no. 1 (2000): 13.

5. Cynthia Young, *Culture, Radicalism, and the Making of a U.S. Third World Left* (Durham, NC: Duke University Press, 2006).

6. Elizabeth Robinson, "Twenty-Five Years of the Third World News Review," *Race and Class* 47, no. 2 (2005): 80.

7. Patterson and Kelley, "Unfinished Migrations," 13.

8. Ibid., 18.

9. Ibid, 19.

10. The most important studies of this kind have been produced by George Fredrickson, Christopher Saunders, Anthony Marx, and the contributors to *Safundi: Journal of South African and American Studies*. But similar studies have been conducted that examine gendered racial politics and racism in the United States and Brazil, the United States and Cuba, and throughout the Americas by Nikol Alexander-Floyd, Nira Yuval-Davis, David Covin, Michael Hanchard, Michael Mitchell, Bernd Reither, Gladys L. Mitchell, Nancy Mirabal, Lisa Brock and Digna Castañeda Fuertes, Nancy Stepan, Mark Sawyer, Kia Lilly Caldwell, and Kheisha-Khan Perry, among many others.

11. Nahum Chandler, *Toward an African Future—Of the Limit of World,* Preface Denise Ferreira Da Silva (New York: Living Commons Collective, 2013); Marilyn Lake and Henry Reynolds, *Drawing the Global Colour Line: White Men's Countries and the International Challenge of Racial Equality* (Cambridge: Cambridge University Press, 2008); W.E.B. Du Bois, *The World and Africa* (New York: International Publishers, 1979).

12. Political ideas about the relationship between race and nation allegedly reinforce the idea of one nation for one territory. And yet the concepts "Anglo-Saxon solidarity," the "white man's burden," *"raza cósmica,"* the "wretched of the earth," the "3/5 compromise," the "one drop rule," "kill the Indian, save the man," "beaten men from beaten races," and others too numerous to name, reveal the influence of a global racial order. These political ideas manifest as policies and practices that must address or pivot around slavery, forced labor, and colonialism and typically only achieve visions of emancipation with indenture, emancipation with debt peonage, emancipation with increased carcerality, erasure of records of state genocide, forced removals and spatial detention on reservations, premature death, and vigilante violence. Gendered black internationalism (and its insistence that we prioritize race over empire and reject settler colonialism) unequivocally rejects the national project that relies on de jure and de facto slave making and occupation of the land by settlers.

13. Kersten Biehn, "Improving Mankind: Philanthropic Foundations and the Transformation of American University Research between the World Wars" (Ph.D. diss., Rice University, 2006); Jonathan Hyslop, "Imperial Working Class Makes Itself 'White': White Labourism in Britain, Australia and South Africa before the First World War," *Journal of Historical Sociology* 12, no. 4 (2002): 398–421; William Watkins, *The White Architects of Black Education: Ideology and Power in America, 1865–1954* (New York: Teachers College Press, 2001); Lee Baker, *From Savage to Negro: Anthropology and the Construction of Race, 1896–1954* (Berkeley: University of California Press, 1998); Sue Krige, "Segregation, Science, and Commissions of Enquiry: Contestation of Native Educational Policy in South Africa, 1930–1936," Seminar Paper No. 398 (University of Witwatersrand, Institute for Advanced Social Research, Education Department, April 29, 1996); Saul Dubow, *Illicit Union: Scientific Racism in Modern South Africa* (Johannesburg: University of Witwatersrand Press, 1995); Brahm David Fleish, "Social Scientists as Policy Makers: E.G. Malherbe and the National Bureau for Education and Social Research, 1929–1943," *Journal of Southern African Studies* 21, no. 3 (1995): 349–72; Ellen Condliffe Lagemann,

The Politics of Knowledge: The Carnegie Corporation, Philanthropy, and Public Policy (Chicago: University of Chicago Press, 1992); Walter Jackson, *Gunnar Myrdal and America's Conscience: Social Engineering and Racial Liberalism, 1938–1987* (Chapel Hill: University of North Carolina Press, 1990); C. J. Groenewald, "Methodology of Poverty Research in South Africa: The Case of the First Carnegie Investigation, 1929–1932," *Social Dynamics* 13, no. 2 (1987): 60–74; Paul Rich, *White Power and the Liberal Conscience: Racial Segregation and South African Liberalism* (Johannesburg: Ravan Press, 1984); Edward Berman, *Ideology of Philanthropy: The Influence of the Carnegie, Ford, and Rockefeller Foundations on American Foreign Policy* (Albany: State University of New York Press, 1983); Thomas J. Noer, *Briton, Boer, and Yankee: The United States and South Africa, 1879–1914* (Kent, OH: Kent State University Press, 1978); Martin Legassick, "The Rise of Modern South African Liberalism: Its Assumptions and Its Social Base," paper presented at the Ideology and Social Structure in Twentieth-Century Africa Seminar, Institute of Commonwealth Studies, University of London, 1973.

14. Charles Van Onselen, *New Babylon, New Nineveh* (Cape Town: Jonathan Ball, 2001). Van Onselen describes several forms of economic support initiated to benefit landowning, tenant, and impoverished rural white people from the 1890s on. These included concessions for liquor distilleries to absorb agriculture from Transvaal farmers and concessions for brick building, promises of jobs and housing, and guaranteed seats on the town council.

15. The debate over which countries could receive Carnegie Corporation Funds and whether they qualified as British dominions (the Philippines, Mexico, and Palestine were rejected) pivoted on whether the New York state charter enabled international philanthropy and permitted more than building libraries and shipping church organs. In 1917, $10 million was set aside as the Special Fund to meet the new needs in Canada, the United Kingdom, and the British colonies in any way the organization decided. See Columbia University, Manuscripts and Archives, Carnegie Corporation of New York Grant Files, Carnegie Corporation of New York Printed Material, Robert M. Lester, ed., *The Corporation and Its Counsel* (New York: CCNY, 1940), Secretary Box 3, File 3.5, RS no. 31.

16. Race relations scholarship includes concepts such as assimilation, race contact, and racial distance. These ideas traveled by means of publications, professional associations, national advisers to philanthropic organizations, and, more important, personnel trained to take up the same social forces, identities, ideologies, and phenomena.

17. Lagemann, *Politics of Knowledge,* 11.

18. Pearl Robinson, "Area Studies in Search of Africa," in *The Politics of Knowledge: Area Studies and the Disciplines,* ed. David Szanton (Berkeley: University of California Press in collaboration with e-scholarship, 2004), 1–41; Watkins, *The White Architects;* Joyce Ladner, ed., *The Death of White Sociology: Essays on Race and Culture* (Baltimore, MD: Black Classic Press, 1998); John Stanfield, *Philanthropy and Jim Crow in American Social Science* (Westport, CT: Greenwood Press, 1985); Carol Taylor, "W. E. B. Du Bois's Challenge to Scientific Racism," *Journal of Black Studies* 11, no. 4 (1981): 449–60; Edward

H. Berman, "Tuskegee—in—Africa," *Journal of Negro Education* 41, no. 2 (1972): 99–112.

19. Robinson's term *racial regimes* is defined as unstable truth claims about political authority that rest on several national myths linked to the "invention of the Negro" as a hapless antithesis to human progress. Cedric J. Robinson, *Forgeries of Memory and Meaning: Blacks and the Regimes of Race in American Theater and Film before World War II* (Chapel Hill: University of North Carolina Press, 2007). Further, racial regimes rest on the belief that republican nationalism signals an exceptional form of European qua white political maturity, indeed the very bedrock upon which modernity and order is based. See Saidiya Hartman, *Scenes of Subjection: Terror, Slavery, and Self-Making in Nineteenth-Century America* (New York: Oxford University Press, 1997); and Cedric Robinson, *Terms of Order: Political Science and the Myth of Leadership* (Albany: State University of New York Press, 1980), for a discussion of how political authority reifies national exceptionalism. The most important of these myths is the seeming resolution of white on white violence in national histories of settler societies; such resolution normalizes white fraternity, subjectivity, agency, sociality, goodheartedness, individuality, innocence, vulnerability, and humanity.

20. These include analysis of the written correspondence between members of the Carnegie Corporation of New York Board of Directors and South African personnel, research reports by Carnegie personnel, oral histories conducted with research team members, pamphlets by the Overseas Visitors Grant Program recipients, records of the Carnegie Corporations Dominions and Colonies Fund, Union of South Africa National Archives, Pretoria Depot, Poor White Collection, Reports from the Inspectorate of White Labor File.

21. Grace Hong and Roderick Ferguson, eds., *Strange Affinities: The Gender and Sexual Politics of Comparative Racialization,* (Durham, NC: Duke University Press, 2011); Michael West, William Martin, and Fanon Che Wilkins, eds., *From Toussaint to Tupac: The Black International since the Age of Revolution* (Chapel Hill: University of North Carolina Press, 2009); Denise Da Silva, *Toward a Global Idea of Race* (Minneapolis: University of Minnesota Press, 2007); Katherine McKittrick, *Demonic Ground: Black Women and the Cartographies of Struggle* (Minneapolis: University of Minnesota Press, 2006); Ruth Wilson Gilmore, "Race and Globalization," in *Geographies of Global Change: Remapping the World,* ed. R. J. Johnston et al. (Malden: Blackwell, 2002).

22. Charles Mills and Carole Pateman, *Contract and Domination* (London: Polity Press, 2007); Tryon Woods, "The Fact of Anti-Blackness: Decolonization in Chiapas and the Niger River Delta," *Human Architecture: Journal of the Sociology of Self-Knowledge* 5, no. 3 (2007): 32, http://scholarworks.umb.edu/humanarchitecture/vol5/iss3/29, accessed April 30, 2013; Kia Lilly Caldwell, *Negras in Brazil: Re-envisioning Black Women's Citizenship and the Politics of Identity* (New Brunswick, NJ: Rutgers University Press, 2006); Penny Von Eschen, *Race against Empire: Black Americans and Anticolonialism, 1937–1957* (Ithaca, NY: Cornell University Press, 1997); Avery Gordon and Chris Newfield, eds., *Multiculturalism* (Minneapolis: University of Minnesota Press, 1996).

23. Patterson and Kelley, "Unfinished Migrations," 13.

24. Robinson, *Forgeries of Memory*, xiii; G.E.M. de Ste. Croix, *The Class Struggle in the Ancient Greek World: From the Archaic Age to the Arab Conquests* (Ithaca, NY: Cornell University Press, 1989); I.F. Stone, *The Trial of Socrates* (New York: Anchor Books, 1989); Hannah Pitkin, *Fortune Is a Woman: Gender and Politics in the Work of Nicollo Machiavelli* (Chicago: University of Chicago Press, 1999); Joanne Wright, *Origin Stories in Political Thought: Discourses on Gender, Power, and Citizenship* (Toronto: University of Toronto Press, 2004); Michael Meckler, *Classical Antiquity and the Politics of America: From George Washington to George W. Bush* (Waco, TX: Baylor University Press, 2006).

25. Arturo Escobar, *Encountering Development: The Making and Unmaking of the Third World* (Princeton, NJ: Princeton University Press, 1995); Keletso Atkins, *The Moon Is Dead! Give Us Our Money! The Cultural Origins of an African Work Ethic, Natal, South Africa, 1843–1900* (Portsmouth, NH: Heinemann, 1993); Walter Rodney, *How Europe Underdeveloped Africa* (Washington, DC: Howard University Press, 1974).

26. Da Silva, *Toward a Global Idea of Race*, 175.

27. Pal Ahluwalia, "When Does a Settler Become a Native? Citizenship and Identity in a Settler Society," *Pretexts: Literary and Cultural Studies* 10, no. 1 (2001): 63–73.

28. W.M. Macmillan, *My South African Years* (Cape Town: David Philip, 1975), explains that the term *race* came to be equated with *Anglo* rather than *Afrikaner*. Afrikaner origin stories of conquest rely on theological claims of having been ordained as inheritors and God's proprietors and managers of *terra nullius*, defending and legitimizing European migration, mobility, and conquest while erasing the existence of economically and culturally hardy black people. However, South African history has had the unenviable and rarely convincing burden of suggesting that white people, even such white people as the Afrikaners were perceived to be in the white global imaginary, were the engines of the region's history. In the world of international affairs, the Afrikaner republics and the Afrikaner people were seen as incapable of self-governance, particularly because of their reliance on an obligation to defend "traditionalism" as a justification for their autonomy. Noer, *Briton, Boer, and Yankee*, 65. The Afrikaners were interested in trying to preserve what they argued was their unique culture, language, religious pietism, political independence, and theologically justified hierarchy of races against British expansionism, industrialization, and control over Southern Africa. The British imperialist notion of uplifting the African as the white man's burden was beyond the borders of Afrikaner ethical systems, which positioned religiously devoted Afrikaners as the wardens of a hopelessly savage race. The Afrikaners were seen as anachronistic for failing to embrace the terms of empire, which somehow was figured as a modernizing presence not a return of an ancient regime of brutality. As the United States, Portugal, and Germany vied for market share of global capital on the African continent, the Afrikaners instead refused to announce that they had a special white man's burden to supervise Africans' move toward development. Instead they articulated a crude and explicitly violent tendency toward genocide and reducing all

African resistance to a theologically justified slavery. Making no such pronouncements, proclamations, declarations, or guarantees about a white responsibility to a civilizing mission made the Afrikaners expendable, though as white people the Afrikaners were also subject to potential extermination. By rejecting Anglophile empire, the Afrikaners were poised to stand in as against civilization. In this moment, we have a powerful illustration of the ways that the racial order associated with white people can produce both white privilege and white misery. To construct the former, white social identity has to be seen as superior and inherently constitutive of progress and futurity and modernity. To construct the latter, it has to be racialized, seen as uniquely vulnerable to degeneration into blackness and inherently constitutive of everything antithetical to civilization—wildness, barbarism, primitivism, superstition, lasciviousness, lawlessness, belligerence, and a lack of noble sentiments to protect the weak. And while the British imperialists could claim to be living up to their civilizational duty in the white global imaginary, the Afrikaner was reviled for marshaling these views in the service of republicanism but not in the service of a well-articulated Afrikaner vision of empire. The British in South Africa cultivated an international reputation for taking on the lofty moral burden of civilizing and characterized their presence as a mission and a moral obligation to the Africans. The Afrikaners were relegated to an international reputation for being capricious and uniquely brutal—and by the end of World War II infamous as "exceptional"— exploiters who saw the African people as a damned obstruction to be disposed of according to Thomas Noer. Though Timothy Keegan has demonstrated that the role of enlightened missionaries of civilization was certainly not less antagonistic to black human being than the idea that black people were perpetually the damned humanoid creatures of the earth, the historiographic distinction that has been posed as a battle between ethnic nationalisms, British and Afrikaner, was far more continuous than dichotomous. The British considered those willing to take on the lofty moral burden of civilization simply less crude than the Afrikaners, who viewed the African as a cursed obstacle to be removed or contained. The subtle difference between these two white nationalisms notwithstanding, for the many African peoples and individual people subject to rule by either or both, their common roots were far more important than the ideological hair-splitting that was said to mark as different the enlightened British and the backward Afrikaners. the United States, a "sister republic" that failed to honor its sibling obligations to South Africa, allied itself with the British Empire in its role as parental origin of Anglo-Saxon solidarity. Noer explains that imperialist Cecil Rhodes had a vision of "Anglo-American world domination" but also saw the United States as a potential threat in the profitable South African Republics. See Noer, *Briton, Boer, and Yankee,* 32. Great Britain supported the United States in the Spanish-American War and aided U.S. missionaries in South Africa. At the same time people in the United States expressed hesitation about British imperialism over whites.Ultimately, the Americans sided with the British in South Africa against the Afrikaners in hope that the former could more likely guarantee efficient good governance, a better environment for free trade, implanting and maintaining the organizations of the Christian gospel of wealth, and access to penetrate the South African consumer market. Noer writes,

"American policy toward southern Africa in the period 1870–1914 reflected prevailing concepts of economic expansion, worldwide evangelism to the heathen, and racism. There was little conflict between the desire to create a market for American goods in South Africa and the sincere belief in Americas mission to shape the area into a Christian, capitalistic, 'civilized' nation on the American model." See Noer, *Briton, Boer, and Yankee,* x. Americans trafficking in the logic of empire, expansionism, industrialization, and the hierarchy of race were much closer to the tendencies and politics of British empire than to the commercial expediency that guided Portuguese and German interests in the African continent, according to Noer. Though British rule might not give the United States carte blanche, it was believed that Britain would create fair rules so that Germany, the United States, and the United Kingdom could have "nearly equitable competition" in the scramble for South Africa. See Noer, *Britain, Boer, Yankee,* xi. In this fashion, the United States would benefit from British imperialism and military invasion, via hitchhiking imperialism, but not be explicitly allied with it.

29. Beverly Crawford and Ronnie D. Lipschultz, eds., The *Myth of "Ethnic Conflict": Politics, Economics, and Cultural Violence* (Berkeley: International and Area Studies, University of California Press, 1998). See also Heribert Adam and Hermann Giliomee, *Ethnic Power Mobilized: Can South Africa Change?* (New Haven, CT: Yale University Press, 1979).

30. Lake and Reynolds, *Drawing the Global Color Line,* 103–4; Robinson, *Forgeries of Memory;* Brenda Gayle Plummer, *Rising Wind: Black Americans and U.S. Foreign Affairs, 1935–1960* (Chapel Hill: University of North Carolina Press, 1996).

31. Robinson, *Forgeries of Memory,* 101–8; Douglas Daniels, *Charlemagne Peralte and the First American Occupation of Haiti,* translation of *Charlemagne Peralte: Un Centenaire, 1885–1995,* by Georges Michel (Dubuque, IA: Kendall-Hunt, 1996).

32. Wilson, cited in Linda Martín Alcoff, *Visible Identities: Race, Gender, and the Self* (London: Oxford University Press, 2006), 21; Robert Bates, "Modernization, Ethnic Competition, and the Rationality of Politics in Contemporary Africa," in *State versus Ethnic Claims: African Policy Dilemmas,* ed. Donald Rothchild and Victor A. Olorunsola (Boulder, CO: Westview Press, 1983), 152–71.

33. Afrikaners were caricatured as awed, defeated, and broken by the sublimely catastrophic and hostile southern African landscape and peoples, thus differing from other white settler communities around the world. Afrikaners seemed to have been *Africanized* by their experiences on the African continent—Africanized, by being subdued by nature and subdued by the continued existence of the African people they wished to dominate. Afrikaners were caricatured as "stupid," as "dupes," and as an "embittered minority" that "detest[s] civilization" (Noer, *Briton, Boer, and Yankee,* 68). Their failure to adequately dominate the landscape and the humanscape reflected something inherently defeated and deficient about the Afrikaners. Many scholars distinguished between South Africa on the one hand and Australia, New Zealand, Canada, and the United States on the other. Trollope wrote that the burden of living

alongside African people had condemned the Europeans in southern Africa. Anthony Trollope, *South Africa* (1877), 235–36. The South African novelist Sarah Gertrude Millin explained Afrikaners' difference from other settler societies as a consequence of frightful practices of miscegenation occurring generation after generation and hoped in her novels to provide a moral prophylaxis. See Sarah Gertrude Millin, *God's Stepchildren* (London: Constable & Co., 1924) and *The Fiddler* (London: Constable & Co., 1929). Writing in 1941, the American university president Cornelis De Kiewiet blamed Afrikaners' economic and social backwardness on having to negotiate with African people about the terms on which proletarianization would occur; see De Kiewiet's *History of South Africa: Social and Economic* (Oxford: Oxford University Press, 1950).

34. Kenan Malik, *The Meaning of Race: Race, History, and Culture in Western Society* (New York: New York University Press, 1996), 135–44, 174; Michael Omi and Howard Winant, *Racial Formation in the United States: From the 1960s to the 1990s* (New York: Routledge, 1994), 4–5, 14–23.

35. This community was so designated to point to their being a mixed-race or "Bastard" community having Dutch fathers and African mothers, mostly occupying the Karoo and Namibia.

36. Van Onselen, *New Babylon, New Nineveh;* Solomon Plaatje, *Mafeking Diary,* Centenary ed., ed. John Comaroff and Brian Willan (Suffolk: James Currey, 1999); Timothy Keegan, *Colonial South Africa and the Origins of the Racial Order* (Charlottesville: University of Virginia Press, 1996); Timothy Keegan, *Rural Transformations in Industrializing South Africa: The Southern Highveld to 1914* (Johannesburg: Ravan Press, 1986).

37. Gqola, *What Is Slavery to Me?*

38. Robinson, *Forgeries of Memory,* 7–8.

39. Ibid.

40. Thomas Arne set the British military anthem "Rule, Britannia," by James Thomson, to music in 1740.

41. Woods, "The Fact of Anti-Blackness," 32;

42. Charles S. Mills, *Racial Contract* (Ithaca, NY: Cornell University Press); Ira Katznelson, *When Affirmative Action Was White: An Untold History of Racial Inequality in Twentieth-Century America* (repr. New York: Norton, 2006); Melissa Steyn, *Whiteness Just Isn't What It Used to Be: White Identity in a Changing South Africa* (Albany: State University of New York Press, 2001); Thandeka, *Learning to Be White: Race, Money and God in America,* 2nd ed. (New York: Continuum, 2000); George Lipsitz, *Possessive Investment in Whiteness* (Philadelphia: Temple University Press, 1998); Noel Ignatiev, *Race Traitor* (New York: Routledge, 1996); Cheryl I. Harris, "Whiteness as Property," in *Critical Race Theory: The Key Writings That Formed the Movement,* ed. Kimberle Crenshaw and Neil Gotanda et al. (New York: New Press, 1995); Ruth Frankenberg, *White Women, Race Matters: The Social Construction of Whiteness* (Minneapolis: University of Minnesota Press, 1994); David Roediger, "From the Social Construction of Race to the Abolition of Whiteness," in *Towards the Abolition of Whiteness: Essays on Race, Politics, and Working-Class History* (New York: Verso, 1994), 1–18; Catherine Hall, *White Male and*

Middle Class: Explorations in Feminism and History (New York: Routledge, 1992); David Roediger, *The Wages of Whiteness: Race and the Making of the American Working Class* (London: Verso, 1991); Richard Sennett and Jonathan Cobb, *The Hidden Injuries of Class* (New York: Norton, 1972); James, *Black Jacobins;* W.E.B. Du Bois, *Black Reconstruction in America: 1860–1880,* Introd. David Levering-Lewis (New York: Simon and Schuster, [1935] 1992).

43. Wilma A. Dunaway, "Slavery and Poor Whites in the Mountain South," in *Slavery in the American Mountain South* (Cambridge: Cambridge University Press, 2003), 139–62; Cedric Robinson, *Black Marxism,* 2nd ed., Foreword Robin Kelley (Chapel Hill: University of North Carolina Press, 2000), 124.

44. Damien Riggs, "Benevolence and the Management of Stake: On Being 'Good White People,'" *Philament* 4 (2004): 1–10.

45. Thandeka, *Learning to Be White,* 9.

46. Marlene Van Niekerk, *Triomf,* trans. Leon de Kock (Johannesburg: Jonathon Ball, [1994] 1999); Carnegie Corporation, "Joint Recommendations and Findings," in *Report of the Carnegie Commission of Investigation on the Poor White Question in South Africa* (Stellenbosch: Pro-Ecclesia-Drukkery, 1932).

47. Robyn Wiegman, *Object Lessons* (Durham, NC: Duke University Press, 2012); Gqola, *What Is Slavery to Me?;* Jared Sexton, *Amalgamation Schemes: Anti-Blackness and the Critique of Multiracialism* (Minneapolis: University of Minnesota Press, 2008); Magubane, *Bringing the Empire Home;* Simon Lewis, *White Women Writers and Their African Invention* (Gainesville: University Press of Florida, 2003).

48. New white nationalisms rely on being able to claim that aspirational white people have not been enslaved or have overcome their former status as slaves. Robinson, *Black Marxism;* Malik, *The Meaning of Race;* Omi and Winant, *Racial Formation.*

49. Pumla Gqola's work on the question of slavery in postapartheid South Africa gives testimony to this effect. White claims to an enslaved history via the Khoi woman "Krotoa" are mounted in order to elicit postracialist sympathy and give legitimacy to white people who submit to a one-man/one-vote electoral system. White people's slave history is intraracial.

50. Wiegman, *Object Lessons,* 29.

51. Robinson, *Black Marxism,* xxx.

52. Annabel Cooper, "Poor Men in the Land of Promises: Settler Masculinity and the Male Breadwinner Economy in Late Nineteenth-Century New Zealand," *Australian Historical Studies* 39, no. 2 (2008): 247.

53. Gqola, *What Is Slavery to Me?;* Ciraj Rassool and Patricia Hayes, "Science and the Spectacle: Khanako's South Africa, 1936–1937," in *Deep Histories: Gender and Colonialism in Southern Africa,* ed. Wendy Woodward, Patricia Hayes, and Gary Minkley (Amsterdam: Rodopi, 2002, 117–161). Many scholars are more recently pointing to the meaning of slavery in southern Africa.

54. Matthew Jacobson, *Barbarian Virtues: The United States Encounters Foreign Peoples at Home and Abroad, 1876–1917* (New York; Hill and Wang, 2000).

55. Robinson, *Black Marxism,* xxix.

56. Ibid.

57. Tiffany Willoughby-Herard, ed. *Theories of Blackness: On Life and Death* (San Diego, CA: Cognella, 2011); Sexton, *Amalgamation Schemes;* Robin Kelley, *Freedom Dreams: The Black Radical Imagination* (Boston: Beacon Press, 2003); Clyde Woods, *Development Arrested: The Blues and Plantation Power in the Mississippi Delta* (New York: Verso, 2000); Cedric Robinson, *Black Movements in America* (New York: Routledge, 1997).

58. Caldwell, *Negras in Brazil;* Mark Sawyer, *Racial Politics in Post-Revolutionary Cuba* (Cambridge: Cambridge University Press, 2005); Alejandro de la Fuente, "Myths of Racial Democracy: Cuba, 1900–1912," *Latin American Research Review* 34, no. 3 (1999): 39; Hartman, *Scenes of Subjection.*

59. Plummer, *Rising Wind,* 128.

60. Wilderson's critique of Gramsci's notion of exploitation posits that "Black death is the modern bourgeois state's recreational past-time" and that "slavery . . . is closer to capital's primal obsession than waged oppression. . . . The worker demands that productivity be fair and democratic [and] . . . the slave demands that production stop; stop without recourse to its ultimate democratization." Frank Wilderson, "Gramsci's Black Marx: Whither the Slave in Civil Society?," *We Write* 2, no. 1 (2005): 6. In such a structural antagonism, white pleasure relies on black suffering. Similarly, Denise Da Silva has argued in "The Dead Do Fly Planes" that premature death is precisely the set of relations and practices and the context for institutional life that best explains the murder of the Guinean immigrant Amadou Diallo (February 4, 1999). The police who shot Diallo over forty times at close range described their fear of entering a literal and figurative "state of nature" in the neighborhood where he resided. Thus Silva makes the claim that for the only people empowered to use force of arms in civil society to refer to "places where blacks reside" as akin to the state of nature suggests that black people are not recognizable as human and thus are scheduled for inevitable and juridically legitimated premature death. Denise Da Silva, "The Dead Do Fly Planes," paper presented at (T)races Conference, University of California, Irvine Humanities Research Institute, April 11, 2003, http://vimeo.com/album/163167o/video/25726623, accessed June 12, 2012.

61. These mobile keywords each have particular histories, but their mobility is quite important for tracking the deployment of the poor white idea. As Magubane explains, *vagrant* was a term used by defenders of the Cape Colony 1838 Vagrancy Law throughout the empire that erroneously compared Khoikhoi people and English paupers such that by the 1850s the comparison had become paradigmatic (Magubane, *Bringing the Empire Home,* 54). The term *heathen at home* was used by nineteenth- and early-twentieth-century English photographers to explain both the white working class and the nonwhite subject of empire. Sally Gaule, "Poor White, White Poor: Meanings in the Differences of Whiteness," *History of Photography* 25, no. 4 (2001): 334–47.

62. When Magubane investigates all the groups that came to stand in for black suffering in the imperial age in Britain—white workers who are called slaves, white married and unmarried women who are called white slaves—she is explaining a feature of this mechanism of deploying the white primitive as an evocative symbolic reminder of a collective consciousness that reminds white people to avert their eyes while engaging in a pretense of charitable looking that

is fundamentally pathologizing and demonizing. This scopophilic attention is regularly converted into the currency of expertise, guardianship, and protection.

63. Frank Gilliam, "The 'Welfare Queen' Experiment: How Viewers React to Images of African-American Mothers on Welfare," *Nieman Reports* (Nieman Foundation for Journalism at Harvard University) 53, no. 2 (1999): 5–6.

64. Duchess Harris, "Kathryn Stockett Is Not My Sister and I Am Not Her Help," *Feminist Wire,* August 12, 2011, http://thefeministwire.com/2011/08 /kathryn-stockett-is-not-my-sister-and-i-am-not-her-help/, accessed May 21, 2012.

65. Ange-Marie Hancock, *The Politics of Disgust: The Public Identity of the Welfare Queen* (New York: New York University Press, 2004).

66. Duchess Harris, *Black Feminist Politics from Kennedy to Obama* (New York: Palgrave Macmillan, 2011); Harris, "Kathryn Stockett Is Not My Sister"; Christina Sharpe, *Monstrous Intimacies: Making Post-Slavery Subjects* (Durham, NC: Duke University Press, 2010); Julia Jordan-Zachery, *Black Women, Cultural Images, and Social Policy* (New York: Routledge, 2008); Thavolia Glymph, *Out of the House of Bondage: The Transformation of the Plantation Household* (New York: Cambridge University Press, 2008); Nikol Alexander-Floyd, *Gender, Race, and Nationalism in Contemporary Black Politics* (New York: Palgrave Macmillan, 2007); France Winddance Twine, *Racism in a Racial Democracy: The Maintenance of White Supremacy in Brazil* (New Brunswick, NJ: Rutgers University Press, 1998); Valerie Smith, *Not Just Race, Not Just Gender: Black Feminist Readings* (New York: Routledge, 1998); Nell Irvin Painter, "Introduction: The Journal of Ella Gertrude Glanton Thomas: An Educated White Woman in the Eras of Slavery, War, and Reconstruction," in *The Secret Eye: The Journal of Ella Gertrude Clanton Thomas, 1848–1889,* ed. Virginia Burr (Chapel Hill: University of North Carolina Press, 1990), 1–70.

67. Toni Morrison, *Beloved* (New York: Knopf, 1987).

68. Hartman, *Scenes of Subjection,* 49–78.

69. Sindiwe Magona, *To My Children's Children,* reissue (Northhampton, MA: Interlink, 2006); Andrea Smith, *Conquest: Sexual Violence and American Indian Genocide* (Cambridge, MA: South End Press, 2005); Wendy Woodward, "Contradictory Tongues: Torture and the Testimony of Two Slave Women in the Eastern Cape Courts in 1833 and 1834," in *Deep Histories: Gender and Colonialism in Southern Africa,* Cross/Cultures: Readings in the Post/Colonial Literatures in English 57, ed. Wendy Woodward, Patricia Hayes, and Gary Minkley (Amsterdam: Rodopi, [1994] 2002), 55–84; Rassool and Hayes, "Science and Spectacle"; T. Denean Sharpley-Whiting, *Frantz Fanon: Conflicts and Feminisms* (Lanham, MD: Rowman and Littlefield, 1997); Angela Davis, *Woman, Race and Class* (New York: Vintage, 1983).

70. Robinson's "terms of order" refers to the institutions, practices, and cultural and racial logics that prop up domination and dehumanization. Social science in the United States, out of deference to its own making in the culture of corporations transforming themselves into philanthropies—what some of us might call the ancestors of the privatization of the public—did everything to mask its own manufacture. Gilmore describes the contemporary operating "order" as a gulag, in two senses: (a) a set of institutions and practices, and (b) a cultural mind-

set. See Robinson, *Terms of Order*; Ruth Wilson Gilmore, *Golden Gulag: Prisons, Surplus, Crisis, and Opposition in Globalizing California* (Berkeley: University of California Press, 2007); and Setsu Shigematsu, Cameron Granadino, and Jolie Chea. *Visions of Abolition: From Critical Resistance to a New Way of Life* (DVD: Critical Resistance/PM Press, 2011). Like the spectacle of bourgeois society itself, social science in the United States adorned itself with the pretense that Magubane describes as "one of the cornerstones in the ideological justification of capitalism: that the appropriation of another person's labor can be treated as equivalent to the performance of the activity of labor." Magubane, *Bringing the Empire Home*, 67. Thus social science in the United States was concerned most of all with providing cover for the market and the bourgeois state through securing for itself the coveted position of propagandist for technocratic rule masquerading as democracy. Having sold its birthright in the decision to enslave, again and again, as a basis for the republic, the United States was certainly in need of such public relations as social science could provide. Barbara Christian describes this process as the substitution by which "works (a word that evokes labor) have become texts. . . . [F]or the critic yearning for attention has displaced the writer and has conceived of herself or himself as the center." Barbara Christian, "Race for Theory," *Cultural Critique* 6 (1987): 67. These various interpretations cumulatively explain the nature of the terms of order.

71. Black women's status can be used to spectacularize myths about black male and black female sexual and gender deviance and non-normative relations of social reproduction. Noting the consistency of this juridical illegibility within the site of domestic safety, the domestic violence shelter, Kimberle Crenshaw made visible the contours of anti-blackness that entrap black women and Latinas into sites of unenviable exception. Kimberle Crenshaw, "Mapping the Margins: Intersectionality, Identity Politics, and Violence against Women of Color," in Crenshaw, Gotanda, et al., *Critical Race Theory*, 357–83.

72. Angela Davis, *Are Prisons Obsolete?* (New York: Seven Stories Press, 2003), 82, 124 n. 98, citing Amanda George, "Strip Searches: Sexual Assault by the State," 211–12, www.aic.gov.au/publications/proceedings/20/george.pdf.

73. Ibid.

74. Ayelet Waldman and Robin Levi, eds., *Inside This Place Not of It: Narratives from Women's Prisons* (San Francisco: McSweeneys, 2011). I am reminded of the value attached to Dominique Strauss-Kahn's reputation as more vulnerable than Nafissatou Diallo's body (*People of the State of New York v Strauss-Kahn*, May 14, 2011), DNA evidence and all, and the lack of value (girlhood) assigned to Quvenzhané Wallis, a nine-year-old African American actress and Oscar nominee, publicly referred to by a derogatory name for female anatomy. Tressie McMillan Cottom, "Did White Feminists Ignore Attacks on Quvenzhané Wallis? That's an Empirical Question," *Tressie MC Blog*, February 28, 2013, http://tressiemc.com/2013/02/28/did-white-feminists-ignore-attacks-on-quvenzhane-wallis-thats-an-empirical-question/, accessed May 21, 2013. On the issue of black women and reputation, see Toni Morrison, ed., *Race-ing Justice, En-gendering Power* (New York: Pantheon, 1992). In the past black critiques of attacks on reputation have been chalked up to frustrated assimilation into masculine nationalism and patriarchal domesticity. Kevin Gaines,

Uplifting the Race: Black Leadership, Politics, and Culture in the Twentieth Century (Chapel Hill: University of North Carolina Press, 1996), provides extensive discussion of masculinist attempts at "uplifting the race" and "dissemblance." See also Darlene Clark Hine, "Rape and the Inner Lives of Black Women in the Middle West: Preliminary Thoughts on the Culture of Dissemblance," in *Words of Fire: An Anthology of African-American Feminist Thought,* ed. Beverly Guy-Sheftall (New York: New Press, 1995). Nafissatou Diallo and Quvenzhané Wallis and the everyday sexual violence that structures policing, surveillance, media trashing, and incarceration get closer to what has compelled this sustained attempt to resist attacks on the black reputation, i.e., antiblack gratuitous sexual violence. This is not merely a question of pluralistic competition over resources and over the content of the political agenda, it is a question of whether or not black people's main role in this social order is to sustain sexual and gender injury.

75. Sharpe, *Monstrous Intimacies*; Robinson, *Forgeries of Memory*, 15–81; Gargi Bhattacharyya, *Tales of Dark Skinned Women: Race, Gender, and Global Culture* (New York: Routledge, 1998); Hortense Spillers, "Mama's Baby, Papa's Maybe," *Diacritics* 17, no. 2 (1987): 64–81.

76. Lagemann, *Politics of Knowledge,* 57.

77. James Jennings, *Welfare Reform and the Revitalization of Inner City Neighborhoods* (Lansing: Michigan State University Press, 2003).

78. Harris draws on Locke's (1886–1954) point that though the social sciences originated in humanities subjects (classics and Egyptology), the foundations launched a role for the social scientists in governance. Leonard Harris, ed. *The Philosophy of Alain Locke: Harlem Renaissance and Beyond* (Philadelphia: Temple University Press, 1991). Nikol Alexander-Floyd (2012, 17) concurs that the Greek meaning of empiricism is "experience"—a key part of data gathering in "Disappearing Acts: Reclaiming Intersectionality in the Social Sciences in a Post-Black Feminist Era" *Feminist Formations* 24, no.1. See also Lagemann, *Politics of Knowledge,* 70; Jacobson, *Barbarian Virtues,* 165. Jacobson explains that even lay social scientists—craniometric statisticians—benefited handsomely from the vigorous interest in their expertise. Thus, the overvalorization of the social sciences as absolutely necessary for fixing social problems instead of the philosophical, aesthetic, affective, or experiential is arbitrary, ethnocentric, and explicitly manufactured through the influence harvesting by foundations.

79. Alice O' Connor, *Poverty Knowledge: Social Science, Social Policy, and the Poor in Twentieth-Century U.S. History* (Princeton, NJ: Princeton University Press, 2002).

80. Lagemann, *Politics of Knowledge,* 67–68; Harris, ed., *Philosophy of Alain Locke,* 12. This knowledge elite maligned the New Deal administration's policy pragmatism as "ad hoc tinkering," marginalized vindicationist nationalism by black intellectuals, and vilified the economic justice research agenda of the settlement house movement. Houston Baker describes black intellectuals' difference from the professionalized status seekers funded by the Carnegie Corporation as "radical marronage." Such critical cultural examinations and their alternative models of social research enabled communities to work together to learn to solve problems that immediately affected them. Carnegie's men deemed

this sort of cultural examination and settlement house social research as anti-American hubs of wayward socialistic women.

81. Lagemann, *Politics of Knowledge*, 45. Classical art and architecture, scientific research, economic and legal analyses, and professional education were to be disseminated to the masses via schools, museums, and libraries but not to black people, who were believed to be incapable of benefiting from civilization.

82. Berman, *Ideology of Philanthropy*, 15.

83. Lageman, *Politics of Knowledge*, 67–68.

84. Harris, ed., *Philosophy of Alain Locke*, 19.

85. The Carnegie Corporation literally built these new disciplines from the ground up by being a major donor to research scientists and universities, taking on the expense of publishing their work for academic and nonacademic audiences, and creating policy and research institutes.

86. Berman, *Ideology of Philanthropy*, 4. According to Robinson in *Terms of Order*, unlike "the medieval Church and the Absolut[ist] State . . . the development of industrial organization . . . presupposed a different order of discipline and civility. . . . The bourgeoisie mystified their expropriation of wealth by accruing to themselves the function of rational, scientific management. In this way, the mystification of the ruling class of industrial society became the historical and political basis for the mystification of leadership in contemporary Western thought. Concomitant to this mystification was the conduction of the discipline of the industrial work place to the regions of social and political behavior" (56–57). See also Paul Feyeraband, "Consolations for the Specialist," in *Criticism and the Growth of Knowledge: Proceedings of the International Colloquium in the Philosophy of Science*, ed. Imre Lakatos and Alan Musgrave (Cambridge: Cambridge University Press, 1970) 214.

87. As a radical pragmatist, Locke criticized American pragmatism for its "ethnocentrism and privileging [of] experimentalism and the scientific method" while explaining that constantly changing features of human experience were linked to specific historical moments and values and feelings specific to human groups. Locke's political project was to examine black humanity without "prescribing cultural uniformity" or maligning group membership resulting from "objectively calculated social choices." See Harris, ed., *Philosophy of Alain Locke*, 17–18.

88. Berman, *Ideology of Philanthropy*, 5. Pearl Robinson's "Area Studies in Search of Africa" echoes this point in great detail.

89. Berman, *Ideology of Philanthropy*, 30.

90. Ibid., 45.

91. Lagemann, *Politics of Knowledge*, 65. Having demobilized local and neighborhood community-based social research and also representative government, the foundation sector inserted itself as the most salient professional expertise in public life. See Stanfield's *Philanthropy and Jim Crow*, William Watkin's *The White Architects*, and Henry Yu's *Thinking Orientals: Migration, Contact, and Exoticism in Modern America* (Oxford: Oxford University Press, 2001).

92. The nomenclature of a "Gilded Age," and "The Nadir" largely fail. The former does not tend to the level of violence that created such upholstered lives;

the latter needs more specific articulation linking lynching to the production and extension of wealth, social identities, and carceral institutions.

93. Jacqueline Goldsby's *A Spectacular Secret: Lynching in American Life and Literature* (Chicago: University of Chicago Press, 2006), 27; and Hartman's *Scenes of Subjection* get at this in the most sustained fashion and echo the enduring specificity described in the discussion above of gendered blackness. But others have taken up this point: Sharpe, *Monstrous Intimacies;* Morgan, *Laboring Women;* Avery Gordon, *Ghostly Matters: Haunting and the Sociological Imagination,* 2nd ed. (Minneapolis: University of Minnesota Press, 2008); Grace Hale, *Making Whiteness: The Culture of Segregation in the South, 1890–1940* (New York: Vintage Press, 1999). In their attention to the enduring legacies of sexual torture as constitutive of each postemancipation moment, Yvette Abrahams, "'Ambiguity' Is My Middle Name: A Research Diary," in *Hear Our Voices: Race, Gender, and the Status of Black South African Women in the Academy,* ed. Reitumetse Mabokela and Zine Magubane (Pretoria and Leiden: University of South Africa Press and Koninklijke Brill, 2004), 10–24; and Wendy Woodward, "Contradictory Tongues," make it plain that the practices of violence itself are perhaps the most essential though largely overlooked and denied component of technopolitical progress narratives.

94. David Roediger and Elizabeth Esch, *The Production of Difference: Race and the Management of Labor in US History* (Oxford: Oxford University Press); Lisa Yun, *The Coolie Speaks: Chinese Indentured Laborers and African Slaves in Cuba* (Philadephia: Temple University Press, 2008); Gerald Horne, *White Pacific: U.S. Imperialism and Black Slavery in the South Seas after the Civil War* (Honolulu: University of Hawai'i Press, 2007); Mark Aldrich, "Progressive Economists and Scientific Racism: Walter Willcox and Black Americans, 1895–1910," *Phylon* 40 (1979): 1.

95. Ibid.

96. Rebecca Hill, *Men, Mobs, and Law: Anti-Lynching and Labor Defense in US Radical History* (Durham, NC: Duke University Press, 2009).

97. Goldsby, *Spectacular Secret,* 23–24.

98. Bridget Cooks, "Confronting Terrorism: Teaching the History of Lynching through Photography," Pedagogy 8, no. 1 (2008): 135–45; Ken Gonzales-Day, *Lynching in the West, 1850–1935* (Durham, NC: Duke University Press, 2006).

99. Goldsby, *Spectacular Secret;* Gerald Horne, *Black and Brown: African Americans and the Mexican Revolution, 1910–1920* (New York: New York University Press, 2005); Roediger, *Wages of Whiteness.*

100. Roediger and Esch, *The Production of Difference;* Alex Lichtenstein, *Twice the Work of Free Labor: The Political Economy of Convict Labor in the New South* (New York: Verso, 1996).

101. Robinson, *Forgeries of Memory.*

102. Lagemann, *Politics of Knowledge,* 128. Liberals such as Newton Baker, infamously known for referring to black people as merely "uncaged animals," articulated his naive political liberalism by legitimizing race riots, lynchings, the hardships of the Great Migration, and the hideous public policies of the eugenics movement. For Baker, the United States was experiencing a period of incredible progress in this age of lynching.

103. Plummer, *Rising Wind,* 20. In the end, Japan failed to have the subsequent League of Nations adopt a (racial) equality clause. The United States and Britain opposed the measure, but when it came to a vote, it was passed by a majority. Woodrow Wilson, presiding, then declared that only unanimity could make the principle binding and refused to recognize it. In so doing, he blatantly departed from past parliamentary practice.

104. Goldsby, *Spectacular Secret,* 11.

105. For example, the South African campaigns against imperialism often ignored the processes by which Afrikaner capitalists had cheated Afrikaner miners from titles to their lands via the institution of the Diggers Committees organized to turn prospecting Afrikaners off the mining lands.

106. Lagemann, *Politics of Knowledge,* 6.

107. By "racial development," I mean segregationist philanthropy's role in legitimating the racial labor hierarchy of black people in the United States and globally. Knut G. Nustad, "Politics of Development: Power and Changing Discourses in South Africa," *Cambridge Anthropology* 19 (1996): 1; Escobar, *Encountering Development;* Rodney, *How Europe Underdeveloped Africa.*

108. Robinson, *Forgeries of Memory,* xii.

109. The Rosenwald Foundation–launched academic Rose Butler Browne offers a useful account: *Love My Children: An Autobiography* (New York: Meredith Press, 1969).

110. Laura Putnam, "Nothing Matters but Color: Transnational Circuits, the Interwar Caribbean, and the Black International," in West, Martin, and Wilkins, *From Toussaint to Tupac,* 107–29.

111. Forms of bondage included debt peonage, the convict lease system, lynching in the South and West, the Dawes Act, systematic violence against domestic and household workers, destruction of black landowning neighborhoods, and bloody antiblack race riots. Marco Williams, dir., *Banished: How Whites Drove Blacks out of Town in America* (DVD, Independent Lens, 2006).

112. Debs's speech was published in 1901. Eugene V. Debs, "Crimes of Carnegie: Protest against Condoning Crime in the Name of Philanthropy" (March 30, 1901), *Missouri Socialist,* April 1, 1901.

113. Du Bois, *Black Reconstruction.*

114. Hill, *Men, Mobs, and Law;* Hyslop, "Imperial Working Class Makes Itself 'White'"; Deborah Posel, "Whiteness and Power in the South African Civil Service: Paradoxes of the Apartheid State," *Journal of Southern African Studies* 25, no. 1 (1999): 99–119; Pieter C. Van Duin, "'Workers of All Colours Unite!': South African Communism, the White Working Class, and the Ideology of Proletarian Non-Racialism, 1917–1943," *South Asia Bulletin, Comparative Studies of South Asia, Africa and the Middle East* 15, no. 2 (1996): 64–71. For contemporary examples of this articulation and for historical work on this, see Robert F. Castro, "Busting the Bandido Boyz: Militarism, Masculinity, and the Hunting of Undocumented Persons in the U.S.-Mexico Borderlands," *Journal of Hate Studies* 6, no. 1 (2007–8): 7–30; and Mike Davis and Justin Chacon, *No One Is Illegal: Fighting Racism and State Violence on the U.S. Mexico Border* (Chicago: Haymarket Books, 2006).

115. Columbia University, Manuscripts and Archives, Carnegie Corporation of New York Grant Files, Poor White Study, Keppel Loram Correspondence,

1927–29; C.T. Loram to CCNY President Dr. F.P. Keppel, Students reject higher diploma in Jeannes School in Nyasaland, Series I. Box 295, File 295.8.

116. Raymond Wolters, *The New Negro on Campus: Black College Rebellions of the 1920s* (Princeton, NJ: Princeton University Press, 1975).

117. Andrew Carnegie, "Mr. Carnegie's Address," in *Presentation of the Carnegie Library to the People of Pittsburgh, with a Description of the Dedicatory Exercises* (Pittsburgh: City of Pittsburgh, November 5, 1895), 13–14.

118. Robinson, *Forgeries of Memory;* Meckler, *Classical Antiquity;* Pitkin, *Fortune Is a Woman;* Cynthia Farrar, *Origins of Democratic Thinking: The Invention of Politics in Classical Athens* (London: Cambridge University Press, 1989).

119. Robinson, *Forgeries of Memory,* xiii.

120. Paul Ramsey, "Wrestling with Modernity: Philanthropy and the Children's Aid Society in Progressive-Era New York City," *New York History* 88, no. 2 (2007): 153–74; Davis and Chacon, *No One Is Illegal;* David Leverenz, *Paternalism Incorporated: Fables of American Fatherhood, 1865–1940* (Ithaca, NY: Cornell University Press, 2003); Gaines, *Uplifting the Race;* Mark Twain and Charles Dudley, The Project Gutenberg EBook of *The Gilded Age: A Novel About Today* ([1873] 2006), www.gutenberg.org/files/3178/3178-h/3178-h.htm, accessed October 13, 2013.

121. I challenge the representation of scientific racist discourse as a marginalized and defeated mode of inquiry. As early as the 1870s European scientific authority agreed on the unitary origins of all human beings. However, at each moment of its supposed repudiation, the same body of authorities continued to rank levels of civilization, studying "contemporary savages" and calling them the "missing link," "living fossils," "cultural fossils," and the past of civilized society. But even though scientific racism most often shows up to superintend white people in order to ultimately benefit them, the history of white people as targets of scientific racism indicates important tendencies in the institutionalization of white vulnerability and the process through which a social formation was made into an ideological goad. Dorothy Roberts, *Fatal Invention: How Science, Race, and Big Business Re-Create Race in the Twenty-First Century* (New York: New Press, 2011); Troy Duster, *Backdoor to Eugenics,* 2nd ed. (New York: Routledge, 2003); Regna Darnell, *Invisible Genealogies: A History of Americanist Anthropology,* Critical Studies in the History of Anthropology (Lincoln: University of Nebraska Press, 2001); Regna Darnell, *And Along Came Boas: Continuity and Revolution in Americanist Anthropology,* Studies in the History of the Language Sciences (Amsterdam: John Benjamins, 1998); Jacobson, *Barbarian Virtues,* 141, 148; Joyce Ladner, ed., *The Death of White Sociology: Essays on Race and Culture* (Baltimore, MD: Black Classic Press, 1998).

122. Robinson, *Forgeries of Memory,* contends, "Anti-black racism, then, is a tool to legitimate decisive transformations in power relations, not a universally inherent code of belief," and also warns against "mistaking an inventory of how raced subjects are invented" as the same thing as "Black resistance to each historical moment of Negrophobic impulses." In order to foreground black resistance to Negrophobic impulses, the Negrophobic impulse and its "patchwork, masquerade of history" cannot be ceded all the ground that it seeks to claim (xvi). The demeaned state of the black body causes perhaps the most con-

fusion here because so much of white humanitarianism has been organized by preventing so-called white people from being treated "like" black people.

123. Racialization of poor whites is fundamentally a variant of antiblackness, albeit one whose target is white people.

CHAPTER 1

1. Malherbe was far junior to Stellenbosch University faculty member R.W. Wilcocks. In many ways the study could have been more closely associated with Wilcocks. However, this was not the way the study was funded or marketed. Columbia University, Manuscripts and Archives, Carnegie Corporation of New York Grant Files, Poor White Study, Africa: Cooperative Research Poor White Study, Wilcox [sic] 12/12/29, 11/21/29, 10/4/29, Series I, Box 295, File 295.4.

2. William Watkins, *The White Architects of Black Education: Ideology and Power in America, 1865–1954* (New York: Teachers College Press, 2001); Paul Rich, *White Power and the Liberal Conscience: Racial Segregation and South African Liberalism* (Johannesburg: Ravan Press, 1984); Edward Berman, *The Ideology of Philanthropy: The Influence of the Carnegie, Ford, and Rockefeller Foundations on American Foreign Policy* (Albany: State University of New York Press, 1983).

3. I return to why the Carnegie Corporation was in South Africa at the end of this chapter and again in chapter 6.

4. Charlie Johnson and Gerry Mooney, "'Problem' People, 'Problem' Spaces? New Labour and Council Estates," in *Securing an Urban Renaissance: Crime Community, and British Urban Policy,* ed. Rowland Atkinson and Gesa Helms (Bristol: Policy Press, 2007): 125–39; W.E.B. Du Bois, "Strivings of the Negro People," *Atlantic Monthly,* 1897, www.theatlantic.com/magazine/archive1897/08/strivings-of-the-negro-people/5446/, accessed June 15, 2012.

5. J.F.W. Grosskopf, "Economic Report: Rural Impoverishment and Rural Exodus. Part I," in *Report of the Carnegie Commission of Investigation on the Poor White Question in South Africa* (Stellenbosch: Pro-Ecclesia-Drukkery, 1932).

6. Carnegie Commission, "Joint Findings and Recommendations of the Commission," in *Report of the Carnegie Commission,* vii.

7. Neil Roos, "Some Preliminary Notes on Work Colonies and Apartheid Culture," paper presented at South African Historical Society Biennial Conference, University of South Africa, Tshwane, Sunnyside Campus, June 22–24, 2009; Linda Chisholm, "Themes in the Construction of Compulsory Education for the White Working Class on the Witwatersrand, 1886–1907," paper presented at History Workshop and Wits Institute for Social and Economic Research, Class, Community and Conflict: Local Perspectives, Johannesburg, January 31–February 4, 1984); H.C. Hopkins, *Kakamas—From the Wilderness an Oasis* (in Afrikaans) (Cape Town: National Book Press, 1978); Nicholaas Jacobus De Wet, Officer Administering the Government, and A.M. Conroy, Officer Administering the Government-in-Council, Union of South Africa, Letters of Appointment to Commission of Enquiry Kakamas Labour Colony (1945) to Mr. Justice Jean Etienne De Villiers, Marthinus Johannes Van Den Berg, Esquire, M.P., Hendrik Johannes Nel, Esquire, Michael Daniel Otto Klopper, Lt.-Col and Paul Jacobus Burger, Esquire, and to Captain James Watts Butler (June 16, 1945).

8. Cedric J. Robinson, *Forgeries of Memory and Meaning: Blacks and the Regimes of Race in American Theater and Film before World War II* (Chapel Hill: University of North Carolina Press, 2007), 62.

9. Zine Magubane, *Bringing the Empire Home: Race, Class, and Gender in Britain and Colonial South Africa* (Chicago: University of Chicago Press, 2003), 177. This leadership class has been considered extensively through Robinson's concept of the renegade black intelligentsia. See Cedric Robinson, *Black Marxism,* 2nd ed., foreword Robin Kelley (Chapel Hill: University of North Carolina Press, 2000), 181–82. Berman's treatment of the "native informant" concept explains the significance of Jomo Kenyatta's role in liberal and Marxist intellectual debates. See Bruce Berman, "Ethnography as Politics, Politics as Ethnography: Kenyatta, Malinowki, and the Making of Facing Mount Kenya," *Canadian Journal of African Studies* 30, no. 3 (1996): 313–44.

10. According to Malherbe, the most acclaimed member of the *Poor White Study* research team, the dependency that poor whites manifested made them an insult to the noble memory of the Trekboers, the 1830s generation of Afrikaner nationalist pioneers whose migration from British-dominated coastal colonial cities has a central place in South African racial historiography. Malherbe's complaint about poor white dependency was steeped in a racialist logic about white people and their innate superiority and innate independence. He was deeply disturbed by the existence of any people who confirmed that whites were not conquerors bringing civilization, urban cosmpolitanism, and industrial progress to South Africa. Indeed, Malherbe's comments reflected yet another mystification about the origins of white poverty that located it in hereditary, genetic, and character flaws. Poor whites were a threat to the idea of white supremacy in South Africa because they suggested that whiteness in and of itself guaranteed nothing. They revealed that whiteness was a sham, a case of false advertising that was believed in only by those who had the most to gain from it.

11. Paul Rich, "Ministering to the White Man's Needs: Development of Urban Segregation in South Africa, 1913–1923," *African Studies* 37, no. 2 (1978): 177–92.

12. Neil Roos, "Some Preliminary Notes on Work Colonies and Apartheid Culture"; Shurlee Swain, "The Value of the Vignette in the Writing of Welfare History," *Australian Historical Studies* 39, no. 2 (2008): 199–212; Louise Vincent, "Bread and Honor: White Working Class Women and Afrikaner Nationalism in the 1930s," *Journal of Southern African Studies* 26, no. 1 (2000): 61–78; Louise Vincent, "A Cake of Soap: The Volksmoeder Ideology and Afrikaner Women's Campaign for the Vote," *International Journal of African Historical Studies* 32, no. 1 (1999): 1–17; H.C. Hopkins, *Kakamas—From the Wilderness an Oasis* (Afrikaans) (Cape Town: National Book Press, 1978); Nicholaas Jacobus De Wet, Officer Administering the Government, and A.M. Conroy, Officer Administering the Government-in-Council, Union of South Africa, Letters of Appointment to Commission of Enquiry Kakamas Labour Colony 1945 to Mr. Justice Jean Etienne De Villiers, Marthinus Johannes Van Den Berg, Esquire, M.P., Hendrik Johannes Nel, Esquire, Michael Danicl Otto Klopper, Lt.-Col., and Paul Jacobus Burger, Esquire, and to Captain James Watts Butler, 16 June, 1945.

13. Malherbe's records document an unseemly obsession with self-promotion.

14. As late as 1999 one of the agencies that Malherbe initiated, which eventually became the Human Sciences Research Council (HSRC), was still cramped by the main legacy of apartheid social science: job protection for apartheid social scientists. Reeling from the effects of trying to employ hundreds of highly trained researchers in some other task than statistical justifications for apartheid, the agency had to reckon with Malherbe's "contributions."

15. Andrew Zimmerman, *Alabama in Africa: Booker T. Washington, the German Empire, and the Globalization of the New South*, Reprint Edition (Princeton, NJ: Princeton University Press, 2012); Richard Glotzer, "The Career of Mabel Carney: The Study of Race and Rural Development in the United States and South Africa," *International Journal of African Historical Studies* 29, no. 2 (1996): 309–36; Edward Berman, *The Ideology of Philanthropy: The Influence of the Carnegie, Ford, and Rockefeller Foundations on American Foreign Policy* (Albany: State University of New York Press, 1983); Thomas J. Noer, *Briton, Boer, and Yankee: The United States and South Africa, 1879–1914* (Kent, OH: Kent State University Press, 1978).

16. Pearl Robinson, "Area Studies in Search of Africa," in *The Politics of Knowledge: Area Studies and the Disciplines,* ed. David Szanton (Berkeley: University of California Press in collaboration with e-scholarship, 2004), 1–41; Ellen Condliffe Lagemann, *The Politics of Knowledge: The Carnegie Corporation, Philanthropy, and Public Policy* (Chicago: University of Chicago Press, 1992), 65–68; Leonard Harris, ed., *The Philosophy of Alain Locke: Harlem Renaissance and Beyond* (Philadelphia: Temple University Press, 1991).

17. Edward Berman, "Tuskegee—in—Africa," *Journal of Negro Education* 41, no. 2 (Spring 1972): 102; Richard Glotzer, "A Long Shadow: Frederick P. Keppel, the Carnegie Corporation, and the Dominions and Colonies Fund Area Experts, 1923–1943," *History of Education* 38, no. 5 (2009): 621–48; Watkins, *The White Architects;* Lagemann, *Politics of Knowledge,* 19–20; Edward Berman, "American Influence on African Education: The Role of the Phelps-Stokes Fund's Education Commissions," *Comparative Education Review, Colonialism and Education* 5, no. 2 (1971): 132–45.

18. Ernest Malherbe, "The Carnegie Poor White Investigation: Its Origin and Sequels," Columbia University, CCNY Grant Files 295.7, n.d., 83.

19. Ibid.

20. Maria Lis Lange, *White, Poor and Angry: White Working-Class Families in Johannesburg,* (Aldershot: Ashgate, 2003); Judith Tayler, "Aspects of Social Welfare and Poor White Rehabilitation in South African Railways and Harbours, 1934–1952" (Master's thesis, University of South Africa, 1992); Charles Van Onselen, *New Babylon, New Nineveh* (Cape Town: Jonathan Ball, 2001); Colin Bundy, "Vagabond Hollanders and Runaway Englishmen: White Poverty in the Cape before Poor Whiteism," *Second Carnegie Inquiry into Poverty in South Africa* (Cape Town: University of Cape Town, 1984); B.H. Kinkead-Weekes, "History of Vagrancy in Cape Town," in *Second Carnegie Inquiry;* Pieter Le Roux, "Poor White," *Second Carnegie Inquiry;* Vivian Bickford-Smith, "Dangerous Cape Town: Middle Class Attitudes to Poverty in Cape Town in the

late Nineteenth Century," in *Studies in the History of Cape Town,* vol. 4, ed. Christopher Saunders (Cape Town: University of Cape Town Press, 1981), 29–65; N.G. Garson, "Political Role of the White Working Class in South Africa, 1902–1924," paper presented at African Studies Institute Conference on Southern African Labor History, Johannesburg, University of Witwatersrand, April 8–10, 1976; J.G. Potgieter, "From the Rand War to the Rand Revolt: Overview of the Convergence and Divergence of White Interests" (Ph.D. diss., University of Cape Town, 1976).

21. However, prior to these new employment patterns, in rural areas white women's main task was not to contribute to the household economically but to spend and demonstrate the social and economic status of the household. Magubane, *Bringing the Empire Home.*

22. Trends like women's public service as charity workers, bilingual and bicultural whites' whites championing of monolingual education and cultural events, and the increasing legitimacy granted to universities and researchers over churches and state agencies in responding to social problems can all be observed among the research team members and their contributions to the study. See Bickford-Smith, "Dangerous Cape Town"; Potgieter, "From the Rand War to the Rand Revolt."

23. Researchers overlooked the ways in which religious philanthropy and its proto-social work had actually provided more sustainable and long-term conditions of overall support and stability for urban and rural poor whites. Religious charities, unlike secular ones, were always quite explicit about their belief that poverty was a moral failure to be overcome. Secular antipoverty bureaucracies had similarly freighted accounts of poor people, albeit without the redemptive qualities associated with religious antipoverty programs.

24. Malherbe, "The Carnegie Poor White Investigation," 83. The American sociologist Charles W. Coulter also raised this issue; see his "Problem of Judicious Charity," *Social and Industrial Review* 2 (1930).

25. David Roediger and Elizabeth Esch, *The Production of Difference: Race and the Management of Labor in US History* (Oxford: Oxford University Press, 2012).

26. Robinson, "Area Studies in Search of Africa."

27. While looking at documents on South Africa's history of racial proletarianization—in this case the history of the black industrial worker—in the South African National Archives, I returned numerous times to the Inspectorate of White Labor, a government agency designed to replace African and Indian and Colored laborers with white laborers, the so-called poor whites, in unskilled work in order to institutionalize the color bar in the workplace, thus writing non-Europeans out of the history of industrial, working-class, and socialist histories of the country. Black people remain in many of these histories as traitors to the working-class cause. More important, during the interwar years in South Africa, cross-race workers' movements repeatedly were sabotaged by their inability to immobilize the proliferation of global whiteness.

28. Keletso Atkins, *The Moon Is Dead! Give Us Our Money! The Cultural Origins of an African Work Ethic, Natal, South Africa, 1843–1900* (Portsmouth, NH: Heinemann, 1993).

29. Matthew Frye Jacobson, *Barbarian Virtues: The United States Encounters Foreign Peoples at Home and Abroad, 1876–1917* (New York: Hill and Wang, 2000), 156.

30. Rehana Ebr.-Vally, *Kala Pani: Caste and Colour in South Africa* (Cape Town and Maroelana: Kwela Books and South African History Online, 2001); John S. Sharp, "The Roots and Development of Volkekunde in South Africa," *Journal of Southern African Studies* 8, no.1 (1981): 16–36.

31. The Homestead Act provisions in the U.S. Reconstruction era offer a convenient comparison of postwar wealth redistribution to the wealthy. The main beneficiaries of the Homestead Act in the former Confederacy, deeply indebted planters, were able to avoid bankruptcy and the public humiliation of complete loss of economic status. Nell Irvin Painter, Introduction to *Secret Eye: The Journal of Ella Gertrude Clanton, Thomas, 1848–1889*, ed. Virginia Burr (Chapel Hill: University of North Carolina Press, 1990). From blackbirding of dark-skinned labor in the Pacific and theft of Chinese people into Cuban bondage to state-funded prison and penal labor in the South, Northern capital investing in the newly industrializing South and its "labor" methods under bondage in industries as varied as coal, timber, iron, and real estate drew on the financial networks of the impoverished planter class and a new class of attorneys, insurance brokers, and journalists who could now enter the wealthy classes through their investments. Lisa Yun, *The Coolie Speaks: Chinese Indentured Laborers and African Slaves in Cuba* (Philadephia: Temple University Press, 2008); Gerald Horne, *White Pacific: U.S. Imperialism and Black Slavery in the South Seas after the Civil War* (Honolulu: University of Hawai'i Press, 2007); Alex Lichtenstein, *Twice the Work of Free Labor: The Political Economy of Convict Labor in the New South* (New York: Verso, 1996).

32. Pamela Brooks, *Boycotts, Buses, and Passes: Black Women's Resistance in the U.S. South and South Africa* (Amherst: University of Massachusetts Press, 2008), 81–82; Rich, *White Power*.

33. C.W. De Kiewiet, "Gold Mining," "Poor Whites and Poor Blacks," "Civilized Labor," in *History of South Africa: Social and Economic* (Oxford: Oxford University Press, 1950), 158–77, 179–206, 209–45; Robert Morrell, ed., *White but Poor: Essays on the History of Poor Whites in Southern Africa, 1880–1940* (Pretoria: UNISA, 1992); Robert H. Davies, *Capital, State, and White Labour in South Africa, 1900–1960: An Historical Materialist Analysis of Class Formation and Class Relations* (Brighton: Harvester Press).

34. Stephen Steinberg, *The Ethnic Myth: Race, Ethnicity and Class in America*, 3rd ed. (Boston, MA: Beacon Press, 2001); Beverly Crawford and Ronnie D. Lipschultz, eds., *The Myth of "Ethnic Conflict": Politics, Economics, and Cultural Violence* (Berkeley: International and Area Studies, University of California Press, 1998); Kenan Malik, *The Meaning of Race: Race, History and Culture in Western Society* (New York: New York University Press, 1996), 135–44, 174; J. Sakai, *Settlers: The Mythology of the White Proletariat* (Rogue River, OR: Morningstar Press, 1989); Donald Horowitz, *Ethnic Groups in Conflict* (Berkeley: University of California Press, 1985); Robert Bates, "Modernization, Ethnic Competition, and the Rationality of Politics in Contemporary Africa," in *State versus Ethnic Claims: African Policy Dilemmas,* ed. Donald

Rothchild and Victor A. Olorunsola (Boulder, CO: Westview Press, 1983), 152–71.

35. Van Onselen, *New Babylon, New Nineveh*, 27.

36. A wide range of scholars have worked very diligently to disprove these notions. See Timothy Keegan, *Colonial South Africa and the Origins of the Racial Order* (Charlottesville: University of Virginia Press, 1996); Charles Van Onselen, *The Seed Is Mine: The Life of Kas Maine, a South African Sharecropper, 1894–1985* (Cape Town: David Philip, 1996); Saul Dubow, *Illicit Union: Scientific Racism in Modern South Africa* (Johannesburg: University of Witwatersrand Press, 1995); Atkins, *The Moon Is Dead!;* Timothy Keegan, *Rural Transformations in Industrializing South Africa: The Southern Highveld to 1914* (Johannesburg: Ravan Press, 1986); Rich, *White Power;* Peter Kallaway, "Black Responses to an Industrializing Economy: 'Labour Shortage' and 'Native Policy' in Griqualand West, 1870–1900," paper presented at the African Studies Institute Conference on Southern African Labor History, Johannesburg, University of Witwatersrand, April 8–10, 1976.

37. Keegan, *Colonial South Africa.* Unable to represent whatever factors and dimensions of Western civilization their settlement was supposed to guarantee, they were recoverable, in the eyes of Eurocentric global history, if conceived of as another tribe of Africa, albeit the white tribe. See Andre Du Toit and Hermann Giliomee, *Afrikaner Political Thought: Analysis and Documents* (Cape Town: David Philip, 1983); Andre Du Toit, "No Chosen People: The Myth of the Calvinist Origins of Afrikaner Nationalism and Racial Ideology," *American Historical Review* 88, no. 4 (1983): 920–52; David Harrison, *The White Tribe of Africa: South Africa in Perspective* (Berkeley: University of California Press).

38. W. M. Macmillan, *My South African Years* (Cape Town: David Philip, 1975).

39. Keegan, *Colonial South Africa;* Rich, *White Power;* Berman, *The Ideology of Philanthropy.*

40. Rich, *White Power.*

41. Du Bois rewrote the historiography of the U.S. Civil War and the nation rebuilding project of the Radical Reconstruction by challenging the ahistorical trope/analytic about an epic sibling rivalry between white men, made spatial through the geographic analytics of political conflict between North and South. Rewritingthe historiography of South Africa should foreground gendered black identities and struggles within racial capitalism. See W. E. B. Du Bois, "The Propaganda of History," in *Black Reconstruction in America: 1860–1880,* Introd. David Levering-Lewis (New York: Simon and Schuster, [1935] 1992), 711–30.

42. Leon De Kock, Louise Bethlehem, and Sonja Laden, eds., *South Africa in the Global Imaginary* (Leiden: Brill Academic, 2004); Keegan, *Colonial South Africa;* Brenda Gayle Plummer, *Rising Wind: Black Americans and U.S. Foreign Affairs, 1935–1960* (Chapel Hill: University of North Carolina Press, 1996); Noer, *Briton, Boer, and Yankee.*

43. Frederick Cooper and Ann Stoler, eds., *Tensions of Empire: Colonial Cultures in a Bourgeois World* (Berkeley: University of California Press, 1997), 5; Robinson, *Black Marxism,* xxx; Lisa Brock and Digna Castañeda Fuertes,

eds., *Between Race and Empire: African Americans and Cubans before the Cuban Revolution* (Philadelphia: Temple University Press, 1998); Penny Von Eschen, *Race against Empire: Black Americans and Anticolonialism, 1937–1957* (Ithaca, NY: Cornell University Press, 1997).

44. C. R. D. Halisi, *Black Political Thought in the Making of South African Democracy* (Bloomington: Indiana University Press, 1999); Bernard Magubane, *The Ties That Bind: African-American Consciousness of Africa* (Trenton, NJ: Africa World Press, 1987).

45. Part of the logic of this ethnicity account has been to foreground a history of "good white people" versus "bad white people." The former are politically mature and astute and have been "Friends of the Negro," while the latter are politically immature and naive about their role in the permanence of racial regimes. Cleveland Hayes and Brenda G. Juárez, "You Showed your Whiteness: You Don't Get a 'Good' White People's Medal," *International Journal of Qualitative Studies in Education* 22, no. 6 (2009): 729–44; Damien Riggs, "Benevolence and the Management of Stake: On Being 'Good White People,'" *Philament* 4 (2004): 1–10.

46. Malik, *Meaning of Race,* 135–44, 174; Michael Omi and Howard Winant, *Racial Formation in the United States: From the 1960s to the 1990s* (New York: Routledge, 1994), 4–5; George Fredrickson, *White Supremacy: A Comparative Study in American and South African History* (Oxford: Oxford University Press, 1982).

47. On the other hand, Marxist historicism has contributed greatly to the demythologization of South African white identity by insisting that culture is an agreed upon set of practices that has the goal of creating a group identity. What was once considered an ancient ethnic minority guided solely by a Calvinist manifest destiny philosophy, the whites in South Africa were revealed to be a manufactured community with shifting and changing political interests. T. Dunbar Moodie, *The Rise of Afrikanerdom: Power, Apartheid, and the Afrikaner Civil Religion* (Berkeley: University of California Press, 1975). In this way white identity in Africa was denaturalized, and we could begin the practice of explaining the social forces and the politics of knowledge that produced "white people" and especially "poor whites." Jacobson (*Barbarian Virtues*) insists that ethnicity was a manufactured identity created when racialization of European immigrants to the United States was no longer effective as a measure of social control. The conception of Europeans as belonging to different races was folded into the conception of ethnic differences because all European immigrants were being molded into Caucasians. Esch describes Ford workers attending Americanization schools of the Ford Motor Company (Elizabeth Esch, "Fear of a Miscege-Nation: Henry Ford and 'Poor Whites' from Detroit to Port Elizabeth," paper presented at the History Workshop and Wits Institute for Social and Economic Research, University of the Witwatersrand, conference "Burden of Race? 'Whiteness' and 'Blackness' in Modern South Africa," Johannesburg, July 5–8, 2001). Upon graduation these students walked across the stage and into a giant cauldron and out again, symbolic of their immersion in the American melting pot. This melting pot metaphor—a traveling race relations concept—for theorizing the rationalization of an immigrant workforce and circumscribing the access of black and other

nonwhite workers in the industrial workforce ironically enabled the software of black and white to be the only social categories for determining quality of life. For me the attention to disabling these concepts, "ethnicity" and "inevitable ethnic conflict," is critical to understanding how white identity was used, marked, and created. Ethnicity has been used in two primary ways: first, it was used globally to distinguish between Europeans and give them richer social history while African groups were described simply as the generic "natives"; and second, it was applied to Africans to shore up customary law and crush mobilizations for autonomy, self-determination, and Pan-Africanist humanism against forced labor and land theft. Ethnicity has been used to pathologize Africans and other Third World people as "tribal."

48. Jack Simons and Ray Simons offer an important and clarifying distinction in *Job Reservation and the Trade Unions* (Woodstock, Cape Town: Enterprise Publishing, 1959). Having failed to understand the contemporaneousness of the peasant, the wife, the slave, the child, the domestic servant, the unmarried family member, the indentured, the refugee, the prostitute, the criminal, the exiled, the outcast, the orphan, the insane, the mystic, the sick, and the multitude of figures propping up the household (the *oikos,* or the Greek linguistic derivation of the economy) by their unwaged labor and wageless availability for consumption and fungibility, Marxist historicism planted the seeds of its own irrelevance. Robinson writes, "Fully aware of the constant place women and children held in the workforce, Marx still deemed them so unimportant as a proportion of wage labor he tossed them, with slave labor and peasants into the imagined abyss signified by precapitalism, noncapitalist, and primitive accumulation." Robinson, *Black Marxism,* xxix. As a methodology Marxist historicists underestimated their generative capacities, their discernment, their memories, and their familiarity with trafficking between the dialectic of the living (worker) and the dead (property-/wageless affective laborer, the possession) which workers claim in their pay packet.

49. Hortense Spillers, "Mama's Baby, Papa's Maybe," Culture and Countermemory: The American Connection, *Diacritics* 17, no. 2 (1987): 64–81.

50. Johan Geerstema, "White Natives? Dan Roodt, Afrikaner Identity and the Politics of the Sublime," *Journal of Commonwealth Literature* 41, no. 3 (2006): 103–20. The Afrikaners, in particular, were reputed in global history as having shown themselves to be incapable of self-governance and to reflect the epitome of cultural anachronism. Noer, *Briton, Boer, and Yankee, 65.*

51. Robinson, *Forgeries of Memory.*

52. Rural white women, for example, were rarely tended by doctors during their confinement and when giving birth. Instead their sole medical care came from black and colored midwives.

53. Deborah Posel, "Whiteness and Power in the South African Civil Service: Paradoxes of the Apartheid State," *Journal of Southern African Studies* 25, no. 1 (1999): 99–119.

54. Richard Sennett and Jonathan Cobb, *The Hidden Injuries of Class* (New York: Norton, 1972), 20.

55. Derrick Bell coined this term in his "Racial Preference Licensing Act," in *Faces at the Bottom of the Well: The Permanence of Racism* (New York: Basic Books, 1993).

56. Pumla Gqola, *What Is Slavery to Me? Postcolonial/Slave Memory in Post-Apartheid South Africa* (Johannesburg: Wits University Press, 2010); Posel, "Whiteness and Power"; Janis Grobbelaar, "Afrikaner Nationalism: End of a Dream" (Inaugural Lecture, Department of Sociology, University of South Africa, 1995).

57. Thandeka, *Learning to Be White: Race, Money and God in America,* 2nd ed. (New York: Continuum, 2000), 8.

58. Sennett and Cobb, *Hidden Injuries of Class,* 32.

CHAPTER 2

1. I have adapted Goldsby's "cultural logic" concept to hone in on a racial analytic that explores the social projects around poor whites (Jacqueline Goldsby, *A Spectacular Secret: Lynching in American Life and Literature* [Chicago: University of Chicago Press, 2006]); the repetitiveness of these images in political cartoons via Josh Greenberg's "Framing and Temporality in Political Cartoons: A Critical Analysis of Visual News Discourse," *Canadian Review of Sociology and Anthropology* 39, no. 2 (2002): 181–98; and psychic pleasure associated with these cultural representations following Toni Morrison's *Playing in the Dark: Whiteness and the Literary Imagination* (Cambridge, MA: Harvard University Press, 1992).

2. Max Weber, "Asceticism and the Spirit of Capitalism," in *The Protestant Ethic and the Spirit of Capitalism,* trans. Talcott Parsons (New York: Scribner, [1905] 1958), 81, http://xroads.virginia.edu/~HYPER/weber/toc.html; Jim Sidanius et al., "The Interface between Ethnic and National Attachment," *Public Opinion Quarterly* 61 (1997): 102–33. See also David Roediger and Elizabeth Esch, *The Production of Difference: Race and the Management of Labor in US History* (Oxford: Oxford University Press, 2012).

3. Weber "Asceticism and the Spirit of Capitalism," 5. Also T. Dunbar Moodie's *The Rise of Afrikanerdom: Power, Apartheid, and the Afrikaner Civil Religion* (Berkeley: University of California Press, 1975), among many others, explores religiosity as a key feature of Afrikaner Nationalist politics.

4. The papers are available in the Boonzaier Cartoons Collection, Museum Africa, Johannesburg; and the T. Dunbar Moodie Collection, Cullen Library, University of Witwatersrand Historical Papers Room.

5. Robyn Wiegman, *Object Lessons* (Durham, NC: Duke University Press, 2012); Ruth Frankenberg, ed., *Displacing Whiteness* (Durham, NC: Duke University Press, 1997); Cheryl Harris, "Whiteness as Property," in *Critical Race Theory: The Key Writings That Formed the Movement,* ed. Kimberle Crenshaw, Neil Gotanda, et al. (New York: New Press, 1995): 276–91; Sandra Harding, *Whose Science, Whose Knowledge: Thinking from Women's Lives* (Ithaca, NY: Cornell University Press, 1991).

6. Edward Said, "Media, Margins, and Modernity: Raymond Williams and Edward Said, 1978," Appendix to Raymond Williams, *The Politics of Modernism: Against the New Conformists* (London: Verso, 1989): 177–97.

7. E. Michele Ramsey, "Inventing Citizens during World War I: Suffrage Cartoons in the Woman Citizen," *Western Journal of Communication* 64, no. 2

(2000): 113–47; Jeraine R. Root, "Is a Picture Worth a Thousand Words? A Methodological Study of Political Cartoons" (Ph.D. diss., University of Houston, 1995), reviewed in *Political Communication* 13 (1995): 363–64.

8. Josh Greenberg, "Framing and Temporality in Political Cartoons: A Critical Analysis of Visual News Discourse," *Canadian Review of Sociology and Anthropology* 39, no. 2 (2002): 182, 186; Ken Gonzales-Day, *Lynching in the West, 1850–1935* (Durham, NC: Duke University Press, 2006), 56, 184.

9. Andy Mason, *What's So Funny? Under the Skin of South African Cartooning* (Claremont, CA: Double Storey Press, 2010).

10. Greenberg, "Framing and Temporality."

11. Murray Schoonraad and Elzabé Schoonraad, *Companion to South African Cartoonists* (Johannesburg: A.D. Donker, 1989); Cedric J. Robinson, *Forgeries of Memory and Meaning: Blacks and the Regimes of Race in American Theater and Film before World War II* (Chapel Hill: University of North Carolina Press, 2007); Gonzales-Day, *Lynching in the West;* L.E. Neame, *Some South African Politicians,* illus. Quip (Cape Town: Maskew Miller, 1929).

12. Susan Sontag, "Looking at War: Photography's View of Devastation and Death," *New Yorker* (December 9, 2002): 87.

13. Greenberg, "Framing and Temporality," 181; Rey Chow, "Seminal Dispersal, Fecal Retention, and Related Narrative Matters: Eileen Chang's Tale of Roses in the Problematic of Modern Writing," *differences: Journal of Feminist Cultural Studies* 11, no. 2 (1999): 156.

14. Rachel Adams, *Sideshow USA: Freaks and the American Cultural Imagination* (Chicago: University of Chicago Press, 2001), 115.

15. Ibid., 121; Cedric Robinson, *Black Marxism,* 2nd ed., foreword Robin Kelley (Chapel Hill: University of North Carolina Press, 2000).

16. Robinson, *Forgeries of Memory;* Sontag, "Looking at War," 87–90.

17. In 1906, following on the heels of the St. Louis World's Fair, Bronx Zoo director William Hornaday built an exhibit featuring Ota Benga, a Central African man who was a captive in the zoo. Hornaday's exhibit placed Ota Benga in the same cage as an orangutan dressed in human clothes, which served to convey to viewers the notion that the highest genus of animals was far superior to the lower classes of human beings (Adams, *Sideshow USA,* 39).

18. C.J. Groenewald, "Methodology of Poverty Research in South Africa: The Case of the First Carnegie Investigation, 1929–1932." *Social Dynamics* 13, no. 2 (1987): 60–74.

19. This racist gaze exceeds the extent to which the *Poor White Study* was part of a segregationist research agenda. Sue Krige, "Segregation, Science and Commissions of Enquiry: Contestation of Native Educational Policy in South Africa, 1930–1936," Seminar Paper No. 398, presented at Institute for Advanced Social Research, Education Department, University of Witwatersrand, Johannesburg, April 29, 1996; Brahm David Fleish, "Social Scientists as Policy Makers: E.G. Malherbe and the National Bureau for Education and Social Research, 1929–1943," *Journal of Southern African Studies* 21, no. 3 (1995): 349–72; Paul Rich, *White Power and the Liberal Conscience: Racial Segregation and South African Liberalism* (Johannesburg: Ravan Press, 1984); Edward Berman, *Ideology of Philanthropy: The Influence of the Carnegie, Ford, and Rockefeller*

Foundations on American Foreign Policy (Albany: State University of New York Press, 1983), 14; Thomas J. Noer, *Briton, Boer, and Yankee: The United States and South Africa, 1879–1914* (Kent, OH: Kent State University Press, 1978); W. M. Macmillan, *My South African Years* (Cape Town: David Philip, 1975).

20. Sally Gaule, "Poor White, White Poor: Meanings in the Differences of Whiteness," *History of Photography* 25, no. 4 (2001): 35; Sam Radithlalo, "Vanishing Cultures? Authority, Authorising, Representation in South African Photography," paper presented at the conference "Encounters with Photography: Photographing People in Southern Africa, 1860–1999," Iziko Museum and South African Museum, Capetown, July 14–17, 1999.

21. Adams, *Sideshow USA,* 18, 26–27, 119–21. According to Roland Barthes's essay "Great Family of Man," the tragedy of photographic representations that appeal to representations of nature is photographers' unwillingness to scrutinize history and the time-bound histories that emerge from it. See Roland Barthes, *Mythologies,* trans. Annette Lavers (New York: Noonday Press, 1993), 100–102. New research by Marijke Du Toit argues that the realism of natural settings reflected ideologies significant at that time: "'*Binnelandse Reise*' (Journeys to the Interior): Photographs from the Carnegie Commission of Investigation into the Poor White Problem, 1929/1932," *Kronos,* no. 32 (November 2006): 58]).

22. Gaule, "Poor White, White Poor," 35.

23. Zine Magubane, *Bringing the Empire Home: Race, Class, and Gender in Britain and Colonial South Africa* (Chicago: University of Chicago Press, 2003), 47.

24. Pumla Gqola, *What Is Slavery to Me? Postcolonial/Slave Memory in Post-Apartheid South Africa* (Johannesburg: Wits University Press, 2010), 8, 10–11.

25. Ibid., 7.

26. Ibid.; Jared Sexton, *Amalgamation Schemes: Anti-Blackness and the Critique of Multiracialism* (Minneapolis: University of Minnesota Press, 2008); Eduardo Bonilla-Silva, *Racism without Racists: Color-Blind Racism and the Persistence of Racial Inequality in the United States* (Lanham, MD: Rowman and Littlefield, 2003).

27. Keisha-Khan Perry, *Black Women against the Land Grab: The Fight for Racial Justice in Brazil* (Minneapolis: University of Minnesota Press, 2013); Kia Lilly Caldwell, *Negras in Brazil: Re-envisioning Black Women's Citizenship and the Politics of Identity* (New Brunswick, NJ: Rutgers University Press, 2006), Mark Sawyer, *Racial Politics in Post-Revolutionary Cuba* (Cambridge: Cambridge University Press, 2005); France Winddance Twine and Jonathan W. Warren, *Racing Research, Researching Race: Methodological Dilemmas in Critical Race Studies* (New York: New York University Press, 2000); C.L.R. James, *Black Jacobins: Toussaint L'Ouverture and the San Domingo Revolution* (repr., New York: Vintage, [1938] 1989).

28. Ida B. Wells, *Southern Horrors: Lynch Law in All Its Phases* (Seattle: Create Space Press, [1894] 2011); Ange-Marie Hancock, *The Politics of Disgust: The Public Identity of the Welfare Queen* (New York: New York University Press, 2004); Simon Lewis, *White Women Writers and Their African Invention* (Gainesville: University Press of Florida, 2003); Louise Vincent, "Bread and

Honor: White Working-Class Women and Afrikaner Nationalism in the 1930s,"*Journal of Southern African Studies* 26, no. 1 (2000): 61–78; Marijke Du Toit, "Women, Welfare and the Nurturing of Afrikaner Nationalism: A Social History of ACVV, 1879–1939" (Ph.D. diss. University of Cape Town, 1996); Ann DuCille, "Dyes and Dolls: Multicultural Barbie and the Merchandising of Difference," *differences: Journal of Feminist Cultural Studies* 6, no. 1 (1994): 48–68; Morrison, *Playing in the Dark.*

29. Magubane, *Bringing the Empire Home,* 64–66; Vron Ware, *Beyond the Pale: White Women, Racism, and History* (New York: Verso, 1992); Ruth Frankenberg, *White Women, Race Matters: The Social Construction of Whiteness* (Minneapolis: University of Minnesota Press, 1994); Mab Segrest, *Memoir of a Race Traitor* (Boston: South End Press, 1994).

30. In his oppositional history of the South African war, Solomon Plaatje (1876–1932), a founding member of the South African Native National Congress, recounted the deliberate and intentional starvation and ejection of the Barolong people, protected subjects of the British Empire (Solomon Plaatje, *Mafeking Diary,* Centenary ed., ed. John Comaroff and Brian Willan [Suffolk: James Currey, 1999]). The Barolong, some of the most productive agriculturalists of colonial-era South Africa, were starved to safeguard food supplies for white people. The work I do with this image points to the illegibility of Barolong hunger in a political system organized around extension of white life through the inclusion of starving but unsympathetic black people.

31. In postapartheid shopping malls and tourist venues in South Africa circa 1999 one could find giant cannibal pots with elaborate jungle sets that presumably white tourists could take pictures standing inside of for a small fee. Such globally circulated Negrophobic souvenirs figure tourists as playfully risking being eaten by cannibals. Gqola, *What Is Slavery to Me?;* Robinson, *Forgeries of Memory,* 227; Gehard Schutte, "Tourists and Tribes in the 'New' South Africa, "*American Society for Ethnohistory* 50, no. 3 (2003): 473–87; Maurice Manning, *Slave in a Box: The Strange Career of Aunt Jemima* (Charlottesville: University of Virginia Press, 1998); Jan Nederveen Pieterse, *White on Black: Images of Africa and Blacks in Western Popular Cultures* (New Haven, CT: Yale University Press, 1992); Morrison, *Playing in the Dark.*

32. Mason, *What's So Funny?,* 16–17.

33. Frantz Fanon, *The Wretched of the Earth* (New York: Grove Press, 1963), 38–39.

34. Theorists of Athenian democracy have enshrined by Western tradition have hidden that part of the struggle for democracy led by the poor and the enslaved. Indeed the false history of Athenians never having been enslaved and the false history of the natural slave has outlasted this particular slave system. See Robinson, *Forgeries of Memory;* Cynthia Farrar, *Origins of Democratic Thinking: The Invention of Politics in Classical Athens* (London: Cambridge University Press, 1989).

35. *As die Tuig Skawe* won the prestigious Hertzog Award for drama in 1926 and thus played its role in the consolidation of the cultural practices of Afrikaner Nationalism.

36. Neame, *Some South African Politicians;* Schoonraad and Schoonraad, *Companion to South African Cartoonists.*

37. Beverly Crawford and Ronnie D. Lipschultz, eds., *The Myth of "Ethnic Conflict": Politics, Economics, and Cultural Violence* (Berkeley: International and Area Studies, University of California Press, 1998).

38. Neame, *Some South African Politicians*, 78, 79, 84.

39. For narrow racialists, Afrikaners were defined only as South Africa–born descendants of Europeans. Neame, *Some South African Politicians*, 79.

40. South Africa has been marked in the global imaginary as a "backward" white man's country—when championing both "racial narrowness" and expansionist white men's countries in southern Africa. Figuring out which of these positionalities, racial colony or heroic, independence-seeking white republic, better describes South Africa is less important than seeing how the historical writing about South Africa constructs it in relation to the rest of the white global imaginary and the antagonistic black global imaginary.

41. Building on the history of crushing political mobilization, passive resistance, and congress movements led by Indian, Colored, and black people for decades, this act was particularly spectacular.

42. Robert Vosloo, "The Dutch Reformed Church and the Poor White Problem in the Wake of the first Carnegie Report (1932): Some Church-Historical and Theological Observations," *Studia Historiae Ecclesiasticae* 37, no. 2 (September 2011), 67–85, http://uir.unisa.ac.za/bitstream/handle/10500/5121/Vosloo.pdf?sequence=1, accessed May 1, 2012; Pieter G.R. De Villiers, "A Spirituality of Mercy in a Time of War," *Religion and Theology* 18, no. 1–2 (2011): 147–72.

43. Translations by Frederick Backman. The self-help organization focused on community development for the entire rural community rather than solely the poor. Du Toit notes that much of such an organization's work would have been done by women and entailed shared or communal food preparation, land clearance, and providing health care for families. Such an organization would have been a bit less plagued by middle-class finger wagging about what poorer families ought to be doing.

44. Johan Geerstema, "White Natives? Dan Roodt, Afrikaner Identity and the Politics of the Sublime," *Journal of Commonwealth Literature* 41, no. 3 (2006): 103–20.

45. Pierterse, *White on Black*, 69.

46. Saul Dubow, *Illicit Union: Scientific Racism in Modern South Africa* (Johannesburg: University of Witwatersrand Press, 1995), 9, 166, 173.

47. Mass media and political leadership discussed poor whites as being "like slaves" and "worse off than slaves," lending validity to the practice of drawing comparisons between the racially "vagrant" Khoikhoi people and English paupers, who were said to have the same disposition. Johan Geerstema, "White Natives?"; Magubane, *Bringing the Empire Home*, 54.

48. By August 1931, some 469,000 European women were added to the South African electorate. Du Toit, "Women, Welfare and the Nurturing of Afrikaner."

49. Magubane, *Bringing the Empire Home*.

50. J.R. Albertyn, "The Poor White and Society, Part V, Section A," in *Report of the Carnegie Commission of Investigation on the Poor White Question in South Africa* (Stellenbosch: Pro-Ecclesia-Drukkery, 1932),1.

51. The most damning piece of evidence of the disdain shown toward poor whites by their wealthy brethren is the quotation of an anonymous Ministry of Railways administrator who exclaimed, "Why would I hire a lazy poor white in exchange for a hard working Indian or Native who speaks many languages and has a family to provide for." See Susan Parnell, "Slums, Segregation and Poor Whites in Johannesburg, 1920–1934," in *White but Poor: Essays on the History of Poor Whites in Southern Africa, 1880–1940,* ed. Robert Morrell (Pretoria: UNISA, 1992), 115–29. Meanwhile the White Labor Bureau documented narrow and short-lived schemes by businesses to hire poor whites. IWL 1915, SA/NA, MNW 295 File 2457/15–2534/15, December 8, 1915. See also Judith Tayler, "'Our Poor:' Politics of the Poor White Problem, 1932–1942," *KLEIO* 24 (1992): 42–65.

52. Morrell, *White but Poor;* John Bottomley, "The South African Rebellion of 1914: The Influence of Industrialization, Poverty and 'Poor Whiteism,'" Research Seminar Paper, presented at the African Studies Institute and Wits Institute for Social and Economic Research, Johannesburg, 1982.

53. Translation by Frederick Backman.

54. They were constituted as independent republics in 1907, before South Africa was a united country. Until 1910 South Africa was comprised four provinces—Transvaal, the Orange Free State, and the British Crown Colonies, Natal and the Cape—semiautonomous mission territories, and several Crown Territories where Xhosa and Zulu royalty were guaranteed exclusive holdings by treaty to their land, where the majority of voters were whites. The Cape Colony was the only place where educated landholding black people could vote.

55. Denis-Constant Martin, "What's in the Name 'Coloured,'" *Social Identities: Journal of the Study of Race, Nation and Culture* 4, no. 5 (1998): 23–540; Rehana Ebr.-Vally, *Kala Pani: Caste and Colour in South Africa* (Cape Town and Maroelana: Kwela Books and South African History Online, 2001).

56. Solomon Plaatje, *Native Life in South Africa, before and since the European War and the Boer Rebellion* (New York: Negro Universities Press, 1969).

57. Until very recently the Afrikaans *Taal Woordeboek*—the official dictionary of the language—noted that it did not include Cape Afrikaans, Namaqua, or Griqua Afrikaans.

58. Marilyn Lake and Henry Reynolds, *Drawing the Global Colour Line: White Men's Countries and the International Challenge of Racial Equality* (Cambridge: Cambridge University Press, 2008); Gerald Horne, *The White Pacific: U.S. Imperialism and Black Slavery in the South Seas after the Civil War* (Honolulu: University of Hawai'i Press, 2007); Gerald Horne, *The Deepest South: The United States, Brazil, and the African Slave Trade* (New York: New York University Press, 2007); Jonathan Hyslop, "Imperial Working Class Makes Itself 'White': White Labourism in Britain, Australia and South Africa before the First World War," *Journal of Historical Sociology* 12, no. 4 (2002): 398–421; Matthew Frye Jacobson, *Barbarian Virtues: The United States Encounters Foreign Peoples at Home and Abroad, 1876–1917* (New York: Hill and Wang, 2000).

59. Elizabeth Esch's study of this company reflects the symbiosis between these white nationalisms. Elizabeth Esch, "Fear of a Miscege-Nation: Henry

Ford and 'Poor Whites' from Detroit to Port Elizabeth," paper presented at the History Workshop and Wits Institute for Social and Economic Research, University of the Witwatersrand conference "Burden of Race? 'Whiteness' and 'Blackness' in Modern South Africa," Johannesburg, July 5–8, 2001.

60. David Goldblatt, *Some Afrikaners Photographed* (Johannesburg: M. Crawford, 1975); Peter Magubane, *Magubane's South Africa,* with a foreword by Ambassador Andrew Young (New York: Knopf, 1978).

61. Gaule reiterates a point made by bell hooks that the act of observing and scrutinizing was an exclusive preserve of white people. "Wearing the mask" was not simply an act of dissembling or creating space for tricksterism, but it was the required uniform for survival. In the post–World War II era, Native Affairs Commissioners sternly shut down any black photographers of Magubane's generation who had begun to take pictures of whites. Gaule, "Poor White, White Poor, 335. See also bell hooks, "Representing Whiteness in the Black Imagination," in *Black on White: Black Writers on What It Means to Be White,* ed. David Roediger (New York: Schocken Books, 1998) 38–53.

62. U.S. Ambassador Andrew Young's foreword to *Magubane's South Africa* (1978) illustrated in pointed detail that a major audience for Magubane was the black radical intelligentsia working to sustain the international antiapartheid movement and exiled South African dissidents around the world. Magubane's embrace of cultural activism, using photography as a medium to represent widespread resistance to apartheid, foregrounded the dignity of black people in South Africa. See John Henrik Clarke, ed., *Dimensions of the Struggle against Apartheid: A Tribute to Paul Robeson: Proceedings of Special Meeting of the Special Committee against Apartheid on the 80th Anniversary of the Birth of Paul Robeson, 10 April 1978* (New York and Washington, DC: African Heritage Studies Association in Cooperation with the United Nations Centre against Apartheid, 1979).

63. Quoted in Tiffany Willoughby-Herard, "Visualizing the Aesthetics of the World Culture of Poverty: Interview with Roger Ballen," Unpublished interview, Johannesburg, South Africa, June 30, 2002, 18.

64. David Harrison, *The White Tribe of Africa: South Africa in Perspective* (Berkeley: University of California Press, 1983). Ballen described poor whites as a tribe vulnerable to disappearance after reflecting on the similarity between his photos and the themes in the *Poor White Study.*

65. Quoted in Willoughby-Herard, "Visualizing the Aesthetics," 8, 9.

66. Ibid., 18.

67. Cynthia Young, *Soul Power: Culture, Radicalism, and the Making of a U.S. Third World Left* (Durham, NC: Duke University Press, 2006).

68. Reitumetse Obakeng Mabokela and Zine Magubane, eds., *Hear Our Voices: Race, Gender and the Status of Black South African Women in the Academy* (Pretoria: University of South Africa Press, 2004); Pal Ahluwalia, "When Does a Settler Become a Native? Citizenship and Identity in a Settler Society," *Pretexts: Literary and Cultural Studies* 10, no. 1 (2001): 65; Lewis, *White Women Writers and Their African Invention;* Nancy Scheper-Hughes, "On the Call for a Militant Anthropology: The Complexity of 'Doing the Right Thing,'" *Current Anthropology* 37, no. 2 (1996): 341–46; Rosemary Jolly,

Colonization, Violence, and Narration in White South African Writing (Athens: Ohio University Press, 1996); J. Sakai, *Settlers: The Mythology of the White Proletariat* (Rogue River, OR: Morningstar Press, 1989); John Coetzee, *White Writing: on the Culture of Letters in South Africa* (New Haven, CT: Yale University Press, 1988); Frantz Fanon, "The Negro and Language," in *Black Skin, White Masks* (New York: Grove Press, 1967), 17–40.

69. Willoughby-Herard, "Visualizing the Aesthetics," 16–17.

70. Sontag, "Looking at War," 87.

71. Adams, *Sideshow USA*, 15, 126.

72. In the United States, Dorothea Lange (1895–1965) and Walker Evans (1903–75) are the most often cited documentary photographers of the poor. As members of Roosevelt's New Deal Works Progress Administration Photographic Corps, Lange and Evans contributed to the alleviation of poverty among the millions of unemployed, domestics, agricultural workers, and migrants who would not become beneficiaries of labor rights under the 1935 Wagner Act that guaranteed some workers the right to organize and provided employment, health, and retirement insurance and income. Jacob Holdt's traveling photography series, *American Pictures* (1979), documented conditions that shaped the lives of poor and wealthy people in the United States in a decidedly antiaesthetic paradigm mobilizing in response to a national welfare rights movement for economic justice. Adams, *Sideshow USA*, 15, concludes that the antiaesthetics of placing sideshow and circus performers in their working lives and "not hiding people with disabilities from sight, but granting them visibility without perceiving them as freaks," goes a long way toward uncoupling the colonial capacities of documentary photography.

73. Liese Van Der Watt, "'Making Whiteness Strange': White Identity in Post-Apartheid South African Art," *Third Text* 56 (2001): 68, 73. Again, the black feminist lens on power relations in spaces designated as intimate leads me to ask what else is not captured by the photograph and what visual practices and techniques are used to distract us from that. Darlene Clark Hine, "Rape and the Inner Lives of Black Women in the Middle West: Preliminary Thoughts on the Culture of Dissemblance," *Signs* 14, no. 4 (1989): 912–20.

74. Coetzee, *White Writing*.

75. Orlando Patterson, *Slavery and Social Death: A Comparative Study* (Cambridge, MA: Harvard University Press, 1985). This is a powerful antecedent of Rachel Adams's question about who enters the racial and sexual economy in which recurring ways.

76. In all likelihood, Ballen's images of poor people with freakish bodies would have been of black people, except the white world had been hyperproductive at circulating images of South Africa's "savage paupers" for nearly seven decades and the black world had been successful at circulating humanizing images of black people.

77. Willoughby-Herard, "Visualizing the Aesthetics," 5–6, 7–8, 11.

78. Audre Lorde, "The Uses of the Erotic: The Erotic as Power," in *The Lesbian and Gay Studies Reader*, ed. Henry Abelove (New York: Routledge, 2012), 340; Audre Lorde, "The Uses of Anger: Women Responding to Racism," in *Sister Outsider: Essays and Speeches* (Berkeley, CA: Crossing Press, 1984).

79. Johan Geertsema, "White Natives? Dan Roodt, Afrikaner Identity and the Politics of the Sublime," *Journal of Commonwealth Literature* 41, no. 3 (2006): 103–20; John W. Crawford, "South Africa Is a Confused and Very Confusing Place: Sarah Gertrude Millin Writes an Illuminating Study of Its People and Their Problems" (Review of Sarah Gertrude Millin's *The South Africans*), *New York Times,* April 3, 1927, BR3. After nearly a half century of depicting poor white people and African people and Colored people as antihuman in *The Fiddler* (London: Constable & Co., 1929) and *God's Stepchildren* (London: Constable & Co., 1924), Millin strives to depict white people as victims and as human in *White People Are Also People* (Cape Town: Howard Timmins, 1966). Of course at this moment she is focused on recovering upper-class white people by identifying them with destitute and impoverished white people.

CHAPTER 3

1. Columbia University, Manuscripts and Archives, Carnegie Corporation of New York Grant Files, Carnegie Corporation of New York Graphic Materials, South African Council for Scientific and Industrial Research—Mobile Testing Laboratory for Research on Mentality, 1952–60; Carnegie Mobiele Sielkundige Laboratorium Nasionale Instituut vir Personeelnavorsing, WNNR or Carnegie Mobile Psychological Laboratory National Institute for Personnel Research, Box 2, File 2.63.

2. Liese Van Der Watt, "'Making Whiteness Strange': White Identity in Post-Apartheid South African Art," *Third Text* 56 (2001): 63–74; Melissa Steyn, *Whiteness Just Isn't What It Used to Be: White Identity in a Changing South Africa* (Albany: State University of New York Press, 2001); Sally Gaule, "Poor White, White Poor: Meanings in the Differences of Whiteness," *History of Photography* 25, no. 4 (2001): 334–47; Matthew Frye Jacobson, *Barbarian Virtues: The United States Encounters Foreign Peoples at Home and Abroad, 1876–1917* (New York: Hill and Wang, 2000); Thandeka, *Learning to Be White: Race, Money and God in America,* 2nd ed. (New York: Continuum, 2000); Marlene Van Niekerk, *Triomf,* trans. Leon de Kock (Johannesburg: Jonathon Ball, [1994] 1999); George Lipsitz, *Possessive Investment in Whiteness* (Philadelphia: Temple University Press, 1998); David Roediger, ed., *Black on White: Black Writers on What It Means to Be White* (New York: Random House, 1998); Ruth Frankenberg, ed., *Displacing Whiteness: Essays in Social and Cultural Criticism* (Durham, NC: Duke University Press, 1997); Neil Foley, *The White Scourge: Mexicans, Blacks, and Poor Whites in Texas Cotton Culture* (Berkeley: University of California Press, 1997); Richard Dyer, *White* (London: Routledge, 1997); Ian Haney-Lopez, *White by Law: Legal Constructions of Race* (New York: New York University Press, 1996); Noel Ignatiev and John Garvey, eds., *Race Traitor* (New York: Routledge, 1996); Robert Fikes, "Escaping the Literary Ghetto: African American Authors of White Life Novels, 1946–1994," *Western Journal of Black Studies* 19, no. 2 (1995): 105–12; Ann DuCille, "Dyes and Dolls: Multicultural Barbie and the Merchandising of Difference," *differences: Journal of Feminist Cultural Studies* 6, no. 1 (1994): 48–68; Mab Segrest, *Memoir of a Race Traitor* (Boston: South End Press, 1994); Cheryl Harris, "Whiteness as

Property," in *Critical Race Theory: The Key Writings that Formed the Movement,* ed. Kimberle Crenshaw, Neil Gotanda, et al. (New York: New Press, 1995): 276–92; Dorothy Allison, *Skin: Talking about Sex, Class, and Literature* (Ithaca, NY: Firebrand Books, 1994); Dorothy Allison, *Bastard out of Carolina* (New York: Plume Books, 1993); Toni Morrison, *Playing in the Dark: Whiteness and the Literary Imagination* (Cambridge, MA: Harvard University Press, 1992); Robert Morrell, ed., *White but Poor: Essays on the History of Poor Whites in Southern Africa, 1880–1940* (Pretoria: UNISA, 1992); W.E.B. Du Bois, *Black Reconstruction in America: 1860–1880,* Introd. David Levering-Lewis (New York: Simon and Schuster, [1935] 1992); David Roediger, *The Wages of Whiteness: Race and the Making of the American Working Class* (London: Verso, 1991); Nell Irvin Painter, "Introduction: The Journal of Ella Gertrude Glanton Thomas: An Educated White Woman in the Eras of Slavery, War, and Reconstruction," in *The Secret Eye: The Journal of Ella Gertrude Clanton, Thomas, 1848–1889,* ed. Virginia Burr (Chapel Hill: University of North Carolina Press, 1990); Dorothy Allison, *Trash* (Ithaca, NY: Firebrand Books, 1988).

3. On scientific racism, see Edwin Black, *War against the Weak: Eugenics and America's Campaign to Create a Master Race* (Westport, CT: Dialog Press, [2003] 2012); Dorothy Roberts, *Fatal Invention: How Science, Race, and Big Business Re-Create Race in the Twenty-First Century* (New York: New Press, 2011); Laura Lovett, *Conceiving the Future: Pro-Natalism, Reproduction, and the Family, 1890–1938* (Chapel Hill: University of North Carolina Press, 2007); Alexandra Stern, *Eugenic Nation: Faults and Frontiers of Better Breeding in Modern America* (Berkeley: University of California Press, 2005); Troy Duster, *Backdoor to Eugenics,* 2nd ed. (New York: Routledge, 2003); Sandra Harding, *The "Racial" Economy of Science: Toward a Democratic Future* (Bloomington: Indiana University Press, 1993); Sandra Harding, *Whose Science, Whose Knowledge: Thinking from Women's Lives* (Ithaca, NY: Cornell University Press, 1991); Nancy Stepan, *The Hour of Eugenics: Race, Gender, and Nation in Latin America* (New York: Cornell University Press, 1981); Stephen Jay Gould, *The Mismeasure of Man* (New York: Norton, 1981). Though some have argued that scientific racism is dead and gone (this case has been made since the 1930s, in fact), it is a stubborn and necessary feature of the present. Ultimately, scientific racism is a positivist and systematic way of naturalizing the social and political status of a group, which may be considered alternately subhuman and superhuman.

4. Black feminist and African gender studies theorists have found that "bio-logic or body-logic" is pervasive and that the "obsession with spectacular looking" and biological explanations for race support enduring distinctions between the "body and the flesh" that persist as the afterlife of chattel slavery and racial colonial relations. Oyèrónké Oyěwùmí, *The Invention of Women: Making an African Sense of Western Gender Discourses* (Minneapolis: University of Minnesota Press, x, 11); Gargi Bhattacharyya, *Tales of Dark Skinned Women: Race, Gender, and Global Culture* (New York: Routledge, 1998), 77–78; Hortense Spillers, "Mama's Baby, Papa's Maybe," *Diacritics* 17, no. 2 (1987): 64–81; Kenan Malik, *The Meaning of Race: Race, History and Culture in Western Society* (New York: New York University Press, 1996), 135–44, 174; George

Stocking, *The Ethnographer's Magic and Other Essays in the History of Anthropology* (Madison: University of Wisconsin Press, 1992); Patricia Hill Collins, *Black Sexual Politics: African Americans Gender, and the New Racism* (New York: Routledge, 2004), 34; Duster, *Backdoor to Eugenics;* Howard Winant, "White Racial Projects," in *The Making and Unmaking of Whiteness,* ed. Birgit Brander-Rasmussen et al. (Durham, NC: Duke University Press, 2001); Howard Winant, "Behind Blue Eyes: Whiteness and Contemporary Racial Politics," *New Left Review* 225 (September–October 1997): 73–88. Though scholars define whiteness as naturalized property rights and invisible privilege, this "body-logic" is operative in the tropes about "white racial degeneration." Such tropes reveal that white privilege is embodied, highly visible, and associated with the risk of proximity to blackness by which it is defined.

5. Robert Park and Ernest Burgess's *Introduction to the Science of Sociology* (Chicago: University of Chicago Press, 1921), the so-called Green Book, provides the best comparison of the influence of the *Poor White Study* on social policy and the training of academics in South Africa. The Carnegie Corporation disseminated the findings globally and especially to universities in North America. Mogens Blegvad, "A Simmel Renaissance," *Acta Sociologica* 32, no. 2 (1989): 203–9. There were many theses and dissertations on poor whites that reiterated its basic findings, ambivalence about the "Noble Boer," and eugenic caricatures of poor whites. See, e.g., Harcourt Eustace Rudd, "The Poor White Problem with Special Reference to the Educational Bearings" (Master's thesis, University of South Africa, 1928).

6. Natalie Ring, *The Problem South: Region, Empire, and the New Liberal State, 1880–1930* (Athens: University of Georgia Press, 2012); Andrew Zimmerman, *Alabama in Africa: Booker T. Washington, the German Empire, and the Globalization of the New South,* Reprint Edition (Princeton, NJ: Princeton University Press, 2012); Marilyn Lake and Henry Reynolds, *Drawing the Global Colour Line: White Men's Countries and the International Challenge of Racial Equality* (Cambridge: Cambridge University Press, 2008); Thomas Borstelmann, *The Cold War and the Color Line: American Race Relations in the Global Arena* (Cambridge, MA: Harvard University Press, 2001); Thomas Borstelmann, *Apartheid's Reluctant Uncle: The United States and Southern Africa in the Early Cold War* (New York: Oxford University Press, 1993); Cedric Robinson, *Black Marxism,* 2nd ed., foreword Robin Kelley (Chapel Hill: University of North Carolina Press, 2000 [1980]); Ellen Condliffe Lagemann, *The Politics of Knowledge: The Carnegie Corporation, Philanthropy, and Public Policy* (Chicago: University of Chicago Press, 1992); Edward Berman, *The Ideology of Philanthropy: The Influence of the Carnegie, Ford, and Rockefeller Foundations on American Foreign Policy* (Albany: State University of New York Press, 1983); Thomas J. Noer, *Briton, Boer, and Yankee: The United States and South Africa, 1879–1914* (Kent, OH: Kent State University Press, 1978). See Appendixes in this book.

7. Cedric J. Robinson, *Forgeries of Memory and Meaning: Blacks and the Regimes of Race in American Theater and Film before World War II* (Chapel Hill: University of North Carolina Press, 2007); Van Der Watt, "Making Whiteness Strange," 68.

8. Robinson, *Forgeries of Memory.*

9. Pearl Robinson, "Area Studies in Search of Africa," in *The Politics of Knowledge: Area Studies and the Disciplines,* ed. David Szanton (Berkeley: University of California Press in collaboration with e-scholarship, 2004), 1–41; William Watkins, *The White Architects of Black Education: Ideology and Power in America, 1865–1954* (New York: Teachers College Press, 2001); Henry Yu, *Thinking Orientals: Migration, Contact, and Exoticism in Modern America* (Oxford: Oxford University Press, 2001); Robert Bates, V.Y. Mudimbe, and Jean O'Barr, eds., *Africa and the Disciplines: The Contributions of Research in Africa to the Social Sciences and Humanities* (Chicago: University of Chicago Press, 1993); Stocking, *The Ethnographer's Magic;* Michael Taussig, *Shamanism, Colonialism, and the Wild Man: A Study in Terror and Healing* (Chicago: University of Chicago Press, 1981); John Stanfield, *Philanthropy and Jim Crow in American Social Science* (Westport, CT: Greenwood Press, 1985).

10. Thus the following questions: How do we account for whiteness that surfaces in the abject station usually understood to be the home of black people? What role did the study of abject whiteness play in the making of both grand apartheid and the social science that found it to be an appropriate accommodative social structure for regulating the impact of laws and policies enforcing racial difference?

11. Woods and Hartman understand antiblackness as white supremacy; social death defined by gratuitous violence, natal alienation, spirit injury, physical abuse, and generalized dishonor; the existence of an antiblack world predicated on slavery and its denial; an ontology that constitutes white civic life and subjectivity; the repressed long memory of enslavement and its present-day afterlife; and imperiled black life. Tryon Woods, "The Fact of Anti-Blackness: Decolonization in Chiapas and the Niger River Delta," *Human Architecture: Journal of the Sociology of Self-Knowledge* 5, no. 3 (2007), 323, Art. 29, http://scholarworks. umb.edu/humanarchitecture/vol5/iss3/29; Saidiya Hartman, *Scenes of Subjection: Terror, Slavery, and Self-Making in Nineteenth-Century America* (New York: Oxford University Press, 1997), 6. Gordon explains that we live in an antiblack world in which white supremacy measures political and social maturation by the willingness to participate and remain entrenched in and *used for* the benefit and maintenance of the system of white supremacy. Lewis Gordon, "The Black and the Body Politic: Fanon's Existential Phenomenological Critique of Psychoanalysis," in *Fanon: A Critical Reader,* ed. Lewis Gordon, T. Denean Sharpley-Whiting, and Renee White (Malden, MA: Blackwell, 1996), 74–84.

12. One variant has been the notorious postracial history entrenched by the Truth and Reconciliation Commission process. Scholars note that the republic was saved and reinaugurated by enshrining a mythology about everyone in South Africa and South African history itself being the ultimate victims of apartheid—not African people, solely or primarily. Scholars explain that the variability of white experience under colonial apartheid or in the post-1948 period does not legitimize taking our focus off the material conditions manufactured for African people in the global racial capitalist order. Bronwyn Leebaw, *Judging State-Sponsored Violence, Imagining Political Change* (New York: Cambridge University Press, 2011); Pumla Gqola, *What Is Slavery to Me? Postcolonial/*

Slave Memory in Post-Apartheid South Africa (Johannesburg: Wits University Press, 2010); Shaun Irlam, "Unraveling the Rainbow: The Remission of Nation in Post-Apartheid Literature," *South Atlantic Quarterly* 103, no. 4 (2004) 695–718; Mahmood Mamdani. "A Diminished Truth," in *After the TRC: Reflections on Truth and Reconciliation in South Africa,* ed. Wilmot James and Linda van de Vijver (Athens: Ohio University Press, 2001), 58–61; Julian Kunnie, *Is Apartheid Really Dead? Pan-Africanist Working-Class Cultural Critical Perspectives* (Boulder, CO: Westview Press, 2000).

13. Thandeka, *Learning to Be White,* 2000.

14. Frank Wilderson, *Red, White, and Black: Cinema and the Structure of U.S. Antagonism* (Durham, NC: Duke University Press, 2010); Robinson, *Forgeries of Memory;* Denise Da Silva, *Toward a Global Idea of Race* (Minneapolis: University of Minnesota Press, 2007).

15. Black, *War against the Weak;* Lake and Reynolds, *Drawing the Global Colour Line;* Duster, *Backdoor to Eugenics;* Jacobson, *Barbarian Virtues;* Saul Dubow, *Illicit Union: Scientific Racism in Modern South Africa* (Johannesburg: University of Witwatersrand Press, 1995).

16. Black, *War against the Weak,* 237.

17. Dorothy Roberts, in *Killing the Black Body: Race, Reproduction and the Meaning of Liberty* (New York: Vintage, 1998) and *Shattered Bonds: The Color of Child Welfare* (repr. New York: Basic Civitas Books, 2003), provides the most comprehensive history of the genocidal impact of an enduring scientific racism. Another potent example of the persistence of scientific racism is provided by the notorious workhouses, Magdalene Asylums/Laundries (1922–96), where unwed Irish women were detained, unpaid, and hidden from public view for generations as forced laborers for "criminalized reproductivity"; Prime Minister Enda Kenny issued a state apology on behalf of the government in February 2013. Susanne Klausen, *Race, Maternity, and the Politics of Birth Control in South Africa, 1910–1939* (Basingstoke: Palgrave Macmillan, 2004); Sue Krige, "Segregation, Science and Commissions of Enquiry: Contestation of Native Educational Policy in South Africa, 1930–1936," Seminar Paper No. 398, presented at University of Witwatersrand Institute for Advanced Social Research, Education Department, Johannesburg, April 19, 1996; Shula Marks and Richard Rathbone, *Industrialization and Social Change, 1870–1930* (New York: Longman, 1982); Linda Chisholm, "Themes in the Construction of Compulsory Education for the White Working Class on the Witwatersrand, 1886–1907," paper presented at History Workshop, "Class, Community and Conflict: Local Perspectives," Johannesburg, January 31–February 4, 1984.

18. Bhattacharyya, *Tales of Dark Skinned Women;* Spillers, "Mama's Baby, Papa's Maybe"; Christina Sharpe, *Monstrous Intimacies: Making Post-Slavery Subjects* (Durham, NC: Duke University Press, 2010). Bhattacharyya speaks to the enforcement of being made to remember everyday gratuitous violence and "flesh-making" by defining blackness as a politics of revolution against global antiblackness. Sharpe's discussion of property explains the antagonism between the flesh and those deemed alive, suggesting that the former are property and the latter are those deemed the inheritors of the former.

19. Cecil Rhodes described his interest in annexing Transvaal and building the South African academy "out of kaffir stomachs." Quoted in Zine Magubane, "Pigment of the Imagination? Race, Subjectivity, Knowledge and the Image of the Black Intellectual," in *Hear Our Voices: Race, Gender, and the Status of Black South African Women in the Academy,* ed. Reitumetse Mabokela and Zine Magubane (Pretoria and Leiden: University of South Africa Press and Koninklijke Brill, 2004), 47. The relationship between these two systems of dehumanization that created the "poor white" and the "detribalized African" are essential keys for understanding the processes by which antiblack racism was simultaneously enacted in rehearsals among those being rehabilitated from whatever they were prior and being made into white people.

20. Keletso Atkins, *The Moon Is Dead! Give Us Our Money! The Cultural Origins of an African Work Ethic, Natal, South Africa, 1843–1900* (Portsmouth, NH: Heinemann, 1993); Belinda Bozzoli, ed., *Class, Community and Conflict: South African Perspectives* (Johannesburg: Ravan Press, 1987).

21. Jacobson, *Barbarian Virtues;* Seppo Sivonen, *White Collar or Hoe Handle: African Education under British Colonial Policy, 1920–1945,* Bibliotheca Historica 4 (Helsinki: Suomen Historiallinen Seura, 1995); Edward H. Berman, ed., *African Reactions to Missionary Education* (New York: Teachers College Press, 1975).

22. Malik, *Meaning of Race,* 84–109; Jacobson, *Barbarian Virtues,* 148–72.

23. Sharpe, *Monstrous Intimacies;*); Hartman, *Scenes of Subjection;* Orlando Patterson, *Slavery and Social Death: A Comparative Study* (Cambridge, MA: Harvard University Press, 1985).

24. Thandeka, *Learning to Be White.*

25. Thavolia Glymph, *Out of the House of Bondage: The Transformation of the Plantation Household* (New York: Cambridge, 2008); Painter, "Introduction."

26. Richard Sennett and Jonathan Cobb, *The Hidden Injuries of Class* (New York: Norton, 1972). Otis Madison has explained this in detail in lectures for over two decades: "Introduction to Black Studies Lectures," University of California, Santa Barbara, 1995–2003, unpublished.

27. Charles S. Mills, *Racial Contract* (Ithaca, NY: Cornell University Press, 1997), 18.

28. Emma Perez, *The Decolonial Imaginary* (Bloomington: Indiana University Press, 1999); Ngugi Wa Thiong'o, "Decolonising the Mind," *Diogenes* 46, no. 184 (1998): 101–4; Jamaica Kincaid, "On Seeing England for the First Time," *Transition Magazine* 51 (1991): 32–40, www.hamiltonunique.com/wp-content/uploads/2013/08/OnSeeingEngland-Kincaid.pdf, accessed June 30, 2014; Frantz Fanon, *The Wretched of the Earth* (New York: Grove Press, 1963); Aimé Césaire, *Discourse on Colonialism* (New York: Monthly Review Press, 2000 [1955]).

29. Ignatiev and among many others have deployed and theorized this concept.

30. Mab Segrest, "The Souls of White Folks," in Brander-Rasmussen, *Making and Unmaking of Whiteness,* 43–71; Frankenberg, *Displacing Whiteness;* Noel Ignatiev and John Garvey, eds., *Race Traitor* (New York: Routledge, 1996); Segrest, *Memoir of a Race Traitor.*

31. Jacqui Alexander, *Pedagogies of Crossing: Meditations on Feminism, Sexual Politics, Memory, and the Sacred* (Durham, NC: Duke University Press, 2006), 301.

32. R.W. Wilcocks,"Intelligence, Environment and Heredity," Presidential Address to Section F, delivered July 9, 1931, *South African Journal of Science* 28 (November 1931): 67, Killie Campbell Collection, Durban, Kwa Zulu Natal, South Africa, Rec. No. 477/6 56979 (263).

33. Susanne Klausen, "The Politics of 'Poor White' Fertility within the South African Birth Control Movement, 1929–1939," paper presented at History Workshop and Wits Institute for Social and Economic Research conference, Burden of Race? "Whiteness" and "Blackness" in Modern South Africa, Johannesburg, July 5–8, 2001, 6.

34. Scott Christianson's 2003 review of this archive is a very helpful introduction to the Jukes controversy and reveals the problems with this sort of research on genetic degeneration. Scott Christianson, "Bad Seed or Bad Science: The Story of the Notorious Jukes Family," *New York Times,* February 8, 2003.

35. Wilcocks applied his data to the 23.3 percent of poor white children who did not score an 89 on the IQ tests, the minimum score to qualify for education beyond the elementary level.

36. Mokubung Nkomo, *Pedagogy of Domination: Toward a Democratic Education in South Africa* (Trenton, NJ: Africa World Press, 1990); Brian P. Bunting, *Education for Apartheid* (London: Christian Action for the Southern Africa Education Fund, 1971); R.W. Wilcocks, *Psychological Report: The Poor White,* vol. 2 of *Report of the Carnegie Commission of Investigation on the Poor White Question in South Africa* (Stellenbosch: Pro-Ecclesia-Drukkery, 1932), 147 n. 9.

37. The mental testing of poor whites resulted from a policy to improve white welfare by ending white poverty and propping up white supremacy. Non-Europeans were believed to be genetically inferior intellectually and to have the cognitive capacity of European minors. Thus justifications for eroding claims for African voting rights were pitted against an ambivalent relationship to hereditary science. Dubow, *Illicit Union.*

38. Dubow, *Illicit Union,* 226.

39. Krige, "Segregation, Science and Commissions of Enquiry"; Stanfield, *Philanthropy and Jim Crow;* Paul Rich, *White Power and the Liberal Conscience: Racial Segregation and South African Liberalism* (Johannesburg: Ravan Press, 1984); Zimmerman, *Alabama in Africa.*

40. Maria Lis Lange, *White, Poor and Angry: White Working Class Families in Johannesburg* (Aldershot: Ashgate, 2003); Charles Van Onselen, *New Babylon, New Nineveh* (Cape Town: Jonathan Ball, 2001).

41. Dubow, *Illicit Union,* 179.

42. The state and the Dutch Reformed Church regularly removed children from homes, encouraged them to take up unsafe forced labor, and separated them from their families to prevent the influence of their parents. *Report of the Carnegie Commission,* Part V, 8–13.This work was also characterized by violence, provoking children to run away from orphanages and children's hostels in ways similar to what has been observed in the Servants and Apprentices Act

used to control African children. Such domestic labor and apprenticeship labor was deemed key to their racial rehabilitation.

43. Klausen, "The Politics of 'Poor White' Fertility," 9.

44. Dubow, *Illicit Union,* 10.

45. Chela Sandoval, "Theorizing White Consciousness for a Post-Empire World: Barthes, Fanon, and Rhetoric of Love." in Frankenberg, *Displacing Whiteness.*

46. Du Bois, *Black Reconstruction in America;* C.L.R. James, *Black Jacobins: Toussaint L'Ouverture and the San Domingo Revolution* (repr. New York: Vintage, [1938] 1989); Roediger, *Black on White;* Ducille, "Dyes and Dolls"; Morrison, *Playing in the Dark;* Painter, "Introduction."

47. Sally Gaule, "Poor White, White Poor: Meanings in the Differences of Whiteness," *History of Photography* 25, no. 4 (2001): 334–47.

48. Fikes, "Escaping the Literary Ghetto"; Morrison, *Playing in the Dark;* Donna Allegra, *Witness to the League of Blond Hip Hop Dancers* (New York: Alyson Books, 2000); Painter, "Introduction."

49. On February 1, 1893, Henry Smith was lynched by a crowd of 10,000 spectators after being hunted by a posse of 2,000 in Paris, Texas. In Seattle some months later, Samuel Burdett noticed a large throng of people crowding close to hear a new entertainment, a re-creation of Smith's murder using new sound technology and people's familiarity with World's Fairs. Goldsby asks, "Was viewing the simulation a way to protest the lynching, or did watching amount to a vicarious act of complicity with the southern mob? [What is to be made of the fact that] the deaths of black people were openly sought out as public events worth seeing and without the risk of legal reprisal?" Jacqueline Goldsby, *A Spectacular Secret: Lynching in American Life and Literature* (Chicago: University of Chicago Press, 2006), 15.

50. Lipsitz, *Possessive Investment,* 18, 20; Richard Dyer, *White* (London: Routledge, 1997); Brenda Gayle Plummer, *Rising Wind: Black Americans and U.S. Foreign Affairs, 1935–1960* (Chapel Hill: University of North Carolina Press, 1996); Jan Nederveen Pieterse, *White on Black: Images of Africa and Blacks in Western Popular Cultures* (New Haven, CT: Yale University Press, 1992).

51. bell hooks, "Representing Whiteness in the Black Imagination," in Roediger, *Black on White,* 41; Fikes, "Escaping the Literary Ghetto"; Morrison, *Playing in the Dark.*

52. Frankenberg, *Displacing Whiteness,* 4; hooks, "Representations of Whiteness in the Black Imagination," *Black on White,* 41.

53. I am reminded of Frantz Fanon's description in *The Wretched of the Earth* of the client he counseled who had discovered that his work of torturing Algerian prisoners of war had become part of his nightly domestic ritual. Shame and humiliation are inherited along with the material benefits of the white man's burden. Tiffany Willoughby-Herard, "The Rape of an Obstinate Woman: Frantz Fanon's *Wretched of the Earth*," in *Shout Out: Women of Color Respond to Violence,* ed. Barbara K. Ige and Maria Ochoa (Berkeley, CA: Seal Press, 2008), 264–80; Roediger, *Black on White;* Sandoval, "Theorizing White Consciousness"; Fikes, "Escaping the Literary Ghetto"; Morrison, *Playing in the Dark.*

54. Robinson, *Forgeries of Memory,* xvi.

55. Ibid., xvi.

56. Ducille, "Dyes and Dolls"; Allison, *Skin;* Allison, *Bastard out of Carolina;* Allison, *Trash.*

57. Jared Sexton, *Amalgamation Schemes: Anti-Blackness and the Critique of Multiracialism* (Minneapolis: University of Minnesota Press, 2008); Glymph, *Out of the House of Bondage;* Simon Lewis, *White Women Writers and Their African Invention* (Gainesville: University Press of Florida, 2003); Uma Narayan, *Dislocating Cultures: Identities, Traditions, and Third World Feminisms* (New York: Routledge, 1997); T. Denean Sharpley-Whiting, *Frantz Fanon: Conflicts and Feminisms* (Lanham, MD: Rowman and Littlefield, 1997); Ducille, "Dyes and Dolls"; Painter, "Introduction"; Gerda Lerner, *Black Women in White America: A Documentary History* (New York: Vintage, 1992); Chandra Mohanty, "Under Western Eyes: Feminist Scholarship and Colonial Discourses," *Feminist Review* 30 (1988): 61–88; Anita Cornwell, *Black Lesbian in White America* (Tallahassee, FL: Naiad Press, 1983); Toni Cade, *The Black Woman: An Anthology* (New York: New American Library, 1970).

58. Athol Fugard, *Master Harold and the Boys,* 12th ed. (New York: Penguin, 1995); Jacklyn Cock, *Maids and Madams: Domestic Workers under Apartheid* (Johannesburg: Ravan Press, 1980).

59. Lewis, *White Women Writers;* Segrest, "The Souls of White Folks"; Van Der Watt, "Making Whiteness Strange"; Allison, *Skin;* Frantz Fanon, "Algeria Unveiled," in *A Dying Colonialism* (New York: Grove Press, 1994), 35–63; Allison, *Bastard out of Carolina;* Lerner, *Black Women in White America;* Allison, *Trash.*

60. Harris, "Whiteness as Property," 284.

61. Lipsitz, *Possessive Investment;* Peggy Pascoe, "Miscegenation Law, Court Cases, and Ideologies of 'Race' in Twentieth-Century America," *Journal of American History* 83 (1996): 44–69.

62. Thandeka, *Learning to Be White.*

63. Harris, "Whiteness as Property," 275.

64. Ibid., 276; Harris suggests that the delimiting constraint, the risk, of "passing" or presenting oneself as white, in this case, is being part of a social category that requires a whole system of exclusion.

65. Jill Nelson, *Volunteer Slavery: My Authentic Negro Experience* (New York: Penguin, 1994).

66. Hartman would have us understand that in no uncertain terms does a contract guarantee any of these things. Power, in fact, merely relies on the contract process and language to exact affective and psychic labor that mystifies the actual relationship between property and owner. Saidya Hartman, "The Burdened Individuality of Freedom" and "Fashioning Obligation: Indebted Servitude and the Fetters of Slavery," in *Scenes of Subjection: Terror, Slavery, and Self-Making in Nineteenth Century America* (New York: Oxford University Press, 1997), 115–24, 125–63.

67. Lipsitz, *Possessive Investment,* viii.

68. Ibid., xix.

69. Van Der Watt, "Making Whiteness Strange," 66.

70. James Weldon Johnson, *The Autobiography of an Ex-Colored Man* (Mineola, NY: Dover, [1912] 1995). Johnson, part of a group that secured a $10,000 Carnegie library grant, used his to make a major contribution to the Schomburg Library, a signature North American library and archive of African American and African Diasporic papers and works.

71. David Roediger, *History against Misery* (Oakland, CA: AK Press, 2006); Derrick Bell, *Faces at the Bottom of the Well: The Permanence of Racism* (New York: Basic Books, 1993); Thandeka, *Learning to Be White;* Ruth Frankenberg, *White Women, Race Matters: The Social Construction of Whiteness* (Minneapolis: University of Minnesota Press, 1994); Segrest, *Memoir of a Race Traitor.*

72. Morrell, *White but Poor.*

CHAPTER 4

1. By using the term *scientific management,* Richards was endorsing a more intensive form of Taylorism and Fordism. Columbia University, Manuscripts and Archives, Carnegie Corporation of New York Grant Files, Carnegie Corporation of New York Printed Material; C.S. Richards, *Graduate Training for Business Management and Administration in Great Britain, Europe and North America* (Pretoria: National Council for Social Research, Department of Education, Arts and Science, 1931), Overseas Travel Grant, Report No. 7, Carnegie Corporation of New York Travel Grants, Box 3, File 3.1. Jacobson writes that civilization was understood as the social force that "had bred into civilized Europeans the instinct of continuous steady labor" and had bred out the "wild untameable restlessness" that was "innate with savages" and locked black people into an anachronistic form of production. Matthew Frye Jacobson, *Barbarian Virtues: The United States Encounters Foreign Peoples at Home and Abroad, 1876–1917* (New York: Hill and Wang, 2000), 154. See also David Roediger and Elizabeth Esch, *The Production of Difference: Race and the Management of Labor in US History* (Oxford: Oxford University Press, 2012); John Benhart, *Appalachian Aspirations: The Geography of Urbanization and Development in the Upper Tennessee River Valley, 1865–1900* (Knoxville: University of Tennessee Press, 2007).

2. As Elizabeth Esch has illustrated, the concern for poor whites was manifested in a moralizing and racialized paternalism to teach them to aspire to middle-class domesticity, which had a price tag. Elizabeth Esch, "Fear of a Miscege-Nation: Henry Ford and 'Poor Whites' from Detroit to Port Elizabeth," paper presented at the History Workshop and Wits Institute for Social and Economic Research conference, "Burden of Race? 'Whiteness' and 'Blackness' in Modern South Africa," Johannesburg, July 5–July 8, 2001. White workers, then, used this to demand greater access to higher-paying jobs with job security. According to Jacobson's *Barbarian Virtues,* the average weekly wages to be expected between 1890 and 1910 for white workers in the United States was $8.82 in 1890, $8.94 in 1900, and $10.68 in 1910, which is in sharp contrast to $2.00 in Ireland, under $2.00 in Italy, and $22.00/year for agricultural workers in Hungary. See also Abe Ignacio et al., *The Forbidden Book: The Philippine American War in Political Cartoons* (San Francisco: T'Boli Publishing, 2004);

Maria Lis Lange, *White, Poor and Angry: White Working Class Families in Johannesburg* (Aldershot: Ashgate, 2003); Jonathan Hyslop, "Imperial Working Class Makes Itself 'White': White Labourism in Britain, Australia and South Africa before the First World War," *Journal of Historical Sociology* 12, no. 4 (2002): 398–421; Jeremy Krikler, "White Working Class Identity and the Rand Revolt," paper presented at History Workshop and Wits Institute for Social and Economic Research conference; Jacobson, *Barbarian Virtues,* 63; Pieter C. Van Duin, "'Workers of All Colours Unite!' South African Communism, the White Working Class and the Ideology of Proletarian Non-Racialism, 1917–1943," *South Asia Bulletin, Comparative Studies of South Asia, Africa and the Middle East* 15, no. 2 (1996): 64–71; Tim A. Nuttall, "'Do Not Accept Kaffir Standards': Trade Unions and Strikes among African Workers in Durban during the Second World War," *South African Historical Journal* 29 (1993): 153–76; David Ticktin, "The White Labour Movement in South Africa, 1902–1910, and Working Class Solidarity," paper presented at African Studies Institute, Conference on Southern African Labor History, April 8–10, 1976.

3. Charles Van Onselen, *New Babylon, New Nineveh* (Cape Town: Jonathan Ball, 2001); Timothy Keegan, *Colonial South Africa and the Origins of the Racial Order* (Charlottesville: University of Virginia Press, 1996); Keletso Atkins, *The Moon Is Dead! Give Us Our Money! The Cultural Origins of an African Work Ethic, Natal, South Africa, 1843–1900* (Portsmouth, NH: Heinemann, 1993); Timothy Keegan, *Rural Transformations in Industrializing South Africa: The Southern Highveld to 1914* (Johannesburg: Ravan Press, 1986); Timothy Keegan, "Lapsed Whites and Moral Panic: An Aspect of One South African Ideological Crisis," paper presented at Second Carnegie Commission on Poverty Conference, Cape Town, April 13–19, 1984. Mark Aldrich explained, "Because such traits as thriftiness, intelligence, and the willingness, and ability to work were all thought to be distributed unequally among the races, race became a significant economic variable and came to play an important role in economists' analyses." Mark Aldrich, "Progressive Economists and Scientific Racism: Walter Willcox and Black Americans, 1895–1910," *Phylon* 40 (1979): 2. See also Charlie Johnson and Gerry Mooney, "'Problem' People, 'Problem' Spaces? New Labour and Council Estates," in *Securing an Urban Renaissance: Crime Community, and British Urban Policy,* ed. Rowland Atkinson and Gesa Helms (Bristol: Policy Press, 2007), 125–39; W. E. B. Du Bois, "Strivings of the Negro People," *Atlantic Monthly,* 1897, www.theatlantic.com/magazine/archive1897/08/strivings-of-the-negro-people/5446/, accessed June 15, 2012.

4. Roediger and Esch, *The Production of Difference;* Esch, "Fear of a Miscege-Nation"; Alex Lichtenstein, *Twice the Work of Free Labor: The Political Economy of Convict Labor in the New South* (New York: Verso, 1996).

5. Annabel Cooper, "Poor Men in the Land of Promises: Settler Masculinity and the Male Breadwinner Economy in Late Nineteenth-Century New Zealand," *Australian Historical Studies* 39, no. 2 (2008): 247; Hyslop, "Imperial Working Class Makes Itself 'White.'"

6. This is a strange political configuration of the enemies of white working-class labor that figures pro-imperial people of color as in league with capital. Notwithstanding the fact that the use of hateful racist nomenclature framing

Chinese labor as akin to capital mystified the reality that both white aristocrats and white male labor had access to legitimized political violence, making this equation, Chinese workers = aristocrats, fly apart. Marilyn Lake and Henry Reynolds, *Drawing the Global Colour Line: White Men's Countries and the International Challenge of Racial Equality* (Cambridge: Cambridge University Press, 2008), 7.

7. Poor whites figured prominently in the consolidation of race relations of settler societies. Cooper calls this an "interlocking knowledge system." Frederick Cooper, "Back to Work: Categories, Boundaries and Connections in the Study of Labour," in *Racializing Class, Classifying Race: Labour and Difference in Britain, the USA, and South Africa,* ed. Peter Alexander and Rick Halpern (New York: St. Martin's Press, 2000), 214; W.E.B. Du Bois, *Black Reconstruction in America: 1860–1880,* Introd. David Levering-Lewis (New York: Simon and Schuster, [1935] 1992); C.L.R. James, *Black Jacobins: Toussaint L'Ouverture and the San Domingo Revolution* (repr. New York: Vintage, [1938] 1989), 33 n. 3.

8. Black workers were caught between being caricatured as lazy, vain dandies who only worked when subjected to extreme violence on the one hand and as parasites whose mere presence undermined the living standard of hardworking white workers struggling to become bourgeois subjects on the other.

9. I am not interested in debating whether black people were workers or whether black people rejected proletarianization and the murder, land theft, theft of entire economic sectors and trades, pass laws, criminalization, and taxation that precipitated it as this question has been decided definitively. This caricature of black workers was consistent across liberal imperialist and historical materialist economic histories. See Kathleen Arnold, *America's New Working Class: Race, Gender, and Ethnicity in a Biopolitical Age* (University Park: Pennsylvania State University Press, 2009); Grace Kyungwon Hong, *The Ruptures of American Capital: Women of Color Feminism and the Culture of Immigrant Labor* (Minneapolis: University of Minnesota Press, 2006); Zine Magubane, *Bringing the Empire Home: Race, Class, and Gender in Britain and Colonial South Africa* (Chicago: University of Chicago Press, 2003); Atkins, *The Moon Is Dead!;* David Roediger, *The Wages of Whiteness: Race and the Making of the American Working Class* (London: Verso, 1991).

10. Cooper, "Back to Work," 227; Seppo Sivonen, *White Collar or Hoe Handle: African Education under British Colonial Policy, 1920–1945,* Bibliotheca Historica 4 (Helsinki: Suomen Historiallinen Seura, 1995); Edward Berman, ed., *African Reactions to Missionary Education* (New York: Teachers College Press, 1975).

11. Voting, landownership, and white skin constituted the three qualifications used to guarantee that these places remained domains of white power. Settlers regardless of their European origins could in one generation, or at least this was the promise and expectation, secure the sort of leisured, owning-class lives that they had not been able to achieve elsewhere.

12. Pamela Brooks, *Boycotts, Buses, and Passes: Black Women's Resistance in the U.S. South and South Africa* (Amherst: University of Massachusetts Press, 2008); Magubane, *Bringing the Empire Home;* Atkins, *The Moon Is Dead!;*

C. W. De Kiewiet, "Gold Mining," "Poor Whites and Poor Blacks," and "Civilized Labor," in *History of South Africa: Social and Economic* (Oxford: Oxford University Press, 1950), 158–77, 179–206, 209–45, respectively.

13. The CCNY *Poor White Study* recommended policy correctives such as institutionalized national government support, employment, guaranteed wages, and work colonies for white workers. However, these forms of national government support for poor whites were short-lived and symbolic, and mining capital was not willing to devote structural solutions to eradicating poor white poverty. Though the apartheid economy created a massive transfer of wealth and infrastructure to white people, South African corporate capital continued to reproduce white economic devastation in every generation. The national debate on the poor white problem was central to obscuring this fact and the fact that the transfer of wealth had been primarily from the poor to international *and* domestic mining capital.

14. Magubane, *Bringing the Empire Home;* Lange, *White, Poor, and Angry;* Van Onselen, *New Babylon, New Nineveh,* 25, 33; Klausen, "The 'Politics' of Poor White Fertility"; Sue Krige, "Segregation, Science and Commissions of Enquiry: Contestation of Native Educational Policy in South Africa, 1930–1936," Seminar Paper No. 398, University of Witwatersrand, Institute for Advanced Social Research, Education Department, April 29, 1996; Susan Parnell, "Slums, Segregation and Poor Whites in Johannesburg, 1920–1934," in *White but Poor: Essays on the History of Poor Whites in Southern Africa, 1880–1940,* ed. Robert Morrell (Pretoria: UNISA, 1992), 115–29.

15. The Phelps-Stokes Fund is one of the most significant examples of this. Its founders established a legacy of relationships between the "rulers and the ruled"—a contemporary racial designation that suggested that some societies and groups of people were fundamentally lords and others fundamentally bondsmen—when they funded the American Colonization Society and the colonization of Liberia by free black people from North America. Free black people in the early-nineteenth-century United States were motivated to escape a treacherous racial state and slave society in order to imagine a free black political entity in Africa, albeit one steeped in Victorian racial capitalism. Planter capital and corporate wealth relied on the mask of charity, humanitarianism, and caretaking to hide their deep investments in disciplining white workers by punishing black people.

16. Andrew Zimmerman, *Alabama in Africa: Booker T. Washington, the German Empire, and the Globalization of the New South,* Reprint Edition (Princeton, NJ: Princeton University Press, 2012); Paullette Dilworth, "Competing Conceptions of Citizenship Education: Thomas Jesse Jones and Carter G. Woodson," *International Journal of Social Education* 18, no. 2 (2003–4): 1–10; William Watkins, *The White Architects of Black Education: Ideology and Power in America, 1865–1954* (New York: Teachers College Press, 2001); William Watkins, "Thomas Jesse Jones, Social Studies, and Race," *International Journal of Social Education* 10, no. 2 (1995–96): 124–34; Sivonen, *White Collar or Hoe Handle;* John Stanfield, *Philanthropy and Jim Crow in American Social Science* (Westport, CT: Greenwood Press, 1985); Paul Rich, *White Power and the Liberal Conscience: Racial Segregation and South African Liberalism* (Johannesburg: Ravan

Press, 1984); Stephen J. Ball, "Imperialism, Social Control and the Colonial Curriculum in Africa," *Journal of Curriculum Studies* 15, no. 3 (1983): 237–63; Edward Berman, ed., *African Reactions to Missionary Education* (New York: Teachers College Press, 1975); Edward H. Berman, "Tuskegee—in—Africa," *Journal of Negro Education* 41, no. 2 (1972): 99–112.

17. They parroted the idea that as subject peoples, black people in Africa and the Americas needed forms of institutionalized social control to become economically productive. These gatekeepers charged that by having accommodated themselves to domination during slavery and racial colonialism, black people were doomed to this station. Gerald Horne, *The White Pacific: U.S. Imperialism and Black Slavery in the South Seas after the Civil War* (Honolulu: University of Hawai'i Press, 2007); Gerald Horne, *The Deepest South: The United States, Brazil, and the African Slave Trade* (New York: New York University Press, 2007); Kevin Gaines, *Uplifting the Race: Black Leadership, Politics, and Culture in the Twentieth Century* (Chapel Hill: University of North Carolina Press, 1996).

18. Maria Lis Lange, "Making of the White Working Class: Class Experience and Class Identity in Johannesburg, 1890–1922" (Ph.D. diss., University of the Witwatersrand, 1998), 221.

19. Ibid., 224.

20. Ibid., 227.

21. Magubane, *Bringing the Empire Home;* Atkins, *The Moon Is Dead!;* Walter Rodney, *How Europe Underdeveloped Africa* (Washington, DC: Howard University Press, 1974).

22. Carnegie Commission, "Joint Findings and Recommendations of the Commission," in *Report of the Carnegie Commission of Investigation on the Poor White Question in South Africa* (Stellenbosch: Pro-Ecclesia-Drukkery, 1932), xix.

23. Robert H. Davies, *Capital, State, and White Labour in South Africa, 1900–1960: An Historical Materialist Analysis of Class Formation and Class Relations* (Brighton: Harvester Press), 77–80.

24. In my research I have engaged the popular scholarship on whiteness studies in order to point to the ways that whiteness, when analyzed in the context of the racialization of poverty, must also theorize white misery. See my chapter "The White Primitive: Whiteness Studies, Embodiment, Invisibility, Property" for an analysis of other accounts of global discourses of whiteness. Lake and Reynolds, *Drawing the Global Colour Line;* Emmanuel Eze, *Race and the Enlightenment: A Reader* (London: Wiley-Blackwell, 1997); Charles S. Mills, *Racial Contract* (Ithaca, NY: Cornell University Press, 1997); George Padmore, *Africa: Britain's Third Empire* (New York: Negro Universities Press, 1969).

25. M. Z. Nkosi, "American Mining Engineers and the Labor Structure in the South African Gold Mines," *African Journal of Political Economy* 1, no. 2 (1987): 73. Emphasis mine.

26. Ibid.; Elaine Katz, "Revisiting the Origins of the Industrial Colour Bar in the Witwatersrand Gold Mining Industry, 1891–1899," *Journal of Southern African Studies* 25, no. 1 (1999): 73–97; Marijke Du Toit, "Women, Welfare and

the Nurturing of Afrikaner Nationalism: A Social History of ACVV, 1879–1939" (Ph.D. diss., University of Cape Town, 1996); Martin Legassick, "The Mining Economy and the White Working Class," paper presented at African Studies Institute, Conference on Southern African Labor History, April 8–10, 1976.

27. E.P. Thompson, *Making of the English Working Class* (New York: Random House, 1966).

28. Katz, "Revisiting the Origins," 79.

29. Magubane, *Bringing the Empire Home;* Keegan, *Colonial South Africa;* Keletso Atkins, *The Moon Is Dead!;* Keegan, *Rural Transformations.*

30. On the role of the black working class, they provided a sustained retort to the myth that "industrious white workers" were responsible for South Africa's mineral wealth while "lazy Africans" had worked sporadically in between running away from work, causing the ensuing terrible labor shortages. The more liberal historians argued that the African working class had been essential to the economic success of South Africa, yet they failed to challenge the overt caricature of the African worker as a tragic "detribalized African." Rejecting as "heartless" and "specious" the apartheid "policy of deliberately separating the Bantu from contact ... with the white man" [because] we must not "turn a Black man into an imitation white man," they pivoted around enduring notions of African culture, in this case the potential cultural loss for Africans not exposed to white ways. Malherbe, author of a volume of the *Poor White Study* and a voice of liberalism, argued that "acquiring White civilization" and "greater contact with whites" was necessary to the livelihood of black people. See Ernest G. Malherbe, *Bantu Manpower and Education: 1969 Conference on Bantu Education* (Johannesburg: South African Institute of Race Relations, 1969), 6; Christopher Saunders, *The Making of the South African Past: Major Historians on Race and Class* (Lanham, MD: Rowman and Littlefield, 1988); Nuttall, "'Do Not Accept'"; Shula Marks and Richard Rathbone, eds., *Industrialization and Social Change in South Africa: African Class Formation, Culture, and Consciousness, 1870–1930* (New York: Longman, 1982), 18; Peter Richardson and Jean Jacques Van Helten, "Labour in the South African Gold Mining Industry, 1886–1914," in Marks and Rathbone, *Industrialization and Social Change in South Africa,* 81–82, 87.

31. Nuttall, "'Do Not Accept.'"

32. These structural disincentives included the lowest unskilled wage rates in a South African urban center, fluctuating labor demand in key sectors where they were employed, high competition for unskilled jobs, exclusion from the Industrial Conciliation Boards that were only open to Indian and white workers, and government targeting of African harbor workers—the most militant of Durban African workers. In response to these structural disincentives, African workers qua workers used oscillating migration between town and countryside, high job turnover, and, labor militancy.

33. The workplace agenda for African workers had to address blacks' limited access to permanent living in urban areas along with workplace barriers and the structure of the racially stratified labor market. African workers were undercut as a workforce by the constantly enforced threat of forced removals. For Nuttall, African workers would be considered a genuine urban proletariat if they met characteristics like equalized male/female ratios and higher migration to urban

areas. However, no matter how high African urban migration skyrocketed, if whiteness in this case—access to the city—was an unspoken defining factor in being recognized as a working class, Africans could not be recognized as being part of a working class. Nuttall focuses on one strategy that African workers used to ameliorate the rigid labor segregation, that of leaving jobs in search of higher wages. While this strategy had obvious strengths, it militated against collective action because workers' ties were not deep enough to make collective action satisfy nonmonetary motivations.

34. Nuttal saw labor militancy as the apex of identification with the worker's movement, even though it was a racially exclusive field of mobilizing.

35. J. F. W. Grosskopf's *Poor White Study* volume concluded that "industrial civilization" was a white gift. Ultimately, in this construction *race means black culture*, while *development means white industrialization*. Grosskopf's volume hailed industrial civilization as a defining fact of the white group. To be fair, Marks and Rathbone were more likely to construe industrialization as a white poison more than a white gift. Nevertheless, that the process of industrialization gets linked to one race is problematic.

36. African culture does not have equal standing because the numerous laws intended to get land away from Africans and into the hands of Europeans had the effect of codifying development for whites and underdevelopment for Africans. Keegan's analysis of the nineteenth-century documents legal procedures that protected settlers in the Cape Crown Colony in their land grabs. Keegan, *Rural Transformations.* See also Aletta Norval, *Deconstructing Apartheid Discourse* (New York: Verso, 1996); Atkins, *The Moon Is Dead!;* Jack Simons and Ray Simons, *Class and Colour in South Africa, 1850–1950* (London: International Defense and Aid Fund for Southern Africa, 1983); Padmore, *Africa.*

37. Marks and Rathbone, in *Industrialization and Social Change in South Africa,* defined culture as group autonomy and agency and not as a set of aesthetic practices and fluid answers to questions about social relations, resources, and rites of passage. The 1988 *South African Keywords: The Uses and Abuses of Political Concepts,* edited by Emile Boonzaier and John Sharp, a poststructuralist project to examine the move away from viewing culture as a group identity came close to defining culture in a new way (Cape Town: David Philip). But, as Nancy Scheper-Hughes rightly critiques in "On the Call for a Militant Anthropology—Reply" *Current Anthropology* 37, no. 2 (April 1996): 344–46, the move away from group identity is not welcomed in many quarters where simple affirmation and rights ascribed to African identity in particular have yet to become guarantees of citizenship.

38. Frederick Cooper, "Back to Work: Categories, Boundaries and Connections in the Study of Labour," in *Racializing Class, Classifying Race: Labour and Difference in Britain, the USA, and South Africa,* ed. Peter Alexander and Rick Halpern (New York: St. Martin's Press, 2000), 216–17.

39. Marks and Rathbone, *Industrialization and Social Change,* 1–3.

40. By not looking at white culture, the authors were able to give authority and recognition to Africans while simultaneously speaking for Africans. More important even than this failed attempt to represent African workers was that Marks and Rathbone created a mythic "African" and "European" in this study

rather than searching for the complicated relationship that both had with culture and industrialization. Ultimately, they reaffirmed the false binary of modern/premodern where Africans were under obligation to aspire to and achieve something to which Europeans inherently had access. Any group who resists industrialization may mobilize as an ethnic identity to justify resistance, but such an identity is likely to be tactical, not permanent. Marks and Rathbone essentialized African culture as being outside of the modern economy, which their labor was central to building. The women, culture, and development school defines culture as the major organizing tool for resisting modernization and as a central feature of the modernizing process. However, by "culture," they do not mean an invocation of traditionalism; rather they are evaluating whether the modern economic system can provide them means for reproducing social relations of value. They define culture as a dynamic set of practices that provide models for development and ways to reckon with modernization *qua* Westernization. Kum-Kum Bhavnani, John Foran and Priya Kurian, eds., *Feminist Futures: Re-Imagining Women, Culture and Development* (London: Zed Books, 2003).

41. Davies, *Capital, State, and White Labour in South Africa,* 55.

42. Roediger and Esch, *The Production of Difference;* Meizhu Lui et al., *The Color of Wealth: The Story behind the U.S. Racial Wealth Divide* (New York: New Press, 2006); Jacobson, *Barbarian Virtues.*

43. Carnegie Commission, "Joint Findings and Recommendations," xix.

44. Magubane, *Bringing the Empire Home;* Peter Limb,"Rethinking Sol Plaatje's Attitudes to Empire, Labour and Gender," *Critical Arts* 16, no. 1 (2002): 23–42; Van Onselen, *New Babylon, New Nineveh;* Jane Starfield, "Rethinking Sol Plaatje's Mafeking Diary," *Journal of Southern African Studies* 27, no. 4 (2001): 855–63; Atkins, *The Moon Is Dead!;* Solomon Plaatje, *Native Life in South Africa, before and since the European War and the Boer Rebellion* (New York: Negro Universities Press, 1969).

45. Typically scholars also point to the fact that unskilled whites were more than willing to take jobs that were designated as "kaffir work" and that the mine power brokers were more than willing to hire them.

46. Davies, *Capital, State, and White Labour,* 57.

47. Saul Dubow, *Illicit Union: Scientific Racism in Modern South Africa* (Johannesburg: University of Witwatersrand Press, 1995).

48. Davies, *Capital, State, and White Labour,* 56. The use of the passive voice should not be ignored. Davies is attempting to convince us that whiteness guaranteed special protection from the violence of capitalism—as if racial capitalism could function without its tendency to render poor whites as racially marked. "Resulted" implies simply that economic forces intended to uplift all whites while erasing the violent and depoliticizing social forces necessary for uplifting. These forces included deliberately applied coercive and repressive apparatuses framed as "good for you" while those used to constrain black people were seen to be benefical but ineffective because blackness was believed to be an impossible, unforgivable corruption. Ken Burns, dir., *Unforgivable Blackness: The Rise and Fall of Jack Johnson* (WETA, Arthur Vining Davis, Corporation for Public Broadcasting, 2004).

49. Neil Roos, "Some Preliminary Notes on Work Colonies and Apartheid Culture," paper presented at South African Historical Society, Biennial Conference,

University of South Africa, Tshwane, June 22–24, 2009; Morrell, *White but Poor;* Union of South Africa National Archives, Pretoria Depot, *Report of the Commission of Enquiry Kakamas Labour Colony* (Cape Town: Cape Times Ltd., 1945), U.G. no. 14.

50. Davies, *Capital, State, and White Labour,* 56.

51. Vic Alhadeff, *A Newspaper History of South Africa* (Cape Town: Don Nelson, 1985), 51.

52. Davies, *Capital, State, and White Labour,* 58.

53. Ibid.

54. Louise Vincent, "Bread and Honor: White Working Class Women and Afrikaner Nationalism in the 1930s," *Journal of Southern African Studies* 26, no. 1 (2000): 61–78.

55. Marijke Du Toit, "The Domesticity of Afrikaner Nationalism: A Social History of ACVV, 1904–1929," *Journal of Southern African Studies* 29, no. 1 (2003): 155–76; Marijke Du Toit, conversation with author, Cape Town, South Africa, week of July 18, 2002; Marijke Du Toit, "'Moedermeesteres': Dutch-Afrikaans Women's Entry into the Public Sphere in the Cape Colony, 1860–1896," paper presented at University of Western Cape, Gender and Colonialism Conference, Cape Town, 1997; Marijke Du Toit, "Women, Welfare and the Nurturing of Afrikaner Nationalism." Rental housing costs provide a useful example: rentals cost 30 shillings/mo. in South Africa and 13 shillings/mo. in Britain.

56. Lange, *White, Poor and Angry;* Katz, "Revisiting the Origins"; Nkosi, "American Mining Engineers"; Elaine Katz, "White Workers Grievances and the Industrial Colour Bar, 1902–1913," unpublished paper, African Studies Institute Seminar, University of the Witwatersrand, 1973.

57. Davies, *Capital, State, and White Labour,* 10.

58. Deirdre Royster, *Race and the Invisible Hand: How White Networks Exclude Black Men from Blue-Collar Jobs* (Berkeley: University of California Press, 2003).

59. Davies, *Capital, State, and White Labour,* 61.

60. Ibid, 62.

61. Ibid, 63.

62. Ibid, 62.

63. Vincent examines the formative role of white women as workers, not simply as Afrikaner Nationalists. Vincent, "Bread and Honor"; Louise Vincent, "A Cake of Soap: The Volksmoeder Ideology and Afrikaner Women's Campaign for the Vote," *International Journal of African Historical Studies* 32, no. 1 (1999): 1–17; Jonathon Hyslop, "Representations of White Working Class Women in the Construction of a Reactionary Populist Movement: 'Purified' Afrikaner Nationalist Agitation for Legislation against 'Mixed' Marriages, 1934–1939," African Studies Institute, University of the Witwatersrand, 1993.

64. Davies, *Capital, State, and White Labour,* 66.

65. Ibid, 67.

66. Ibid.

67. Shula Marks, *Ambiguities of Dependence in South Africa: Class, Nationalism and the State in Twentieth-Century Natal* (Johannesburg: Ravan Press, 1986).

68. Lange, *White, Poor and Angry;* Adam Przeworski, *Democracy and the Market: Political and Economic Reforms in Eastern Europe and Latin America* (Cambridge: Cambridge University Press, 1991); Davies, *Capital, State, and White Labour,* 58.

69. Abebe Zegeye, *Youth and Societal Change in South Africa* (Pretoria: UNISA Press, n.d.), 11.

70. Cooper, "Back to Work," 221.

71. Andre Du Toit, "No Chosen People: The Myth of the Calvinist Origins of Afrikaner Nationalism and Racial Ideology," *American Historical Review* 88, no. 4 (1983): 920–52.

72. Johan Geerstema, "White Natives? Dan Roodt, Afrikaner Identity and the Politics of the Sublime," *Journal of Commonwealth Literature* 41, no. 3 (2006): 103–20.

73. I have in mind citizen, subject, perpetual foreigner, and internal threat, all of which are positions on a racial labor hierarchy and contribute to the production of difference and the racial wealth divide. Dollars and Sense, *The Wealth Inequality Reader,* 3rd ed. (Boston: Dollars and Sense, 2009); Lui et al., *Color of Wealth;* Royster, *Race and the Invisible Hand.* On uplift, see Gaines, *Uplifting the Race.*

74. I am concerned with a whole host of tropes that were offered in popular, legal, parliamentary, and academic debates to explain the origins of white poverty. These tropes include (1) black workers as the cause of white poverty, (2) a white standard of living defined as any wage higher than that paid to a black person, (3) the need to train white people's conspicuous consumption, and (4) white workers as more efficient than black. These tropes have had a long life that extends beyond the idea of civilized labor. The idea of civilized labor identifies classes of work preserved for white people from which black people are excluded. However, analysis of the civilized labor idea has not plumbed the social meanings, and the domestic and international juridical frameworks, that blame the racialized poor and entitle the wealthy. The legacy of blaming the poor for the conditions of poverty and wealth inequality is too often delinked from imperial racial regimes and viewed instead through the lens of the economic development of one state versus that of another state. I am extending theories about civilized labor by looking at the racial wealth divide. The global racial wealth divide is an aspect of racial capitalism that identifies a history of internationally linked, state-sponsored, de jure and de facto policies and norms that have prohibited wealth accumulation by black people and transferred wealth to whites. Moreover, deconstructing the racial formation of poor whites as I have done here attends to the process by which wealth dispossession is linked to a cycle of racial demonization and rehabilitation/redemption. By focusing on the Carnegie Corporation case, I consider the global color line that enables a proper examination of the transnational and international dimensions of what Frederick Cooper calls "processes that are not spatially located," like the poor white racial formation and the idea of cheap black labor.

75. Magubane, *Bringing the Empire Home,* provides excellent examples of this in popular culture and public space where black income accumulation is said to be marked by ignorant extravagance and lacking in a proper understand-

ing of economic development. Whites came to see any claims to work, public goods, or space made by black people as unjustified. Since black people represented an unforgiveable social group the representatives of poor whites came to see black people as legitimate targets of state, employment, and everyday violence.

76. Achola Pala, "Definitions of Women and Development: An African Perspective," in *African Gender Studies: A Reader,* ed. Oyèrónké Oyěwùmí (New York: Palgrave Macmillan, 2005), 299–312.

CHAPTER 5

1. The studies explain Carnegie philanthropy in the following ways: (1) as an exceptional South African type of segregation, (2) as social welfare and social science tools of the white parental state, (3) as mediating industrial relations, and (4) as examples of the significance of race and empire. All agree that eugenics shaped the interwar period decisively. See Natalie Ring, *The Problem South: Region, Empire, and the New Liberal State, 1880–1930* (Athens: University of Georgia Press, 2012); Sue Krige, "Segregation, Science and Commissions of Enquiry: Contestation of Native Educational Policy in South Africa, 1930–1936," Seminar Paper No. 398, presented at Institute for Advanced Social Research, Education Department, University of Witwatersrand, Johannesburg, April 29, 1996; Saul Dubow, *Illicit Union: Scientific Racism in Modern South Africa* (Johannesburg: University of Witwatersrand Press, 1995); Brahm David Fleish, "Social Scientists as Policy Makers: E.G. Malherbe and the National Bureau for Education and Social Research, 1929–1943," *Journal of Southern African Studies* 21, no. 3 (1995): 349–72; C.J. Groenewald, "Methodology of Poverty Research in South Africa: The Case of the First Carnegie Investigation, 1929–1932," *Social Dynamics* 13, no. 2 (1987): 61, 69–70; Paul Rich, *White Power and the Liberal Conscience: Racial Segregation and South African Liberalism* (Johannesburg: Ravan Press, 1984), 7, 73; Edward Berman, *The Ideology of Philanthropy: The Influence of the Carnegie, Ford, and Rockefeller Foundations on American Foreign Policy* (Albany: State University of New York Press, 1983), 21; Thomas J. Noer, *Briton, Boer, and Yankee: The United States and South Africa, 1879–1914* (Kent, OH: Kent State University Press, 1978); C.W. De Kiewiet, "Gold Mining," "Poor Whites and Poor Blacks," "Civilized Labor," in *History of South Africa: Social and Economic* (Oxford: Oxford University Press, 1950), 158–77, 179–206, 209–45, respectively.

2. Groenewald argued that U.S. and British sociology of "social pathology" provided the "conceptualization [and] . . . theoretical framework for data-gathering and interpretation . . . as well as the program for social reform" in South Africa and that the *Poor White Study* "stimulated the institutionalization of social research in South Africa. . . . The Carnegie Commission thus established a theoretical foundation for social research in . . . the pre–World War II period." See "Methodology of Poverty Research," 61, 69–70. However, calling Carnegie the originator of African social science repeated Hegel's claim that Africa had no knowledge systems that existed prior to and alongside the Enlightenment. Emmanuel Eze, *Race and the Enlightenment: A Reader* (London: Wiley-Blackwell, 1997).

3. Robinson's critique of the "Exceptionalism Question" demonstrates that American Exceptionalism provides a national/domestic origin story for global forms of white supremacy. National exceptionalism, then, might be better understood as an unlikely fanciful account that paradoxically unites white men's countries. Gaye Seidman, "Is South Africa Different? Sociological Comparisons and Theoretical Contributions from the Land of Apartheid," *Annual Review of Sociology* 25 (1999): 419–40; Seymour Lipset, *American Exceptionalism: A Double-Edged Sword* (New York: Norton, 1997); Dubow, *Illicit Union;* Cedric Robinson, *Terms of Order: Political Science and the Myth of Leadership* (Albany: State University of New York Press, 1980).

4. A central feature that constitutes these polities is the origin story. Cedric J. Robinson, *Forgeries of Memory and Meaning: Blacks and the Regimes of Race in American Theater and Film before World War II* (Chapel Hill: University of North Carolina Press, 2007). Classicists explain in great detail how origin stories shape our misunderstandings of Greek democracy. Moreover, they address our attempts to justify contemporary politics by suturing them to the illustrious reputation of Greek antiquity. Michael Meckler, *Classical Antiquity and the Politics of America: From George Washington to George W. Bush* (Waco, TX: Baylor Press, 2006); Cynthia Farrar, *Origins of Democratic Thinking: The Invention of Politics in Classical Athens* (London: Cambridge University Press, 1989).

5. While a defender of civil liberties, Malherbe is inconsistent in defending the civil liberties of persons discriminated against because of race, class, and gender; he superintended the systematic strangling of black scholarship in higher education. Compared to William Magkoba's "typically African leadership" as vice-chancellor of the University of Witwatersrand, Malherbe's leadership of the white-dominated university is memorialized by some scholars as the zenith of academic freedom. Other commentators regard Malherbe's liberal racism as the signature mode of his public life—and so view him and other race relations technicians as operatives for white minority rule, or "tokoloshes." See G.A. Duncan, ed., *Lovedale, Coercive Agency: Power and Resistance in Mission Education* (Pietermaritzburg: Cluster, 2003); Hassim Kader, "No Moral Highground at UKZN," *Witness Newspaper Online,* December 10, 2008, www.witness.co.za/index.php?showcontent&global[_id] = 17103, accessed March 1, 2012; Frank Wilderson, *Incognegro: A Memoir of Exile and Apartheid* (Boston: South End Press, 2008), 139–41.

6. White liberalism is no benefit to poor whites for it uses them to mobilize systematic antiblack hatred while clearly arresting development. My interest is in the mechanisms of this process.

7. Lipset, *American Exceptionalism;* Seymour Lipset and Stein Rokkan, *Party Systems and Voter Alignments* (New York: Free Press, 1967).

8. Marilyn Lake and Henry Reynolds, *Drawing the Global Colour Line: White Men's Countries and the International Challenge of Racial Equality* (Cambridge: Cambridge University Press, 2008); Charles Mills and Carole Pateman, *Contract and Domination* (London: Polity Press, 2007); Zine Magubane, *Bringing the Empire Home: Race, Class, and Gender in Britain and Colonial South Africa* (Chicago: University of Chicago Press, 2003); Jonathan Hyslop,

"Imperial Working Class Makes Itself 'White': White Labourism in Britain, Australia and South Africa before the First World War," *Journal of Historical Sociology* 12, no. 4 (2002): 398–421; Matthew Frye Jacobson, *Barbarian Virtues: The United States Encounters Foreign Peoples at Home and Abroad, 1876–1917* (New York: Hill and Wang, 2000); Tim A. Nuttall, "'Do Not Accept Kaffir Standards': Trade Unions and Strikes among African Workers in Durban during the Second World War," *South African Historical Journal* 29 (1993): 153–76.

9. Indebted to these agencies, many scholars reiterated this point to sell American educational philanthropy, the empirical voice for liberal apartheid. By the late 1970s, several manuscripts argued that the Carnegie presence in Africa was an extension of U.S. empire.

10. Kersten Biehn, "Improving Mankind: Philanthropic Foundations and the Transformation of American University Research between the World Wars" (Ph.D. diss., Rice University, 2006).

11. According to Dr. R.W. Wilcocks's letter of gratitude, the South Africa–based team requested American sociologists to correct for the Dutch Reformed Church's Chief of Poor Relief Rev. J.R. Albertyn, who viewed poor whites as racial degenerates. The CCNY sent Dr. Charles W. Coulter and Dr. Kenyon L. Butterfield. Butterfield spent fourteen days in the field with the researchers, and he investigated their work twice. Described as charming, tactful, enthusiastic, and devoted during his three-month participation, Coulter brought the comparison with the United States "in the study of such questions as those of our Juvenile Courts, our Charitable Institutions and Miscegenation in South Africa." CCNY Grant Files, Series I, *Poor White Study,* Box 295.4. As it turns out, Albertyn actually wrote the sociological volume. So much for the tact and enthusiasm of the Americans. See also John Henrik Clarke, ed., *Dimensions of the Struggle against Apartheid: A Tribute to Paul Robeson: Proceedings of Special Meeting of the Special Committee against Apartheid on the 80th Anniversary of the Birth of Paul Robeson, 10 April 1978* (New York and Washington, DC: African Heritage Studies Association in Cooperation with the United Nations Centre Against Apartheid, 1979).

12. C.J. Groenewald, "Methodology of Poverty Research in South Africa: The Case of the First Carnegie Investigation, 1929–1932," *Social Dynamics* 13, no. 2 (1987): 61. The Carnegie Corporation spent R200,000 for "black Africans" in South Africa and East Africa in 1928 values while expending only R8,000 for poor whites. The Carnegie Corporation funded the Non-European Library Service, Transkeian Territories General Council, Native Night Schools, the South African Institute of Race Relations, the Joint Councils, the National Bureau for Educational and Social Research (known today as the Human Sciences Research Council), the Overseas Visitors Program, and the New Education Fellowship, all of which were helmed by Carnegie philanthropy operatives, especially Charles T. Loram and Malherbe. Krige's study of the racist bases of the Native Economic Commission, the Phelps-Stokes Fund, and the Native Affairs Commission argues that Loram and Malherbe transmitted Columbia Teachers College theories about race and primitive peoples to the South African context. See Krige, "Segregation, Science and Commissions of Enquiry." These reformers went on to be very important in terms of social research and social

policy, which silenced educated franchise-seeking urban Africans and consigned black people to the coverture-like status of retribalization and racial conciliation. The Carnegie Corporation sponsored numerous campaigns that were profoundly influenced by U.S. segregationist philanthropy and were often called by the same names as their U.S.-based sister organizations, including improving urban slum conditions, founding urban civic organizations, destroying opposing black newspapers and creating ones more conciliatory in tone, removing urban Africans to agricultural cooperatives, promoting autonomous trade between the reserves and the Southern African Protectorates to guarantee a merchant class sympathetic to Anglo-American interests throughout the region, collaborating with chiefs in the rural areas, prioritizing cultural cohesion and squashing cultural variation and experimentation, and electing segregationist Native Representatives. Such strategies co-opted radical black leaders, imposed upon the black political agenda, tamped down the influence of an emerging class of radical black people, and shaped black public opinion.

13. Government administration, public policy, and social welfare for African people reflected the Milner administration's colonial racial logics about the white man's burden in societies where segregation persisted through colonial custom, law, and economic order. Marijke Du Toit, "The Domesticity of Afrikaner Nationalism: A Social History of ACVV, 1904–1929," *Journal of Southern African Studies* 29, no. 1 (2003): 155–76; William Watkins, *The White Architects of Black Education: Ideology and Power in America, 1865–1954* (New York: Teachers College Press, 2001); Mahmood Mamdani, "Teaching Africa at the Post-Apartheid University of Cape Town: A Critical View of the 'Introduction to Africa' Core Course in the Social Science and Humanities Faculty's Foundation Semester, 1998," *Critical Exchanges* 24, no. 2 (1998): 1–32, http://web.uct.ac.za/depts/cas/sd/vol24no2.htm, accessed September 15, 2013; Mahmood Mamdani, "Is African Studies to Be Turned into a New Home for Bantu Education at UCT?," *Critical Exchanges* 24, no. 2 (1998): 63–75, accessed September 15, 2013; Timothy Keegan, *Colonial South Africa and the Origins of the Racial Order* (Charlottesville: University Press of Virginia, 1996); Krige, "Segregation, Science and Commissions of Enquiry"; Fleish, "Social Scientists as Policy Makers"; Rich, *White Power and the Liberal Conscience;* Kevin Gaines, *Uplifting the Race: Black Leadership, Politics, and Culture in the Twentieth Century* (Chapel Hill: University of North Carolina Press, 1996); Stephanie J. Shaw, *What a Woman Ought to Be and to Do: Black Professional Women Workers during the Jim Crow Era* (Chicago: University of Chicago Press, 1995); Hazel V. Carby, "Policing the Black Woman's Body in an Urban Context," *Critical Inquiry,* 18, no. 4 (1992): 738–55.

14. See Rich's discussion of "the Helping Hand Club for Native Girls in Hans Street, Fairview[,] . . . [which] sought to insulate African female domestic servants from the pressures of city life" via organized social monitoring, class surveillance, and political guidance by a class of white women carving space for themselves in the public sphere. Rich, *White Power and the Liberal Conscience,* 13. See DuToit's study of Afrikaner Nationalist women's self-help/ charity groups like the Helpmekaar Club: "The Domesticity of Afrikaner Nationalism."

15. Henry Yu, *Thinking Orientals: Migration, Contact, and Exoticism in Modern America* (Oxford: Oxford University Press, 2001); John Stanfield, *Philanthropy and Jim Crow in American Social Science* (Westport, CT: Greenwood Press, 1985).

16. Ange-Marie Hancock, "Beyond the Oppression Olympics: Seeking Intersectional Solidarity among Black Women in the Academy," paper presented at the panel "The Politics of Political Science in the Academy," Black Women in the Ivory Tower: Research and Praxis Conference, Rutgers University Douglass Campus, March 5–6, 2009, http://www.youtube.com/watch?v = 5lvomJnkPq4, accessed March 2012; Sanford Schram, *Welfare Discipline: Discourse, Governance, and Globalization* (Philadelphia: Temple University Press, 2006); Sanford Schram, *Words of Welfare: The Poverty of Social Science and the Social Science of Poverty* (Minneapolis: University of Minnesota Press, 1995).

17. Dubow, *Illicit Union.*

18. Edwin Black, *War against the Weak: Eugenics and America's Campaign to Create a Master Race* (Westport, CT: Dialog Press, [2003] 2012).

19. Dubow, *Illicit Union,* 11, 15. See also Dipesh Chakrabarty, *Provincializing Europe: Postcolonial Thought and Historical Difference* (Princeton, NJ: Princeton University Press, 2007).

20. Dubow, *Illicit Union,* 14.

21. Ibid., 43–4.

22. Robinson, *Forgeries of Memory;* George Stocking, *The Ethnographer's Magic and Other Essays in the History of Anthropology* (Madison: University of Wisconsin Press, 1992); Jan Nederveen Pieterse, *White on Black: Images of Africa and Blacks in Western Popular Cultures* (New Haven, CT: Yale University Press, 1992); Michael Taussig, *Shamanism, Colonialism, and the Wild Man: A Study in Terror and Healing* (Chicago: University of Chicago Press, 1981); Winthrop Jordan, *White over Black: American Attitudes toward the Negro, 1550–1812* (Chapel Hill: University of North Carolina Press, 1968).

23. Robinson, *Forgeries of Memory;* Cedric Robinson, *Black Marxism,* 2nd ed., Foreword Robin Kelley (Chapel Hill: University of North Carolina Press, 2000); David Roediger, ed., *Black on White: Black Writers on What It Means to Be White* (New York: Random House, 1998); Martin Bernal, *Black Athena: The Afroasiatic Roots of Classical Civilization* (New Brunswick, NJ: Rutgers University Press, 1987); William Leo Hansberry and Joseph E. Harris, *Africa and Africans as Seen by Classical Writers* , vol. 2 (Washington, DC: Howard University Press, 1977).

24. This is a strange disavowal by a scholar with a scholarly commitment to examining and ending racial segregation.

25. Dubow, *Illicit Union,* 227. So while Groenewald insists that Carnegie's largesse benefited mostly black people, Dubow finds that mostly poor white people benefited. Neither of these statements about sets of beneficiaries addresses the racial logic of white vulnerability or the cultural work that was effected by this segregationist philanthropy. Both naturalize these donations and the claims made by the corporation about them.

26. This is a subtle instruction to disregard white poverty as a phenomenon. A recent book on the racialization of welfare, Cybelle Fox's *Three Worlds of Relief* (Princeton: Princeton University Press, 2012) suggests that scientific racist

policies of sterilization did not target blacks until the 1930s in the United States because they were believed to be irredeemable—ignoring the entire history of carceral sexual and reproductive control and manipulation under chattel slavery and war against First Nations women that Harriet Washington has so powerfully detailed in *Medical Apartheid: The Dark History of Medical Experimentation on Black Americans from Colonial Times to the Present* (New York: Doubleday, 2006). Fox explains that it is more pressing to focus on white and Mexican American targets of sterilization as there has been an "African American exceptionalism," ie. as too much attention to their experiences of sterilization.

27. The postemancipation state, for example, claims to have achieved progress while utilizing domestic labor, indentured labor, detained and convict labor, sharecropping and tenant labor, reserve labor, child labor, and myriad other forms of unfree and forced labor that reinforce race, class, sexual, and gender hierarchies. The seemingly innocuous, even accidental, blackening of poor whites has warranted a host of racial legitimations of antiblackness. Emancipation in the Americas and in Southern Africa featured continuities of the logic of enslavement, especially the "afterlife of slavery" in which human freedom is still predicated on black unfreedom coordinated by the parental state that uses proximity to blackness to exact violence. Wendy Woodward, Patricia Hayes, and Gary Minkley, eds., *Deep Histories: Gender and Colonialism in Southern Africa* (Amsterdam: Rodopi, [1994] 2002); Ciraj Rassool and Patricia Hayes, "Science and the Spectacle:/Khanako's South Africa, 1936–1937," in Woodward, Hayes, and Minkley, *Deep Histories;* Charles S. Mills, *Racial Contract* (Ithaca, NY: Cornell University Press, 1997); Saidiya Hartman, *Scenes of Subjection: Terror, Slavery, and Self-Making in Nineteenth-Century America* (New York: Oxford University Press, 1997); Orlando Patterson, *Slavery and Social Death: A Comparative Study* (Cambridge, MA: Harvard University Press, 1985).

28. Dubow's tracing of the "selective absorption" of eugenics and Groenewald's attention to the "American inheritance" of social science converge in this point about "South Africanization" because neither expected European settlers to take on the scientific practices of the African peoples of southern Africa. Cheikh Anta Diop, *The African Origin of Civilization: Myth or Reality,* ed. Mercer Cook (New York: Lawrence Hill Books, 1989); W.E.B. Du Bois, *The World and Africa* (New York: International Publishers, 1979).

29. Dubow explains that according to J.H. Hofmeyr of the South African Institute of Race Relations, "The challenge of science in Africa was to determine the lines along which white and colored races could best live together in harmony and to their common advantage" (Dubow, *Illicit Union,* 15). At this time period international social science did not look kindly on "races" living in close contact unless one was clearly the subordinate and the other clearly the dominant. The CCNY, proponents of this view, frowned on miscegenation in the *Poor White Study,* and what was called the South African "laboratory of racial and cultural relations" would have been eschewed by most social scientists in the world (Dubow, *Illicit Union,* 14). The mingling of the white and nonwhite worlds was anathema. Rehana Ebr.-Vally, *Kala Pani: Caste and Colour in South*

Africa (Cape Town and Maroelana: Kwela Books and South African History Online, 2001), 58–61; Yu, *Thinking Orientals;* Regna Darnell, *Invisible Genealogies: A History of Americanist Anthropology* (Lincoln: University of Nebraska Press, 2001); Regna Darnell, *And Along Came Boas: Continuity and Revolution in Americanist Anthropology* (Amsterdam: John Benjamins, 1998); France Winddance Twine, *Racism in a Racial Democracy: The Maintenance of White Supremacy in Brazil* (New Brunswick, NJ: Rutgers University Press, 1998); Denis-Constant Martin, "What's in the Name 'Coloured,'" *Social Identities: Journal of the Study of Race, Nation and Culture* 4, no. 3 (1998): 523–40; Krige, "Segregation, Science and Commissions of Enquiry"; Stocking, *The Ethnographer's Magic.*

30. Several scholars have traced the intellectual history of the multiple projects in which hybridity was deployed in North Africa by European-descent immigrants, the so-called *pied-noirs,* in order to cultivate new cosmopolitan social identities for themselves that had the effect of pathologizing Arab and Muslim and African identities in North Africa, continentally, and in the French metropole. Predictably, this project of hybridity and postidentity did not remain within the domain of the French colonial world. Instead it traveled and has been used as a retort to all manner of black consciousness and anticolonial knowledge projects. See Pal Ahluwalia, *Out of Africa: Post-Structuralism's Colonial Roots* (New York: Routledge, 2010); Avery Gordon and Chris Newfield, eds., *Mapping Multiculturalism* (Minneapolis: University of Minnesota Press, 1996).

31. The novelist Sarah Gertrude Millin is useful on this point. Africa literally forces white people to go mad and to decay in her major novels, *God's Stepchildren* and *The Fiddler.*

32. Marilyn Lake and Henry Reynolds, *Drawing the Global Colour Line: White Men's Countries and the International Challenge of Racial Equality* (Cambridge: Cambridge University Press, 2008); Brenda Gayle Plummer, *Rising Wind: Black Americans and U.S. Foreign Affairs, 1935–1960* (Chapel Hill: University of North Carolina Press, 1996).

33. Noer, *Briton, Boer, and Yankee.*

34. Dubow, *Illicit Union,* 49.

35. The notion of nonproductive black labor insisted that African workers were not in high-status and high-ranking work categories—the recently reclassified ones—because they lacked the capacity to do those jobs. This description echoed the policies defending "civilized labor" as more efficient.

36. Moreover, these debates about the racial *cum* cultural distinctiveness of Africans entrenched "retribalization" as an aim of segregation. The goal of segregation was to discern the "primitive mentality" and reinscribe notions of an inscrutable, unfathomable backward Other. The African urban middle class resisted the application of the Tuskegee model and demanded rights to the city. Tuskegee model propped up philanthropy-funded colonial education globally and across the U.S. South in the aftermath of the Radical Reconstruction. The Political historian Otis Madison insists that Booker T. Washington's economic philosophy called for using black artisanal skills to compel white industry to employ black workers, while segregationist philanthropy used Washington's philosophy against black people. Otis Madison, "Introduction to Black Studies

Lectures, 1995–2003," University of California, Santa Barbara, unpublished; Robert Vinson, *The Americans Are Coming! Dreams of African American Liberation in Segregationist South Africa* (Athens: Ohio University Press, 2012); Andrew Zimmerman, *Alabama in Africa: Booker T. Washington, the German Empire, and the Globalization of the New South,* Reprint Edition (Princeton, NJ: Princeton University Press, 2012); Penny Von Eschen, *Race against Empire: Black Americans and Anticolonialism, 1937–1957* (Ithaca, NY: Cornell University Press, 1997); Kevin Gaines, *Uplifting the Race: Black Leadership, Politics, and Culture in the Twentieth Century* (Chapel Hill: University of North Carolina Press, 1996); Sue Krige, "Segregation, Science and Commissions of Enquiry," 5–6; Edward H. Berman, "Tuskegee—in—Africa,"*Journal of Negro Education* 41, no. 2 (1972): 99–112.

37. South African liberals feigned sympathy about the consequences of urbanization and industrialization for African peasants. Moreover, they were concerned that Africans might not be equipped to develop appropriate moral and aesthetic sensibilities without the social control of traditional gendered class and status hierarchies (Magubane, *Bringing the Empire Home*). Their policy intervention then was "managing inter-ethnic and racial relations," which had the potential to be explosive and produce unexpected social and political outcomes (Rich, *White Power and the Liberal Conscience,* 4). Liberals feared that the very features of industrial modernization that created opportunities for status, wealth, and accumulation for European migrants and immigrants would destroy Africans people. The urge to protect Africans while at the same time providing elaborate mechanisms for social control reveals how liberal philanthropy proliferated denser and more bureaucratic practices for domination of black people.

38. The oft-repeated joke by U.S. comedian Wanda Sykes describes the difference between being robbed by an ordinary mugger and by a CEO: "a mugger will take what you have in your pockets, a CEO will steal your future" (http://www.last.fm/music/Wanda+Sykes/+wiki). Cornell University Africana Studies founding chair, Professor James Turner, has described this type of theft as "intergenerational emiseration" that takes absurd and vicious turns.

39. Government officials believed the myth of the "pound per day" white wage earner. They campaigned for a white standard of living that would be shored up by internationally comparable white wages and benefits. Such compensation was believed to guarantee access to the manual labor of the African workforce, and to high-quality housing defined as stand-alone bungalows with electricity. In reality, white workers in the period before World War II earned only a bit more than African workers: the wages for the former ranged between 17s 6d and 25s per week while the wages for the latter ranged between 15s 8d and 23s 9d per week. Most of the state public policy for poor whites included resettlement on labor colonies, detention in institutions for the feeble-minded, and remanding children to youth labor and detention facilities. Where one landed depended on racial and gender bias that pivoted around preventing this group from reproducing. Neil Roos, "Some Preliminary Notes on Work Colonies and Apartheid Culture," paper presented at the University of South Africa, South African Historical Society Biennial Conference, Tshwane, Sunnyside, June 22–24, 2009; Maria Lis Lange, *White, Poor and Angry: White Working Class Families in*

Johannesburg (Aldershot: Ashgate, 2003); Annika Teppo, "'Good White Times': The Production of Whiteness in a Former Poor White Area, 1938–2000," paper presented at History Workshop and Wits Institute for Social and Economic Research conference, "Burden of Race? 'Whiteness' and 'Blackness' in Modern South Africa," Johannesburg, July 5–8, 2001; Gordon Pirie, "White Railway Labour in South Africa, 1873–1924," in *White but Poor: Essays on the History of Poor Whites in Southern Africa, 1880–1940,* ed. Robert Morrell (Pretoria: UNISA, 1992), 101–14; Susan Parnell, "Slums, Segregation and the Poor Whites in Johannesburg, 1920–1934," in Morrell, *White but Poor,* 115–29; Linda Chisholm, "Themes in the Construction of Compulsory Education for the White Working Class on the Witwatersrand, 1886–1907," History Workshop, "Class, Community and Conflict: Local Perspectives," University of Witwatersrand, January 31–February 4, 1984.

40. "Job protection" was one of the conditions of union under which the Afrikaner republics joined the British part of the country, 1911–12.

41. The White Labour Department drew on this governmental failure to successfully advocate for sick pay, holiday leave, medical care, coal, money, seed for employee gardens, night schools for employees, and elementary schools for their children.

42. Lange, *White, Poor and Angry;* Morrell, *White but Poor;* Pirie, "White Railway Labour."

43. While workplace segregation was a fairly evident matter of policy and black people were no longer a job competition threat after 1912 when job titles above manual laborer were no longer available to them as a matter of national labor policy, segregated housing was not very evident because poor people all lived together in the same tin and wood houses near each other. One major indicator of white poverty was residing in integrated neighborhoods. In the 1934 Slums Act city officials acknowledged that whites were not "inveterate or hereditary" slum dwellers. But, they argued, it was close association with black city dwellers (a "scientific" measure for the level of poverty) that was the real social problem. The presence of black people represented a threat to the *white living standard.* That is to say, blacks represented the living standards that white urban working people would have to endure as poor people. The government officials were motivated to "protect" poor whites because, in fact, whites were not a coherent or unique group, but the poor were. Why the same whites that had a decade earlier complained of wage competition with blacks did not associate housing segregation as a part of maintaining the "European standard of living" is a striking contradiction. White urban dwellers, single men and women, rented houses from Indians, so-called Coloreds, and Africans. In the rural community of Knysna, Grundlingh documented through survey data that "subsistence craft dwellers practiced very little color discrimination and numbered a rather undifferentiated spectrum from white to colored." Albert Grundlingh, "'God het ons arm mense die houtjies gegee': 'Poor White' Woodcutters in the Southern Cape Forest Area, c. 1900–1939," in Morrell, *White but Poor,* xv.

44. Rebekah Lee, *African Women and Apartheid: Migration and Settlement in Urban South Africa* (London: I.B. Tauris, 2009); Sindiwe Magona, *To My Children's Children,* Reissue (Northhampton, MA: Interlink, 2006); Franco

Frescura, "The Spatial Geography of Urban Apartheid," in *Social Identities in the New South Africa,* ed. Abebe Zegeye (Cape Town: Kwela, 2001), 99–125.

45. It was not until the 1934 Slums Act that Johannesburg Town Council officials successfully took measures to rehabilitate the "deserving" white poor: local authorities were empowered to seize land and put low-cost housing on it; and the Central Housing Board offered low-interest loans for housing schemes. By this time, the Johannesburg Housing Utility Company had been founded with its inaugural campaign, "To Hell with Slums." In booklets announcing this campaign, the company attacked slums as confining poor whites to mental and moral degradation, as products of a capitalist society ignoring the very poor, and as "fertile fields for subversive propaganda." See Morrell, *White but Poor,* 127.

46. Dorothy Roberts, *Fatal Invention: How Science, Race, and Big Business Re-Create Race in the Twenty-First Century* (New York: New Press, 2011); Rebecca Skloot, *The Immortal Life of Henrietta Lacks* (repr. New York: Broadway Books, 2011); Nthabiseng Motsemme, "Loving in a Time of Hopelessness: On Township Women's Subjectivities in a Time of HIV/AIDS," in *Basus'iimbokodo, bawel'imilambo/They remove boulders and cross rivers: Women in South African History,* ed. Nomboniso Gasa (Pretoria: Human Sciences Research Council Press, 2007), 346–68; Troy Duster, *Backdoor to Eugenics,* 2nd ed. (New York: Routledge, 2003); Charles Jones, *Bad Blood: The Tuskegee Syphilis Experiment: A Tragedy of Race and Medicine* (New York: Free Press, 1982).

47. This may be a counterintuitive finding given the successful meeting of racism and white Labour ideology that was captured in the 1922 Rand Rebellion and their slogan, "White Workers of the World Unite."

48. In 1920 the Johannesburg Town Council filed its application to the national funding agency late, and in 1923 their application was again rejected because the national agency claimed that the city had enough resources to provide housing for all its residents and that there were plenty of unoccupied dwellings that could be used to accommodate poor whites.

49. Parnell, "Slums, Segregation and Poor Whites in Johannesburg."

50. E. G. Malherbe, "The Carnegie Poor White Investigation: Its Origin and Sequels," Columbia University: CCNY Grant Files 295.7, n.d., 83.

51. Watkins, *White Architects;* Stanfield, *Philanthropy and Jim Crow.*

52. Ebr.-Vally, *Kala Pani;* Martin, "What's in the Name 'Coloured'"; Dubow, *Illicit Union;* John S. Sharp, "The Roots and Development of Volkekunde in South Africa," *Journal of Southern African Studies* 8, no.1 (1981): 16–36.

53. Thomas Borstelmann, *Apartheid's Reluctant Uncle: The United States and Southern Africa in the Early Cold War* (New York: Oxford University Press, 1993); Noer, *Briton, Boer, and Yankee.*

54. Watkins, *White Architects;* John Higginson, "Upending the Century of Wrong: Agrarian Elites, Collective Violence, and the Transformation of State Power in the American South and South Africa, 1865–1914," *Social Identities* 4, no. 3 (1998): 399–415; Krige, "Segregation, Science and Commissions of Enquiry"; Paul Rich, "Whites against Apartheid," *South African Historical Journal* 32, no. 1 (1995): 206–16; Rich, *White Power and the Liberal Conscience.*

55. Rich's *White Power and the Liberal Conscience* mentions this work in the Institute of Race Relations, the Joint Councils, the Native Representative Councils, the civic organizations, the research institutes, and the lobbying campaigns and as articulated in the educational buildings and infrastructure funded by the CCNY.

CHAPTER 6

1. The Carnegie Commission had just completed Gunnar Myrdal's *American Dilemma* (1944), which reiterated behaviorism's practice of overlooking black political organization. Based on his role as the chief field researcher on the Myrdal Study, Ralph Bunche's *The Political Status of the Negro in the Age of FDR* (1973) is a necessary corrective to Myrdal's sanitizing approach to state criminality and V.O. Key's defense of New South modernity in *Southern Politics* (1984). Joseph McCormick, personal conversation via email, September 9–11, 2010; Kimberley Johnson, *Reforming Jim Crow: Southern Politics and State in the Pre-Brown South* (New York: Oxford, 2010); Bernard Magubane, *The Making of a Racist State: British Imperialism and the Union of South Africa, 1875–1910* (Trenton, NJ: Africa World Press, 1996); Cedric Robinson, *Terms of Order: Political Science and the Myth of Leadership* (Albany: State University of New York Press, 1980).

2. Cornelis De Kiewiet was an American university president at the height of U.S. anticommunism during the era of Carnegie Corporation "strategic philanthropy" for the benefit of human welfare and world peace. Arguably, nothing could have done more for human welfare and world peace than a study that delegitimized Afrikaner Nationalism. Cornelis De Kiewiet, "The Reminiscences of Cornelis de Kiewiet," Interviewed by Isabel Grossamer (Columbia University, Oral History Collection, 1969), 5; Cornell University, History of Cornell's Provosts, "Cornelis W. de Kiewiet, 1948–1951," www.cornell.edu/provost/history.cfm, Accessed June 13, 2012.

3. Though De Kiewiet went on to join the research stable of other Carnegie-made race relations technocrats in Africa, his journey was more arduous since his devotion to U.S. expansionism did not prove to be as useful. He was regarded by his peers as a "militant anti-communist" who had directed Area and Language Programs during World War II. www.cornell.edu/provost/history.cfm; Richard Glotzer, "American Educational Research in the Dominions: Making the Case for Decentralization in Interwar South Africa," *Educational Change* (1997): 52–65, www.oneonta.edu/library/edchange/1997/art05.pdf; De Kiewiet, "The Reminiscences," 11–12.

4. Apparently, there was very little political influence to be achieved internationally by examining segregation in South Africa as an authoritarian or anti-democratic form of governance. Though black radical scholars had argued that apartheid was continuous with Jim Crow discrimination, this position was largely suppressed.

5. According to a deferential De Kiewiet, this was "characteristic . . . of a corporation that must be careful not to tread heavily on a local susceptibilities, particularly when there was coming to be expressed in South Africa, such very

controversial ideas." Shepardson later introduced him to Paul Hoffman, who was the head of the Mutual Security Agency on whose board De Kiewiet eventually served. De Kiewiet repeatedly tried to capture what struck him as the generosity and magnanimity of these men, who were mostly businessmen and academics. When he returned from a CCNY trip and had $300 to $400 left over, he wanted to return the money and told Mr. Hoffman that. Hoffman instructed him to keep the money because he probably "had some expenses that were forgotten." Oral History Collection of Columbia University, *The Reminiscences of Cornelius de Kiewiet* (1969), 8–9.

6. Poverty was viewed as inherent in tribal blackness, whereas poor whites were viewed as salvageable, potentially autonomous white republican citizen-workers (through discipline and punishment).

7. This is documented through analysis of the written correspondence between members of the Carnegie Corporation of New York Board of Directors and South African personnel, research reports by Carnegie personnel, oral histories conducted with research team members, pamphlets by the Overseas Visitors Grant Program recipients, records of the Carnegie Corporations Dominions and Colonies Fund, Reports from the Inspectorate of White Labor. Examples include a host of programs founded in the 1920s and 1930s to promote "indigenous economies," the Non-European Library Service, the Transkeian Territories General Council, Native Night Schools, the South African Institute of Race Relations, the Jeannes Schools for domestic worker training, and the interracial, though predominantly white, Joint Councils. Extant anthropological notions about group cohesion, group preservation, and group-scale economic development undergirded the popular education. See Ellen Hellman, *History of the Institute*, South African Institute of Race Relations (n.d.), www .sairr.org.za/profile/history, accessed, June 13, 2012; Maxine Rochester, "The Carnegie Corporation and South Africa: Non-European Library Services," *Libraries & Culture* 34, no. 1 (1999): 27–51; Paul Rich, *White Power and the Liberal Conscience: Racial Segregation and South African Liberalism* (Johannesburg: Ravan Press, 1984); Marguerite Andrée Peters, *The Contribution of the (Carnegie) Non-European Library Service, Transvaal, to the Development of Library Services for Africans in South Africa* (Pretoria: State Library, 1975); Robert M. Lester, *The Corporation and Its Counsel* (New York: CCNY, 1940), Secretary, CCNY, Printed Material, Box 3, File 3.5, RS no. 31; Frank Brownlee, "The Administration of the Transkeian Native Territorities," *African Affairs* 36, no. 144 (1937): 337–46; Charles Templeman Loram, "The Education of the South African Native" (Ph.D. diss., Columbia University, 1915), published in book form under the same title by Longmans in London in 1917.

8. Richard Glotzer, "A Long Shadow: Frederick P. Keppel, the Carnegie Corporation, and the Dominions and Colonies Fund Area Experts, 1923–1943," *History of Education* 38, no. 5 (2009): 621–48; Lisa Brock and Digna Castañeda Fuertes, eds., *Between Race and Empire: African Americans and Cubans before the Cuban Revolution* (Philadelphia: Temple University Press, 1998); Penny Von Eschen, *Race against Empire: Black Americans and Anticolonialism, 1937–1957* (Ithaca, NY: Cornell University Press, 1997); Brenda Gayle Plummer,

Rising Wind: Black Americans and U.S. Foreign Affairs, 1935–1960 (Chapel Hill: University of North Carolina Press, 1996).

9. Richard Glotzer, "The Career of Mabel Carney: The Study of Race and Rural Development in the United States and South Africa," *International Journal of African Historical Studies* 29, no. 2 (1996): 309–36; Rich, *White Power;* C.T. Loram to CCNY President Dr. F.P. Keppel, Letter from Loram and Keppel, Columbia University Manuscripts and Archives, CCNY Grant Files Series I, *Poor White Study,* Box 295, File 295.8, Keppel Loram Correspondences 1927–1929.

10. Noer paints a vivid picture of the zeitgeist of the age of American Empire, which was shaped by nineteenth-century memory of the extermination of First Nations people, the occupation of Haiti and the Philippines, and the exportation of Southern planters to the Pacific and South America. Thomas J. Noer, *Briton, Boer, and Yankee: The United States and South Africa, 1879–1914* (Kent, OH: Kent State University Press, 1978), xii–xiii. White settler communities were uniquely aware of their potential vulnerability to extermination, having defended barbarian virtues seen as necessary to defend civilization. Berman explains that the "foundation educational ventures coincided with the demise of the colonial empires of Britain, France, and the Netherlands after 1945. The resultant educational and cultural programs were a reflection of the belief that America's post-WWII interests could be served by aligning the evolving third world nations to the United States through the provision of social services (particularly education), which had been limited by the former colonial powers, thereby fulfilling an articulated local need and at the same time weaning these nations from flirtation with socialist doctrine. The extension of a sophisticated form of cultural imperialism also had the advantage of obfuscating the continuance of discredited and crude forms of economic and military imperialism." Edward Berman, *The Ideology of Philanthropy: The Influence of the Carnegie, Ford, and Rockefeller Foundations on American Foreign Policy.* (Albany: State University of New York Press, 1983), 14. See also Lester, *The Corporation and Its Counsel.*

11. Saul Dubow, *Illicit Union: Scientific Racism in Modern South Africa* (Johannesburg: University of Witwatersrand Press, 1995); Berman, *Ideology of Philanthropy;* Noer, *Briton, Boer, and Yankee.*

12. Marilyn Lake and Henry Reynolds, *Drawing the Global Colour Line: White Men's Countries and the International Challenge of Racial Equality* (Cambridge: Cambridge University Press, 2008); Melissa Steyn, *Whiteness Just Isn't What It Used to Be: White Identity in a Changing South Africa* (Albany: State University of New York Press, 2001); George Lipsitz, *Possessive Investment in Whiteness* (Philadelphia: Temple University Press, 1998); David Roediger, *Black on White: Black Writers on What It Means to Be White* (New York: Schocken Books, 1998).

13. Although other research team members, including R.W. Wilcocks, J.F.W. Grosskopf, J.R. Albertyn, and M.E. Rothmann, had more training and experience with charity programs for poor whites, the Carnegie Corporation appointed the South African E.G. Malherbe, a Columbia University Teacher's College alumnus, to lead the study that endorsed the narrow policies of the faction of

Afrikaner Nationalism that ushered in apartheid. Keppel had solid intelligence about the stakes of his support for particular personnel on this project.

14. Consider this a prequel to Cold War–era U.S. legislators' claims that they just could never figure out the "right side" when voting and advocating for savage military interventions and propping up authoritarian anti-communist leaders on the African continent. This dilemma is so consistent as to have been massified at the level of comedy: a common joke 1970s Africanists told to each other in their attempts to support the "right governments." Immanuel Wallerstein, *Africa and the Modern World* (Trenton, NJ: Africa World Press, 1986).

15. CCNY Grant Files, Series I, *Poor White Study,* Box 295, File 295.4. Letters by R.W. Wilcocks, author of the volume on mental health and hygiene, C.T. Loram, and Frederick Keppel himself indicated that the government would not budge. In a memo of December 12, 1929, Keppel expressed his plan for collaboration with the Union Government based on an incentive of L1,000 to encourage the latter to contribute to the *Poor White Study.*

16. Wilcocks itemized the gifts in kind that had been received from the University of Cape Town, the Dutch Reformed Church, and the Union Departments of Health, Education, and Railways—mostly gifts of stipend, salary, and release time for research team members Malherbe, director of national education, and to State Medical Officer W.A. Murray, train passes for Dr. Coulter and some Ford automobiles that had been made available so they could travel around the country documenting the experiences and lives of poor whites. These gifts "ha[d] enabled the members of the Research Committee to devote either the whole or, at least, a considerable portion of their time to the Research." Wilcocks reported that they had spent L2,614 pounds. From September 30 to December 31, 1929, they were budgeted to use L1,091, but they were sure that the Joint Board would be able to meet this expense as the budget still had L1,585 unspent either in funds or assets.

17. Wilcocks thanked the CCNY for lending the support of Coulter and Kenyon Butterfield. He reported that Butterfield spent fourteen days in the field with the researchers and investigated their work in a systematic fashion twice. Coulter had been collaborating with researchers for the several months he was in South Africa. Wilcocks also reported that Coulter's charm and tact and enthusiasm and devotion to the project had been helpful to researchers. Also, Coulter had proved to be of great use because he brought the comparison with the United States especially with regard to the "the study of such questions as those of our Juvenile Courts, our Charitable Institutions and Miscegenation in South Africa." As Wilcocks was the major correspondent with Frederick Keppel, president of the Carnegie Corporation, it is even stranger that Malherbe was designated as head of this study. Wilcocks, oddly, doesn't even warrant entries in the *South African Year Book* in the years immediately following the publication of the *Poor White Study*. Malherbe, on the other hand, the junior scholar on the research team, parlayed his international connections into becoming the scholar most associated with this study and with the many financial rewards that continued to come from the Carnegie Corporation's interest in South Africa.

18. David Roediger and Elizabeth Esch, *The Production of Difference: Race and the Management of Labor in US History* (Oxford: Oxford University Press,

2012); Judith Carney, *Black Rice: The African Origins of Rice Cultivation in the Americas* (Cambridge, MA: Harvard University Press, 2002); Matthew Frye Jacobson, *Barbarian Virtues: The United States Encounters Foreign Peoples at Home and Abroad, 1876–1917* (New York: Hill and Wang, 2000); Elaine Katz, "Revisiting the Origins of the Industrial Colour Bar in the Witwatersrand Gold Mining Industry, 1891–1899," *Journal of Southern African Studies* 25, no. 1 (1999): 73–97; Elaine Katz, "White Workers' Grievances and the Industrial Colour Bar, 1902–1913," paper presented at the African Studies Institute Seminar, University of the Witwatersrand, 1973.

19. Zine Magubane, *Bringing the Empire Home: Race, Class, and Gender in Britain and Colonial South Africa* (Chicago: University of Chicago Press, 2003), 37.

20. In Port Elizabeth, South Africa, Ford Motors subjected workers to U.S. and South African segregation laws and to Americanization programs. Ford Motors ceremonies involved workers walking into and out of a giant cauldron, symbolic of their immersion in the American melting pot, which rationalized an immigrant European workforce and circumscribed the access of black workers in the industrial workforce. Elizabeth Esch "Fear of a Miscege-Nation: Henry Ford and 'Poor Whites' from Detroit to Port Elizabeth," paper presented at the History Workshop and Wits Institute for Social and Economic Research, University of the Witwatersrand, Burden of Race? 'Whiteness' and 'Blackness' in Modern South Africa Conference, Johannesburg, July 5–8, 2001.

21. Carnegie Commission. "Joint Findings and Recommendations of the Commission," in *Report of the Carnegie Commission of Investigation on the Poor White Question in South Africa* (Stellenbosch: Pro-Ecclesia-Drukkery, 1932).

22. Robinson explains that in North America members of the black radical intelligentsia "came through an apprenticeship with Marxism, w[ere] deeply affected by the crisis in world capitalism, and the responses of workers' and anti-colonial movements, and produced, in the midst of depression and war, important books that challenged Marxism and tried to grapple with the historical consciousness embedded in the Black Radical Tradition. W. E. B. Du Bois, C. L. R. James and Richard Wright eventually revised their positions on Western Marxism or broke with it altogether and, to differing degrees, embraced Black radicalism." Cedric Robinson, *Black Marxism,* 2nd ed., Foreword Robin Kelley (Chapel Hill: University of North Carolina Press, 2000), 308; Kelley, Foreword to Robinson, *Black Marxism,* xv; Andrew Zimmerman, *Alabama in Africa: Booker T. Washington, the German Empire and the Globalization of the New South*, Reprint Edition (Princeton, NJ: Princeton University Press, 2012); Rich, *White Power and the Liberal Conscience,* 19, 27, 28; W. E. B. Du Bois, *Black Reconstruction in America: 1860–1880,* Introd. David Levering-Lewis (New York: Simon and Schuster, [1935] 1992).

23. Noer, *Briton, Boer, and Yankee,* 35.

24. Indeed, the prominent South African representative of the African National Congress, Solomon Plaatje (1876–1932) toured the United States (1920–22) and provided detailed coverage and analysis of the consequences of the 1913 Land Act for black South Africans. Molema's study of black history,

Jack Simons and Ray Simons's studies of the effects of discrimination on Xhosa immigrants to Cape Town, Alain Locke's studies of black aesthetics and culturally relevant adult education, Leo Hansberry's studies of the African roots of Western civilization, Carter G. Woodson's studies of black people's history since 1865, Du Bois's study of the role of the black worker in the U.S. Reconstruction and of black communities in Philadelphia, the poverty reduction research at the Lovedale College (the British Missionary College for the education of Africans), and Horace Cayton and St. Clair Drake's class and social status research on black migrants in Chicago, despite their various methodologies and sites of inquiry, all articulated a consistent position against racial accommodationism in the context of both Jim Crow and racial colonialism. See Rich, *White Power and the Liberal Conscience,* 147 nn. 28, 29, 30, 31, all of which reference major research by U.S. philanthropies in South Africa. By World War I substantial numbers of black Americans had traveled to South Africa to aid, uplift, convert, and spread some type of gospel message—finding themselves radicalized and politicized against racial colonialism in the process. Robert Vinson, *The Americans Are Coming! Dreams of African American Liberation in Segregationist South Africa* (Athens: Ohio University Press, 2012); G.A. Duncan, ed., *Lovedale, Coercive Agency: Power and Resistance in Mission Education* (Pietermaritzburg: Cluster, 2003); Du Bois, *Black Reconstruction;* Jack Simons and Ray Simons, *Class and Colour in South Africa, 1850–1950* (London: International Defense and Aid Fund for Southern Africa, 1983); Christopher Saunders, *Black Leaders in Southern African History* (London: Heinemann Educational Books, 1979); William Leo Hansberry and Joseph E. Harris, *Africa and Africans as Seen by Classical Writers,* vol. 2 (Washington, DC: Howard University Press, 1977); St. Clair Drake and Horace Cayton, *Black Metropolis: A Study of Negro Life in a Northern City,* Introd. Richard Wright, Foreword William Julius Wilson (Chicago: University of Chicago Press, [1945] 1993); Howard Pim, *A Transkei Enquiry* (Alice: Lovedale, 1934); Silas Modiri Molema, *The Bantu, Past and Present: An Ethnographical and Historical Study of the Native Races of South Africa* (Edinburgh: Green and Son, 1920); W.E.B. Du Bois, *The Philadelphia Negro* (Millwood: Kraus-Thomson, [1899] 1973).

25. Edward H. Berman, "Tuskegee—in—Africa," *Journal of Negro Education* 41, no. 2 (1972): 99–112.

26. Kelley, "Foreword," xv; Pearl Robinson, "Area Studies in Search of Africa," in *The Politics of Knowledge: Area Studies and the Disciplines,* ed. David Szanton, (Berkeley: University of California Press in collaboration with e-scholarship, 2004), 1–41. Robinson argues that the ranking and power of "three worlds" of area studies research formations explains Carnegie suppression of a black radical social research agenda. Pearl Robinson, former president (2007–8) and vice president (2006–7) of the African Studies Association, explained that the "first world" included well-funded top tier U.S. research universities providing data for anticommunism in Africa via language training, geographic and spatial mapping, and social and demographic data gathering and analysis. This world had a parasitic relationship to black scholars and their writings, which were parroted and praised when useful for endorsing leadership by white "Friends of the Negro" and suppressed when they exceeded that. Carter G.

Woodson wrote of Thomas Jesse Jones, for example: "His published works on his efforts and results there from were of the type claiming credit for what others achieved." Carter G. Woodson, "Thomas Jesse Jones," *Journal of Negro History* 35 (1950): 108. See Nomboniso Gasa, "Let Them Build More Gaols," in *Basus'iimbokodo, bawel'imilambo/They remove boulders and cross rivers: Women in South African History,* ed. Nomboniso Gasa (Pretoria: Human Sciences Research Council Press, 2007): 138; Troy Duster, *Backdoor to Eugenics,* 2nd ed. (New York: Routledge, 2003); Paullette Dilworth, "Competing Conceptions of Citizenship Education: Thomas Jesse Jones and Carter G. Woodson," *International Journal of Social Education* 18, no. 2 (2003–4): 1–10; Lerone Bennett, "Carter G. Woodson: A Profile of the Founder of Black History Month" (East Carolina University, Laupus Library, 1993), www.ecu.edu/cs-dhs/laupuslibrary/diversity/0910/CarterGWoodson.cfm, accessed September 15, 2013; Ellen Condliffe Lagemann, *The Politics of Knowledge: The Carnegie Corporation, Philanthropy, and Public Policy* (Chicago: University of Chicago Press, 1992), 124–26, 129–30. Moreover, Jones's stratagem of domination used philanthropic largesse and research funding to promote a culture of surveillance and compliance. Though biographers have explained that Carnegie funds dried up for Woodson because he was "too volatile," it does seem that his unwillingness to be plagiarized for the express benefit of Jim Crow may be the root of his agitation and decided turn toward black community funding for the Association of African American Life and History. Pearl Robinson's "second world" comprised black internationalist, Pan Africanist, Garveyite scholars, including historically black college faculty and independent researchers galvanized by the Harlem Renaissance, the New Negro artistic scene. Pearl Robinson writes that "pan-Africanist scholars—for reasons of their own history, location and social position—have often willingly embraced 'rejected forms of wisdom' concerning Africa. And it was through their World that African Studies first entered the US academy" to mobilize against Jim Crow. Such persons as Wilmot Blyden, Leo Hansberry, Pearl Primus, Zora Neale Hurston, Alain Locke, Ralph Bunche, E. Franklin Frazier, Melville Herskovits, and Franz Boas and important universities such as Lincoln University in Pennsylvania, Spelman College, and Atlanta University played critical roles in the continuation of this research agenda. Though wide ranging in political ideologies at a fundamental level, they constituted a vibrant scholarly conversation about black life and material conditions under the global racial order. The third world, comprising African universities and research networks, like their diasporic brethren, had to overcome pro-imperial and colonial missionary scholars and have arguably achieved "the African university" in the postcolonial period. On postcolonial African humanities, see Abebe Zegeye and Maurice Vambe, *Close to the Sources: Essays on Contemporary African Culture, Politics, and Academy* (Pretoria: UNISA Press, 2009); Richard Pithouse, ed., *Asinamali: University Struggles in Post-Apartheid South Africa* (Trenton, NJ: Africa World Press, 2006); Mahmood Mamdani, "Teaching Africa at the Post-Apartheid University of Cape Town: A Critical View of the 'Introduction to Africa' Core Course in the Social Science and Humanities Faculty's Foundation Semester, 1998." *Critical Exchanges* 24, no. 2 (1998): 1–32, http://web.uct.ac.za/depts/cas/sd/vol24no2.htm, accessed

September 15, 2013; Mahmood Mamdani, "Is African Studies to Be Turned into a New Home for Bantu Education at UCT?," *Critical Exchanges* 24, no. 2 (1998): 63–75, accessed September 15, 2013. See the critical work that has been done on Mable Palmer, which addresses the construction and meanings of the "three worlds" of knowledge making in the relationship between Mable Palmer, Lily Patience Moya, and Sibusisiwe Makhanya. Shula Marks, ed., *Not Either an Experimental Doll: The Separate Worlds of Three South African Women* (Bloomington: Indiana University Press, 1987). These literatures address the structure of suppression of other knowledge worlds as described by Pearl Robinson, the plagiarism and theft from these knowledge worlds as described by Woodson, and the misapprehension that is caused by cultural imperialism.

27. The actual language used in the introduction to the *Poor White Study* calls the Carnegie Corporation "generous" for bearing the greatest part of the costs and says that "from various quarters the *Poor White Question* was proposed to representatives of the Corporation as one in urgent need of investigation, and a request was addressed to the Corporation by the Dutch Reformed Church asking for support towards this intervention." Carnegie Commission, "Joint Findings and Recommendations of the Commission," 1.

28. Unlike the claims about nation-specific scientific racisms, Noer's *Briton, Boer, and Yankee* and Edwin Black's *War Against the Weak* identified numerous ways in which scientific racism matched international incarnations. Indeed, the obsession with rediscovering and monitoring white settler communities such as the poor whites in South Africa that shaped the compulsion that drew the Carnegie Corporation into this moment in African history rested on the notions that proximity to blackness and residing in that part of the world inhabited by the ruled resulted in white racial degeneration.

29. These scholars argue that philanthropy acts as a social palliative for generalized dissent in response to racial wealth inequality, gratuitous violence, and bondage. William Watkins, *The White Architects of Black Education: Ideology and Power in America, 1865–1954* (New York: Teachers College Press, 2001); Joyce Ladner, ed., *The Death of White Sociology: Essays on Race and Culture* (Baltimore, MD: Black Classic Press, 1998); Brian P. Bunting, *Education for Apartheid* (London: Christian Action for the Southern Africa Education Fund, 1971).

30. Berman, *Ideology of Philanthropy*, 15.

31. The presence of the Carnegie Corporation in South Africa reveals world visions in antagonism—one concerned with shoring up white supremacy and one concerned with black freedom. Emancipation for black people and black peoples is concerned with many dimensions of accompaniment, experimentation, autonomy, healing, and the permanent paradox of fragmentation, but in an initial instance it is typically concerned with pushing against white interference and molestation and the dangerous implications of paternalistic assistance for black people who are believed to be inferior. White interference of this sort animates white nationalisms and white global imaginaries; it exists in contradistinction to the ethics of black liberation. Harriet Washington, *Medical Apartheid: The Dark History of Medical Experimentation on Black Americans from*

Colonial Times to the Present (New York: Doubleday, 2006); Jacqui Alexander, *Pedagogies of Crossing: Meditations on Feminism, Sexual Politics, Memory, and the Sacred* (Durham, NC: Duke University Press, 2006), 301, 310, 327; Fred Moten, *In the Break: The Aesthetics of the Black Radical Tradition* (Minneapolis: University of Minnesota Press, 2003); Carney, *Black Rice;* Robert Farris Thompson, *Flash of the Spirit: African and Afro-American Art and Philosophy* (New York: Random House, 1983); Toni Cade Bambara, *The Salt Eaters* (New York: Random House, 1980); Zora Neale Hurston and Alice Walker, *I love myself when I am laughing . . . and then again when I am looking mean and impressive: A Zora Neale Hurston Reader* (Old Westbury: Feminist Press, 1979); Zora Neale Hurston, *Tell My Horse* (Philadelphia: J.B. Lippincott Co., 1938).

32. Watkins, *White Architects;* John Stanfield, *Philanthropy and Jim Crow in American Social Science* (Westport, CT: Greenwood Press, 1985); Noer, *Briton, Boer, and Yankee,* 41–42.

33. There is abundant evidence in the print journalism record of the success of these strategies, especially to the extent that they could be replicated by the same personnel across geographical terrain, from the American South to the British colonies and dominions. In many ways propagandizing about their success contributed to the suppression of distribution of information about black radical resistance to modes of co-optation and deracination. Black American missionaries circulated Booker T. Washington's 1895 Atlanta Compromise speech in South Africa and throughout West Africa, for example. See Rich, *White Power and Liberal Conscience,* 2, 15, 16, 18, 19, 22, 27, 51, 65, 100, 106, 183; Magubane, "What Is (African) America to Me? African Americans, and the Rearticulation of Blackness," in *Bringing the Empire Home,* 153–84; Vinson, *The Americans Are Coming!;* Magubane, *Bringing the Empire Home;* Kevin Gaines, *Uplifting the Race: Black Leadership, Politics, and Culture in the Twentieth Century* (Chapel Hill: University of North Carolina Press, 1996); James Campbell, *Songs of Zion: The African Methodist Episcopal Church in the United States and South Africa* (New York: Oxford University Press, 1995).

34. Vinson, *The Americans Are Coming!,* xxx.

35. Gaines, in *Uplifting the Race,* explains that self-help was not the same thing as racial accommodationism although they articulate with each other. See also Kathleen Arnold, *America's New Working Class: Race, Gender, and Ethnicity in a Biopolitical Age* (University Park: Pennsylvania State University Press, 2009); Grace Kyungwon Hong, *The Ruptures of American Capital: Women of Color Feminism and the Culture of Immigrant Labor* (Minneapolis: University of Minnesota Press, 2006); Jacobson, *Barbarian Virtues;* Ladner, *Death of White Sociology;* Gaines, *Uplifting the Race;* Mokubung Nkomo, *Pedagogy of Domination: Toward a Democratic Education in South Africa* (Trenton, NJ: Africa World Press, 1990).

36. The thought that an entire society, or that multiple new nations in the Americas, could export the political complexities raised by the capture and enslavement of Africans by ejecting said Africans after emancipation was an important rallying cry and mobilizing agenda for the white nationalist independence movements across the Americas. Isoke offers a stinging history of this urge to deport for colonial New Jersey, where public calls for the deportation of free

blacks began immediately after some few black people became free in 1737. After all black people were emancipated in 1804, the legislature banned black voting in 1807, and calls for deportation increased in force, volume, and violence at all levels of state government by 1824. By 1854 the state dedicated substantial sums to deporting black people under the perverse logic that the costs associated with their deportation was a small repayment for all their unpaid labor during slavery. This, all given that the land of New Jersey was stolen from the Lenape people and ownership of one slave, could be used to appeal for a seventy-five-acre grant of land from the Crown. Indeed, enslaved Africans were given as donations for the building of a white school. Once black people were free and no longer fungible as currency their presence was resented, and sustained attempts to remove them continued unabated for generations. White nationalist independence movements in the Americas in pursuit of sovereignty and international recognition from their former colonial masters could earn sovereign status or satisfy the prerequisites of sovereignty in part through their management of enslaved Africans, autonomous indigenous communities, maroon territories, and emancipation. The notion that an entire society could eject Africans, those peoples most animated by the pursuit of human freedom and upon whom modern notions of human freedom were constructed, would be ironic if it were not such a common solution central to the making of the nation-state, national identities, and international relations in the period after the American Revolution, the so-called age of revolution. In this way, modern notions of human freedom in this revolutionary period were structured by the constitutional and cultural denial of that freedom and the paradox of continuing African enslavement. The descendants of enslaved Africans could be put to work maintaining this system of unfreedom, as evidence of the progress wrought by American empire. Individual republican freedom, a freedom contingent on ideas about black nonhumanity, and a freedom contingent on the belief that all black people ranked *dead* last on any index of racial hierarchy and human capacity. Zenzele Isoke, "Historicizing Resistance: The Makings of a Marginal Community in the Central Ward," in *Urban Black Women and the Politics of Resistance* (New York: Palgrave Macmillan, 2013), 40–43; Michael West, William Martin, and Fanon Che Wilkins, eds., *From Toussaint to Tupac: The Black International since the Age of Revolution* (Chapel Hill: University of North Carolina Press, 2009); Gerald Horne, *The White Pacific: U.S. Imperialism and Black Slavery in the South Seas after the Civil War* (Honolulu: University of Hawai'i Press, 2007); Gerald Horne, *The Deepest South: The United States, Brazil, and the African Slave Trade* (New York: New York University Press, 2007); Paul Keal, *European Conquest and the Rights of Indigenous Peoples: The Moral Backwardness of International Society* (Cambridge: Cambridge University Press, 2003); Robinson, *Black Marxism;* Saidiya Hartman, *Scenes of Subjection: Terror, Slavery, and Self-Making in Nineteenth-Century America* (New York: Oxford University Press, 1997); Charles S. Mills, *Racial Contract* (Ithaca, NY: Cornell University Press, 1997); Walter Mignolo, *The Idea of Latin America* (London: Wiley-Blackwell, 1991).

37. On "providential design," see Robert Vinson, "Providential Design: American Negroes and Garveyism in South Africa," in West, Martin, and Wilkins, From Toussaint to Tupac, 130–54. On the "courage" and "vigor" dis-

played by white American nationalism to bringing "uncaged animals" into contact with white families, see Lagemann for how this idea endured in the writings and thinking of liberal racists. Lagemann covers many, but Cleveland mayor and Carnegie head, Newton Baker, is particularly illustrative because of his vile post-Harlem Renaissance language. Ellen Condliffe Lagemann, *The Politics of Knowledge: The Carnegie Corporation, Philanthropy, and Public Policy* (Chicago: University of Chicago Press, 1992), 128.

38. Cedric Robinson, *Black Movements in America* (New York: Routledge, 1997), 50.

39. David Brion Davis, "Slavery and the Post World War II Historians," in *Slavery, Colonialism, and Racism,* ed. Sidney Mintz (New York: Norton, 1974), cited in Robinson, *Black Movements in America,* 50.

40. Berman, *Ideology of Philanthropy*, 14.

41. South African development, De Kiewiet argued, should be compared to other settler colonies, as nonwhites under colonialism typically were, not to the industrialized European countries. South African exports were minimal in comparison to those of Australia, New Zealand, Canada, Argentina, and the United States. The United States was invested in helping South Africa advance because its lack of development threatened the stability of U.S. economic and political interests in the region.

42. U.S. federal government attempts to protect workers' rights almost always excluded domestic, agricultural, migrant, and other nonwhite workers whose labor was commercialized, commodified, and provided the actual base for the superstructure of industrial waged work. Lagemann, *The Politics of Knowledge,* 128; William Beinart and Peter Delius, Introduction to *Putting a Plough to the Ground: Accumulation and Dispossession in Rural South Africa, 1850–1930,* ed. William Beinart, Peter Delius, and Stanley Trapido (Johannesburg: Ravan Press, 1986), 7.

43. Noer, *Briton, Boer, and Yankee,* 35.

44. Ibid., xiii.

45. Von Eschen, *Race against Empire;* Gaines, *Uplifting the Race;* Plummer, *Rising Wind.*

46. Vinson, *The Americans Are Coming!;* Zimmerman, *Alabama in Africa.*

47. Vinson, *The Americans Are Coming!;* Pumla Gqola, *What Is Slavery to Me? Postcolonial/Slave Memory in Post-Apartheid South Africa* (Johannesburg: Wits University Press, 2010).

48. Noer, *Briton, Boer, and Yankee,* 133.

49. Lake and Reynolds, *Drawing the Global Colour Line.*

50. By 1913 there were thirteen different types of permits and passes imposed on black women, which created an extra taxation and funding stream for local government. These included "stand permits, residential passes, visitor's passes, seeking work passes, employment registration certificates, permits to reside on employers' premises and entertainment permits." Gasa, "Let Them Build More Gaols," 137.

51. The only role that this racial divide did not preclude black membership from of course was the constabulary and the military, which from the days of Shakespeare's *Othello* and the constitution of the modern era reserved this

work category and social role, among others, for the black body in the maintenance of white men's countries. Cedric J. Robinson, *Forgeries of Memory and Meaning: Blacks and the Regimes of Race in American Theater and Film before World War II* (Chapel Hill: University of North Carolina Press, 2007); Mark Sawyer, *Racial Politics in Post-Revolutionary Cuba* (Cambridge: Cambridge University Press, 2005).

52. Noer, *Briton, Boer, and Yankee,* 134.

53. Discussionsof Wilmot Blyden, Henry McNeal Turner, James Dwane, Jonas Godluka, and Kirkland Soga, editor of the black press organ, *Izwi Labantu,* are helpful on this point as they describe black activists rejection of the liberal welfare and missionary schemes in place to guide black communities. Noer, *Briton, Boer, and Yankee,* 117–20; Rich, *White Power and Liberal Conscience,* 14–20.

54. Noer, *Briton, Boer, and Yankee,* 13, 32, 38.

55. Setting up such linkages and associations among English-speaking intellectuals was not a new procedure or practice. After the Anglo-Boer War, the British Association for the Advancement of Science founded the South African Association for the Advancement of Science, reiterating a process that had occurred in Canada and Australia. "The Colonial Office encouraged scientific exchanges as a means by which links between the imperial motherland and colony could be sustained and differences transcended." Dubow, *Illicit Union,* 34. But South Africa often was figured in "picturesque" fashion in these associations. Chris Morton, "'Interesting and Picturesque': Staging Encounters for the British Association in South Africa, 1905," paper presented at the Iziko Museum and South African Museum conference, Encounters with Photography: Photographing People in Southern Africa, 1860–1999, Cape Town,, July 14–17, 1999).

56. Columbia University, Manuscripts and Archives, Carnegie Corporation of New York Grant Files, Carnegie Corporation of New York Printed Material, "Memo from Pritchett," in *The Corporation and Its Counsel,* ed. Robert M. Lester, Secretary (New York: CCNY, 1940), 147, Box 3, File 3.5, RS no. 31. The real issue of course was deciding whether the Philippines, Puerto Rico, Palestine, and Mexico were also British possessions.

57. Lester, *The Corporation and Its Counsel,* 147.

58. Berman, *Ideology of Philanthropy,* 14.

59. Critical scholarship on Alain Locke is useful on this point. Locke documents and to some extent analyzes campaigns by students at historically black colleges and universities in the United States in the 1920s. These students were incensed by their accommodationist and Victorian professors and university administrators. See Raymond Wolters, *The New Negro on Campus: Black College Rebellions of the 1920s* (Princeton: Princeton University Press, 1975). See also Alain Locke and Jeffrey Stewart, ed., *Race Contacts and Interracial Relations: Lectures on the Theory and Practice of Race* (Washington, DC: Howard University Press, 1992); Leonard Harris, ed. *The Philosophy of Alain Locke: Harlem Renaissance and Beyond* (Philadelphia: Temple University Press, 1991).

60. W. M. Robb, "Some Impressions of Overseas Universities and Their Significance for New England," Columbia University, CCNY Archives, n.d., CCNY File, Box 3, Travel Grants, File 3.2, pp. 68–69.

61. Seppo Sivonen, *White Collar or Hoe Handle: African Education under British Colonial Policy, 1920–1945,* Bibliotheca Historica 4 (Helsinki: Suomen Historiallinen Seura, 1995); Nkomo, *Pedagogy of Domination;* Stephen J. Ball, "Imperialism, Social Control and the Colonial Curriculum in Africa," *Journal of Curriculum Studies* 15, no. 3 (1983): 237–63; Edward Berman, ed., *African Reactions to Missionary Education* (New York: Teachers College Press, 1975); Bunting, *Education for Apartheid.*

62. C.S. Richards, *Graduate Training for Business Management and Administration in Great Britain, Europe and North America* (Pretoria: National Council for Social Research.Department of Education, Arts and Science, 1931); Overseas Travel Grant, Report No. 7, CCNY Travel Grants File, Box 3, File 3.1.

63. Robinson's report included six pictures of libraries around New Zealand that reveal the varying successes of these projects. Patea Public Library is a stone building with a modest clock tower. Otane Public Library is a plaster building with Art Deco lettering in the frieze. Fielding Public Library, Martinborough Public Library, and Greymouth Public Library look as though they are from the old American West with white wood siding and a few curlicues in the doorways made out of wood to make it look fancy. The humble Turakina Public Library pictured was dingy and in need of whitewashing. CCNY Graphic Materials, Box 2, File 2.3.5, New Zealand Library Association, 1938. One fabulous photograph (n.d.) is of the McMillan Memorial Library in presumably postindependence Kenya. This five-columned building looks just like the main buildings at Columbia University, New York; the University of Cape Town, South Africa; or the University of the Witwatersrand, South Africa; or any other major learning institution for that matter. Greco-Roman architecture continues to be the sine qua non of public repositories of knowledge in Western civilization. Building, endowing, or funding a library with Carnegie money in Kenya or New Zealand meant adopting this architectural tradition as well as the entire world sense of the culture that sought to preserve its scholarly traditions in this way. The building epitomizes the role that knowledge from the West had in Africa; it was not supposed to be related in any way to the cultural production of knowledge in Kenya itself. Even the flora and fauna surrounding the building reflect the jarring difference between the buildings and the built landscape. Rather than complement long-standing cultural or epistemic traditions of reasoning, sustained inquiry, social analysis, or contemplation or gathering exemplary models of aesthetic provenance or wisdom from the immediate surroundings, the libraries as physical structures are situated on top of whatever existed before them. There is none of the syncretism so much in evidence in the libraries designed to serve white populations. Columbia University, CCNY, Box 2, Graphic Materials File 2.4, Kenya Colony Library Development. In stark contrast, a file on Museum Development at Ife included 25 photographs of sculptures of the head and one photo of wood carvings the height of pilings. Thus installations of Nigerian cultural production in museums probably affected ideas about Nigerian artistic directions. CCNY Graphic Materials, Box 2, File 2.37, Nigeria Museum Development at Ife (n.d.).

64. Melanie Kimbell, "From Refuge to Risk: Public Libraries and Children in WWI," *Library Trends* 55, no. 3 (2007): 454–63; H.H. Wheaton, "An Americanization Program for Libraries," *Bulletin of the American Library Association* 10, no. 4 (1916): 265–68.

65. H.M. Robinson, Library Organizer, "Report on the Transvaal Provincial Library Service in Light of a Visit to the U.S.A. and Canada," Columbia University, CCNY Files, April–October 1957, 2, 4, CCNY File Box 3, Travel Grants File 3.7.

66. These were the words of one employee, a Public Service inspector, V.G. Chowles. Columbia University, Manuscripts and Archives, Carnegie Corporation of New York Grant Files, Carnegie Corporation of New York Printed Material, H.M. Robinson, Library Organizer (April–October 1957), "Report on the Transvaal Provincial Library Service in Light of a Visit to the U.S.A. and Canada," CCNY File, Box 3, Travel Grants File 3.7. pp. 2, 4. In 1927 S.A. Pitt, described by Robinson as a "Scotchman," and Milton J. Ferguson, State Librarian of California, who had organized the first South African Library Association, were dispatched on a "CCNY Mission." Until 1937 they dutifully and successfully advocated for public libraries in each province that were supported by the province, not by the federal government and not by international philanthropic organizations. Robinson noted with special pride that communities with more than 50,000 Europeans did not rely on the provincial library service for the upkeep of their libraries at all.

67. Austin Roberts, "Museums, Higher Vertebrate Zoology, and Their Relationships to Human Affairs," Carnegie Visitors' Grants Committee, Pretoria, South Africa, CCNY File, Box 3, Travel Grants File 3.3, 1935, pp. 12, 52.

68. Ibid., 50. The idea of fund-raising by offering South Africa up as an "experimental laboratory" reached its high point in the acclaim its scientists received in 1923 for Raymond Dart's Taung Man archaeological excavations. Dubow, *Illicit Union*.

69. Between 1949 and 1951 De Kiewiet's lobbying for a proposed African Studies Program at Cornell University failed to secure Carnegie funding. However, the Carnegie Corporation in partnership with the CIA hired De Kiewiet to guide a trip with Commonwealth Fund representatives to introduce them to East African officials. The CIA thought that East Africa would be a good "staging area[,] . . . a place where troops might be deployed or might be assembled in case of a crisis, in case they had to fall back from the Mediterranean or from the Near East as had been done during World War II." Grossamer interrogated De Kiewiet as to whether the proposal to Shepardson had not been the East Africa project and not the work he described on Black poverty in South Africa. De Kiewiet, "The Reminiscences," 19, 26–28, 30.

70. De Kiewiet was president of American University and of the American Council of Learned Societies. He reported, for example, that when the Afro-Asian Institute, headed by John B. George, was established he did not join because of its CIA support. De Kiewiet, "The Reminiscences," 30.

71. Pearl Robinson, "Area Studies in Search of Africa," in Szanton, *The Politics of Knowledge*, 130–31.

72. Vernon J. Williams, "Was There a Distinct 'African American Sociology'?," *Western Journal of Black Studies* 35, no. 1 (2011): 39–43.

73. Reitumetse Obakeng Mabokela and Zine Magubane, eds., *Hear Our Voices: Race, Gender and the Status of Black South African Women in the Academy* (Pretoria: University of South Africa, 2004).

74. Oyèrónké Oyèwùmí, ed., *African Gender Studies: A Reader* (New York: Palgrave Macmillan, 2005); Emmanuel Eze, *Race and the Enlightenment: A Reader* (London: Wiley-Blackwell Press, 1997); Cheikh Anta Diop, *The African Origin of Civilization: Myth or Reality,* ed. and introd. Mercer Cook (New York: Lawrence Hill Books, 1989); W.E.B. Du Bois, *The World and Africa* (New York: International Publishers, 1979); Walter Rodney, *How Europe Underdeveloped Africa* (Washington, DC: Howard University Press, 1974).

75. Locke and Stewart, ed., *Race Contacts and Interracial Relations;* Harris, ed., *Philosophy of Alain Locke;* Wolters, *The New Negro on Campus.*

76. Henry Yu, *Thinking Orientals: Migration, Contact, and Exoticism in Modern America* (Oxford: Oxford University Press, 2001); Watkins, *White Architects;* Ladner, *Death of White Sociology;* Nkomo, *Pedagogy of Domination;* Stanfield, *Philanthropy and Jim Crow;* Bunting, *Education for Apartheid.*

CHAPTER 7

1. Irma Du Plessis, "Family Sagas: Afrikaner Nationalism and the Politics of Reproduction in Marlene van Niekerk's *Agaat,*" *Litnet Akademies:'n Joernaal vir de Geesteswetenskappe* 7, no. 3 (2010): 152–94; Jackie Grobler, "Between Wonderful Relief and Bitter Disappointment: The Reaction of Afrikaner Women to the Peace of Vereeniging, May 31, 1902," paper presented at the University of South Africa, South African Historical Society Biennial Conference, Tshwane, June 22, 2009; Georgina Horrell, "A Whiter Shade of Pale: White Femininity as Guilty Masquerade in 'New' (White) South African Women's Writing," *Journal of Southern African Studies* 30, no. 4 (2004): 765–76; Marijke Du Toit, "The Domesticity of Afrikaner Nationalism: A Social History of ACVV, 1904–1929," *Journal of Southern African Studies* 29, no. 1 (2003): 155–76; Maria Lis Lange, *White, Poor and Angry: White Working-Class Families in Johannesburg* (Aldershot: Ashgate, 2003); Annika Teppo, "'Good White Times': The Production of Whiteness in a Former 'Poor White' Area, 1938–2000," paper presented at History Workshop and Wits Institute for Social and Economic Research conference, "Burden of Race? 'Whiteness' and 'Blackness' in Modern South Africa," July 5–8, 2001); Jonathan Hyslop, "Imperial Working Class Makes Itself 'White': White Labourism in Britain, Australia and South Africa before the First World War," *Journal of Historical Sociology* 12, no. 4 (2002): 398–421; Marlene van Niekerk, "Afrikaner Woman and Her 'Prison': Afrikaner Nationalism and Literature," in *Afrikaans Literature: Recollection, Restitution, Redefinition,* ed. Robert Kreiger and Ethel Kreiger (Amsterdam: Rodopi, 1996): 141–54; Jonathon Hyslop, "Representations of White Working-Class Women in the Construction of a Reactionary Populist Movement: 'Purified' Afrikaner Nationalist Agitation for Legislation against 'Mixed' Marriages, 1934–1939," paper presented at African Studies Institute, University of the Witswatersrand,1993; Lou-Marie Kruger, "Gender, Community, and Identity: Women and Afrikaner Nationalism in the Volksmoeder Discourse of *Die Boerevrou,* 1919 –1931"

(M.A. thesis, University of Cape Town, 1991); Elsabé Brink "The Garment Workers and Poverty on the Witwatersrand, 1920–1945," paper presented at the African Studies Seminar Paper, University of Virginia, 1986.

2. Such disavowals take two forms, claiming that all evil is the same and is banal and that there is no cause for even minor redistribution.

3. Marijke Du Toit, "'Die Bewustheid Van Armoed': The ACVV and the Construction of Afrikaner Identity, 1904–1928," Social Dynamics 18, no. 2 (1992): 1–25. Du Toit helpfully explains in an analysis of Malherbe's photo albums that are not included in the Poor White Study that the images reinforce ideas about poor white people as negligent parents *and* as mothers who are "slum-makers." See "Binnelandse Reise (Journeys to the Interior): Photographs from the Carnegie Commission of Investigation into the Poor White Problem, 1929/1932," Kronos, no. 32 (November 2006): 58. There is a notion that such persons need to be civilized and corrected. Ange-Marie Hancock's analysis of the "politics of disgust" powerfully demonstrates how and why a black feminist approach is so useful.

4. Elaine Katz, "Revisiting the Origins of the Industrial Colour Bar in the Witwatersrand Gold Mining Industry, 1891–1899," *Journal of Southern African Studies* 25, no. 1 (1999): 73–97.

5. Du Toit, "Binnelandse Reise (Journeys to the Interior)," 56, 61, 66, 68. Du Toit goes further urging that one should read the *Poor White Study* along with *Huis Genoot,* a ladies' homemaking magazine, Malherbe's own family vacation album, "snapshot portraiture," and "amateur landscape photography." Du Toit identifies representational continuities that show "smooth transitions between using the camera as social science and as adventurous traveler" (66). All of these photographic forms kitschified poor whites and their relationship to the land as part of developing what Zine Magubane has explained as the masculine bourgeois aesthetic tastes of the new Afrikaner Nationalist middle class. Zine Magubane, *Bringing the Empire Home: Race, Class, and Gender in Britain and Colonial South Africa* (Chicago: University of Chicago Press, 2004), 156.

6. Louise Vincent, "Bread and Honor: White Working-Class Women and Afrikaner Nationalism in the 1930s," *Journal of Southern African Studies* 26, no. 1 (2000): 61–78; Hyslop, "Representations of White Working-Class Women."

7. Ann DuCille, "Dyes and Dolls: Multicultural Barbie and the Merchandising of Difference," *differences: Journal of Feminist Cultural Studies* 6, no. 1 (1994): 48–68.

8. Zenzele Isoke, *Urban Black Women and the Politics of Resistance* (New York; Palgrave Macmillan), 14; Ange-Marie Hancock, "Beyond the Oppression Olympics: Seeking Intersectional Solidarity among Black Women in the Academy," paper presented on the panel, The Politics of Political Science in the Academy, Rutgers University, Black Women in the Ivory Tower: Research and Praxis Conference, Douglass Campus, March 5–6, 2009, www.youtube.com/watch?v = 5lvomJnkPq4, accessed March 5, 2012; Latoya Peterson, "Re-examining the Phrase 'Oppression Olympics,'" *Racialicious Blog,* December 23, 2009, www .racialicious.com/2008/05/06/re-examining-the-phrase-oppression-olympics/; Jared Sexton, *Amalgamation Schemes: Anti-Blackness and the Critique of*

Multiracialism (Minneapolis: University of Minnesota Press, 2008); Andrea Smith, "Heteropatriarchy and the Three Pillars of White Supremacy: Rethinking Women of Color Organizing," in *The Color of Violence: The Incite! Anthology,* ed. B. Richie, J. Sudbury, and A. Smith (Boston: South End Press, 2006), 66–73; Angela Davis and Elizabeth Martinez, "Coalition Building among People of Color: A Conversation with Angela Davis and Elizabeth Martinez," in *Enunciating Our Terms: Women of Color in Collaboration and Conflict,* ed. Maria Ochoa and Teresia Teaiwa (Santa Cruz: University of California, Santa Cruz. Center for Cultural Studies, 1994); Audre Lorde, "There Is No Hierarchy of Oppressions," in *Homophobia and Education,* ed. Leonore Gordon (New York: Council on Interracial Books for Children, 1983), n.p.

9. Marijke Du Toit, "Women, Welfare and the Nurturing of Afrikaner Nationalism: A Social History of ACVV, 1879–1939" (Ph.D. diss., University of Cape Town, 1996).

10. Vincent, "Bread and Honor"; Hyslop, "Representations of White Working-Class Women."

11. Horrell, "A Whiter Shade of Pale," 769.

12. Barbara Katz Rothman examines the devastatingly predetermined scripts that emerge from a 400-year history of white tutelage of black dependents in the context of U.S. slavery. As she illustrates the journey to becoming the blackened white mother of a black child through political choices, not simply through adopting a black child or having a black lover, she cautions that the white mother might be unconsciously motivated by a desire to shortcut social, economic, and political change and justice by rearing a child that becomes forever lost to the black community, or in Katz Rothman's words, "Gone from the black community as surely as if she'd been exiled. She had been exiled" (178). In the process of imagining what it means to debate the domestic and to interrogate the way we think about who has power in the domestic and what the base and superstructure of that power is realizing that the domestic is always one of the most fraught zones of political inequality is essential. Barbara Katz Rothman, *Weaving a Family: Untangling Race and Adoption* (Boston: Beacon Press, 2005).

13. *Agaat,* van Niekerk's 2006 novel, touches on precisely why the relationship between black children and white women has such a troubling history: it is the line between the nurtured child and the despised, underpaid, and often detained servant. Twine discusses the paradoxical situation in which the *criada* practice of Afro-Brazilian girls being raised as part of Euro-Brazilian families places them as domestic laborers once they reach between eight and eleven years of age. At that time these children, who are dubbed "members of the family," no longer attend school and begin to provide full-time child care and other domestic labor for the family. Twine notes incredulously that none of the adult women raised in these homes regard this system as a type of institutionalized antiblack female violence that prevents the transmission of knowledge, self-actualization, human dignity, creativity, acquisition of wealth, and so on. Like other practices of creating outsiders within and maintaining a rigid color line, criada simply reaffirms that the political, social, economic, and status differences that constitute Brazilian society are "victimless crimes" perpetrated in the private sphere of

the household by "innocent" white women. Romero's classic *Maid in the U.S.A.* (New York: Routledge, 2002) and her analysis of the poet Audre Lorde's account of her 1967 experience wheeling her daughter through the aisles of a supermarket contextualizes the ugly misrecognition of Lorde's black daughter by a white child as "a baby maid" in a racialized and gendered global economy. Frances Winddance Twine, *Racism in a Racial Democracy: The Maintenance of White Supremacy in Brazil* (New Brunswick, NJ: Rutgers University Press, 1998); Audre Lorde, "The Uses of Anger: Women Responding to Racism," in *Sister Outsider: Essays and Speeches*, Foreword Cheryl Clarke (Berkeley: Crossing Press, [1984] 2007) 124–33.

14. Van Niekerk, "Afrikaner Woman and Her 'Prison.'"

15. Jacqueline Bobo, *Black Women as Cultural Readers* (New York: Columbia University Press, 1995), 42.

16. Zine Magubane, "The American Construction of the Poor White Problem in South Africa," South Atlantic Quarterly 107, no. 4 (2008): 691–713; Du Toit, "The Domesticity of Afrikaner Nationalism"; Louise Vincent, "A Cake of Soap: The Volksmoeder Ideology and Afrikaner Women's Campaign for the Vote, "*International Journal of African Historical Studies* 32, no. 1 (1999): 1–17.

17. Segregationist economic development always implies underdevelopment and emiseration for the racialized poor.

18. Lynn Fujiwara, *Mothers without Citizenship: Asian Immigrant Families and the Consequences of Welfare Reform* (Minneapolis: University of Minnesota Press, 2008); Ange-Marie Hancock, *The Politics of Disgust: The Public Identity of the Welfare Queen* (New York: New York University Press, 2004); Sanford Schram, *Words of Welfare: the Poverty of Social Science and the Social Science of Poverty* (Minneapolis: University of Minnesota Press, 1995).

19. Shurlee Swain, "The Value of the Vignette in the Writing of Welfare History," *Australian Historical Studies* 39, no. 2 (2008): 202.

20. The sustained critique of the role that whiteness and white supremacy have played in Western philosophy, property rights, and academic disciplines (as social, cultural, aesthetic, juridical, and national capital) has undoubtedly provided some of the more important scholarly criticism of the past two decades. Melissa Steyn, *Whiteness Just Isn't What It Used to Be: White Identity in a Changing South Africa* (Albany: State University of New York Press, 2001); Birgit Brander-Rasmussen et al., *The Making and Unmaking of Whiteness* (Durham, NC: Duke University Press, 2001); David Roediger, *Black on White: Black Writers on What It Means to Be White* (New York: Random House, 1998); Ruth Frankenberg, ed., *Displacing Whiteness: Essays in Social and Cultural Criticism* (Durham, NC: Duke University Press, 1997); Cheryl Harris, "Whiteness as Property," in *Critical Race Theory: The Key Writings That Formed the Movement*, ed. Kimberle Crenshaw and Neil Gotanda et al. (New York: New Press, 1995), 276–91.

21. W.M. Macmillan is useful here, lamenting that at major Volkskongres meetings sectional anti-British sentiment forestalled any meaningful policy solutions to white poverty—which he concluded could not be addressed without changing the practices of farming on shares and tenancy rights.

22. See Alba Bouwer, *Dictionary of South African Biography* 5 (n.d.), 661–63. I am not sure whether Rothmann had more than one Overseas Visitors

Grant, but it is clear that her relationship with Carnegie as a researcher lasted over three decades and that the Carnegie Corporation's research agenda on race and poverty still accommodated Afrikaner Nationalist segregationism and its proponents throughout this period. See M.E. Rothmann, "A Comparison: Report on Certain Social and Economic Conditions seen from a Social Workers Point of View in Two Areas, Leslie County, Kentucky, U.S.A., and Knysna District, South Africa," Carnegie Corporation Visitors Grants Committee, 1940, Travel Grants Box 3, File 3.9; M.E. Rothmann, *The Mother and Daughter in the Poor Family,* Part V, Section B, of *Report of the Carnegie Commission of Investigation on the Poor White Question in South Africa* (Stellenbosch: Pro-Ecclesia-Drukkery, 1932).

23. William Watkins, *The White Architects of Black Education: Ideology and Power in America, 1865–1954* (New York: Teachers College Press, 2001); Manthia Diawara, dir., *Rouch in Reverse* (Formation Films for ZDF/ARTE, Library of African Cinema, 1995); Nkomo, *Pedagogy of Domination;* Stephen J. Ball, "Imperialism, Social Control and the Colonial Curriculum in Africa," *Journal of Curriculum Studies* 15, no. 3 (1983): 237–63.

24. Matthew Frye Jacobson, *Barbarian Virtues: The United States Encounters Foreign Peoples At Home and Abroad, 1876–1917* (New York: Hill and Wang, 2000); Magubane, "The American Construction"; Tiffany Willoughby-Herard, "South Africa's Poor Whites and Whiteness Studies: Afrikaner Ethnicity, Scientific Racism, and White Misery," *New Political Science* 29, no. 3 (2007): 479–500.

25. Rothmann, *Mother and Daughter,* 152.

26. Gloria Naylor's *Women of Brewster Place* (repr. New York: Penguin 1983), 115, has just such a rendering of sympathy toward a mother who is a welfare recipient. A community worker queries a social worker: "You're going to write the woman off as a human being just because she has dirty dishes in the sink?" Naylor reminds that the social worker's task is to see the human dignity in a person's life, not the lack. It is not clear that Rothmann had this much sympathy for poor whites because her insistence that the wife and daughter be controlled and managed smacks of control of reproduction and sexuality, classically means to secure eugenic control. Nevertheless, her role as a charity worker and not a social worker places her outside the circle of authority automatically granted to the male researchers, even though she did the most home visits of any of them.

27. Neil Roos, "Some Preliminary Notes on Work Colonies and Apartheid Culture," paper presented at the University of South Africa, South African Historical Society Biennial Conference, Tshwane, June 22–24, 2009; Betty Valentine, *Hustling and Other Hard Work: Lifestyles of the Ghetto* (New York: Free Press, 1980).

28. Roos, "Preliminary Notes."

29. Rothmann, *Mother and Daughter,* 155.

30. Hyslop, "Imperial Working Class Makes Itself 'White'"; Mab Segrest, "The Souls of White Folks," in Brander-Rasmussen et al., *Making and Unmaking of Whiteness,* 43–71; W.E.B. Du Bois, *Black Reconstruction in America: 1860–1880,* Introd. David Levering-Lewis (New York: Simon and Schuster, [1935] 1992); David Roediger, *The Wages of Whiteness: Race and the Making of the American Working Class* (London: Verso, 1991).

31. This complex discourse analysis is certainly justified through the scholarship on white union workers' complicated rejections and responses to the color bar in various sectors. The presumption that all whites endorsed white supremacist attitudes and ideologies in the same ways and for the same reasons has been disproved by Elaine Katz and Lis Lange. Lis Lange, *White, Poor and Angry;* Katz, "Revisiting the Origins"; Elaine Katz, "White Workers Grievances and the Industrial Colour Bar, 1902–1913," paper presented at the African Studies Institute Seminar, University of the Witwatersrand, 1973.

32. Keegan documents economic distress among poor whites who depended extensively on Basotho grain farming and sharecropping on Basotho landholdings. As transport riders poor whites had a role in the distribution and sale of Basotho crops. As Keegan explained, not only was the Basotho rural economy flourishing, but it was also key to bywoner economic survival: "The more recent interpretations reflect to a greater degree than the inter-war generation of liberals.... In the view of contemporary whites, there was nothing stagnant or decaying about the black rural economy." Timothy Keegan, *Rural Transformations in Industrializing South Africa: The Southern Highveld to 1914* (Johannesburg: Ravan Press, 1986), xvi. Keegan writes further, "However, the Sotho were not only potential labourers in Boer eyes. It is apparent that in the early decades of Boer settlement on the Highveld they were largely reliant for their grain supplies on their Sotho neighbors, who were producing substantial surpluses of maize and wheat, as well as wool and mohair ... for colonial markets" (8). When the roles of transport riders and sharecroppers were eliminated by railroads, white tenant farmers economic dependency on black people was revealed more plainly.

33. Du Toit, "Women, Welfare and the Nurturing of Afrikaner Nationalism," 147.

34. Vincent, "Bread and Honor"; Hyslop, "Representations of White Working-Class Women."

35. Rothmann, *Mother and Daughter,* 156.

36. Valentine, *Hustling and Other Hard Work.*

37. Alice O'Connor, *Poverty Knowledge: Social Science, Social Policy, and the Poor in Twentieth-Century U.S. History* (Princeton, NJ: Princeton University Press, 2002).

38. Lange, *White, Poor, and Angry.*

39. Du Toit, "Women, Welfare and the Nurturing of Afrikaner Nationalism."

40. Robert Morrell, ed., *White but Poor: Essays on the History of Poor Whites in Southern Africa, 1880–1940* (Pretoria.: UNISA, 1992); Belinda Bozzoli, ed., *Class, Community and Conflict: South African Perspectives* (Johannesburg: Ravan Press, 1987); Keegan, *Rural Transformations.*

41. Magubane, *Bringing the Empire Home.*

CONCLUSION

1. Edward Berman, *The Ideology of Philanthropy: The Influence of the Carnegie, Ford, and Rockefeller Foundations on American Foreign Policy* (Albany: State University of New York Press, 1983), 4.

2. Brenda Gayle Plummer, *Rising Wind: Black Americans and U.S. Foreign Affairs, 1935–1960* (Chapel Hill: University of North Carolina Press, 1996), 111.

3. Thomas J. Noer, *Briton, Boer, and Yankee: The United States and South Africa, 1879–1914* (Kent, OH: Kent State University Press, 1978), 133.

4. Gerald Horne, *The Deepest South: The United States, Brazil, and the African Slave Trade* (New York: New York University Press, 2007).

5. Plummer, *Rising Wind,* 96.

6. Marilyn Lake and Henry Reynolds, *Drawing the Global Colour Line: White Men's Countries and the International Challenge of Racial Equality* (Cambridge: Cambridge University Press, 2008), 44.

7. Abebe Zegeye and Maurice Vambe, *Close to the Sources: Essays on Contemporary African Culture, Politics, and Academy* (Pretoria: UNISA Press, 2009), 17.

8. Ann Stoler, "State Racism and the Education of Desires: A Colonial Reading of Foucault," in *Deep Histories: Gender and Colonialism in Southern Africa,* ed. Wendy Woodward, Patricia Hayes, and Gary Minkley, Cross/Cultures: Readings in the Post/Colonial Literatures in English 57 (Amsterdam: Rodopi, 2002), 6.

9. Uma Narayan, *Dislocating Cultures: Identities, Traditions, and Third World Feminisms* (New York: Routledge, 1997).

10. Cynthia Young, *Soul Power: Culture, Radicalism, and the Making of a U.S. Third World Left* (Durham, NC: Duke University Press, 2006); Kia Lilly Caldwell, *Negras in Brazil: Re-envisioning Black Women's Citizenship and the Politics of Identity* (New Brunswick, NJ: Rutgers University Press, 2006); Penny Von Eschen, *Satchmo Blows Up the World: Jazz Ambassadors Play the Cold War* (Cambridge, MA: Harvard University Press, 2006); Mark Sawyer, *Racial Politics in Post-Revolutionary Cuba* (Cambridge: Cambridge University Press, 2005); Brent Hayes Edwards, *Practice of Diaspora: Literature, Translation, and the Rise of Black Internationalism* (Cambridge, MA: Harvard University Press, 2003); James H. Meriwether, *Proudly We Can Be Africans: Black Americans and Africa* (Chapel Hill: University of North Carolina Press, 2002); Charles P. Henry, ed., *Foreign Policy and the Black (Inter) National Interest* (Albany: State University of New York Press, 2000); T. Denean Sharpley Whiting, *Black Venus: Sexualized Savages, Primal Fears, and Primitive Narratives in French* (Durham, NC: Duke University Press, 1999); France Winddance Twine, *Racism in a Racial Democracy: The Maintenance of White Supremacy in Brazil* (New Brunswick, NJ: Rutgers University Press, 1998); Penny Von Eschen, *Race against Empire: Black Americans and Anticolonialism, 1937–1957* (Ithaca, NY: Cornell University Press, 1997); Plummer, *Rising Wind.*

11. Frederick Cooper, "Back to Work: Categories, Boundaries and Connections in the Study of Labour," in *Racializing Class, Classifying Race: Labour and Difference in Britain, the USA, and South Africa,* ed. Peter Alexander and Rick Halpern (New York: St. Martin's Press, 2000), 229.

12. Henry, *Foreign Policy and the Black (Inter) National Interest,* 7.

Selected Bibliography

ARCHIVAL COLLECTIONS

Columbia University, Manuscripts and Archives, Carnegie Corporation of New York Grant Files

   Poor White Study

Africa: Cooperative Research Poor White Study, Wilcox [sic] 12/12/29; 11/21/29; 10/4/29. Series I. Box 295, File 295.4.

Malherbe, E.G. "The Carnegie Poor White Investigation: Its Origin and Sequels." n.d., 1–83, 295.7.

Keppel Loram Correspondence, 1927–29; C.T. Loram to CCNY President Dr. F.P. Keppel. Students reject higher diploma in Jeannes School in Nyasaland. Series I. Box 295, File 295.8.

Carnegie Corporation of New York Graphic Materials

Kenya Colony Library Development, Box 2, File 2.4.

Loram, Charles Templeman. n.d. Box 2, File 2.11. C.T. Loram.

New Zealand Library Association. 1938. Box 2, File 2.3.5.

Nigeria Museum Development at Ife. n.d. Box 2, File 2.37.

Pim, Howard. Box 2, File 2.38. North American Indian Conference, n.d.

Pim, Howard. Box 2, File 2.50. Howard Pim, n.d.

Progressive Education Association—Program in Art for Indians. Box 2, File 2.53.

South African Council for Scientific and Industrial Research—Mobile Testing Laboratory for Research on Mentality, 1952–60. Carnegie Mobiele Sielkundige Laboratorium Nasionale Instituut vir Personeelnavorsing, WNNR or Carnegie Mobile Psychological Laboratory National Institute for Personnel Research. Box 2, File 2.63.

South Australian Museum. Box 2, File 2.64. n.d.

Carnegie Corporation of New York Printed Material

Carnegie Corporation Overseas Travel Grants and Visitor's Grants Committee File.

Lester, Robert M., ed. *The Corporation and Its Counsel.* New York: CCNY, 1940. Secretary Box 3, File 3.5, RS no. 31.

Pritchett. "Memo from Pritchett." In *The Corporation and Its Counsel,* ed. Robert M. Lester, Secretary. New York: CCNY, 1940. 147, Box 3, File 3.5, RS no. 31.

Richards, C.S. *Graduate Training for Business Management and Administration in Great Britain, Europe and North America.* National Council for Social Research. Department of Education, Arts and Science, Pretoria: Carnegie Corporation Visitors Grants Committee, April–December 1931. Report no. 7. Box 3, File 3.1.

Robb, W.M. "Some Impressions of Overseas Universities and Their Significance for New England." Pretoria: Carnegie Corporation Visitors Grants Committee, n.d. Box 3, File 3.2, pp. 68–69.

Roberts, Austin. "Museums, Higher Vertebrate Zoology, and Their Relationships to Human Affairs." Carnegie Visitors' Grants Committee. Pretoria: Carnegie Corporation Visitors Grants Committee, 1935. Box 3, File 3.3.

Robinson, H.M., Library Organizer. "Report on the Transvaal Provincial Library Service in Light of a Visit to the U.S.A. and Canada." Pretoria: Carnegie Corporation Visitors Grants Committee, April–December 1931. Box 3, File 3.7.

Rothmann, M.E. 1940. *A Comparison: Report on Certain Social and Economic Conditions Seen from a Social Workers Point of View in Two Areas: Leslie County, Kentucky, U.S.A., and Knysna District, South Africa.* Pretoria: Carnegie Corporation Visitors Grants Committee, 1940. Box 3, File 3.9.

Columbia University, Oral History Research Office,
Oral History Collection

The Reminiscences of Cornelis de Kiewiet. Interviewed by Isabel Grossamer, 1969.

The Reminiscences of E.G. Malherbe. Interviewed by Isabel Grossamer, 23 June 1967. Rec. No. 519/3 5698343.

McGregor Museum, Kimberley, South Africa, Kakamas Land Settlement
Scheme Collection

"Kakamas." In *Standard Encyclopedia of Southern Africa* 6:272–75. n.d.

Union of South Africa National Archives, Pretoria Depot, Poor White
Collection

Inspectorate of White Labor. White Labor Bureau to the Inspectorate of White Labor. Acting Assistant Inspector for the White Labor Bureau reported on Mr. Maggs' Silverton Tannery scheme to hire an additional 20–30 whites. IWL 1915, SA/NA, MNW 295 File 2457/15–2534/15, 8 December 1915.

Report of the Commission of Enquiry Kakamas Labour Colony. Cape Town: Cape Times Limited. U.G. No. 14, 1945.

University of Kwa Zulu Natal, Killie Campbell Library, Ernest Gideon Malherbe Papers

Malherbe, E.G. "Afrikaner Economic Movement." Unpublished, 1940. Rec. No. 446/456975 460C.

Malherbe, Ernest G. *Autonomy of Our Universities and Apartheid.* No publication information available. May 1957.

Malherbe, Ernest G. *Bantu Manpower and Education. 1969 Conference on Bantu Education.* Johannesburg: South African Institute of Race Relations, 1969.

Malherbe, E.G. "Broederbond Bamboozling." Unpublished, 1970. Rec. No. 446/4B 56975 45a.

Malherbe, Ernest G. *Demographic and Socio-Political Forces Determining the Position of English in the South African Republic: English as Mother Tongue.* Publication No. 3 of the English Academy of Southern Africa and the Institute for the Study of English in Africa Grahamstown: Rhodes University, 1966.

Malherbe, E.G. "The Poor White Problem." *African Observer* 4, no. 6 (n.d.: 16–27). Rec. No. 477/3 56979 235.

Malherbe, E.G. "Race and Education." Hoernle Memorial Lecture. South African Institute of Race Relations Johannesburg: Natal Witness Ltd., 1946.

Malherbe, E.G. Table Showing Size of Family in Relation to Economic Condition in Each Province. "Education and Economic Condition in Relation to Family Size," n.d. Rec. No. 477/4 56979 240.

Malherbe, Ernest G., with J.J.G. Carson and J.D. Rheinallt Jones. *Educational Adaptations in a Changing Society: Report of the South African Education Conference held in Capetown and Johannesburg in July 1934.* New Education Fellowship. Cape Town: Juta & Co, 1937.

University of Kwa Zulu Natal, Killie Campbell Library, Raymond William Wilcocks Papers

Wilcocks, R.W. November 1931. "Intelligence, Environment and Heredity." Presidential Address to Section F, delivered 9 July 1931. *South African Journal of Science* 28.63–76. Rec No. 477/6 56979 263.

Wilcocks, R.W. "Psychological Observations on the Relation between Poor Whites and Non-Europeans." *Social and Industrial Review* (May 1930): 1–8. Rec. No. 477/6 56979 265.

Wilcocks, R.W. "Rural Poverty among Whites in South Africa and in the South of the United States." Unpublished MS. Rec. No. 477/6 56979 267.

University of the Witwatersrand, William Cullen Historical Papers, Poor White Collection

Albertyn, J.R. *The Poor White and Society.* Part V, Section A, of *Report of the Carnegie Commission of Investigation on the Poor White Question in South Africa.* Stellenbosch: Pro-Ecclesia-Drukkery, 1932.

Carnegie Commission. "Joint Findings and Recommendations of the Commission." In *Report of the Carnegie Commission of Investigation on the Poor White Question in South Africa*. Stellenbosch: Pro-Ecclesia-Drukkery, 1932.

Grosskopf, J. F. W. *Economic Report: Rural Impoverishment and Rural Exodus*. Part I of *Report of the Carnegie Commission of Investigation on the Poor White Question in South Africa*. Stellenbosch: Pro-Ecclesia-Drukkery, 1932.

Malherbe, E. G. *Educational Report: Education and the Poor White*. Part III of *Report of the Carnegie Commission of Investigation on the Poor White Question in South Africa*. Stellenbosch: Pro-Ecclesia-Drukkery, 1932.

Murray, W. A. *Health Report: Health Factors in the Poor White Problem*. Part IV of *Report of the Carnegie Commission of Investigation on the Poor White Question in South Africa*. Stellenbosch: Pro-Ecclesia-Drukkery, 1932.

Rothmann, M. E. *The Mother and Daughter in the Poor Family*. Part V, Section B, of *Report of the Carnegie Commission of Investigation on the Poor White Question in South Africa*. Stellenbosch: Pro-Ecclesia-Drukkery, 1932.

Wilcocks, R. W. *Psychological Report: The Poor White*. Vol. II of the *Report of the Carnegie Commission of Investigation on the Poor White Question in South Africa*. Stellenbosch: Pro-Ecclesia-Drukkery, 1932.

INTERVIEWS

Ballen, Roger. "Visualizing the Aesthetics of the World Culture of Poverty: Interview with Roger Ballen," unpublished interview by author, Johannesburg, South Africa, 30 June 2002.

Cuthbertson, Greg. Interview by author, UNISA, 31 May and 7 June 2002.

Du Toit, Marijke. Conversation with author. Cape Town, South Africa, week of 18 July 2002.

Goldblatt, David. Interview by author. Johannesburg, South Africa, 25 June 2002.

McCormick, Joseph. Email conversation with author, 9–11 September 2010.

Simon, Mary. Conversation with author, University of Cape Town, week of 19 July 2002.

Tayler, Judith. Conversation with author, University of South Africa, 8 June 2002.

PUBLICATIONS

Abrahams, Yvette. "'Ambiguity' Is My Middle Name: A Research Diary." In *Hear Our Voices: Race, Gender, and the Status of Black South African Women in the Academy*, ed. Reitumetse Mabokela and Zine Magubane, 10–24. Pretoria and Leiden: University of South Africa Press and Koninklijke Brill, 2004.

Adam, Heribert, and Hermann Giliomee. *Ethnic Power Mobilized: Can South Africa Change?* New Haven, CT: Yale University Press, 1979.

Adams, Rachel. *Sideshow USA: Freaks and the American Cultural Imagination*. Chicago: University of Chicago Press, 2001.

Ahluwalia, Pal. *Out of Africa: Post-Structuralism's Colonial Roots*. New York: Routledge, 2010.

Alcoff, Linda Martín. *Visible Identities: Race, Gender, and the Self.* London: Oxford, 2006.

Alexander, M. Jacqui. *Pedagogies of Crossing: Meditations on Feminism, Sexual Politics, Memory, and the Sacred.* Durham, NC: Duke University Press, 2006.

Alexander, Ray, and Jack Simons. *Job Reservation and the Trade Unions.* Woodstock, Cape Town: Enterprise Publishing, 1959.

Alexander-Floyd, Nikol. *Gender, Race, and Nationalism in Contemporary Black Politics.* New York: Palgrave Macmillan, 2007.

Alhadeff, Vic. *A Newspaper History of South Africa.* Cape Town: Don Nelson, 1986.

Allegra, Donna. *Witness to the League of Blond Hip Hop Dancers.* New York: Alyson Books, 2000.

Allison, Dorothy. *Bastard out of Carolina.* New York: Plume Books, 1993.

———. *Skin: Talking about Sex, Class, and Literature.* Ithaca, NY: Firebrand Books, 1994.

———. *Trash.* Ithaca, NY: Firebrand Books, 1988.

Arnold, Kathleen. *America's New Working Class: Race, Gender, and Ethnicity in a Biopolitical Age.* University Park: Pennsylvania State University Press, 2009.

Atkins, Keletso. *The Moon Is Dead! Give Us Our Money! The Cultural Origins of an African Work Ethic, Natal, South Africa, 1843–1900.* Portsmouth, NH: Heinemann, 1993.

Baker, Lee. *From Savage to Negro: Anthropology and the Construction of Race, 1896–1954.* Berkeley: University of California Press, 1998.

Ballen, Roger. *Dorps: Small Towns of South Africa.* Cape Town: Clifton Publications, 1986.

———. *Outland.* London: Phaidon Press, 2001.

———. *Platteland: Images of Rural South Africa.* New York: St. Martin's Press, 1996.

Bambara, Toni Cade. *The Salt Eaters.* New York: Random House, 1980.

Bates, Robert, V. Y. Mudimbe, and Jean O'Barr. *Africa and the Disciplines: The Contributions of Research in Africa to the Social Sciences and Humanities.* Chicago: University of Chicago Press, 1993.

African American Performance. Durham, NC: Duke University Press, 2012.

Beinart, William. *Political Economy of Pondoland, 1860 to 1930.* Johannesburg: Ravan Press, 1982.

Beinart, William, Peter Delius, and Stanley Trapido, eds. *Putting a Plough to the Ground: Accumulation and Dispossession in Rural South Africa, 1850–1930.* Johannesburg: Ravan Press, 1986.

Bell, Derrick. *Faces at the Bottom of the Well: The Permanence of Racism.* New York: Basic Books, 1993.

———. *Gospel Choirs: Psalms of Survival in an Alien Land Called Home.* New York: Basic Books, 1997.

Benhart, John. *Appalachian Aspirations: The Geography of Urbanization and Development in the Upper Tennessee River Valley, 1865–1900.* Knoxville: University of Tennessee Press, 2007.

Berman, Edward. *The Ideology of Philanthropy: The Influence of the Carnegie, Ford, and Rockefeller Foundations on American Foreign Policy.* Albany: State University of New York Press, 1983.

———, ed. *African Reactions to Missionary Education.* New York: Teachers College Press, 1975.

Bhattacharyya, Gargi. *Tales of Dark Skinned Women: Race, Gender, and Global Culture.* New York: Routledge, 1998.

Black, Edwin. *War against the Weak: Eugenics and America's Campaign to Create a Master Race.* Westport, CT: Dialog Press, [2003] 2012.

Blackwell, Maylei. *¡Chicana Power! Contested Histories of Feminism in the Chicano Movement.* Austin: University of Texas Press, 2011.

Bobo, Jacqueline. *Black Women as Cultural Readers.* New York: Columbia University Press, 1995.

Bonilla-Silva, Eduardo. *Racism without Racists: Color-Blind Racism and the Persistence of Racial Inequality in the United States.* Lanham, MD: Rowman and Littlefield, 2003.

Boonzaier, Daniel Cornelis. *Rand Faces.* With an Introduction by J.H. Hofmeyr. Cape Town: Boonzaier, 1915.

Boonzaier, Emile, and John Sharp. *South African Keywords: The Uses and Abuses of Political Concepts.* Cape Town: David Philip, 1988.

Borstelmann, Thomas. *Apartheid's Reluctant Uncle: The United States and Southern Africa in the Early Cold War.* New York: Oxford University Press, 1993.

———. *The Cold War and the Color Line: American Race Relations in the Global Arena.* Cambridge, MA: Harvard University Press, 2001.

Bozzoli, Belinda. *Political Nature of a Working Class: Capital and Ideology in South Africa, 1890–1933.* London: Routledge and Kegan Paul, 1981.

———, ed. *Class, Community and Conflict: South African Perspectives.* Johannesburg: Ravan Press, 1987.

Breman, Jan, Piet de Rooy, Ann Stoler, and Wim F. Wertheim, eds. *Imperial Monkey Business: Racial Supremacy in Social Darwinist Theory and Colonial Practice.* Amsterdam: V.U. University Press, 1990.

Brock, Lisa, and Digna Castañeda Fuertes, eds. *Between Race and Empire: African Americans and Cubans before the Cuban Revolution.* Philadelphia: Temple University Press, 1998.

Brooks, Pamela. *Boycotts, Buses, and Passes: Black Women's Resistance in the U.S. South and South Africa.* Amherst: University of Massachusetts Press, 2008.

Browne, Rose Butler. *Love My Children: An Autobiography.* New York: Meredith Press, 1969.

Bunche, Ralph. *An African American in South Africa: The Travel Notes of Ralph J. Bunch, 28 September 1937–January 1938.* Contributor Robert J. Edgar. Athens: Ohio University Press, [1992] 2001.

———. *The Political Status of the Negro in the Age of FDR.* Chicago: University of Chicago Press, 1973.

Bundy, Colin. *Rise and Fall of South African Peasantry.* Berkeley: University of California Press, 1979.

Bunting, Brian P. *Education for Apartheid*. London: Christian Action for the Southern Africa Education Fund, 1971.

Cade, Toni. *The Black Woman: An Anthology*. New York: New American Library, 1970.

Caldwell, Kia. *Negras in Brazil: Re-envisioning Black Women's Citizenship and the Politics of Identity*. New Brunswick, NJ: Rutgers University Press, 2006.

Carney, Judith. *Black Rice: The African Origins of Rice Cultivation in the Americas*. Cambridge, MA: Harvard University Press, 2002.

Césaire, Aimé. *Discourse on Colonialism*. New York: Monthly Review Press, [1955] 2000.

Chakrabarty, Dipesh. *Provincializing Europe: Postcolonial Thought and Historical Difference*. Princeton, NJ: Princeton University Press, 2007.

Chandler, Nahum. *Toward an African Future—Of the Limit of World*. Preface by Denise Ferreira Da Silva. New York: Living Commons Collective, 2013.

Coetzee, John M. *White Writing: On the Culture of Letters in South Africa*. New Haven, CT: Yale University Press, 1988.

Collins, Patricia Hill. *Black Feminist Thought: Knowledge, Consciousness, and the Politics of Empowerment*. Boston: Unwin Hyman, 1990.

———. *Black Sexual Politics: African Americans, Gender, and the New Racism*. New York: Routledge, 2004.

Cornwell, Anita. *Black Lesbian in White America*. Tallahassee, FL: Naiad Press, 1983.

Crapanzano, Vincent. *Waiting: The Whites of South Africa*. New York: Random House, 1985.

Crawford, Beverly, and Ronnie D. Lipschultz, eds. *The Myth of "Ethnic Conflict": Politics, Economics, and Cultural Violence*. International and Area Studies. Berkeley: University of California Press, 1998.

Daniels, Douglas. *Charlemagne Peralte and the First American Occupation of Haiti*. Translation of *Charlemagne Peralte: Un Centenaire, 1885–1995*, by Georges Michel. Dubuque, IA: Kendall-Hunt, 1996.

Darnell, Regna. *And Along Came Boas: Continuity and Revolution in Americanist Anthropology*. Studies in the History of the Language Sciences. Amsterdam: John Benjamins, 1998.

———. *Invisible Genealogies: A History of Americanist Anthropology*. Lincoln: University of Nebraska Press, 2001.

Da Silva, Denise. *Toward a Global Idea of Race*. Minneapolis: University of Minnesota Press, 2007.

Davies, Carole Boyce. *Left of Karl Marx: The Political Life of Black Communist Claudia Jones*. Durham, NC: Duke University Press, 2008.

Davies, Robert H. *Capital, State, and White Labour in South Africa, 1900–1960: An Historical Materialist Analysis of Class Formation and Class Relations*. Brighton: Harvester Press, 1979.

Davis, Angela. *Are Prisons Obsolete?* New York: Seven Stories Press, 2003.

———. *Blues Legacies and Black Feminism: Gertrude "Ma"Rainey, Bessie Smith, and Billie Holiday*. New York: Vintage, 1998.

———. *Woman, Race, and Class*. New York: Vintage, 1983.

Davis, Mike, and Justin Chacon. *No One Is Illegal: Fighting Racism and State Violence on the U.S.-Mexico Border.* Chicago: Haymarket Books, 2006.

De Kiewiet, C.W. *History of South Africa: Social and Economic.* Oxford: Oxford University Press, 1950.

De Kock, Leon, Louise Bethlehem, and Sonja Laden, eds. *South Africa in the Global Imaginary.* Leiden: Brill Academic, 2004.

De Wet, Nicholaas Jacobus, Officer Administering the Government, and A.M. Conroy, Officer Administering the Government-in-Council, Union of South Africa, Letters of Appointment to *Commission of Enquiry Kakamas Labour Colony* 1945 to Mr. Justice Jean Etienne De Villiers, Marthinus Johannes Van Den Berg, Esquire, M.P., Hendrik Johannes Nel, Esquire, Michael Daniel Otto Klopper, Lt.-Col., and Paul Jacobus Burger, Esquire, and to Captain James Watts Butler, 16 June, 1945.

Diawara, Manthia. *Rouch in Reverse.* Formation Films for ZDF/ARTE. Library of African Cinema, 1995.

Diop, Cheikh Anta. *The African Origin of Civilization: Myth or Reality.* Edited and with an Introduction by Mercer Cook. New York: Lawrence Hill Books, 1989.

Dollars and Sense. *The Wealth Inequality Reader.* 3rd ed. Boston: Dollars and Sense, 2009.

Drake, St. Clair, and Horace Cayton. *Black Metropolis: A Study of Negro Life in a Northern City.* Introduction by Richard Wright. Foreword by William Julius Wilson. Chicago: University of Chicago Press, [1945] 1993.

Du Bois, W.E.B. *Black Reconstruction in America: 1860–1880.* With an Introduction by David Levering-Lewis. New York: Simon and Schuster, [1935] 1992.

———. *The Philadelphia Negro.* Millwood: Kraus-Thomson, [1899] 1973.

———. *The World and Africa.* New York: International Publishers, 1979.

Dubow, Saul. *Illicit Union: Scientific Racism in Modern South Africa.* Johannesburg: University of Witwatersrand Press, 1995.

Duncan, G.A., ed. *Lovedale: Coercive Agency, Power and Resistance in Mission Education.* Pietermaritzburg: Cluster, 2003.

Duster, Troy. *Backdoor to Eugenics.* 2nd ed. New York: Routledge, 2003.

Du Toit, Andre, and Hermann Giliomee. *Afrikaner Political Thought: Analysis and Documents.* Cape Town: David Philip, 1983.

Dyer, Richard. *White.* London: Routledge, 1997.

Ebr.-Vally-Rehana. *Kala Pani: Caste and Colour in South Africa.* Cape Town and Maroelana: Kwela Books and South African History Online, 2001.

Edwards, Brent Hayes. *Practice of Diaspora: Literature, Translation, and the Rise of Black Internationalism.* Cambridge, MA: Harvard University Press, 2003.

Erasmus, Zmitri. *Coloured by History, Shaped by Place: New Perspectives on Coloured Identities in Cape Town.* Cape Town: Kwela Books, 2001.

Escobar, Arturo. *Encountering Development: The Making and Unmaking of the Third World.* Princeton, NJ: Princeton University Press, 1995.

Eze, Emmanuel. *Race and the Enlightenment: A Reader.* London: Wiley-Blackwell, 1997.

Fanon, Frantz. *The Wretched of the Earth*. New York: Grove Press, 1963.

Farrar, Cynthia. *Origins of Democratic Thinking: The Invention of Politics in Classical Athens*. London: Cambridge University Press, 1989.

Foley, Neil. *The White Scourge: Mexicans, Blacks, and Poor Whites in Texas Cotton Culture*. Berkeley: University of California Press, 1997.

Frankenberg, Ruth, ed. *Displacing Whiteness: Essays in Social and Cultural Criticism*. Durham, NC: Duke University Press, 1997.

———. *White Women, Race Matters: The Social Construction of Whiteness*. Minneapolis: University of Minnesota Press, 1994.

Fredrickson, George. *White Supremacy: A Comparative Study in American and South African History*. Oxford: Oxford University Press, 1982.

Fugard, Athol. *Master Harold and the Boys*. 12th ed. New York: Penguin, 1995.

Fujiwara, Lynn. *Mothers without Citizenship: Asian Immigrant Families and the Consequences of Welfare Reform*. Minneapolis: University of Minnesota Press, 2008.

Gaines, Kevin. *Uplifting the Race: Black Leadership, Politics, and Culture in the Twentieth Century*. Chapel Hill: University of North Carolina Press, 1996.

Gilmore, Ruth Wilson. *Golden Gulag: Prisons, Surplus, Crisis, and Opposition in Globalizing California*. Berkeley: University of California Press, 2007.

Glymph, Thavolia. *Out of the House of Bondage: The Transformation of the Plantation Household*. New York: Cambridge University Press, 2008.

Goldblatt, David. *Some Afrikaners Photographed*. Johannesburg: M. Crawford, 1975.

Goldsby, Jacqueline. *A Spectacular Secret: Lynching in American Life and Literature*. Chicago: University of Chicago Press, 2006.

Gonzales-Day, Ken. *Lynching in the West, 1850–1935*. Durham, NC: Duke University Press, 2006.

Gordon, Avery. *Ghostly Matters: Haunting and the Sociological Imagination*. 2nd ed. Minneapolis: University of Minnesota Press, 2008.

Gordon, Avery, and Chris Newfield, eds. *Multiculturalism*. Minneapolis: University of Minnesota Press, 1996.

Gore, Dayo. *Radicalism at the Crossroads: African American Women Activists in the Cold War*. New York: New York University Press, 2012.

Gore, Dayo, Jeanne Theoharis, and Komozi Woodard, eds. *Want to Start a Revolution: Radical Women in the Black Freedom Struggle*. New York: New York University Press, 2009.

Gould, Stephen Jay. *The Mismeasure of Man*. New York: Norton, 1981.

Goyal, Yogita. *Romance, Diaspora, and Black Atlantic Literature*. New York: Cambridge University Press, 2010.

Gqola, Pumla. *What Is Slavery to Me? Postcolonial/Slave Memory in Post-Apartheid South Africa*. Johannesburg: Wits University Press, 2010.

Hale, Grace. *Making Whiteness: The Culture of Segregation in the South, 1890–1940*. New York: Vintage, 1999.

Halisi, C.R.D. *Black Political Thought in the Making of South African Democracy*. Bloomington: Indiana University Press, 1999.

Hancock, Ange-Marie. *The Politics of Disgust: The Public Identity of the Welfare Queen*. New York: New York University Press, 2004.

Haney-Lopez, Ian. *White by Law: Legal Constructions of Race*. New York: New York University Press, 1996.

Hansberry, William Leo, and Joseph E. Harris, eds. *Africa and Africans as Seen by Classical Writers*, vol. 2. Washington, DC: Howard University Press, 1977.

Harding, Sandra. *The "Racial" Economy of Science: Toward a Democratic Future*. Bloomington: Indiana University Press, 1993.

———. *Whose Science, Whose Knowledge: Thinking from Women's Lives*. Ithaca, NY: Cornell University Press, 1991.

Harris, Duchess. *Black Feminist Politics from Kennedy to Obama*. New York: Palgrave Macmillan, 2011.

Harris, Leonard, ed. *The Philosophy of Alain Locke: Harlem Renaissance and Beyond*. Philadelphia: Temple University Press, 1991.

Harrison, David. *White Tribe of Africa*. Berkeley: University of California Press, 1983.

Hartman, Saidiya. *Lose Your Mother: A Journey along the Atlantic Slave Route*. New York: Farrar, Straus and Giroux, 2008.

———. *Scenes of Subjection: Terror, Slavery, and Self-Making in the Nineteenth-Century*. New York: Oxford University Press, 1997.

Henry, Charles P., ed. *Foreign Policy and the Black (Inter)National Interest*. Albany: State University of New York Press, 2000.

Higashida, Cheryl. *Black Internationalist Feminism: Women Writers of the Black Left, 1945–1995*. Champaign: University of Illinois Press, 2013.

Hill, Rebecca. *Men, Mobs, and Law: Anti-Lynching and Labor Defense in U.S. Radical History*. Durham, NC: Duke University Press, 2009.

Hong, Grace Kyungwon. *The Ruptures of American Capital: Women of Color Feminism and the Culture of Immigrant Labor*. Minneapolis: University of Minnesota Press, 2006.

Hong, Grace, and Roderick Ferguson. *Strange Affinities: The Gender and Sexual Politics of Comparative Racialization*. Durham, NC: Duke University Press, 2011.

Hopkins, H.C. *Kakamas—From the Wilderness an Oasis*. (Afrikaans.) Cape Town: National Book Press, 1978.

Horne, Gerald. *Black and Brown: African Americans and the Mexican Revolution, 1910–1920*. New York: New York University Press, 2005.

———. *The Deepest South: The United States, Brazil, and the African Slave Trade*. New York: New York University Press, 2007.

———. *The White Pacific: U.S. Imperialism and Black Slavery in the South Seas after the Civil War*. Honolulu: University of Hawai'i Press, 2007.

Horowitz, Donald. *Ethnic Groups in Conflict*. Berkeley: University of California Press, 1985.

Hurston, Zora Neale. *Tell My Horse*. Philadelphia: J.B. Lippincott, 1938.

Hurston, Zora Neale, and Alice Walker. *I Love Myself When I Am Laughing . . . and Then Again When I Am Looking Mean and Impressive: A Zora Neale Hurston Reader*. Old Westbury: Feminist Press, 1979.

Hutton, Dean. *"I have fallen": Photographs of South Africa's White Poor*. London: Oodee Books, 2013.

Ignacio, Abe, Enrique de la Cruz, Jorge Emmanuel, and Helen Toribio, eds. *The Forbidden Book: The Philippine American War in Political Cartoons*. San Francisco: T'Boli Publishing, 1985.

Ignatiev, Noel, and John Garvey, eds. *Race Traitor*. New York: Routledge, 1996.

Iris Films-Feminist Collective. *Long Nights Journey into Day*. VHS. California Newsreel, San Francisco, 2000.

Isoke, Zenzele. *Urban Black Women and the Politics of Resistance*. New York: Palgrave Macmillan, 2013.

Jackson, Walter. *Gunnar Myrdal and America's Conscience: Social Engineering and Racial Liberalism, 1938–1987*. Chapel Hill: University of North Carolina Press, 1990.

Jacobson, Matthew Frye. *Barbarian Virtues: The United States Encounters Foreign Peoples at Home and Abroad, 1876–1917*. New York: Hill and Wang, 2000.

James, C.L.R. *Black Jacobins: Toussaint L'Ouverture and the San Domingo Revolution*. Reprint. New York: Vintage Press, [1938] 1989.

Jennings, James. *Welfare Reform and the Revitalization of Inner City Neighborhoods*. Lansing: Michigan State University Press, 2003.

Johnson, James Weldon. *The Autobiography of an Ex-Colored Man*. Mineola, NY: Dover, [1912] 1995.

Johnson, Kimberley. *Reforming Jim Crow: Southern Politics and State in the Pre-Brown South*. New York: Oxford University Press, 2010.

Jolly, Rosemary. *Colonization, Violence, and Narration in White South African Writing*. Athens: Ohio University Press, 1996.

Jones, Charles. *Bad Blood: The Tuskegee Syphilis Experiment. A Tragedy of Race and Medicine*. New York: Free Press, 1982.

Jordan, Winthrop. *White over Black: American Attitudes toward the Negro, 1550–1812*. Chapel Hill: University of North Carolina Press, 1968.

Jordan-Zachery, Julia. *Black Women, Cultural Images, and Social Policy*. New York: Routledge, 2008.

Katznelson, Ira. *When Affirmative Action Was White: An Untold History of Racial Inequality in Twentieth-Century America*. Reprint. New York: Norton, 2006.

Keal, Paul. *European Conquest and the Rights of Indigenous Peoples: The Moral Backwardness of International Society*. Cambridge: Cambridge University Press, 2003.

Keegan, Timothy. *Colonial South Africa and the Origins of the Racial Order*. Charlottesville: University of Virginia Press, 1996.

———. *Rural Transformations in Industrializing South Africa: The Southern Highveld to 1914*. Johannesburg: Ravan Press, 1986.

Kelley, Robin. *Freedom Dreams: The Black Radical Imagination*. New ed. Boston: Beacon Press, 2003.

Key, V.O. *Southern Politics in State and Nation*. With Contributions from Alexander Heard. Knoxville: University of Tennessee Press, 1984.

Kihato, Caroline Wanjiku. *Migrant Women of Johannesburg: Everyday Life in an In-Between City*. New York: Palgrave Macmillan, 2013.

Klausen, Susanne. *Race, Maternity, and the Politics of Birth Control in South Africa, 1910–1939.* Basingstoke: Palgrave Macmillan, 2004.

Kunnie, Julian. *Is Apartheid Really Dead? Pan-Africanist Working-Class Cultural Critical Perspectives.* Boulder, CO: Westview Press, 2000.

Ladner, Joyce, ed. *The Death of White Sociology: Essays on Race and Culture.* Baltimore, MD: Black Classic Press, 1998.

Lagemann, Ellen Condliffe. *The Politics of Knowledge: The Carnegie Corporation, Philanthropy, and Public Policy.* Chicago: University of Chicago Press, 1992.

Lake, Marilyn, and Henry Reynolds. *Drawing the Global Colour Line: White Men's Countries and the International Challenge of Racial Equality.* Cambridge: Cambridge University Press, 2008.

Lange, Maria Lis. *White, Poor and Angry: White Working-Class Families in Johannesburg.* Aldershot: Ashgate, 2003.

Lazerson, Joshua. *Against the Tide: Whites against Apartheid.* Bellville: Mayibuye Books, 1994.

Lee, Rebekah. *African Women and Apartheid: Migration and Settlement in Urban South Africa.* London: I.B. Tauris, 2009.

Leebaw, Bronwyn. *Judging State-Sponsored Violence, Imagining Political Change.* New York: Cambridge University Press, 2011.

Lerner, Gerda. *Black Women in White America: A Documentary History.* New York: Vintage Press, 1992.

Leverenz, David. *Paternalism Incorporated: Fables of American Fatherhood, 1865–1940.* Ithaca, NY: Cornell University Press, 2003.

Lewis, Simon. *White Women Writers and Their African Invention.* Gainesville: University Press of Florida, 2003.

Lichtenstein, Alex. *Twice the Work of Free Labor: The Political Economy of Convict Labor in the New South.* New York: Verso, 1996.

Lipset, Seymour. *American Exceptionalism: A Double-Edged Sword.* New York: Norton, 1997.

Lipsitz, George. *Possessive Investment in Whiteness.* Philadelphia: Temple University Press, 1998.

Locke, Alain, and Jeffrey Stewart, ed. *Race Contacts and Interracial Relations: Lectures on the Theory and Practice of Race.* Washington, DC: Howard University Press, 1992.

Lovett, Laura. *Conceiving the Future: Pro-Natalism, Reproduction, and the Family, 1890–1938.* Chapel Hill: University of North Carolina Press, 2007.

Lui, Meizhu, B. Robles, and B. Leonard-Wright, eds. *The Color of Wealth: The Story behind the U.S. Racial Wealth Divide.* New York: New Press, 2006.

Mabokela, Reitumetse Obakeng, and Zine Magubane, eds. *Hear Our Voices: Race, Gender and the Status of Black South African Women in the Academy.* Pretoria: University of South Africa Press, 2004.

Macmillan, W.M. *My South African Years.* Cape Town: David Philip, 1975.

Magona, Sindiwe. *To My Children's Children.* Reissue. Northhampton, MA: Interlink, 2006.

Magubane, Bernard. *The Making of a Racist State: British Imperialism and the Union of South Africa, 1875–1910.* Trenton, NJ: Africa World Press, 1996.

————. *The Ties That Bind: African-American Consciousness of Africa*. Trenton, NJ: Africa World Press, 1987.

Magubane, Peter. *Magubane's South Africa*. With a Foreword by Ambassador Andrew Young. New York: Knopf, 1978.

Magubane, Zine. *Bringing the Empire Home: Race, Class, and Gender in Britain and Colonial South Africa*. Chicago: University of Chicago Press, 2004.

Malik, Kenan. *The Meaning of Race: Race, History, and Culture in Western Society*. New York: New York University Press, 1996.

Manning, Maurice. *Slave in a Box: The Strange Career of Aunt Jemima*. Charlottesville: University of Virginia Press, 1998.

Marks, Shula. *Ambiguities of Dependence in South Africa: Class, Nationalism and the State in Twentieth-Century Natal*. Johannesburg: Ravan Press, 1986.

Marks, Shula, and Richard Rathbone. *Industrialization and Social Change, 1870–1930*. New York: Longman, 1982.

Maseko, Zola, dir. *The Life and Times of Sara Baartman*. First Run/Icarus Films, New York, 1998.

Mason, Andy. *What's So Funny? Under the Skin of South African Cartooning*. Claremont, CA: Double Storey Press, 2010.

Matebeni, Zethu. *Black Lesbian Sexualities and Identity in South Africa: An Ethnography of Black Lesbian Urban Life*. n.p.: Lambert Academic Publishing, 2012.

McDuffie, Erik. *Sojourning for Freedom: Black Women, American Communism, and the Making of Black Left Feminism*. Durham, NC: Duke University Press, 2011.

McKittrick, Katherine. *Demonic Ground: Black Women and the Cartographies of Struggle*. Minneapolis: University of Minnesota Press, 2006.

Meckler, Michael. *Classical Antiquity and the Politics of America: From George Washington to George W. Bush*. Waco, TX: Baylor University Press, 2006.

Meriwether, James H. *Proudly We Can Be Africans: Black Americans and Africa*. Chapel Hill: University of North Carolina Press, 2002.

Mignolo, Walter. *The Idea of Latin America*. London: Wiley-Blackwell, 1991.

Millin, Sarah Gertrude. *The Fiddler*. London: Constable & Co., 1929.

————. *God's Stepchildren*. London: Constable & Co., 1924.

Mills, Charles S. *Blackness Visible: Essays on Philosophy & Race*. Ithaca, NY: Cornell University Press, 1998.

————. *Racial Contract*. Ithaca, NY: Cornell University Press, 1997.

Mills, Charles, and Carole Pateman. *Contract and Domination*. London: Polity Press, 2007.

Molema, Silas Modiri. *The Bantu, Past and Present: An Ethnographical and Historical Study of the Native Races of South Africa*. Edinburgh: Green & Son, 1920.

Moodie, T. Dunbar. *The Rise of Afrikanerdom: Power, Apartheid, and the Afrikaner Civil Religion*. Berkeley: University of California Press, 1975.

Morgan, Jennifer. *Laboring Women: Reproduction and Gender in New World Slavery*. Philadelphia: University of Pennslvania Press, 2004.

Morrell, Robert. *White but Poor: Essays on the History of Poor Whites in Southern Africa, 1880–1940*. Pretoria: UNISA, 1992.

Morrison, Toni. *Beloved*. New York: Knopf, 1987.

———. *Playing in the Dark: Whiteness and the Literary Imagination*. Cambridge, MA: Harvard University Press, 1992.

———, ed. *Race-ing Justice, En-gendering Power*. New York: Pantheon, 1992.

Moten, Fred. *In the Break: The Aesthetics of the Black Radical Tradition*. Minneapolis: University of Minnesota Press, 2003.

Moya, Lily Patience, Mable Palmer, and Sibusisiwe Makhanya. *Not Either an Experimental Doll: The Separate Worlds of Three South African Women*. Edited by Shula Marks. Bloomington: Indiana University Press, 1987.

Myrdal, Gunnar. *An American Dilemma: The Negro Problem and Modern Democracy*. New York: Harper, 1944.

Narayan, Uma. *Dislocating Cultures: Identities, Traditions, and Third World Feminisms*. New York: Routledge, 1977.

Neame, L.E. *Some South African Politicians*. Illustrated by Quip. Cape Town: Maskew Miller, 1929.

Nelson, Jill. *Volunteer Slavery: My Authentic Negro Experience*. New York: Penguin, 1994.

Nkomo, Mokubung, ed. *Pedagogy of Domination: Toward a Democratic Education in South Africa*. Trenton, NJ: Africa World Press, 1990.

Noer, Thomas. *Briton, Boer, and Yankee: The United States and South Africa, 1879–1914*. Kent, OH: Kent State University Press, 1978.

Norval, Aletta. *Deconstructing Apartheid Discourse*. New York: Verso, 1996.

O' Connor, Alice. *Poverty Knowledge: Social Science, Social Policy, and the Poor in Twentieth-Century U.S. History*. Princeton, NJ: Princeton University Press, 2002.

Omi, Michael, and Howard Winant. *Racial Formation in the United States: From the 1960s to the 1990s*. New York: Routledge, 1994.

Oyěwùmí Oyèrónké, ed. *African Gender Studies: A Reader*. New York: Palgrave Macmillan, 2005.

———. *The Invention of Women: Making an African Sense of Western Gender Discourses*. Minneapolis: University of Minnesota Press, 1997.

Padmore, George. *Africa: Britain's Third Empire*. New York: Negro Universities Press, 1969.

Park, Robert, and Ernest Burgess. *Introduction to the Science of Sociology*. Project Gutenberg. Chicago: University of Chicago Press, 1921.

Patterson, Orlando. *Slavery and Social Death: A Comparative Study*. Cambridge, MA: Harvard University Press, 1985.

Perez, Emma. *The Decolonial Imaginary*. Bloomington: Indiana University Press, 1999.

Perry, Keisha-Khan. *Black Women against the Land Grab: The Fight for Racial Justice in Brazil*. Minneapolis: University of Minnesota Press, 2013.

Peters, Marguerite Andrée. *The Contribution of the Carnegie Non-European Library Service, Transvaal, to the Development of Library Services for Africans in South Africa*. Pretoria: State Library, 1975.

Pieterse, Jan Nederveen. *White on Black: Images of Africa and Blacks in Western Popular Cultures*. New Haven, CT: Yale University Press, 1992.

Pim, Howard. *A Transkei Enquiry*. Alice: Lovedale, 1934.

Pithouse, Richard, ed. *Asinamali: University Struggles in Post-Apartheid South Africa*. Trenton, NJ: Africa World Press, 2006.

Pitkin, Hannah. *Fortune Is a Woman: Gender and Politics in the Work of Niccolo Machiavelli*. Chicago: University of Chicago Press, 1999.

Plaatje, Solomon. *Mafeking Diary*. Centenary ed. Edited by John Comaroff and Brian Willan. Suffolk: James Currey, 1999.

———. *Native Life in South Africa, before and since the European War and the Boer Rebellion*. New York: Negro Universities Press, 1969.

Plummer, Brenda Gayle. *Rising Wind: Black Americans and U.S. Foreign Affairs, 1935–1960*. Chapel Hill: University of North Carolina Press, 1996.

Polanyi, Karl. *The Great Transformation: The Political and Economic Origins of Our Time*. Boston: Beacon Press, 1957.

Popay, Jennie, Fiona William, and Ann Oakley. *Welfare Research: A Critical Review*. London: University College of London Press, 1957.

Prashad, Vijay. *Darker Nations: A People's History of the Third World*. New York: New Press, 2008.

Przeworski, Adam. *Democracy and the Market: Political and Economic Reforms in Eastern Europe and Latin America*. Cambridge: Cambridge University Press, 1991.

Rasmussen, Birgit Brander, et. al. *The Making and Unmaking of Whiteness*. Durham, NC: Duke University Press, 2001.

Rich, Paul. *White Power and the Liberal Conscience: Racial Segregation and South African Liberalism*. Johannesburg: Ravan Press, 1984.

Riggs, Marlon, dir. *Ethnic Notions*. California Newsreel, San Francisco, 1986.

Ring, Natalie. *The Problem South Region, Empire, and the New Liberal State, 1880–1930*. Athens: University of Georgia Press, 2012.

Roberts, Dorothy. *Fatal Invention: How Science, Race, and Big Business Re-Create Race in the Twenty-First Century*. New York: New Press, 2011.

———. *Killing the Black Body: Race, Reproduction and the Meaning of Liberty*. New York: Vintage, 1998.

———. *Shattered Bonds: The Color of Child Welfare*. Repr. New York: Basic Civitas Books, 2003.

Robinson, Cedric. *Black Marxism*. 2nd ed. Foreword by Robin Kelley. Chapel Hill: University of North Carolina Press, 2000.

———. *Black Movements in America*. New York: Routledge, 1997.

———. *Forgeries of Memory and Meaning: Blacks and the Regimes of Race in American Theater and Film before World War II*. Chapel Hill: University of North Carolina Press, 2007.

———. *Terms of Order: Political Science and the Myth of Leadership*. Albany: State University of New York Press, 1980.

Rodney, Walter. *How Europe Underdeveloped Africa*. Washington, DC: Howard University Press, 1974.

Roediger, David. *Black on White: Black Writers on What It Means to Be White*. New York: Schocken Books, 1998.

———. *History against Misery*. Oakland, CA: AK Press, 2006.

———. *The Wages of Whiteness: Race and the Making of the American Working Class*. London: Verso, 1991.

Roediger, David, and Elizabeth Esch. *The Production of Difference: Race and the Management of Labor in US History.* Oxford: Oxford University Press, 2012.

Romero, Mary. *Maid in the U.S.A.* New York: Routledge, 2002.

Roos, Neil. *Ordinary Springboks: White Servicemen and the Social Justice in South Africa, 1939–1961.* Aldershot: Ashgate, 2005.

Rothman, Barbara Katz. *Weaving a Family: Untangling Race and Adoption.* Boston: Beacon Press, 2005.

Royster, Deirdre. *Race and the Invisible Hand: How White Networks Exclude Black Men from Blue-Collar Jobs.* Berkeley: University of California Press, 2003.

Sakai, J. *Settlers: The Mythology of the White Proletariat.* Rogue River, OR: Morningstar Press, 1989.

Saunders, Christopher. *Black Leaders in Southern African History.* London: Heinemann Educational Books, 1979.

———. *The Making of the South African Past: Major Historians on Race and Class.* Lanham, MD: Rowman and Littlefield, 1988.

Sawyer, Mark. *Racial Politics in Post-Revolutionary Cuba.* Cambridge: Cambridge University Press, 2005.

Schoonraad, Murray, and Elzabé Schoonraad. *Companion to South African Cartoonists.* Johannesburg: A.D. Donker, 1989.

Schram, Sanford. *Welfare Discipline: Discourse, Governance, and Globalization.* Philadelphia: Temple University Press, 2006.

———. *Words of Welfare: The Poverty of Social Science and the Social Science of Poverty.* Minneapolis: University of Minnesota Press, 1995.

Segrest, Mab. *Memoir of a Race Traitor.* Boston: South End Press, 1994.

Sennett, Richard, and Jonathon Cobb. *The Hidden Injuries of Class.* New York: Knopf, 1972.

Sexton, Jared. *Amalgamation Schemes: Anti-Blackness and the Critique of Multiracialism.* Minneapolis: University of Minnesota Press, 2008.

Sharpe, Christina. *Monstrous Intimacies: Making Post-Slavery Subjects.* Durham, NC: Duke University Press, 2010.

Sharpley-Whiting, T. Denean. *Black Venus: Sexualized Savages, Primal Fears, and Primitive Narratives in French.* Durham, NC: Duke University Press, 1999.

———. *Frantz Fanon: Conflicts and Feminisms.* Lanham, MD: Rowman and Littlefield, 1997.

Shaw, Stephanie J. *What a Woman Ought to Be and to Do: Black Professional Women Workers during the Jim Crow Era.* Chicago: University of Chicago Press, 2010.

Simons, H.J., and Ray Simons. *Class and Colour in South Africa, 1850–1950.* London: International Defense and Aid Fund for Southern Africa, 1983.

Singh, Nikhil P. *Black Is a Country: Race and the Unfinished Struggle for Democracy.* Cambridge, MA: Harvard University Press, 2004.

Sivonen, Seppo. *White Collar or Hoe Handle: African Education under British Colonial Policy, 1920–1945.* Bibliotheca Historica 4. Helsinki: Suomen Historiallinen Seura, 1995.

Skloot, Rebecca. *The Immortal Life of Henrietta Lacks*. Reprint. New York: Broadway Books, 2011.

Smith, Andrea. *Conquest: Sexual Violence and American Indian Genocide*. Cambridge, MA: South End Press, 2005.

Smith, Valerie. *Not Just Race, Not Just Gender: Black Feminist Readings*. New York: Routledge, 1998.

Stanfield, John. *Philanthropy and Jim Crow in American Social Science*. Westport, CT: Greenwood Press, 1985.

Ste. Croix, Geoffrey de. *The Class Struggle in the Ancient Greek World: From the Archaic Age to the Arab*. Ithaca, NY: Cornell University Press, 1989.

Steinberg, Stephen. *The Ethnic Myth: Race, Ethnicity and Class in America*. 3rd ed. Boston, MA: Beacon Press, 2001.

Stepan, Nancy. *The Hour of Eugenics: Race, Gender, and Nation in Latin America*. New York: Cornell University Press, 1985.

Stevens, E.J.C. *White and Black: An Inquiry into Africa's Greatest Problem*. Cape Town: Darter Bros., 1914.

Steyn, Melissa. *Whiteness Just Isn't What It Used to Be: White Identity in a Changing South Africa*. Albany: State University of New York Press, 2001.

Stocking, George. *The Ethnographer's Magic and Other Essays in the History of Anthropology*. Madison: University of Wisconsin Press, 1992.

Stone, I.F. *The Trial of Socrates*. New York: Anchor Books, 1985.

Stern, Alexandra. *Eugenic Nation: Faults and Frontiers of Better Breeding in Modern America*. Berkeley: University of California Press, 2005.

Taussig, Michael. *Shamanism, Colonialism, and the Wild Man: A Study in Terror and Healing*. Chicago: University of Chicago Press, 1991.

Thandeka. *Learning to Be White: Race, Money and God in America*. 2nd ed. New York: Continuum, 2000.

Thompson, E.P. *Making of the English Working Class*. New York: Random House, 1966.

Thompson, Robert Farris. *Flash of the Spirit: African and Afro-American Art and Philosophy*. New York: Random House, 1983.

Twine, France Winddance. *Racism in a Racial Democracy: The Maintenance of White Supremacy in Brazil*. New Brunswick, NJ: Rutgers University Press, 1998.

Twine, Winddance, and Jonathan W. Warren. *Racing Research, Researching Race: Methodological Dilemmas in Critical Race Studies*. New York: New York University Press, 2000.

Vale, Peter. *Keeping a Sharp Eye: A Century of Cartoons on South Africa's International Relations, 1910–2010*. Bloomington, IN: XLIBRIS, 2012.

Valentine, Betty. *Hustling and Other Hard Work: Lifestyles of the Ghetto*. New York: Free Press, 1980.

van Niekerk, Marlene. *Triomf*. Translated by Leon de Kock. Johannesburg: Jonathon Ball, 1980.

Van Onselen, Charles. *New Babylon, New Nineveh*. Cape Town: Jonathan Ball, 1996.

———. *The Seed Is Mine: The Life of Kas Maine, a South African Sharecropper, 1894–1985*. Cape Town: David Philip, 1996.

Vinson, Robert. *The Americans Are Coming! Dreams of African American Liberation in Segregationist South Africa*. Athens: Ohio University Press, 2012.

Von Eschen, Penny. *Race against Empire: Black Americans and Anticolonialism, 1937–1957*. Ithaca, NY: Cornell University Press, 1997.

———. *Satchmo Blows Up the World: Jazz Ambassadors Play the Cold War*. Cambridge, MA: Harvard University Press, 2006.

Waldman, Ayelet, and Robin Levi, eds. *Inside This Place not of It: Narratives from Women's Prisons*. San Francisco: McSweeneys, 2011.

Wallerstein, Immanuel. *Africa and the Modern World*. Trenton, NJ: Africa World Press, 1986.

Ware, Vron. *Beyond the Pale: White Women, Racism, and History*. New York: Verso, 1992.

Washington, Harriet. *Medical Apartheid: The Dark History of Medical Experimentation on Black Americans from Colonial Times to the Present*. New York: Doubleday, 2006.

Watkins, William. *The White Architects of Black Education: Ideology and Power in America, 1865–1954*, New York: Teachers College Press, 2001.

Wells, Ida B. *Southern Horrors: Lynch Law in All Its Phases*. Seattle: Create Space Press, [1894] 2011.

West, Michael, William Martin, and Fanon Che Wilkins, eds. *From Toussaint to Tupac: The Black International since the Age of Revolution*. Chapel Hill: University of North Carolina Press, 2009.

Wiegman, Robyn. *Object Lessons*. Durham, NC: Duke University Press, 2012.

Wilderson, Frank. *Incognegro: A Memoir of Exile and Apartheid*. Boston: South End Press, 2008.

———. *Red, White, and Black: Cinema and the Structure of U.S. Antagonism*. Durham, NC: Duke University Press, 2010.

Williams, Marco, dir. *Banished: How Whites Drove Blacks Out of Town in America*. DVD. Independent Lens, 2006.

Willoughby-Herard, Tiffany. *Theories of Blackness: On Life and Death*. San Diego: Cognella, 2011.

Wolters, Raymond. *The New Negro on Campus: Black College Rebellions of the 1920s*. Princeton, NJ: Princeton University Press, 1975.

Woods, Clyde. *Development Arrested: The Blues and Plantation Power in the Mississippi Delta*. New York: Verso, 2000.

Wray, Matt. *Not Quite White: White Trash and the Boundaries of Whiteness*. Durham, NC: Duke University Press, 2006.

Wright, Joanne. *Origin Stories in Political Thought: Discourses on Gender, Power, and Citizenship*. Toronto: University of Toronto Press, 2004.

Young, Cynthia. *Soul Power: Culture, Radicalism, and the Making of a U.S. Third World Left*. Durham, NC: Duke University Press, 2006.

Yu, Henry. *Thinking Orientals: Migration, Contact, and Exoticism in Modern America*. Oxford: Oxford University Press, 2001.

Yun, Lisa. *The Coolie Speaks: Chinese Indentured Laborers and African Slaves in Cuba*. Philadelphia: Temple University Press, 2008.

Zegeye, Abebe. *Youth and Societal Change in South Africa*. Pretoria: UNISA Press, n.d.

Zegeye, Abebe, and Maurice Vambe, eds. *Close to the Sources: Essays on Contemporary African Culture, Politics, and Academy.* Pretoria: UNISA Press and New York: Routledge, 2009.

Zimmerman, Andrew. *Alabama in Africa: Booker T. Washington, the German Empire, and the Globalization of the New South.* Reprint Edition. Princeton, NJ: Princeton University Press, 2012.

Index

CPSIA information can be obtained
at www.ICGtesting.com
Printed in the USA
FSHW012059140219
55692FS